READING SHAKESPEARE'S WILL

12⁵⁰

R E A D I N G

Shakespeare's Will

THE THEOLOGY OF FIGURE FROM

AUGUSTINE TO THE SONNETS

Lisa Freinkel

COLUMBIA UNIVERSITY PRESS NEW YORK

Columbia University Press
Publishers Since 1893
New York   Chichester, West Sussex

Library of Congress Cataloging-in-Publication Data

Freinkel, Lisa.
Reading Shakespeare's will :
the theology of figure from Augustine to the sonnets /
Lisa Freinkel.
p. cm.
Includes bibliographical referencees (p.) and index.
ISBN 0–231–12324–8 (cloth) – ISBN 0–231–12325–6 (pbk)
1. Shakespeare, William, 1564–1616–Religion.
2. Shakespeare, William, 1564–1616. Merchant of Venice.
3. Christianity and literature–England–History.
4. Augustine, Saint, Bishop of Hippo–Influence.
5. Petrarca, Francesco, 1304–1374–Influence.
6. Shakespeare, William, 1564–1616. Sonnets.
7. Christianity and other religions–Judaism.
8. Luther, Martin, 1483–1546–Influence.
9. Sonnets, English–History and criticism.
10. Theology in literature. 11. Figures of speech.
12. Allegory. I. Title.

PR3011 .F65   2001
822.3'3–dc21   2001017255

Columbia University Press books are printed
on permanent and durable acid-free paper.

Printed in the United States of America
c 10 9 8 7 6 5 4 3 2 1
p 10 9 8 7 6 5 4 3 2 1

"Veritas tua nec mea est nec illius aut illius, sed omnium nostrum."

for my father, Norbie, in memory
for my mother, Ruth, in love

CONTENTS

ACKNOWLEDGMENTS

Truth, Augustine teaches us, is a possession of the community at large; it is falsehood alone to which we can lay private claim. "For whoever speaks a lie," he writes in *The Confessions*, "does so of his own." I feel blessed by the support of family, friends, and colleagues who, over the years, have made thinking these thoughts possible. This book is a better and truer book for their sake, and its weaknesses are all my own.

I wish to thank the teachers who encouraged this study in its earliest, troglodyte phases, and especially Christopher Braider and Stephen Greenblatt, for whose continuing mentorship I am always grateful. Paul Alpers, Albert Ascoli, Louise George Clubb, Timothy Hampton, Victoria Kahn, and Richard Strier read portions of this study in those early days, as did my coconspirators at Berkeley and Chicago: Douglas Bruster, Michel Chaouli, Elizabeth Dillon, Jonathan Elmer, Michael Harrawood, Steven Pincus, Elizabeth Scala, and Rochelle Tobias. To their patient interest in this project I remain deeply indebted.

Early versions of arguments in chapters 4 and 5 first appeared in *Graven Images* 2 (1995): 31–47, under the title "Shakespeare and the Theology of Will"; in James Schiffer, ed., *The Sonnets: Critical Essays*, 241–61 (New York: Garland Publishing, 1999), under the title "The Name of the Rose: Christian Figurality and Shakespeare's Sonnets"; and in Hugh Grady, ed., *Modern and Postmodern Shakespeares*, 122–41 (London: Routledge, 2000), under the title "The Merchant of Venice: 'Modern' Anti-Semitism and the Veil of Allegory." I am grateful to the editors of those volumes–Andrew Weiner, James Schiffer, and Hugh Grady respectively–for their reading and support. I wish likewise to thank my fellow seminarians at the 1999 Shakespeare Association of America conference for their comments on that initial *Merchant* essay. Thanks as well to Marcel Dubbelman and the Siamdutch Mosquito Netting Company, for their gracious permission to use the illustrations in chapter 5.

I owe a special debt of gratitude to my colleagues and friends at the University of Oregon. I wish especially to acknowledge Karen Jackson Ford, George Rowe, and Forest Pyle, who are quite simply the most generous and careful readers I have ever known, and Kenneth Calhoon, Roland Greene, Sara Hodges, Linda Kintz, Clare Lees, John Lysaker, Karen McPherson, Monica Szurmuk, and Mary Wood for their guidance at critical stages in this project. In ways too numerous to recount I remain indebted to John Gage and the University of Oregon Department of English; without the support I have received here, both tangible and intangible, this mammoth undertaking would have gone the way of the woolly. Research grants from the University of Oregon Humanities Center, College of Arts and Sciences, and Office of Research and Sponsored Programs have proved likewise invaluable. I wish, further, to thank my students and especially to acknowledge the members of my "Lyric Shakespeare" and "Shakespeare and Usury" graduate seminars, who helped midwife many of the arguments that follow. I owe a special debt to Gary Bodie for his tireless research assistance and to Jan McInroy for her patient and painstaking copyediting. I remain lastingly indebted to Brian Manning Delaney, whose love and inspiration sustained me through the bulk of this project.

Finally, to my sister, Susan and brother, Andrew, to the lovely Barbara and my dogged ally Ezra: *Gott sei dank.*

PREFACE

It is customary to preface a work with an explanation of the goal [*Zweck*] in view of which the author wrote, as well as whatever occasioned him to do so, and the relationship to other earlier or contemporary treatises on the same subject in which he believes the work to stand. In the case of a philosophical work, however, such an explanation seems not only superfluous but, in view of the nature of the subject-matter, even unsuitable and inappropriate [*unpassend und zweckwidrig*]. For whatever might fittingly be said about philosophy in a preface–say a historical *account* of the main drift and the point of view. . . .–none of this can be accepted as the way in which to expound philosophical truth. . . .

The True is the whole. But the whole is only the essence consummating itself through its development.

–G. W. F. Hegel, *The Phenomenology of Spirit,* "Preface"[1]

"What matter who's speaking, someone said, what matter who's speaking."

–Samuel Beckett, *Texts for Nothing,* cited in
Michel Foucault, "What Is an Author?"[2]

BACKWARDS AND FOREWORDS:
HEGEL AND FOUCAULT

I write this preface at the very end of almost a decade of reading and writing–a decade that has produced the study that you are about to read. This is all "customary," as Hegel would tell us, and to us postmoderns an even more familiar line of argument has customarily deconstructed Hegel's *Gewohnheit.* Following after custom, *nach der Gewohnheit,* the preface is, in the truest sense of the word, *preposterous:*[3] as "before-sayings" (*prae-fatio*'s), prefaces are always in truth postscripts, forced to begin at the end, rump, as it were, facing forward. This problem of the backwards foreword doesn't even begin to surprise us anymore. In theory and practice we are all well accustomed to the paradoxes of the future anterior. And so we cheerfully begin the books we write at their end in order to give our readers, who tend to begin at the beginning, a sense of the whole that *will have been*.[4]

For the study that follows, however, it is fruitful to begin by once again parsing Hegel's logic. As Hegel tells us in his preface, any causal story of why the work was written, under what circumstances or with what purpose (*Zweck*) or intention in mind—any such historical account can only be *zweckwidrig*, inappropriate (literally: *contrary to purpose*) when it comes to explaining a discourse that seeks, like philosophy, to expound the truth. For the truth is universal, essential, while the material of history consists in mere particulars. Any empirical story—even a story about *Zweck*, about the purpose or intention that informed the author's endeavors—any such story will only run counter to the *Zweck* of expounding truth. The truth is whole, and hence its exposition cannot proceed from the vantage of historical beginnings; to tell the story of truth, we cannot, in other words, assume the piecemeal, particularized vantage of history, with its empirical language of cause and effect. Instead our story must begin at the end—not the end that this particular author had, as a matter of historical fact, in mind, but instead the end in view of which these beginnings are justified. Our story must be told from the vantage of an end that has finally revealed, under the veil of historical accident, the self-consummating path of essence.

As a reading of Shakespeare's w/Will—both "will" as *voluntas*, as the intentionality of a historical writing agent, and "Will" as proper name, as the authoritative mark of that agent for later readers—this study purports to offer something like a history of the dilemma described by Hegel. In my readings of Augustine, Petrarch, Luther, and Shakespeare, I trace the evolution of that teleological exchange whereby the "historical accounts" of a writer writing are superseded in the name of the Book's "self-consummating" truth. I offer, in short, something *like* a history of this teleo-logic; indeed something *like* the histories that Foucault proposes when he adopts a Nietzschean "genealogy" in order to demystify just such teleologies.[5] "The genealogist needs history to dispel the chimeras of the origin," Foucault writes.[6] The genealogist records the jolts and quirks and accidents of history in order

to exorcise the phantasm of origins. The genealogist demystifies
the illusion that interpretation merely unveils a meaning that, like
Hegel's self-consummating essence or Christianity's Jesus as *Verbum*, has been "with us" all along.

And yet, in order to read Shakespeare's w/Will, we may need
to retain those teleological chimeras after all. As I trace the development in the Christian West of the idea of the author, I offer a
narrative that can be categorized neither as simply Foucauldian
genealogy nor as simply Hegelian phenomenology. Instead, I offer
my narrative as a *reading*: a reading constrained, and necessarily so,
by the same principles of interpretation that–historically, at the
hands of specific readers and writers–have worked to constitute
the subject of that reading. My methodology, in other words, is cut
from the same cloth as my subject. Where a Foucault would
oppose the historical examination of "descent" [*Herkunft*][7] to the
metaphysical inquiry about origins and ends, I find myself constrained to straddle that opposition itself.

"What is an author?" Foucault famously asks. His attempt to
answer that question is propelled, he tells us, by reflections upon
his own methods–by, in particular, his use of "the names of
authors" in *The Order of Things* "in a naive and often crude fashion"
(113).[8] Foucault's efforts in that study, he tells us, had been to
locate discrete "discursive units"–"verbal clusters" such as "natural
history" or the "analysis of wealth"–that belie the categories (a
book, a work, an author) of a traditional history of ideas (113, 115).
Given his project, his reliance on authors' names constitutes an
embarrassing lapse: "I . . . failed to realize that I had allowed their
names to function ambiguously. This has proved an embarassment
[*sic*] to me" (114). His remarks in "What Is an Author?" emerge as
a belated effort to disambiguate his words.

For Foucault, the heart of the ambiguity resides in a failure to
recognize the difference between an author's name and other
proper names. Following John Searle's work, Foucault addresses
the signifying peculiarities of any proper name. Oscillating
"between the poles of description and designation," in Searle's
account the proper name cannot be reduced to simple ostension,
to "a finger pointed at someone" ("Author," 121). Instead, it designates its referent by means of descriptive features associated with
that name. To put the matter differently: at any moment, according to Searle, the proper name can be replaced by other parts of

speech. In this way, the proper name finds its equivalent in a series of descriptive statements. Such statements, in turn, can be subjected to empirical verification and modulation in order, precisely, to secure the name's reference. Who is Jane Doe? She has brown eyes, lives in New York, loves to travel. In effect, the proper name finds its proper substitution through pronoun and predicate. In contrast, however, Foucault suggests that the author's name has no linguistic equivalent: it "is not simply an element of speech" (123). It can never be reduced to a cognitive description, nor can its reference be established by empirical procedures.[9] Indeed, in essence Foucault argues that the author's name is never simply referential. Instead, its function is "classificatory," working not to indicate an empirical agent or an authoritative "genius" outside the text, but instead to demarcate and authenticate texts themselves, setting them into relationship with other texts and securing their cultural and social status. "Unlike a proper name, which moves from the interior of a discourse to the real person outside who produced it, the name of the author remains at the contours of texts—separating one from the other, defining their form, and characterizing their mode of existence" (123).

Foucault's insistence on the "singularity" (122) of the author's name undergirds his essay's central innovation: the replacement of terms like "author" and "author's name" with the idea of an "author-function." The shift in terminology allows Foucault to expose the metaphysics wrongly attributed to his own prior "naive" usage; "Buffon" in *The Order of Things* refers neither to an empirical agent whose intention determines the meanings of a text nor to the transcendent authority who/which authenticates the work's truth. As author-function, "Buffon" never ventures far from that discourse which bears the name; "Buffon" never moves "outside" discourse, neither toward a biological life nor toward a transcendent end. Instead, understood as discursive function, Foucault's conception of the author reveals the ways in which both life and telos (or, in Hegel's terms, both "historical account" and "philosophical truth") are artifacts produced by the varying cultural and social means according to which texts are *authorized*.

At first glance, Foucault's argument—at least as I've extrapolated it here—anticipates my own conclusions. In my reading of *Shakespeare's Sonnets* in chapter 4, for instance, I too consider authorization as a process that antedates and even constructs the

author of that text. Like Foucault, the effort to demystify the
notion of authors as the origin and end of texts proves central to
my argument. But with this important difference: where Foucault
insists on the singularity of the author's name, finding its discursive authority in the peculiar manner in which it resides "at the
contours of texts," I argue instead that the authority of such names
follows problematically from their *non*-singularity. Not only is the
name of the author inescapably referential, pointing toward a lived
life and a historical individual, but it is also inextricable from other
parts of speech. As I demonstrate most clearly in my reading of
the "will" of *Shakespeare's Sonnets*–a word that is simultaneously
authorial signature, proper name, and common noun–the propriety, autonomy, and singularity of the author's name is never
secure. Indeed, it would be impossible to understand the complex
onomastics so central to Petrarchan poetry without taking this
dilemma into account.

Ultimately, however, Foucault's treatment of a sheerly discursive author-function not only elides the problem of reference, it
mistakes the very nature of that problem. By defining the "naive"
conception of author as that "figure who is outside and precedes"
the text (115), Foucault collapses together two distinct, *crucially*
distinct, points of extra-discursive reference: the empirical and the
transcendental. "I had no intention of describing Buffon or Marx
or of reproducing their statements or implicit meanings," he writes
(114). In struggling to disambiguate his own usage of authors'
names, Foucault hopes to secure a distinction between the author
as discursive function and as extra-discursive guarantor of meaning. But what he misses is the crucial difference between "implicit
meaning" and historical "statement." The biographical reference of
names dovetails, in Foucault's account, with the transcendent
guarantee that those names underwrite. His attempted critique falters, then, by eliding the very question in answer to which the
name of the author is invoked: how is it possible that the historically contingent inscription of texts can yield, in the equally historically contingent readings of others, anything like a unified and
non-arbitrary meaning? How can the historical statements of indi-
viduals be reconciled with the implicit meanings found in their
texts? With his notion of an author-function Foucault hopes to
resituate the author in history, "reveal[ing] the manner in which
discourse is articulated on the basis of social relations" (137). Yet it

is already in the name of the author that our relationship *to* history is mediated. Foucault elides, in short, the very questions that a Hegel (or a Beckett, for that matter) asks, and in doing so he loses the contours of his *own* question: "What is an author?" What Foucault elides, then, is the question of history as it already animates the concept of the author.

Ultimately, by foreclosing the twin reference of the author's name both toward history and beyond history, Foucault's argument fails to capture the logic of authorization itself. Authorization, I maintain, works to resolve the problems of reference–of, let us say, the time-boundedness of texts–by allowing readers to forge a link between history and its beyond. In his treatment of the author-function Foucault loses sight of the *reader's* function. He loses sight, that is to say, of reading *as* authorization: as that activity according to which empirical beginnings are yoked to transcendent ends.

And thus we return to Hegel's chimeras. Entailed in the very concept of the author that Foucault takes to task is a method of interpretation that operates according to Hegelian principles. At stake is that strange transaction between history and *Zweck*, between will and Will, physical body and canonical corpus, that Hegel describes in his preface. If, like Foucault, we want to examine how the concept of the author emerges–within determinate historical contexts, and with precise social functions–we will need to interpret methods of interpretation themselves. Our own methods will engage us from the very start in the same transactions– between "historical statements" and "implicit meanings"–that form the objects of our inquiry. As in Foucault's argument, it will prove impossible in the study that follows to avoid a certain terminological naivety, crudeness, and ambiguity. But unlike Foucault's argument, at the heart of my argument is the presumption that such "lapses" are unavoidable. To examine the readerly nature of authorship, I will have to commit myself in the first place to reading authors.

As Hegel sees it, the problem with authors *is* the problem of the preface: at stake is the difficulty of linking beginnings to ends. As we will see, this is not only a literary problem, it is the problem that for the Christian West inhabits a specific literary mode: *allegory*. "The True is the whole. But the whole is only the essence con-

summating itself through its development." Wholeness and consummation, truth and history: the terms of Hegel's preface, and
indeed of the *Phenomenology of Spirit* itself, are the terms of religious allegory. On the one hand, while identifying the incompatibility of empirical and transcendental discourses–the piecemeal
nature of history versus the wholeness of truth–Hegel nonetheless
spans the chasm between the two by way of *narrative*. The story
of a self-consummating essence unfolding, over time, serves as that
discourse which is simultaneously linear–progressing from one
moment to the next, after the manner of a "historical account"–
and preposterous, retrospectively defining what comes first in
terms of what came last.[10] On the other hand, and even more ger-
mane to the story that *I* want to tell, Hegel's discourse is allegorical in a second, related sense as well: in terms of the relation it
delineates between author, text, and reader. Hegel defines his
authority, his authorship, from the very start, in the transcendent
terms of allegory: he brackets the empirical act of writing with its
historical contingencies and personal *Zweck*, in light of that final
Zweck, that ultimate purpose, that emerges *only after the fact* of his
writing. Such authority defines not only the book's transcendental
origins: it also defines *our* relation to the text in its wholeness,
determining that authoritative position from which we, delivered
from the hold of history, will have understood truth. This is the
future-anterior position from which the text expounds a meaning
"for us" that we cannot fully comprehend until we have completed
our reading; the reader for whom the book was written only
emerges, like the transcendental author, after the empirical fact.

These retrospective constructions of readerly and writerly
authority share the impulse of *allegoria* as it is classically defined:
as *continued metaphor*, allegory forges a bridge between parts and
whole thanks to the narrative movement from one metaphorical
insight to the next. At the same time, given its insistence on a temporally unfolding truth, Hegel's conception of textual authority
even more nearly replicates a specifically *Christian* allegory: the
allegoria that Paul invokes in his efforts to ground the authority of
Christian gospel within the tradition and scriptures of the Jews. By
allegoria I refer to what Erich Auerbach famously calls "*figura*" or
"figural interpretation" and what other modern readers will designate (wrongly, as I argue in chapter 1) as "typology" in an effort to
distinguish it from allegory *tout court*. Such *allegoria* entails a

specifically textual endeavor: an effort to read the text in its whole-ness, delivering from it a truth that is neither partial nor historical, but universal. To read in such terms is to read from a standpoint outside of history—or at least outside of the book's own historical occasions—and yet to read as if this book written *in* history were written *for us* who stand outside. Indeed, Hegel's *"für uns"*—his allu-sions throughout the *Phenomenology* to a meaning only available for "us" who stand outside the text, at the end of the very narrative he recounts—this *für uns* repeats almost to the letter Paul's formula for an allegorical, Christian reading of Jewish scripture: "These things touched them [i.e., the Israelites] in figure, but they were written *for our sake*, in whom the ends of the ages have come" (1 Cor. 10:11, emphasis added). For Hegel, no less than for Paul, to read truth, the whole truth, we must read the text as if it were written *for our sake*.

To read *for our sake* is to take responsibility for the meaning of the text—a responsibility that is infinitely precious and infinitely sweet, for it delivers into our hands a book of infinite meaning: a book that, being whole, is far more than the sum of its parts. At the same time, this responsibility comes at a likewise infinite cost: the present, in all its nontranscendent empirical density, in all of its *zweckwidrig* particularity, is what the infinite meaning of the infinite text gives up. As I sit here, on my porch, under a cool Ore-gon sky, a nighttime winter sky, stars occluded by clouds, the western hills nonetheless studded with lights, Christmas lights, dining room lights, streetlights—as I sit here, shielding my laptop and books from the spatter of rain, a kink in my neck from sitting too long, I am all too aware that, if the study I have just finished writing will have said what I now think I wanted it to say, it will speak more to the infinite cost of a book's meaning, and less to its infinite sweetness.

READING SHAKESPEARE'S WILL

"DR. MOTH sits by the couch, listening to WILL and occasionally making a note on a pad he holds on his knee. What we see here is nothing less than the false dawn of analysis. The session is being timed by an hour-glass."[11] We should not be surprised that within its first ten pages, Marc Norman and Tom Stoppard's screenplay for the 1998 film

Shakespeare in Love puts Will on the couch. From ivory tower to tinsel town, and again from a formalist like Joel Fineman to a cultural materialist like Peter Stallybrass, the most influential recent treatments of the sonnets have all in the first place unearthed in Shakespeare something like the origin of a modern erotic psychology, a modern sexual politics. In the second place, these recent treatments have all presumed, either implicitly or explicitly, that such a modern viewpoint emerges at the expense of a religious worldview. We are a generation of critics who have defined poetic subjectivity–and the subject of Shakespeare's poetry par excellence–in purely secular terms.

Reading Shakespeare's Will, however, questions our contemporary culture's commitment to a "Shakespeare in love" and on the couch: to a lyrical Shakespeare, that is, who prefigures our own secular, post-Freudian age. Challenging the common equation of subjectivity and secularity, the study redefines in theological terms the poetic legacy that Shakespeare both inherits and bequeaths. To read Shakespeare's will is to read his bequest to, and from, literary history–a bequest saturated by religious doctrine.

At the same time that I challenge the contemporary bias toward secularism, my focus throughout is not "subjectivity" so much as intentionality. When literary critics speak of "subjectivity"–a word they adopt from epistemology and psychoanalysis–they do so in order to denote the textual representation of human agency. I, on the other hand, am less concerned with representation than with interpretation. At stake in my argument is the question of "will" as the intention we ascribe to texts; at stake is the active, readerly construction of a meaning before and beyond the text. At stake, in other words, is not the representation of subjects but the construction of authors. Thus, *Reading Shakespeare's Will* offers the first systematic account, in theological terms, of the construction of Shakespeare as author. It is in this light that I examine the "I" of the Sonnets: instead of describing the secular subject, my study offers readings of the theological author.

At the same time, my approach also departs sharply from traditional treatments of early modern religiosity. Traditionally, accounts of the role of theology in Renaissance poetics have hinged upon questions of source and influence, speculating on the interplay between biography and art. The kind of study offered, for instance, in the late seventies by critics like Barbara Lewalski,

Richard Strier, and Andrew Weiner explores the impact of Reformation theology upon an author's poetic practice, choice of
idioms, themes, forms, et cetera. Grounded ultimately in the question of individual belief and practice, such notions of a "Protestant
poetics" work to anchor formal analyses of text within a nuanced
historical and biographical framework. And yet, at the problematic
heart of such research is the same question of history's relation to
meaning that Hegel analyzes in his preface. How is it possible to
relate history to form, causal narrative to textual unity? Ultimately,
by positing a connection between authorial choice, textual form,
and cultural context, such studies revisit the problem that has
vexed modern literary studies since its new critical inception: the
so-called intentional fallacy.

More recently, more material-minded critics have returned to
theological questions, but from the perspective of cultural studies
and new historicism. James Shapiro's important 1996 book, *Shakespeare and the Jews*, is a paradigmatic case in point. Despite its title,
Shapiro's study offers little discussion of Shakespeare per se, focusing instead upon the Reformation's impact on constructions of
English identity. Not unlike Foucault's genealogy, accounts like
Shapiro's sidestep the question of authorial intention, offering a
study of culture as such rather than of individual cultural products.
Yet here too, within the context of cultural materialism, the
dilemma animating Hegel's idealism holds sway: how can a discussion grounded in the contingencies of history warrant a turn—
even if only a titular one—toward the author?[12]

In response I argue that the problem of the author is itself a theological one, and at its core is, indeed, the issue of intentionality. As
I've tried to suggest with my reading of Foucault, the concept of the
author, while historically conditioned, is nonetheless inescapable; it
attends our reading of discourse, enabling that discretion according
to which we define textual unities—"discursive units"—no matter
what our purpose in doing so may be. The theological tradition crucial for my argument is thus not that creed to which individual
authors subscribe so much as it is that doctrinal tradition that makes
the concept of authorship itself available to Western culture. It is
this theological tradition that, I argue, first makes formal textual
analysis possible and justifiable in the Christian West. Finally, I argue
that we must trace this tradition's history if we are to understand the
unique authority our culture has granted Shakespeare.

More precisely, I situate Shakespeare's poetics within the history of *figura*. Originating in the mind/body dualism of the Gospel of John, what Auerbach calls "figural interpretation" takes shape around the claim that the *flesh* is the *figure* (*typos* in Greek; *figura* in Latin) of the *spirit*. My study demonstrates that this tradition of figurality offers the Christian West far more than a mere exegetical method. I argue that *figura* entails a full-fledged theology: what I call the "theology of figure." It is, furthermore, this theology that provides Renaissance Petrarchism with its very themes, tropes, and formal structures. But so too does Petrarchism transform this figural legacy, setting the stage for Martin Luther's redefinition of flesh and spirit in the sixteenth century. Luther, I argue, absolutely shatters the notion of flesh as figure. In so doing, he challenges Christian doctrine and Renaissance poetics at once. Luther's work thus constitutes the crucial intellectual context for Shakespeare's sonnets. Regardless of the poet's own religious beliefs, we cannot properly understand his poetry without recognizing it as a response to Luther. Finally, in my last chapter I consider the political stakes of this poetic response. By way of conclusion, my study moves beyond lyric to the drama, gesturing toward the twentieth century and the darker legacy of Shakespeare's will. In a reading of *The Merchant of Venice* I examine the ways in which Luther's critique of *figura* makes available–for Shakespeare and for us–a newly problematic figure of the Jew.

The central emblem of my study is an orthodox, but seldom cited, figure of figural interpretation: a fantasy that Augustine recounts in his *Confessions*. Struggling to interpret the first book of the Jewish Torah, Augustine imagines for a moment that the (supposed) human author of that text–Moses himself–were present and able to reveal the meaning of the scripture directly to Augustine. In vivid, fleshly terms Augustine imagines taking hold of the author. He imagines Moses' lips "bursting" with words and pressed against his willing ear. The fantasy transforms a relationship mediated by time, culture, and text into a sensual, physical encounter: meaning pours forth into the reader's receptive ear from the author's bursting mouth. But just as soon as Augustine imagines this moment of a direct, unmediated link to the author's will, he abandons the fantasy. Moses' truth would have been particular, private, mortal, and–importantly–*Jewish*, while Augustine seeks a public, eternal, and universal truth. That is to say, he seeks a *Christian* truth. For Augustine, authorial intention is a fallacy because it can only reveal the limits of time and flesh. The real intention of the text is always the spiritual one, and it can only be discovered once we inure ourselves to the siren's call of the long-dead, distant author.

Critics have, of course, for some time now rejected Augustine's allegorical method of interpretation and its notion of a universal truth behind the historical specificities of the text. And yet, we still share with Augustine the sense of an illicit fantasy. We still invoke–with guilt and with qualification–the desire to hear voices long dead; we still reluctantly acknowledge that Moses cannot press his mouth against our ear or that, even if he could, his meaning would not be *the* meaning of the text. Meaning, we still maintain, is discovered in the reading; and it is this primacy and authority of reading that, above all else, Augustine's figural interpretation bequeaths to us. Sixteen centuries before Roland Barthes, Augustine announced "the death of the author"–and, like Barthes, Augustine also declared the reader's birth.

Ultimately I argue that this figural legacy not only informs our modern reading practices; it also informs Renaissance poetic practice by providing writers like Petrarch and Shakespeare with powerful, if ambivalent, fantasies of authorial presence. Indeed, it is my argument in what follows that there is, necessarily, only one way to read Shakespeare's w/Will: that is, to read it as the figural culmination of a history that has called *figura* itself into question. To make that argument I shall require the resources of a figural tradition: a tradition whose central and governing idea, *figura*, is inescapable–not a priori inescapable, to be sure, but inescapable for us ("für uns") who would read it, after the fact. *Figura*, I am arguing, is an idea that can be constructed as a historical phenomenon only by way of the same readerly apparatus it describes.

Shakespeare's *Will*: I mean, in the first place, the *Will* of *Shakespeare's Sonnets*–the almost indecipherable pun that Shakespeare makes of his proper name and his improper pen/penis; but more than that, I mean the authority, the intentionality, the *will* in a sense analogous to Hegel's *Zweck*, Augustine's *arbitrium*, Luther's *Wille* and *Williglichkeit*, that we have come to ascribe to Shakespeare. This is an authority that, I maintain, defines his status for us as the poet of negative capability, as characterless voice (as Keats will call him). Further, it is an authority that has made our attempts to grapple with Shakespeare's first-person—not with his characterless voice in the plays, but with his willful lyrical voice—as thorny and unsatisfying as they are irresistible.

Shakespeare's *Will.* In the second place, I mean the problem of futurity, especially in connection to erotic desire and its consummation (sex, marriage)—a problem that Shakespeare thematizes throughout his work, although perhaps nowhere as resonantly and straightforwardly as he does in the mock wedding scene in *As You Like It.*

> CEL. . . . wil you Orlando, haue to wife this Ros-
> alind?
> ORL. I will.
> ROS. I, but when?
> ORL. Why now, as fast as she can marrie vs.
> ROS. Then you must say, I take thee Rosalind for
> wife.
> ORL. I take thee Rosalind for wife.
>
> (4.1.125–32)

As Shakespeare here reminds us, thanks to the Book of Common Prayer "I will" doesn't simply describe an intention of future compliance: it also performs the present vow of marriage. And yet, almost in anticipation of Derrida's famous response to J. L. Austin's notion of performative utterance, the confusion between Rosalind and Orlando highlights the structural potential for citation and parody that threatens the eventfulness of any speech act. Moreover, given this potential and the way that it casts doubt upon any promise, Rosalind and Orlando's exchange demonstrates that gap between present (e.g., "I will" as performative utterance) and future (e.g., "I will" as statement of intent), which neither human language nor human volition can ever be sure to span. Will our utterances have meant what we mean?

Ultimately at stake for Rosalind—as well as for the *Will* of *Shakespeare's Sonnets*—is the question of temporal constancy. "Was," as Celia reminds us, is not "is":

> CEL. For his [i.e., Orlando's] verity in loue, I doe
> thinke him as concaue as a couered goblet, or
> a Worme-eaten nut.
> ROS. Not true in loue?
> CEL. Yes, when he is in, but I thinke he is not in.
> ROS. You haue heard him sweare downright he was.
> CEL. Was, is not is: besides, the oath of Louer is no
> stronger then the word of a Tapster, they are both
> the confirmer of false reckonings.
>
> (3.4.25–32)[13]

Even in Arden, where supposedly there is no clock to mark the passage of time,[14] time finds its way to mark *us*. No matter how devoutly wished, consummation cannot verify the oaths of lovers; "is" soon becomes "was." Time reveals no "self-consummating" essence, but instead tells only the "false reckonings" of our waste. As Jaques, the melancholic worm at the heart of Arden's nut, reminds us: "And so from houre to houre, we ripe, and ripe, / And then from houre to houre, we rot, and rot" (2.7.28–39).

Shakespeare's *Will*. I mean in the third place, Shakespeare's will as his *legacy*: both what he inherits from tradition and what he bequeaths to us. As I shall argue, this inheritance consists first and foremost in the tradition of *figura*, which construes the authority of the book in terms of the will, the intentionality, that we posit both before and beyond the book, anchoring its legitimacy in history and authorizing its truth in reading. My reading of Shakespeare's *Will*–it will not have escaped notice–promises thus to be unabashedly bardolatrous. But, if I have made my point adequately and correctly, I will by the end of this study have demonstrated why and exactly how such bardolatry is necessary.

Lastly, by invoking Shakespeare's will I invoke not only the *Will* of Will Shakespeare but also the will of the father: the will that *John* Shakespeare is supposed to have left. It is reported that, on April 27, 1757, Joseph Mosely–a builder who was retiling the roof of the Shakespeare house on Henley Street in Stratford– found "wedged between the tiling and the rafters,"[15] a small booklet, handwritten, and seeming to be the Spiritual Last Will and Testament of John Shakespeare. Edmund Malone eventually obtained the manuscript and printed a copy of it in his 1790 edition of Shakespeare's *Plays and Poems*, although he was ultimately dubious of its authenticity. What seemed clear, however, is that, spurious or no, this last will and testament of John Shakespeare's soul was drawn from a religious formulary—and a Catholic one at that: a sort of catechism that the testator was meant to sign in order to declare his adherence to the old faith and to make provisions for death in a Protestant country where, not unlike Old Hamlet, one was liable to die bereft of Catholic sacrament, "cut off euen in the Blossomes of . . . Sinne, / Vnhouzzled, disappointed, vnnaneld" (*Hamlet* 1.5.80–81):

> In the name of God, the father, sonne, and holy ghost, the most holy and blessed Virgin Mary, mother of God, the holy host of archangels, angels, patriarchs, prophets, evangelists, apostles, saints, martyrs, and all the celestial court and company of heaven, I John Shakspear, an unworthy member of the holy Catholick religion, being at this present writing in perfect health of body, and sound mind, memory, and understanding, but calling to mind the uncertainty of life and certainty of death, and that I may be possibly cut off in the blossome of my sins,[16] and called to render an account of all my transgressions externally and internally, and that I may be unprepared for the dreadful trial either by sacrament, pennance, fasting, or prayer, or any other purgation whatever, do in the holy presence above specified, of my own free and voluntary accord, make and ordaine this my last spiritual will, testament, confession, protestation, and confession of faith, hopinge hereby to receive pardon for all my sinnes and offences.[17]

The "John Shakespeare" manuscript itself was lost, but in 1923 a Spanish copy of the formulary upon which the will must have been based was discovered in the British Museum. The formulary was then traced back to Carlo Borromeo, cardinal and archbishop of Milan, who died in 1585 and who has been directly linked to sixteenth-century English Catholics. In 1966, an English translation of Borromeo's formulary, printed in 1638, was finally found—support that copies of the document might have been available to English recusants in John Shakespeare's day.

John Shakespeare's Spiritual Will has, of course, been taken as evidence that the Shakespeare family were Catholics. The evidence is highly debatable, however, and its significance is too: even if we could prove that the father was a Catholic recusant, what would that tell us about the son, and why, how would that information matter? These questions are crucial ones. In what follows I shall be tracing a figural line from Augustine to Petrarch to Luther to Shakespeare, arguing, in effect, that Shakespeare is a Lutheran author. But what does such a claim entail? It does *not*, for instance, entail that Shakespeare was Lutheran, or even Protestant; it does not, in fact, presume anything about the empirical author's actual religious faith. Such empirical facts can be settled only by reference to the historical record, and once having been settled, their relevance remains unclear *for us*, those who seek to read texts not in their piecemeal contingency but rather in their necessary wholeness (even if we come, as poststructuralism has brought us, to define that "wholeness" in terms of a constitutive fragmentation). My argument entails no claims about Shakespeare as empirical author. Instead I am arguing about the kind of author Shakespeare is *for us*. For us, Shakespeare's authority, I argue, can best be described in the theological terms that Luther provides. And indeed, these are terms that preclude our ever closing the gap between empirical questions and transcendental meanings, for it is Luther whose theological insights come at the expense of *figura*'s coherence. It is Luther's reformation, I argue, and the very legacy he leaves behind, that poses a decisive challenge to allegorical teleology, disarticulating any narrative that might take us from the fleshly world of "historical accounts" to the transcendent world of *Geist*, of spirit.

In short, knowing the "actual" William Shakespeare's "actual" religious faith would not change my characterization of him as author. But nonetheless, I find it intriguing that the last testament and spiritual will of Will's father has vanished. When it comes to an author like Shakespeare, our desires for origin and end–for a literary history, a textual authority, secured in the assurance of paternity and pedigree–seem inevitably foreclosed. Will's father's will tantalizes and frustrates, present only as fading memory or spurious myth. But: if like Hegel's chimeras or Hamlet's ghost, the will of the father is a fantasy, it is nonetheless a historically decisive one.

In April of 1989, the author of *Shakespeare's Perjured Eye*, Joel Fineman, died at the age of forty-two. In September of 1989, Norbert

Freinkel, my father, died at the age of sixty-three. The relevance of such sheerly historical occasions for the argument that follows is not at all clear to me. To what extent do such empirical causes stand in for the origins of meaning? As I write this now, I have no answer. But I will say this:

About two weeks ago I dreamed that I was reading Susan Sontag's book, *Illness as Metaphor*. As it turns out, it is a book I have never read, although I am vaguely aware of its content. In the dream, however, I discovered that the book was about a phenomenon that "Sontag," the author I invented in the dream, called *holocemia*. "Holocemia," my dream author explained, was the toxicity from which a post-Holocaust world suffers. *Holocemia*, like *septicemia*, a kind of poisoning of the world's blood, a lingering symptom of the Holocaust. . . . I awoke with a phrase from "Sontag" imprinted in my memory: "The world of deep caring can be built once again out of grieving." I am the daughter of German Jews; the daughter of Holocaust survivors. And the relevance of this "historical account" for the study you are about to read remains, for me, entirely unclear.

READING SHAKESPEARE'S WILL

ONE

Augustine Under the Fig Tree

These things touched them in figure, but they were written for our
sake, in whom the ends of the ages have come.

–1 Corinthians 10:11

When you were under the fig tree, I saw you.

–John 1:48[1]

Figura AS HYBRID: THE PROMISE OF FLESH

As Erich Auerbach tells us, from at least Tertullian onward figurality has been about promises. In his famous essay "Figura," Auerbach charts the development of the Western concept of the figural
from Terence to Dante. Useful for our purposes will be his theo-
rization of what he calls "figural interpretation," but which, as we
shall see, is less an interpretive method than a theory of textuality
and a rationale of textual authority. More commonly referred to as
typology or as Christian allegory (or allegoresis), such figural interpretation takes its cue from Jesus' claim that he comes not to
destroy the law but to fulfill it (cf. Matt. 5:17). The dictum readily
informs Paul's conception of a specifically Christian revelation.
According to Paul, the new covenant, the covenant of grace and
faith, at once surpasses and encompasses, fulfills and annuls, the
Judaic covenant with God, the old covenant of law.[2] But since
even for Paul these covenants were not simply understood as
events but were also seen as *texts*–the texts we have come to call
the *Old Testament* and the *New Testament*[3]–this conception of the

relation between a people and its God immediately bleeds over into a conception of the relation between a people and its *Book*. "As a whole," Auerbach tells us, the Old Testament ceased for Paul "to be a book of the law and history of Israel and became from beginning to end a promise and prefiguration of Christ, in which there is no definitive, but only a prophetic meaning which has now been fulfilled, in which everything is written 'for our sakes.'"[4] To read Scripture, then, is to read it as if written *propter nos*–for our sakes. It is to discern, by light of the New Testament, the figural import of the Old. It is to read the concealed presence of the New in the "figures" (*figurae*) or "types"–the promises–of the Old.

So much is clear even from Paul, but any practical guidelines we might want to establish will be curiously hard to specify. What counts for a figure? An event, a person, a word? What justifies the connection between a given Old Testament type and its New Testament fulfillment or "antitype"?[5] The theory of *figura* is bedeviled in its practical details. Indeed, as I suggested above, Christian figurality will be best understood not as a *practice* of reading but, instead, as a *theory* of reading. Even so, modern literary critics and theologians alike have sought to define figural interpretation as precisely as possible–most often by trying to distinguish it from other forms of allegory. Indeed, many have wanted to differentiate figural interpretation from allegory per se. In large measure thanks not only to Auerbach but also to the important work of the Jesuit theologian Jean Daniélou, modern readers have distinguished between typology, which reads the Old Testament as a prefiguration of the New, and common, so-called moral allegory, which uses events and personae from either testament to illustrate a theological or ethical principle that is in truth extrinsic to the text.[6]

This distinction between allegory and typology is not, however, a neutral one. Indeed, for a reform-minded theologian like Daniélou, the distinction is crucial–a linchpin in his efforts to retrieve an authentic, spiritual sense of Scripture. Beginning in the 1940s, around the same time as Auerbach's work on *figura*, Daniélou, Henri de Lubac, and other affiliates of the Jesuit House in Fourvière, France, urged a renewed Christian humanism, a return *ad fontes*, to the Church's biblical and patristic sources. In patristic discussions of allegory and type, Daniélou finds–almost as if *in figure*–the terms he needs to address the problems of modern exegesis. As he puts it: "Allegory is not a sense of Scripture at all: it is the presentation of philosophy and Christian morality under Biblical imagery" (*Shadows*, 61). In the model of exegesis that Daniélou popularizes, the issues are exceedingly clear-cut: typology provides the sense of Scripture, which, on the other hand, the allegorist simply *fails* to read.

Given this emphasis on allegory's extraneity with respect to the text, one might expect to see typology construed in contrast by writers like Daniélou as an especially literary or textual mode of exegesis. But rather than value a commitment to text and letter, Daniélou and others seem instead to value an interpretation moored in the world of *things*. As Joseph Galdon, S.J., writes:

> Type and antitype are spiritual . . . only with regard to the meaning they embody in the referential context of shadow and fulfillment. In themselves, and of themselves, they remain real things, not abstractions. Indeed, they would have no meaning at all as types if they were not scriptural realities, for the referential meaning of type and antitype rests essentially and necessarily upon the reality or concreteness of both poles of the reference. They are both *things*.[7]

As historical, concrete *things*, scriptural types save us from our-selves, anchoring our reading of the text in an objective, public world–sparing our criticism from the excesses of moral allegory, from, that is to say, an interpretation founded upon the subjective, consisting in the "unwarrantable exercise of private and uncon-trolled ingenuity."[8] Typology is thus opposed to allegory as public is to private, as objective is to subjective, as legitimate use of intel-ligence is to the "unwarrantable" exercise of ingenuity.

At stake here, we might say, is the fantasy of a public lan-guage–and when, in chapter 3, we turn toward Luther's dysphoric image of the "beshitted author," we will see the filthy flip side of such a fantasy in a Reformation print culture. For now, however, we need only note the distance between patristic views of *figura* and modern conceptions of typology. Distinctions between pri-vate and public interpretation, between readings that do and do not attend to history are, to be sure, crucial topics for patristic writ-ers–but not for the reasons a Galdon or a Daniélou presents. Patristic views betray neither anxiety over the "uncontrolled" excesses of subjectivism nor the fantasy of an interpretation grounded in empirical fact. Instead, as I will discuss in more detail below, interpretive authority consists for a writer like Augustine in the plurality of varied and individual interpretations that the community, itself grounded in shared attitudes toward the text and theories of reading, can sustain.[9] Such authority becomes, then, a function of the community, just as the text is conceived as a communal property—and such intersubjectivity is a far cry from the impersonality of a Galdon or Daniélou's historical positivism.[10] As Daniélou writes: "Typology . . . is not an exegesis of the Old Testament; it is an interpretation of the very history which those books recount."[11] As we moderns view it, typology allows us—fantastically—to replace the words of texts with the things of history. To read typologically is to "read" history. Instead of letters, or so the fantasy goes, the typologist "reads" *scriptural realities.*

Strictly speaking, this fantasy is impossible; one cannot rigorously distinguish between typology and allegory any more than one can rigorously demonstrate the legitimacy of a given reading. (Indeed, it is precisely because at some level Luther recognizes this impossibility that his version of the fantasy is so fraught, as we'll see, with anxiety.) More important, however, the desire to replace texts with history precisely inverts the terms of patristic figurality. As Augustine will finally make clear, at stake with figural interpretation is not history as a way out of reading, but reading as a way *into* history. From its Pauline inception Christian figurality grounds itself not in history per se but in the readerly, promissory construction *of* that history.

Thus, when Tertullian sets forth his notion of *figura* as promise in his treatise *Adversus Marcionem*, he is not so much objecting to his opponent Marcion's vision of history as to the way that vision constitutes a refusal to *read.* Thoroughly accepting the Old Testament as history, Marcion and his followers found it impossible to accept as Scripture. As an account of chronological fact the text was true, but as a document of faith, offering deliverance to the believer, the text had no authority for the Christian. In this way, paradoxically owing to his overwhelming piety, to his conception of the Gospel's incomparable goodness and truth, Marcion posited two separate gods, since he could not reconcile the God of creation with the God of salvation. On the one hand, Marcion envisioned a Creator god described in actual, historical terms in the Old Testa-

ment and known to us through his creation; this god Marcion considered as the judicious ruler of the universe and the source of all
that is imperfect, corporeal, corrupt. On the other hand, he posited
a God who was the supreme essence of goodness–a "stranger"
God who was completely unknown to us until the coming of His
Son, Jesus. In this fashion, Marcion glorified the Advent as an
entirely remarkable, unexpected and novel, absolutely incomparable event. The Good News was thus the utterly new good.[12]

Nonetheless, since Marcion accepted the Old Testament as
history, he also noted that the Creator had promised a Christ: a
sort of "parallel universe" Christ, if you will, who, as the political
messiah of the Jews, bore absolutely no relation to the Christ of
the Gospel. Accordingly, Marcion dismissed the Old Testament
christological prophecies as irrelevant. "As the God of the Jews
was radically separate from the Father of the Lord Jesus Christ,"
Jaroslav Pelikan writes, describing Marcionite doctrine, "so the
deposit of the revelations of the former could not be authoritative
for the true disciples of the latter. The Old Testament had not been
fulfilled, but abolished" (*Emergence*, 76). No reason, then, for the
Christian to read the Old: the stranger God of the New Testament
had never been prophesied, had never been promised, had never
done anything before the Advent.

For Tertullian, however, this unknown, inactive God presents
a logical absurdity and a moral outrage; as Tertullian points out,
such divine "idleness" (*otium*) empties out time itself:

> That leisured god of yours, who has neither anything of
> prophecy nor anything of work, and so has nothing of
> time, what has he ever done to cause time to be fulfilled,
> and to justify waiting for its fulfillment?
>
> (*Adversus Marcionem* 5.4.3)[13]

What fills time, what relieves the *otium* of history, is the structure
of prophecy–the way in which we are sustained and supported
through time by the promise of fulfillment. By preaching the radical novelty of Christian salvation, Marcion enforces a discontinuous vision of history whose effect is to evacuate the fullness of
time.

In book 3 of the *Adversus Marcionem*, Tertullian demonstrates
the incoherence of this view. As he points out, Marcion's princi-

ple of historical discontinuity engenders a logical impossibility: for Marcion, the Old Testament must be both read and not read—its authority both accepted and denied. Thus Tertullian uses the notion of Jewish ignorance—of the supposed Jewish failure to recognize Christ as messiah—to split apart the Marcionite idea of a *deus extraneus,* a "stranger God." As Tertullian demonstrates, Jewish ignorance becomes for Marcion both a logically necessary and a logically impossible assumption. We can unpack this aporia as follows: Marcion's notion of a divine duality, of two Fathers and two Sons, two distinct messiahs, was meant to preserve the incomparability of Christian revelation by insisting upon a certain "genetic," if you will, discontinuity: the two filial lines of the Old and New Testaments run parallel to each other but do not intersect. The son of the Old Testament is not the Son of the New; his father is not the Father of Christ. Small wonder then that the Jews did not recognize Christ as their savior: He was literally unknown, *unfamiliar* to them. But in this context, a problem arises: the Old Testament prophets themselves foretell the Jews' failure to recognize their messiah. However, since according to Marcion the Old Testament prophecies do not speak to the New Testament, this foretold ignorance cannot be the same ignorance with which the Jews rejected Christ. Instead, their rejection of Christ must have amounted to a kind of *knowledge*: in failing to recognize Christ, they recognized that He was not the messiah foretold in their scripture. They recognized that Christ was not the son of the Creator. They would have known Christ, then, as unknown.

But as Tertullian sees it, such ignorant knowledge is impossible: if Christ were utterly strange and radically new, strictly speaking there would be no basis for any kind of judgment—including the judgment that He was a stranger. The problem here is that of *knowing a stranger.* If Christ were utterly foreign, entirely unexpected, radically new, how could He possibly be recognized—even to be recognized *as such*? The Jews could not *even* have rejected Christ. As Tertullian puts it:

> It is now apparent why the Jews both rejected Christ and put him to death: not because they understood Christ as a stranger, but because they recognized him as their own. For how could they have understood as a stranger one about

whom there had never been an announcement ... ? For the possibility that something can be understood or not understood comes when, by having a substance [*substantia*] in prophecy, it also will have matter [*materia*] either for acknowledgment or for error. For what lacks matter can't admit the outcome of wisdom. Consequently, it was not as belonging to another god that they objected to Christ and persecuted him, but as being nothing more than a man ... with the result that this very man who was theirs, that is Jewish, but a perverter and destroyer of Judaism, they brought to judgment and punished with their law. A stranger would certainly have not been punished.

(*Adversus Marcionem* 3.6.9–10)

Judgment is only possible on the basis of comparison—what is alien is not familiar, what is new is not old—and for Tertullian it is prophecy, and the temporal distinctions it affords, that provides the ground, the *materia* or *substantia*, for comparative judgments. In this way, the Jews could only reject their own flesh and blood; in Tertullian's hands, the Jews' very ignorance of Christ becomes a proof that He has fulfilled Judaic prophecy. In order to deem Christ a foreigner, a stranger, the Jews would have first had to acknowledge Him as their own.

It is this structure of simultaneous acceptance and denial, acknowledgment and disavowal that disrupts Marcion's logic. Marcion would like to preserve a "genetic" cosmology—a cosmology grounded in a notion of history as the seamless, inevitable consequence of procreation, one generation succeeding the next, defining a *gens*—a people. Such a cosmology is fortified by bloodlines, by the presumably natural order of inheritance and filiation. Ironically, it is upon the basis of the genetic, seemingly irrefutable link between fathers and sons, between one generation and the next, that Marcion defines the strangeness of his stranger Christ: because He has a different Father, the Christ of the Christians is literally *unrelated to* the messiah of the Jews. A "genetic" presumption of historical seamlessness or continuity thus provides the rationale for Marcion's notion of a radical historical *dis*continuity.[14]

It is not hard, however, for Tertullian to unravel this argument. In the end, all he really need remind Marcion is that Jesus was in fact a Jew. Once we recognize the literal heritage of Christ, it becomes impossible to assert the difference between Old and New Testaments, between Jew and Christian in simply genetic terms. In some way, Christ must be conceived as both Jew and non-Jew, as both of his people and a stranger to them. For Tertullian, far from presenting a paradox, this kind of "both-and" logic epitomizes the logic of salvation—a logic that is promissory, i.e., tied to the structure of promising, rather than genetic. Thus, for Tertullian, Christ belongs to the Creator as a fulfillment belongs to a promise: He fulfills the "scripturas creatoris," completes the Creator's words. "In accordance with these scriptures," Tertullian tells us, laying out his battle plan, "I intend to prove that Christ belonged to the Creator since it was in His Christ that these scriptures were afterwards fulfilled" (*Adversus Marcionem* 3.5.1).

The classic statement of this distinction between the genetic and the promissory, however, predates Tertullian by two centuries. It is to be found already with Paul. In his letter to the Galatians, Paul imagines a genealogy without genes, "[so] that the blessing of Abraham might come on the Gentiles through Jesus Christ" (Gal. 3:14). In other words, Paul imagines an order of inheritance that bypasses the dictates of clan: the Christian inherits the Jewish birthright through faith and divine promise instead of through blood. In this way, Paul imagines a continuity between Jew and Christian, between Old and New, that preserves the fruit of genetic affiliation—legacy and birthright—while rejecting its limiting, tribal terms.

At issue here is Paul's conception of Christian liberty: he is at pains to dispel the Galatians' idea that one must be a Jew, devout in adherence to Mosaic law, before one can be a Christian. Instead, the epistle as a whole sets forth the doctrine of *sola fide*, of justification by faith alone. The crux of Paul's argument is his revision of that foundational moment of the Jewish people: Abraham's covenant with God. Paul insists that through faith in Christ—Himself a Jew rejected by Jews—even Gentiles can lay claim to the blessing that is Abraham's divine legacy. "Now to Abraham and his seed were the promises made. He saith not, And to seeds, as of many; but as of one, And to thy seed, which is Christ. . . . And if ye be Christ's, then are ye Abraham's seed, and heirs according to the promise" (Gal. 3:16, 29).

The difference here—and it is a *Christian* difference, we must remember[15]—lies between Judaism as a tribal sect and Christianity as an universalizing world religion. "There is neither Jew nor Greek, there is neither bond nor free, there is neither male nor female: for ye are all one in Christ Jesus" (Gal. 3:28).[16] The Jews are a people insofar as they can trace their lineage back to Abraham; the Christians, on the other hand, can trace their lineage back to Abraham insofar as they are a people, insofar as they are one in Christ Jesus.

We couldn't be further from Marcion's idea of a radical break between Old and New Testaments. Such radical discontinuity, we will remember, was only conceivable according to that logic of historical linearity and racial lineage that I've been calling "genetic." The difference Marcion imagined between Jew and Christian could be understood, that is to say, only on the basis of a genetic principle of similarity. In contrast, Paul exposes the fundamental role of promising in the constitution of a *gens*: God's promise to Abraham is, after all, precisely what founds the Jewish people. Underlying the linear progress of Judaic genealogy is that which is decisively nongenetic: the promise, whose temporality, as we shall see in a moment, is anything but linear. "For if the inheritance be of the law, it is no more of promise: but God gave it to Abraham by promise" (Gal. 3:18). This law is as much the law of nature as it is the law of Moses, and its dictates will contrast sharply with the promise that underlies it. Thus, where Marcion imagined a genetic discontinuity between Jew and Christian, Paul, according to a more complex, hybrid logic, imagines a discontinuity at the heart of the genetic itself. Instead of a radical break between the two, for Paul, the difference between Jew and Christian is thus in an important sense already internal to the Judaic itself.

Paul's hybrid logic and its dependence upon the figurality of Christian reading become more explicit in the very next chapter of Galatians.

> For it is written, that Abraham had two sons, the one by a bondmaid, the other by a freewoman. But he who was of the bondwoman was born after the flesh; but he of the freewoman was by promise. Which things are an allegory: for these are the two covenants; the one from the mount Sinai, which gendereth to bondage, which is Agar. For this Agar is mount Sinai in Arabia, and answereth to Jerusalem which

now is, and is in bondage with her children. But Jerusalem which is above is free, which is the mother of us all. . . . Now we, brethren, as Isaac was, are the children of promise. But as then he that was born after the flesh persecuted him that was born after the Spirit, even so it is now. Nevertheless what saith the scripture? *Cast out the bondwoman and her son: for the son of the bondwoman shall not be heir with the son of the free woman* [Gen. 21:10]. So then, brethren, we are not children of the bondwoman, but of the free.

(Gal. 4:22–31)

Paul's allegory of the difference between the Old and New Testaments glosses the relation between Christian liberty and Hebrew servitude. Ishmael and Isaac, elder and younger, differ as the law of nature differs from, and defers to, the supernatural. Ishmael is born into slavery, as much because he is a bondwoman's son as because he was "born after the flesh"—born, that is, according to the course of nature (*natus secundum carnem*, as the Vulgate has it). Isaac, on the other hand, was born and conceived free—born to a free woman, but born also free of the constraints of the flesh since he was *natus secundum spiritum*, born according to the spirit. As Paul reminds us, Isaac was born by means of a promise (*per repromissionem*): namely, through God's promise that Sarah, although barren, would conceive. "And the Lord visited Sarah as he had said, and the Lord did unto Sarah as he had spoken. For Sarah conceived, and bare Abraham a son in his old age, at the set time of which God had spoken to him" (Gen. 21:1–2). Born out of sync with the course of nature, Isaac is the product of a divine speech-act.

Thus, freedom and slavery are not simply inherited traits for Paul.[17] If Ishmael is a slave, Isaac a free man, the servitude of the one and the liberty of the other do not simply reflect their birth to different mothers; instead, reflected here are their *different births*. Isaac's birth subverts the natural order and sequence of things, bypassing the flesh in order to follow the spirit, just as Christian faith bypasses and surpasses Mosaic law. In contrast, the figure of Ishmael reveals Jewish servitude itself to be a sort of genetic slavery: a commitment to the succession of generations, to the irreversible order of nature and the entrapments of flesh. Paul's allegory, then, provides a powerful rationale for the democratizing, universalizing thrust of this epistle: "There is neither Jew nor Greek, neither bond nor free." Distinctions of birth exist only for those who follow the course of nature—who live *secundum carnem*.[18]

For Paul the difference between Jew and Christian is not, finally, a genetic difference but is rather the difference between the genetic and the promissory. To follow Mosaic law is to be slave to nature, to live according to the flesh; at the same time, the order of Christian faith is an order of the spirit and of freedom, of a life through promise. The two Testaments relate as the flesh does to the spirit that transcends it. Yet it is this very distinction between flesh and spirit—a *New* Testament distinction—that Paul establishes by allegorizing a story from the *Old* Testament. An allegorical reading of the Old, then, provides an allegory of the difference between the Old and the New. But this difference is itself the difference *of* allegory, since, for Paul, what distinguishes the two testaments is the fact that the Old serves the New as its figure. In this way, Paul's allegory of the difference between the two Testaments amounts to an allegory *of* allegory: an allegory, that is to say, of the allegorical or figural reading of the Old in light of the New. The difference between the Old and the New is, then, the difference that allegory makes. It is the way allegory makes the Old *different* by reading it as the promise of the New.

For Paul, then, the difference between two peoples hangs upon a difference of reading: at stake here is a *figural* (and no longer a genetic) difference. In the Epistle to the Romans, Paul offers a striking image for this figural difference. Indeed, Paul's image demonstrates his departure from a Marcionite understanding of genetic difference, literalizing the sense in which the "both-and," promissory logic of *figura* is a *hybrid* logic.

> For I speak to you Gentiles, inasmuch as I am the apostle of the Gentiles, I magnify mine office: If by any means I may provoke to emulation them which are my flesh, and might save some of them. For if the casting away of them be the reconciling of the world, what shall the receiving of them be, but life from the dead? For if the firstfruit be holy, the lump is also holy: and if the root be holy, so are the branches. And if some of the branches be broken off, and thou, being a wild olive tree,

wert graffed in among them, and with them partakest of
the root and fatness of the olive tree; Boast not against
the branches. . . . Thou wilt say then, The branches were
broken off, that I might be graffed in. Well; because of
unbelief they were broken off, and thou standest by faith.
Be not high-minded, but fear: For if God spared not the
natural branches, take heed lest he also spare not thee.

(Rom. 11:13–21)

Paul is peculiarly poised in this passage: a Jew speaking among
Gentiles, acutely aware of his separation from "them which are my
flesh" but at the same time curiously and excessively turned
toward this flesh, "if *by any means* I may provoke [them] to emu-
lation." The conversion of the Jews is of paramount importance for
Paul. But in his simultaneous rejection of and identification with
his people—with his *flesh*—Paul reminds us just how *unkind* Christian nature is. Or rather, he reminds us that such nature is a hybrid
one. Thus Paul tells us of the *oliva*, the cultivated or "true" olive
tree: emblem of a patriarchal, Jewish origin engrafted with its
amputative pagan other—namely, the *oleaster* or "wild" olive.[19] The
intervention of a new species keeps the old root active; at the same
time, the root makes alien branches holy. An unnatural act per-
petuates the order of nature: the insertion[20] of the wild olive in
place of the *oliva*'s broken branches keeps the relation between
root and fruit alive.

    In this way, the order of nature as a genetic transmission from
origin to offshoot is at once sustained and destroyed (it is sustained
because it is destroyed); the hybrid olive at once defies and preserves the claims of lineage. Thus, implicitly, Paul reconsiders
Jesus' caveat regarding false prophets: "Ye shall know them by
their fruits. Do men gather grapes of thorns, or figs of thistles?"
(Matt. 7:16). At stake in the order of nature is also the order of
knowledge: a genetic cosmology precisely vouchsafes our ability
to assert lineage and origin. We can know others by their fruits
because we can deduce kind from kind, parentage from offspring.
We can tell good from bad, true from false because all things
bespeak their source. And yet as Paul considers the new generation of Christians—the pagans who might well be false prophets
and he himself, a Jew among Gentiles—as he positions himself far
from his own kind, he offers an image of the hybrid. In this man-

ner Paul suggests that one *might*, in fact, gather figs from thistles. As it stands, our *oliva* root is yielding *oleaster* branches. At first glance, the fruits of Christianity are unnatural ones indeed.

But the point of the hybrid is that it naturalizes what is potentially unnatural. The hybrid resolves temporal disruption in terms of spatial integration: the diachronic order of natural succession is interrupted and bypassed—but at the same time that order is preserved synchronically in *space*. Because they define a single living organism, root and fruit coexist and are conjoined: *oliva* roots nurture *oleaster* branches. In this way, temporal rupture and disparity condition organic unity: differing in kind, *oliva* and *oleaster* nonetheless are united in the same hybrid tree.

Thus Paul's figures all assume the equivalence of spatial unity and temporal succession: "if the firstfruit be holy, the lump is also holy: and if the root be holy, so are the branches." As Paul sees it, "firstfruit" and "root" are both equally apt images for the Jewish patriarchs in relation to their Christian heirs. But if the root elicits a temporal image of growth and development, the firstfruit invokes the spatial terms of synecdoche. Here Paul calls upon Numbers 15:20: "Ye shall offer up a cake of the first of your dough for an heave offering." Skimmed off the top of one's harvest, if this cake offering, if this so-called firstfruit of one's grain from the threshing floor is holy, then the entire mass of grain is holy. But analogously, as Paul argues, the root sanctifies the branches; thus Paul finds the relation of part to whole, of firstfruit to lump, interchangeable with the relation of origin to offshoot, of root to branch. The Jewish patriarchs are simultaneously parent to a Christian offspring *and* blessed part to an equally sanctified whole. Spatial synecdoche and temporal telos are equivalent; in some sense one might even say that Paul understands time *as* space. At any rate, the temporality of Pauline *figura* takes the form of a hybrid, but unified, spatiality. "And if some of the branches be broken off, and thou, being a wild olive tree, wert graffed in among them, and with them partakest of the root and fatness of the olive tree; Boast not against the branches."

Paul's image of the grafted olive is an image of Christian revisionism, of the retrospective "insertion" of Christian ends in Jewish beginnings. As such it is an image of *figura*—an image of the structure of Christian reading. But if Paul uses the image to warn Christian readers not to "boast against the branches," Augustine reminds us that such anti-Jewish[21] "boasting" is inevitable. The structure of Christian reading, as Augustine understands it, is inescapably *against the Jews*. Thus, when Augustine cites Paul's image of the hybrid tree in his treatise *Adversos Iudaeos* he opposes a salvific Christian figurality to the "fruitless" ("infructuosus") reading of the Jews. Quoting Romans 11:22 ("Behold therefore the goodness and severity of God"), Augustine recalls that Paul was speaking of God's severity against the Jews and his goodness toward the pagans:

> [Paul] said this about the Jews who, as branches of that olive tree which was fruitful in its root of the holy patriarchs, have been broken off on account of their unbelief.
>
> (Adversos Iudaeos 1.1)[22]

And Augustine marvels: "When these Scriptural words are quoted to the Jews, they scorn the Gospel and the Apostle; they do not listen to what we say because what they read, they do not understand [*quoniam quod legunt, non intelligunt*]" (*Adversos Iudaeos* 1.2). The Jews cannot understand the hybrid logic of *figura* because they can only read *secundum carnem*, according to the flesh: they read without revisionism. At the same time, however, to understand *figura* would amount, in Augustine's view, to a capacity for figural reading: in failing to understand what they read, the Jews fail to read figurally. They fail to read with understanding; they read (*legere*) without interpreting (*intellegere*). Blind and sick, *caeci et aegroti* (1.2), the Jews fail to see themselves in Paul's image of the hybrid with its broken branches: *caeci et aegroti*, they fail to see that this figure of figures is a figure of themselves and of their failed "intelligence."

For Augustine, then, the structure of figure is the very structure of intelligibility. Jew opposes Christian as *legere* opposes *intellegere*—as mere reading opposes Pauline exegesis. Just as a genetic sense of order conditions the *legere* of the Jews, a promise-bound sense of figurality conditions Christian *intellegere*. In this way, what the Jewish reader fails to understand in his *legere* is, precisely, the *intellegere* of a hybrid Christian reading.

This emphasis on modes of reading and their relation to knowledge marks Augustine's departure from a strictly Pauline point of view. As we move to Augustine's treatment of *figura* our focus will shift accordingly. Instead of discussing hybrids we will examine the logic of signs. Ever at stake for Augustine will be the status of reading and the place of the reader.

Figura AS TRANSLATION

In book 15 of the *City of God*, Augustine responds to Paul's gloss of the Hagar/Sarah episode. From an Augustinian vantage, the gloss is immediately relevant as a theory of reading–as a theory, that is to say, of *intellegere*.

> This form of understanding [*forma intellegendi*], which comes down to us with apostolic authority [*auctoritate*], reveals to us how we ought to accept the scriptures of the two testaments, the old and the new.
>
> (*Civitate Dei* 15.2)[23]

As an allegorical description of Christian allegory, Paul's reading of Genesis 21 not only *explicates* the proper way to read scriptures: it also *demonstrates* such reading. The *forma intellegendi* that Augustine discusses here thus denotes not only what Paul reads but how he reads it. In other words, as *allegoria*, this "form of understanding" encompasses Paul's "reading" in both senses of the word: *allegoria* refers both to Paul's activity as a glossator, to his allegorizing, and to the gloss itself, to a specific allegorical interpretation of the text. Furthermore, it is because Paul's reading, again in both senses of the word, is exemplary that his *allegoria* comes down to us with apostolic *auctoritas*. Both gloss and glossator have somehow become normative: what we learn from Paul is not how one *might* read Scripture but how one *should* read Scripture. Paul's example, both his reading and his reading, hits us with the force of *ought*.

In general, Augustine's great hermeneutic insight lies in his recognition of the normative authority of allegory: that is, both the authority with which we allegorize and the authority that our allegories wield. As we shall see more clearly when we turn to *Contra Faustum*, this recognition amounts to a theory of the place of the Christian reader. In the *City of God*, however, Augustine suggests that this place–the place of the reader–*takes place* only as a peregrinating no-place, as what somehow lies *between* the city of God and the city of man. Drawing upon the apostolic equation of Hagar with earthly Jerusalem and Sarah with the heavenly kingdom of God–with "the Jerusalem which is above"–Augustine links the question of allegory's *forma intellegendi* to his great theme of the two cities.

> It is written thus that Cain founded a city, whereas Abel, as a pilgrim, did not found one. For the City of the saints is up above, although it produces citizens here below, in whom the City is on pilgrimage [*in quibus peregrinatur*] until the time of its kingdom should come.
>
> (15.1)

Cain's city is the earthly city, the community that testifies to man's self-love and to his sin. But Abel as pilgrim, as figure for Christ and as figure of a self-condemning love of God, has no city. Instead, his pilgrimage is the peregrination of allegory: before the end of time, before the kingdom of God reigns on earth, the heavenly city can be seen only in shadows–in distant images that point to that city, that "peregrinate" it, that set it on a pilgrim's course without serving to actually render it present. *For the City of the saints is up above, although it produces citizens here below.* In this way, allegory joins the two cities even while defining the Christian as simultaneously reader and pilgrim, interpreter and exile. The Christian is he who lives on the road.

It is in this context that Augustine glosses Hagar and Sarah. He argues that the earthly Jerusalem, itself signified by Hagar, serves as an image of the heavenly city of God. "There was certainly a kind of shadow [*umbra*] of this city and a prophetic image [*imago*] which served to signify it rather than to present it on earth" (15.2). Signification is here opposed to presentation: the earthly Jerusalem doesn't bring the holy city down to earth, doesn't make it present in the here and now; instead, it "signifies" that city without drawing it any closer. Thus understood, for Augustine signification amounts to a kind of slavery–a service under which the *imago* labors, indentured to *veritas*. Existing only for the sake of truth, the prophetic image precisely "serves" to prefigure the future rather than to present itself. In this context, the bondwoman Hagar's slavery itself "serves" as a figure for the servitude of *figura*.

Part of the earthly city has been made into an image of
the heavenly city, not by signifying itself, but by signifying
another, and for that reason it is a slave. For it was instituted not for its own sake but for the sake of signifying
another, and thus by means of this other antecedent
signification that prefiguration itself was prefigured.
Hagar, the servant of Sarah, and her son were the image
of this image. . . . Thus we find in the earthly city two
forms: in one respect it displays its own presence, and in
the other it serves by its presence to signify the heavenly
city.

(15.2)

To be a slave is to be a sign. A sign, Augustine tells us in *On Christian Doctrine*, is a thing (*res*) used to signify something (*aliquid*).
"Some things are to be enjoyed, some things are to be used, and
some things are to be both enjoyed and used" (*De Doctrina Christiana* 1.3.3).[24] In view of this rubric, the sign is not a thing-in-itself,
not something to be enjoyed in its own right, but a means to an
end–a means to another's enjoyment. Here clearly the sign is not
its own master. Its very presence serves another and it is instituted
solely for the sake of that other.

But Augustine is talking here about a specific kind of sign: the
figural sign. Like Paul's own gloss of the episode, which offered an
allegory of allegory, or like the hybrid olive tree, which figured
figure, Augustine, in the person of Hagar, presents us with an
image of image, an *imago imaginis*. But Augustine, who explicitly
raises the question of reading Scripture, also complicates the situation: if Paul has revealed "how we ought to take the scriptures of
the two covenants," and if Hagar is a figure for the old covenant,
then she is a figure for that which prefigures the *veritas*, the
fulfillment of promises. Paul, we will remember, allegorized a story
from the Old Testament in order to provide an allegory of the relation between Old and New. Augustine cites Galatians 4:24: "Haec
enim sunt duo testamenta." "For these are the two testaments."
Where Paul indicates the general allegorical value of the episode,
offering an allegory of allegory, Augustine splits the story into its
component parts and reveals a kind of seepage or slippage in its
terms. Abraham's two wives and their children, Augustine reminds
us, are not themselves the two testaments; rather they are *figures*

of the testaments. Paul assumes an interchangeability of his terms, a kind of symmetrical arithmetic: wives and children = testaments. Allegory, consisting in the static equation of two parts, becomes an algorithm: for x, read y. But Augustine reminds us that the parts of the allegory are already themselves allegorical. We can no longer simply replace x with y, because our equation is no longer neat and well behaved. As Augustine views it, a figural wrinkle has entered the equation: Hagar et al. = *figures of* testaments. Allegory has seeped, as it were, out of the equal sign. Hagar, for instance, doesn't simply prefigure the New; instead, as figure of the Old she prefigures prefiguration itself. We have, as Jill Robbins points out, one figure too many:[25] a surplus of figure obtains here, a surplus that unbalances the neat arithmetic of allegory as Paul understands it. Allegory, as the relation between figure and fulfillment, is here unsettled by figurality itself.

To understand this unsettling figurality, we need to look closely at Augustine's treatment of signs in *On Christian Doctrine*. Building upon the fundamental dichotomy with which the treatise begins—"All doctrine is either of things [*res*] or of signs [*signa*]" (*De Doctrina Christiana* 1.2.2)—Augustine tackles the question of figuration in book 2.

> Signs are called proper [*propria*] when they are used to signify those things on account of which they were instituted. . . . Signs are figurative [*translata*] when the things themselves which we signify with proper words are taken up [*usurpantur*] to signify something else.
>
> (2.10.15)

Augustine's example is the word "ox" (*bos*), which we say "when we're thinking of [*intellegimus*] that animal which all men of the Latin tongue call with us by this name." But, Augustine tells us, by this animal itself we understand (*intellegimus*) the evangelist, which, according to Paul, is signified by the words of Deuteronomy 25:4: "Thou shalt not muzzle the ox that treadeth out the corn" (*Doctrina* 2.10.15; cf. 1 Cor. 9:9; 1 Tim. 5:18). Like the ox, Paul argues, the evangelist should not labor in vain, but rather reap material profit for his spiritual work.

In Saussurean terms we might say that Augustine's proper sign operates at the level of the signifier. "Bos," as what Saussure would call, oxymoronically, an "acoustic image" and as what Augustine would call a *vox* or *voice*, thus designates the same *res* to all men of the Latin tongue.[26] On the other hand, the translated sign operates at the level of the signified: to a given interpreter or within a given interpretive community, this *res* itself signifies in a more or less fixed manner.[27] In this way, as a kind of second-order process of signification, the translated sign takes the signified for its signifier. What is translated, then, is the signifying property of the sign; thanks to such translation, the thing designated *by* a sign is in turn treated *as* a sign.

Logically and temporally, the *translatum* sign depends upon the *proprium*: before our words and meanings can be translated they must be properly instituted in the first place. A term like "bos" is, to begin with, established by a given linguistic community to signify a specific thing. Later this thing itself may be taken up–or as Augustine says, *usurped*–by an individual or a community to signify something else. A certain lag time, a certain history even, necessarily separates the first, proper signification from the second, translated one. Translated signs necessarily presuppose the proper, just as the proper use of our words necessarily precedes their usurpation. The order of narrative, of the necssary succession of before by after, precludes the possibility of confusion here. The time line couldn't be straighter. And only time will tell our signs from our things, our proper words from their translated uses.

So much for the theory. But as Augustine himself realizes, *in practice* there can be no rigorous difference between the translated and the proper sign. After all, what Augustine is trying to describe here in terms of translation is nothing other than the figural interpretation of Scripture. In later passages Augustine's terminology even reflects this fact: he refers to translated signs as "figurata" and considers signs proper if they are to be taken literally, "ad litteram" (cf. 3.5.9). In this way, it becomes clear that the distinction between *propria* and *translata* signs is a distinction to be made not in the process of signifying but in the process of *reading*. Such signs aren't so much instituted by sign-makers as they are interpreted by scriptural exegetes.

Thus, one need ask not what a given sign *is* but how it should be *read*, whether as translated or as proper. Should the term "bos," for instance, be understood to refer to a beast of the herd or to an evangelist of the Word? We can read "bos" either way–and here the narrative that would distinguish the proper "ox" from the translated ox is of no help. In readerly practice, *figura* wraps ends in beginnings, defying the straightness of the time line. Indeed, from the standpoint of the reader the two *bos*'s–"bos" as signifier and the *bos* itself as signified–look alike. "For it is written in the law of Moses, *Thou shalt not muzzle the mouth of the ox that treadeth out the corn.* Doth God take care for oxen? Or saith he it altogether for our sakes?" (1 Cor. 9:9–10). Paul's questions are rhetorical: "For our sakes, no doubt, this is written." Obviously Moses was not talking about literal oxen. This image of the ox allowed to eat the grain that he dutifully treads must be meant for us–must be meant as a figure, translated out of its original agricultural context. At the same time, however, the very rhetoricity of Paul's questions and the overwhelming certitude of his response–for our sakes, *no doubt*–precisely leave open the space for doubt. *Does* God take care for oxen? We cannot tell. Either Moses or Paul himself is doing the translating. We cannot tell who the linguistic usurper here is.

Such uncertainty is not happenstance, not an accident, for instance, of Paul's rhetoric, but structured into figurality itself as Augustine comes to understand it and to unpack its aporias. Significantly, it is only in book 3 of the *Doctrine*, where Augustine discusses linguistic ambiguity, that we find his definitive account of the figural sign. It is precisely because such signs are "translated" that they become ambiguous. Furthermore, unlike "ambiguitas in propriis verbis" (3.4.8), unlike ambiguity at the literal level of the text, figural ambiguity cannot be resolved by more careful textual reference. While occasionally caused by a faulty rendering in Latin, ambiguities at the literal level of Scripture, Augustine tells us, are most often due to problems with punctuation (*distinguere*) or with determining word separation (*pronuntiare*) (3.2.2). The lack of either punctuation or word separation in the Latin texts Augustine knew presented specific problems for the *lector* who, reading the text out loud, syllable by syllable, would have needed to insert the proper stops to determine literal sense.[28] In the *Doctrine* Augustine suggests that any ambiguities in this regard can be resolved by a reading more carefully attuned to authorial intention (*scriptorum intentio*) as revealed by context (*circumstantia*) (3.4.8).

Figural uncertainty, on the other hand, proves somewhat more intractable. Reading more carefully cannot help, nor can analyzing context, because figurality itself entails a translation *out* of context. After all, at best *circumstantia* can only reveal an author's intention—and, as we learn in books 12 and 13 of the *Confessions*, to know such intention is not necessarily to know the truth. Rather, as Augustine stresses in those last two books, truth is public—a possession of the community at large—while authorial intention, curiously like mendacity in this regard, is merely private. God's truth, Augustine declares, "is neither mine nor his nor another's, but all of ours." Thus we must *commune* in God's truth, lest by desiring to possess the truth in private we find ourselves deprived of it (*Conf.* 12.25).[29] "For he that speaks a lie, speaks it of his own" (12.25). Even if we knew Moses' intention or his will (*voluntas*) in writing Scripture, any truth therein revealed wouldn't be *Moses'* truth. Instead, the only *voluntas* expansive enough to which we can attribute the truth of Scripture is God's; in this way, the sacred text abounds in meanings, its *veritas* reaching across persons, across circumstance.[30]

Indeed, it would seem that what constitutes figural ambiguity in the first place is this interpersonal aspect of textual truth. The significance, for instance, of "bos" belongs neither solely to Moses nor solely to Paul—nor even to Augustine, who recites and refigures the example for his own purposes. As a function of figurality, *veritas* spans time and persons, entailing the deracination of meaning. No longer understood simply to reside with the author, the text's intentionality is also not understood simply as a readerly fabrication. Instead, *intentio* somehow hovers between author and reader. Like the Christian reader himself, *intentio* is in a certain sense peregrinated, exiled and wandering between two cities.

Thus, as Augustine sees it, *figura* courts ambiguity because it renders signification a collaborative affair, unlike the unilateral exchange we've seen in Paul (i.e., $x = y$). For Paul, meaning resides *with us*: with the Christian reader who knows that $x = y$. But Augustine comes to view figurality as a *bilateral* exchange: instead of being assigned, simply to "us" or to "them," figural meaning takes place as the transaction *between* us and them. Indeed, no longer a matter of simple substitution or replacement, *figura* involves an exchange and even a change: x *turns into* y. Both sides are transformed by the transaction.[31] In this way, Augustine comes to understand *figura* tropologically, as a matter of translations and transactions, conversions and turnings. The figural is not then meaningful because it is "translated"; rather, it produces meaning *as* translation, *in* translation. Meaning resides, then, in the translation from author to reader, from Jew to Christian, from Old to New, letter to spirit. We cannot pin it down to one pole or the other. Instead, *figura* oscillates: defined by a two-way exchange of signs, *figura*, as it were, plays both ends against the middle.

Augustine's shift toward trope entails a similar complication of Pauline temporality. For Paul, we will remember, understood as hybrid, *figura* resolves a temporal rupture with an organic image of spatial unity. The natural branches are replaced by sprigs from the *oleaster: y* displaces *x*, but the vigor and growth of the tree attest to the ease of the transition. Indeed, Paul's figure of the olive tree resembles nothing so much as the structure of synecdoche, where the substitution of parts finds its rationale in the spatial integrity of the whole. For the bishop of Hippo, on the other hand, former teacher of rhetoric and reformed seller of words, *venditor verborum*, as he calls himself in the *Confessions* (cf. 9.5), the rhetorical figure of figure is not synecdoche but chiasmus: the figure of inverted repetition.

Characteristically, then, Augustine's most succinct formula for the connection between the Old and the New Testaments takes chiastic form. "In the Old Testament there is a concealment of the New, in the New Testament there is a revelation of the Old."[32] Jill Robbins views this definition as a standard Pauline sentiment—but it is important to recognize how far we have come from Paul's *allegoria*. Chiasmus, as that rhetorical scheme which inverts the very terms it repeats, mimics this view of *figura* at the level of sentence structure. With chiasmus, repetition undoes itself; the sentence becomes self-reflexive and self-swallowing, initiating an exchange that seems to have no beginning and no end. By inverting the repeated terms, "New" and "Old," Augustine's formulation marks a transfer from "concealment" to "revelation." At the same time, however, the transfer seems to operate in reverse: "revelation" takes us back to our apparent starting point, the "Old," which in turn conceals the "New," which in turn reveals the "Old." In this way, the chiasmus keeps turning upon itself, unfixing reference and sending us from one pole of the sentence to the next. Any loose ends are tucked up in the scheme's beginning while any stray beginnings are enfolded in its end. Thus, where Paul's image of the hybrid transformed temporal difference into spatial unity, Augustine's chiasmus turns temporal difference back upon itself. Repetition becomes inversion and inversion takes us back to where we started.

From Paul we learn revisionism: the Christian message has always been there, the Christian inheritance already promised in the foresight of the patriarchs. But it takes a rhetorical sensibility like Augustine's, steeped in Cicero, trained in oratory, to realize the ambiguating, unsettling force of such revisionism. Especially in his anti-heretical writings and most especially in *Contra Faustum*, Augustine will explore the impossibility of a one-sided allegory: the Old Testament could not have been written *for us*, Augustine will demonstrate, unless the New Testament were also, in a certain sense, written *for them*. To maintain its coherence, Paul's doctrine of *propter nos* must fold back upon itself. In this way, the Pauline notion of a straightforward, one-sided *allegoria* resembles Augustine's theory in *On Christian Doctrine* of the translated sign as a second-order proper sign: both theories imagine figurality as a linear substitution of one term by another, and for both theories this linearity is undermined by the actual practice of reading figurally. On closer inspection, no rigorous distinction obtains between the *proprium* and the *translatum*. On closer inspection, Paul's one-way figural logic necessitates the recursive structure of chiasmus.

Of course, we can run this deconstruction equally well in reverse: if Paul's one-way logic entails an Augustinian chiasmus, so does that chiasmus entail a linearity that renders it, ultimately, off-balance, asymmetrical. A loss is incurred in the production of figural meaning; *figura* produces meaning-as-translation, but something, we might say, gets lost in that translation. Since *figura* has always been about promises—i.e., the Old as promise of the New—we might then want to say that its promises can be kept only by being broken. *figura*'s gains always stand upon loss.

At least this is the sort of formulation suggested by Augustine's arguments in his treatise *Contra Faustum Manicheum, Against Faustus the Manichean*. In the *Confessions*, Faustus is introduced as a great disappointment. Augustine tells us that for almost the whole nine years that he was a disciple of the Manichees, he had been "unsettled in his spirit" (*animo vagabundus*), awaiting the arrival of the Manichean leader Faustus, who could answer his questions and resolve his problems concerning the faith. Other members of the sect, we learn, had been unable to respond adequately to Augustine's concerns. So Faustus, touted as a sage, arrives, amid great fanfare and expectations, only to reveal himself as an "agree-able man with a pleasant manner of talking" but with little on the whole to say (*Conf.* 5.6). Faustus is thus in no position to debate the issues with Augustine, much less to resolve Augustine's problems regarding doctrine. The moment is a turning point for Augustine, taking him one step closer to his eventual conversion: "You turned [*convertebas*] my shameful errors or wanderings [*errores*] before my face then that I might see and hate them" (*Conf.* 5.6).

And thus it is that years later, Augustine, a bishop by this time, reinvents his encounter with Faustus in the treatise *Contra Faustum*. There Augustine imagines a satisfactory discussion with the Manichean sage: a discussion in which the fundamentals of Manicheism are presented intelligently enough that they may be intelligently, and thus completely, refuted. Like Tertullian refuting Marcion, Augustine tries to defeat heresy by demonstrating its log-ical inconsistency. And like Tertullian, the incoherence in question here involves a rejection of the Old Testament.

> Faustus said: "Do you accept the Old Testament? If the inheritance in it is for me, I accept it; if it is not, I don't accept it. For it is indeed too much depravity to take up [*usurpare*] the documents which testify that I am disinherited."
> (*Contra Faustum* 4.1)[33]

Since Christians accept neither the legacy of the Old Testament—i.e., the earthly promised land, Canaan—nor the conditions for that legacy in keeping the law, it is, "Faustus" argues, sheer wickedness to keep the *tabulas* behind the legacy: i.e., the Old Testament itself. The claim of "Faustus," then, is a profoundly moral one. "It is proper," he finally declares, "to give back the documents as well once we refuse the inheritance" (4.1).

In refusing the inheritance, Christianity not only rejects a tem-poral legacy: it rejects the logic of legacy itself. A genetic principle of succession is set aside in favor of Christianity's spiritual bless-ings; indeed, as "Faustus" reminds us, Christian liberty precisely consists in this rejection of birthright. In other words, what makes a Christian free is his knowledge that legacy is a matter of choice and of will. As the fictional Faustus puts it: "This [Old Testament] inheritance is so miserable and fleshly . . . after that blessed offer of the New Testament which promises me the kingdom of heaven and perpetual life, that even if its testator [i.e., Moses] gave me the inheritance without condition [*gratis*] I would scorn it" (4.1). In this way "Faustus" argues that not only do we have no right to the Old Testament, we have no use for it—and we have the freedom to turn it down.

In his initial response Augustine follows traditional Pauline doctrine, demonstrating, in terms of *figura*, both the righteousness and the utility of reading the Old Testament.

> Augustine responded: None of us doubts that promises of temporal things are contained in the Old Testament and that for that reason the testament is called *old*; or that the promise of eternal life and the kingdom of heaven belong to the New Testament. But that in these temporal things were figures of the future which should be fulfilled in us upon whom the ends of the ages are come, is not my suspicion, but the understanding [*intellectus*] of the apostle, when he said of such things, "These things were our figures" and again, "These things touched them in figure, but they were written for our sake in whom the ends of the ages have come" (1 Cor. 10.6, 11). Not therefore for the sake of obtaining these promises do we accept the Old Testament, but for the sake of reading [*ad intellegendas*] in these promises predictions of the New Testament; indeed, the faith of the Old bears witness to the New.
>
> (4.2)

Thus "Augustinus" counters both aspects of his opponent's argument with the doctrine of *propter nos*: the Old Testament is both rightfully and usefully ours since it was written on our behalf, in order to bear witness to the New. Touching the Jews only "in figure," Moses' *tabulae* find their fulfillment and hence their pertinence in a Christian future rather than in a Jewish past.

It is an argument that Paul himself might have made. But it is inadequate as a response to "Faustus." Serving as predictions of the New, it is true, the Old Testament figures find a kind of relevance for the Christian reader. But they don't on that account find their *necessity*. The underlying Manichean criticism remains: now that we have the New Testament, why bother with the Old? The standard consideration of *figura* as a one-way exchange managed *propter nos*, for our sakes, cannot safeguard the importance of the Old. If the laws and observances that bound the Jews were merely figures for Christ, why consider them now, once we have Christ? And even if such figures bear witness to the Advent and thus serve to convert the Jews, what use can the Old Testament have for the already converted Christian reader–much less for a pagan like Faustus? One needn't, the fictional Faustus reminds us, be a Jew in order to be a Christian. "We were not first made Jews that we might follow the faith of the Hebrew prophets and thus reach Christianity," he proclaims (13.1). Unlike Tertullian's opponent Marcion a century earlier, "Faustus" is not denying the Old Testament's authority; instead, he merely denies its exigency in a Christian schema.

But to deny the exigency of the Old is to threaten the coherence of that very schema. I'd like to suggest that, in responding to "Faustus," Augustine inadvertently exposes a stress point in Paul's notion of *figura*. Reading the Old may be a useful or meaningful act, but what makes it a *needful* act? Paul's one-way allegory does not address the question. The problem here is, again, one of normativity: the issue is not how we *might* read the testament of the Jews; the issue is whether we *ought* to read it. As figure of things to come, what authority does the Old Testament have in its own right? And if the Old lacks such authority, if its only authority is prospective, i.e., the authority of the New that it prefigures, how can it possibly bear witness to the New or function as its proof? Lacking any authority of its own, the Old Testament could not command our attention, could not prove or demonstrate a thing. At the same time, it could not provide Christianity with an authoritative base in prophecy and promise. And of course it is precisely such a sense of origin–as well as a break from the bonds of law and lineage–that Christian figurality was meant to provide.

Paul's one-way view of allegory, then, conditions a view of the Old that is purely prospective: its value, its authority, its use completely exhausted by its fulfillment in the New. At the same time this view can't help but call into question the authoritative status of the New itself. In this way the orthodox Pauline sentiment jibes curiously with the Manichean heresy. At stake with both is not only the authority and value of the two testaments but the very conception of Christianity as a scriptural religion. Most important, at stake here is the authority of *reading*. In developing a chiastic, bilateral understanding of *figura* Augustine not only refutes the Manichees, he also supplements Paul, adding an element of normative necessity to the doctrine of *propter nos.*

Thus, in response to the argument that Old Testament *figurae* are needless for the non-Jew—"useless before faith, superfluous after faith" (18.17)—Augustine declares: "Then let those who have believed [*qui crediderunt*] throw away all the books by means of which they have come to believe [*per quos factum est, ut crederent*]. For if this is true, I don't see why the faithful should read the Gospel of Christ itself" (18.18). Pushed to their limits, the Manichean arguments threaten the very notion of the sacred text and its sacred reading. To neutralize this threat, Augustine needs to shift the standard of scriptural authority away from the criterion of utility. Augustine's fictionalized opponent considers only the use-value of the Old Testament; its testimonies, "Faustus" tells us, are "supervacua": superfluous, beyond empty. But use-value alone can never justify a text's status as sacred, even if the use to which the text is put is exalted. Even if, that is to say, the text is used to convert its reader. Instead, Augustine will argue that the sacrality of a text must be a function of the way it positions its reader within a given community and a given faith. In a certain sense the sacred text is sacred because it creates a sacred reader. Such a text was indeed written *for us,* while in reading, we become the audience for which it was written.

It is in such terms that Augustine reinterprets the *propter nos* of Paul's *figura,* reminding us that as testament our holy scriptures are performative and not simply constative documents, embodying as well as constituting our relation to God. In this way, Augustine reimagines the relationship between Old and New in normative terms. Because the sacred text interpellates its reader, making the individual one of the "us" on whose account the text was written, reading becomes compulsory: a matter of *ought* and not *is.* The reader is *compelled* to read. In this way, instead of asking whether the text is useful, in response to "Faustus" Augustine begins to ask whether the text is *binding.* It will turn out that we are bound by, bound up in the New to the extent that we are bound by, bound up in the Old. It is this mutual implication of the two testaments that underlies the new two-sidedness of Augustine's *figura.*

Ultimately, Augustine's most compelling response to "Faustus" sets forth the oddly chiastic sense in which Scripture itself is compelling. In Augustine's terms, the Old Testament compels our reading *now*, even if its laws are mere figures to us and no longer command performance, because it compelled the Jews *then*, on our account.

> Our hope is thus not fixed in the promise of temporal things since we neither believe that those holy and spiritual men of that time, the patriarchs and the prophets, were devoted to these earthly things. For by revelation to them of the spirit of God they understood [*intellegebant*] what was appropriate for that time and in what manner God determined the future by all those acts and sayings to be figured and predicted. Their greater desire was for the New Testament, but a present corporal performance in those promises of the Old was needed to signify the New to come.
>
> (4.2)

No more so than we, were the patriarchs devoted to temporal things. Rather were they bound by the future to observe precepts that the future would annul: bound by the future precisely because it is in light of the future that their present would become meaningful. By the spirit of God they understood their place in the Christian scheme of things–understood their *praesens functio*, their present performance, from the standpoint of a Christian future; understood themselves to be performing the promises of the Old for the sake of the New. Augustine's legal reasoning becomes even more explicit when he discusses the propriety of Old Testament precepts. It was proper [*oportuerit*], he argues, that such rules "were observed at that time when those things which now have shone forth, manifested to us, were predicted as the future by such shadowy figures" (6.2). The Old Testament law–its promises and precepts–was binding for the patriarchs not insofar as they were temporal but because they were figures of things to come. For us, now that all shines forth manifest, these precepts are mere things, and we are not to be bound by mere things; all is pure to the pure, as Augustine tells us (6.3). But because the law is only binding upon the patriarchs insofar as it signifies the future–our present–in light of which the law is void, we cannot dispense with the Old Testament's *figurae* as something that was simply binding *for them* and is now meaningless *for us*. Instead, we must realize that their law was binding then *propter nos*, on our account, for our sakes.

In this way Augustine brings figurality and the law together. The law is only law, is only binding, insofar as it is figure. This formulation marks a departure from the standard Pauline view. According to that view, what existed as law for the patriarchs is revealed in retrospect as mere figure. From our standpoint the law is no longer binding because it is no longer law: for us the law is mere figure, and hence no longer lawful, while for the Jews the law was a carnal thing and hence not yet figural. Christian liberty from the Pauline perspective thus consists in rendering the law figural. For Augustine, on the other hand, the logic is reversed. He argues that the law for the patriarchs was binding only insofar as they recognized it as figure; what's carnal about the Old Testament is that it's *figural* and thus in servitude as a sign.[34] Hence Christian liberty consists not in recognizing the law as figure but in recognizing the law as a mere thing, stripped of its figurality since, in an age of Christian revelation, there is nothing left to figure.[35]

By bringing together law and figure, Augustine effectively refutes the Manichean critique. For all his liberty, the Christian reader cannot reject the *tabulas* of Moses because Mosaic law exists only as such *propter nos*: through reference, that is, to the Christian reader. The law is thus only law insofar as it figures what is non-law: the Gospel. Christianity is already implicated at the heart of the Judaic, just as Judaism finds itself projected forward, at the heart of its Christian fulfillment. Furthermore, this connection between the two religions and their testaments is best understood, for Augustine, in textual terms: as the relation between an author and his reader. The *illud tempus* ("that time") of the patriarchs corresponds to the *now* of writing; in Judeo-Christian myth, according to which Moses is the author of the Old Testament, the *illud tempus* corresponds to the moment of Moses' transcribing the word of God. But Moses' words are only binding, only normative as law, inasmuch as they look ahead to the future that they prefigure: the *praesens* of the patriarchs must pass through that future, defining itself as the future's figural past. Similarly, it is through understanding himself as the future to a patriarchal past that the Christian reader defines his own present as, precisely, a *now* of reading. The *now* of writing and the *now* of reading, the so-called Old and the so-called New, are thus inextricably, chiastically intertwined. Scripture becomes binding across the gap between past and future; textual authority thus transpires, somehow, between writing and reading.

Yet just how "present" is a *now* that defines itself as a forward or backward look? Thanks to the conflation of figure and law, the *now* of textual authority somehow slips out of count: the present gets defined either as the future of the past or as the past of the future. Quoting Isaiah 7:9, Augustine provides a kind of motto for this odd temporality and its relation to reading and belief: "nisi credideritis, non intellegetis" (cf. *Faustum* 4.2). "Unless you have believed, you will not understand." As a formula for reading scripture the verse depicts the logic-defying principle of grace: belief must precede understanding. But furthermore, thanks to Latin grammar rules for the sequence of tenses, the verse offers a grammatical conundrum. In terms of verb tense, the future depends upon the past; but in terms of verb mood, that dependence is reversed. The perfect tense ("you have believed") serves as the condition of possibility for the future ("you will understand"). *Unless* you have believed, you will not understand. Yet at the same time, as a subjunctive expressing doubt and uncertainty, "credideritis" depends precisely upon the certainty of the indicative "intellegetis." In this way, a past belief conditions a future understanding–but at the same time a doubtful belief requires the certainty that such understanding alone can provide. In short, the formula both describes and enacts the chiasmus of Augustinian *figura*: a past faith enables the future revelation, which in turn makes the past faith possible. The tag from Isaiah thus traces that odd hermeneutic circle thanks to which belief is exchanged for understanding and doubt is exchanged for certitude.

Most significant for our purposes, however, is the way in which this exchange somehow precludes a *present*. Where does the reader find himself in this formula for reading scripture? Either in the past or in the future: "Unless you have believed, you will not understand." Neither the moment of belief, nor the moment of exegetical understanding, of *intellegere*, takes place in the *now*. Or rather, consisting in an exchange between the time of writing and the time of reading, this *now* itself never takes place. As the present of textual authority and the place of a Christian reader for whose sake the text was written, this *now*, this place of the reader, has no place. The "you" is a displaced person.

At last we have a good picture of what I have been calling the "promissory" logic of *figura*. Like a promissory note, valuable now because redeemable later, the text extends itself across time and stretches across hands. Its past and its future are bound together and hence the text, again like a promissory note, becomes binding, enacting and embodying an exchange that entails the passage of time even as, chiastically, it folds the temporal back upon itself. But the chiasmus has its price: its seamless, recursive symmetry is unbalanced by loss. In spite of everything, *time passes*; something— the *now* itself—is lost in the translation from past to future. Trope becomes entropy: the turns of *figura*'s chiasmus preclude the present and thus slip forward despite themselves. In theory this lost *now* will be Augustine's problem, threatening his redemption with the taint of mortality. In practice, however, the loss will condition his salvation, endowing his *Confessions* with its distinct ethics and voice.

UNDER THE *Figura* TREE

The *Confessions*, as Eugene Vance reminds us, "is commonly read as an autobiography"; however, the autobiographical content of the text suddenly ceases with the death of Augustine's mother in book 9.[36] Furthermore, Vance points out, "Augustine seems to fail us precisely at the moment when his work is on the verge of fulfilling a narrative structure sustained, up to that point, by the internal logic of autobiography"—at the moment, that is to say, when the "'I' of the narrative past is about to join the 'I' that is writing" ("Augustine's *Confessions*," 6, 5). In other words, Augustine "fails us" at the moment when *then* becomes *now*. A similar perspective on autobiography informs Jill Robbins's account of the *Confessions* as a conversion narrative: "Every story of a conversion is the story of 'how I came to write a narrative of conversion,' or 'how I was a great sinner, then grace intervened, making it possible for me to write the story of how I was a great sinner'" (*Prodigal Son/Elder Brother*, 24). But the *Confessions*, of course, doesn't simply come full circle: when the narrative reaches Augustine's present—the *now* of writing the conversion narrative—Augustine abruptly shifts gears, moving from narrative to an exegesis of Genesis.

Vance suggests that these two modes, the narrative and the exegetical, reflect two fundamentally different orientations toward the Word. He argues that, in shifting from one to the other, Augustine moves from the language of the historical self, to the language of the divine Other. As Vance himself notes, most readers simply ignore the *Confessions'* last three books; those who do wish to salvage a sense of the work's unity, however, tend to adopt his view of a discursive shift in book 11–a shift that corresponds to Augustine's conversion.[37] But even readers like Vance who wish to take the entire text into account proceed, more often than not, straight from book 9 to book 11, leaving out the difficult discussion of memory in book 10. The omission has serious consequences; book 10, after all, begins with Augustine's effort to confess what he now is: "but what I even now am [*quis adhuc sim*], behold even now in the very moment of my confessions [*in ipso tempore confessionum*], many people want to know, both those who know me and those who do not" (10.3). This effort to confess his present state at the very moment of his confessions leads paradoxically into a discussion of memory as that faculty which enables us to review past time. Indeed, as Augustine's narrative approaches the present, the present seems to recede into the reaches of narrative; instead of *then* coming full circle to *now*, *now* seems to lead us back into the past time of memory. In this way book 10, I would argue, again presents us with the chiasmus of *figura*: Augustine's present slips out of count because it is essentially implicated in his past. It is not, then, that Augustine's narrative breaks down because he reaches the present; rather, it is because he is *unable* to reach the present, because the *now* keeps receding from him, that his narrative breaks down.

"Every narrative of conversion," Robbins writes, ". . . reviews a life from the vantage point of its ending and endows it with retrospective coherence" (*Prodigal Son/Elder Brother,* 24). Robbins's comment suggests the extent to which the retrospection of figurality enables a coherent and teleological narrative. Yet for Robbins or Vance this vantage point consists in the *now* of writing; their view of the *Confessions* as autobiography presumes that the moment toward which the narrative tends, the moment that consummates Augustine's life story, is the moment of writing. For them Augustine is first and foremost an *author*. But I would like to suggest that first and foremost Augustine conceives himself as a *reader*. His understanding of his writerly activity is only secondary: the *now* of his writing is always a function of the *now* of his reading—and as such, this *now* is structured as the *now* of *figura*, which is to say: it is a *now* that never takes place.

As a vantage point from which to order narrative, Augustine's *now* is inconclusive and incomplete, too slippery to stabilize the text. And thus it is that Augustine's narrative gives way to an exegesis: the final four books, beginning with book 10 on memory, all assume the effort to present the present of the Christian reader. A narrative detailing not how Augustine has come to write, but how he has come to read, is followed, perhaps even supplemented by an exegesis that also proceeds according to figural principles. In the *Confessions*, we might then say, both narrative and exegesis are figural modes; nonetheless, in some ways the coherence of Augustine's text depends on keeping those modes distinct. The recursive temporality of figural reading, of a reading that tropes ends back into beginnings, must be held at a distance from the linear temporality of a narrative where all takes place *in ordine*. The two modes, narrative and exegesis, are interdependent in Augustine's text; both derive from the retrospection that revises the past in view of the present. Yet this interdependence cannot be avowed: the straightforward, linear order of narrative is belied by the circular exchange of trope; simultaneously, narrative order renders trope's exchanges asymmetrical, marking the temporal difference that exegesis hopes chiastically to bridge. Furthermore, this aporia leaves its mark on Augustine's narrative itself. In book 9, as we shall see, the narrative finds its pivot point, signaling both the necessity of a shift to exegesis and the impossibility of ever completing that shift. The pivotal moment is, not surprisingly, a scene of *reading*, a scene during which the troping of *figura* takes place in linear time.

Now, *figura* figures in the *Confessions* on a variety of levels. As a theory of *translatio* or trope, *figura* informs that "turn" from the *vetus homo* of sin to the *vita nova* of Christian faith. But as such, Augustinian conversion is ever ongoing, never to be completed, since something is always lost in the translation, ever to be recouped. Thus Augustine pleads with God late on in the text: "Pity me . . . and by no means abandoning what you have begun, consummate what remains in me imperfect" (10.4). What is lost in conversion's turn is the *now* of conversion itself: understood figurally, conversion entails a glossing from past to present; a transition that *as* transition can never itself be marked. For Augustine this transitional moment defines the present task, the *praesens functio*, of the successful convert; the *now* of confession is a moment not of writing but of glossing.

It is in this context that Augustine's discourse swerves into the most directly philosophical passages of the text: the discussions in books 10 and 11 of memory and of time. In those books Augustine's confessions become an effort to catch up with a present or to contain a presence that keeps slipping away. "Nor can I grasp what I myself am. The mind is therefore too narrow to possess itself: so where could that be which cannot grasp itself?" (10.8). Thus *figura* informs Augustine's version of the problem of self-consciousness as the problem of self-presence. And it is also in terms of an escaped presence or present that Augustine considers the problem of transitions, defining sin itself as consisting in the transition from one state to the next,[38] and defining the present time as that which "nulla morula extendatur," that which is not extended by the tiniest delay but which nonetheless marks the passage from past to future (11.15). "In truth," Augustine asks, "how do we measure present time when it possesses no space?" (11.21). Characteristically Augustine's answer to this difficulty is to turn back to himself, back to his self-consciousness and self-presence. And equally characteristically because equally influenced by *figura*, such self-presence is the presence to mind of a certain passage or translation: "In you, my mind, I measure my times. . . . The sense which things passing by make in you and which remains when they have passed by, that sense itself I measure as present" (11.27).[39]

Most directly, of course, *figura* enters the *Confessions* as a theory, perhaps even a justification, of textual interpretation. The theme and problematics of presence thus give way to the exegetical practice of the final two books: the *Confessions* close with Augustine beginning to read and learning to put *figura* into effect. In his gloss of Genesis Augustine uses figural structures and principles not only to interpret the letter of the Mosaic text but also, in the process, to outline the standards for doing so: "Let all those depart from me who imagine Moses to have said those things which are false. But let me be joined with them, Lord . . . who in the breadth of charity feed on your truth" (12.23). As Augustine's own reading illustrates, *figura* structures meaning across persons and across circumstance, structuring in the mean while an inter-

pretive community united by a common ethical injunction: "Legitime lege utamur." Let us use the law lawfully. "And in all things let
us honor Scripture's author, ascribing to him only the truest and
most useful intentions" (12.30).

In this way, Augustine demonstrates how the figurality of the
Old Testament enables a reading devoted to truth and governed
by charity. "For a long time now I have been burning to meditate
in your law," he declares in book 11 (11.2), but ultimately his meditation on Mosaic law entails a certain reverence and respect for
the author, Moses, himself. In short, Augustine demonstrates how
figura conditions not only the reception of textual meaning but
also our responsibility as readers to an author. However, for the
bulk of the *Confessions*, Augustine has seemed unconcerned with
the status of the author. Indeed, as we discussed above, his view of
figura undercuts the author's role in the production of meaning:
for Augustine the figural sign signifies almost in spite of authorial
intention.

Paradoxically, it is as a necessarily avoided presence that
authors ultimately matter for Augustine. In his very first attempt to
understand the very first line of the Bible, Augustine imagines an
impossible communication between author and reader, between
Moses and himself:

> Let me hear and understand how in the beginning you
> made heaven and earth. Thus Moses wrote; he wrote and
> he passed away, he passed over hence [*hinc*] from you
> toward you, and he is not now [*nunc*] before me. For if he
> were, I would take hold of him and ask him and for you
> beseech him to reveal these things to me and I would offer
> the ears of my body to the sounds bursting from his
> mouth. . . . But how would I know whether he spoke the
> truth? And if I could know this, would I know it from him?
>
> (11.3)

The vivid wording, the frank sensuousness of this imagined
encounter–Augustine holding his ears to Moses' mouth–will only
serve to highlight the futility of such contact. The truth of the text
cannot be relegated to the relation between author and reader
because, at best, that relation is a matter of speaking bodies–of
the carnal rather than the spiritual. Hence in this passage Augus-

tine reverses the tendency from the *Phaedrus* onward to vilify writing as an imperfect form of speech. For Plato's Socrates, and for the Western metaphysics of presence that, presumably, he typifies,[40] writing is the lesser image of speech—defective since its words are proffered in the absence of a speaker, in the absence of an origin. Their meaning is thus not secured. But for Augustine this independence from origin precisely suggests the greater capacity of the written text to secure meaning. Because written words are free of any given spoken context they achieve a permanence and a certainty unavailable to speech. In the *Doctrine* Augustine thus argues for the merits of inscription: "The signs of words [*signa verborum*] are established by letters since, once the air has been struck [*verberato aerē*], words [*verba*] immediately pass away and last no longer than they sound. Thus words [*voces*] are shown to the eyes, not in themselves, but by the signs which pertain to them" (2.4.5). Language as a visual medium—as a voice (*vox*) that is seen and not heard—proves more reliable than language in its oral/aural mode. Precisely owing to its independence from circumstance, the written sign appears less material, less moored in the space and time that vivifies speech—and thus *more* fixed, more permanent than the words that sound in the air. As a visual, rather than an audible, voice, writing amounts to a more spiritualized medium for truth.

Now, in the early treatise *De Magistro* Augustine does emphasize the primacy of speech over writing, offering the fanciful derivation of *verbum* from *verberare*, "to strike"—the verb that denotes that vibration of air with which our voices resound (*De Magistro*, 4.12).[41] Similarly, he argues, "verba scripta," written signs, are more properly considered "signa verborum," the signs of words, since the word is by definition an artifact of speech; first and foremost, Augustine suggests, language is a matter of voice (*De Magistro*, 4.8). But unlike Socrates' arguments in the *Phaedrus*, such primacy does not indicate a concomitant moral priority: speech is not superior to writing, not closer to truth for being closer to sound. Indeed *De Magistro* is the text in which Augustine first argues that truth cannot be conveyed by external means, but must instead be instilled in our hearts by Christ. In later writings, most notably in book 15 of *De Trinitate*, Augustine identifies this inner teaching with an inner word; what he calls the *verbum in corde*, the word in the heart.[42] A Plotinian distinction between *verbum* and *vox*, between the word as immaterial concept or signified and the word as material signifier, thus animates Augustine's respect for writing. In its freedom from the spatiotemporal constraints of voice, the written sign takes us closer to the immaterial *verbum in corde* and thus closer to the *Verbum Dei*, the Word of God. The truth of the text simply does not lie at the level of corporal reality, at the level of ears and mouths and voices. Augustine's vision of his encounter with Moses thus concludes by dismissing the truth of *vox*:

> And should he speak in Hebrew words [*hebraea voce*], he would strike my sense in vain nor would he ever come near my mind. If however he spoke in Latin, I would know what he said. But how would I know whether he spoke the truth? And if I could know this, would I know it from him? Certainly within me, within that house of my thought, neither in Hebrew nor Greek nor Latin nor in any foreign language, Truth would speak without the help of the mouth and the tongue, and without the sound of any syllable; Truth would say "he speaks truth."
>
> (11.3)

Even if the author were before us, breathing into our ears, the truth, were it to reach us, would somehow bypass his voice. Or rather, as Augustine understands it, the voice of truth is always already the voice of the text, a matter neither of speaking nor of presence, but a "voice" of reading and of absence. Or rather, even more precisely, the voice of the text presents itself, but only by inscribing absence. Such a voice "speaks" in the absent-present *now* of *figura*. The condition for hearing Moses speak is that he is no longer here before us: his words mark his very disappearance. But even if Moses were before us, we would read his words as if he were absent. As if they were merely text. And thus it is that his words are binding, true, lawful. Merely by attending them, we implicate ourselves in the passing of the speaker, taking our place as his future and relegating him to our past. After all, in a larger sense, in a Judeo-Christian context, authority is always mediated, the voice of truth is always scriptural: we are by definition already fallen and God has by definition already withdrawn. He is an absent-present God. His voice only speaks to us ventriloquially; it only sounds in ways that remark its distance.

Ultimately, then, the truth-bearing intersubjective contact that counts for Augustine is that connection most fundamentally structured by *figura*: the connection not between a reader and an author but between a reader and a *text*. It is thus as readers of His Word that we stand *coram Deum*, before God. And it is thus that Augustine tells the story of his conversion. Embedded in the narrative of his life we discern the development and refinement of his own relation to texts. Not only is that narrative itself structured by dint of a figural retrospectivity, so that "colligens [se] a dispersione" (*Conf.* 2.1), collecting or recollecting himself out of dispersion, Augustine can tell his story–but also, as we've already suggested, the vantage point from which Augustine narrates is the conversionary moment of reading: the absent-present *now* of *figura*.

Thus, as he describes it, from his earliest childhood to his time under the fig tree, books affect Augustine powerfully–but not always with moral benefit. From the *Aeneid* to Cicero's *Hortensius* to the books of the Platonists to, finally, Romans 13:13, reading has the status of an event. And by the time Augustine gets to the Pauline epistles, that event has taken on the status of a conversion. Nonetheless, before such a readerly conversion can take place Augustine needs to learn how to read. He knows how to *legere*, how to enunciate what he finds written, but not how to *intellegere*, how to understand what he so finds. Thus he bemoans the recitation of the *Aeneid* by which he was forced as a child to memorize Aeneas's "errores," his own error and wandering having been forgotten, "and to weep for dead Dido because she killed herself for love, while in the meantime with dry eyes for myself I was dying in these things toward you, God my Life" (1.13). As a child the text moves him, but he does not find himself in it; he does not know how to take its terms as allegories, how to see his own moral errancy in Aeneas's *errores*, his own spiritual death in Dido's literal suicide.

After all, what's conversionary about reading is the way in which, as readers, we become implicated in the text, reading our absent-presence in the very words written long ago. Such implication of the self in the text is what Saint Ambrose teaches Augustine, as Augustine recounts in book 6, when he teaches Augustine to read figurally.[43] Even so, what Augustine learns is merely a sacred version of the Virgilian Lots, which he has already described and discounted in book 4. Sometimes, Augustine tells us, a man hits fortuitously upon a passage in a secular work that seems to apply directly to him and to his current business. But such a text's oracular use cannot be sanctioned, the method's success being merely coincidental. The *Aeneid*, we must remember, was not written with our affairs in mind; we may see ourselves in its words, but those words do not for that reason belong to us, nor do we belong to the text. Instead, such a text is consulted "cum forte," haphazardly and by chance (cf. 4.3). With Virgilian Lots what is lacking is the knowledge that the text was written for our sake, *propter nos*. And such knowledge is enough to turn a mere game into grace.[44]

In order to read properly, then, the *Confessions* suggests, we need to read the texts that are proper to us–that were written on our behalf. Once we have done so, the randomness of Virgilian Lots, the *sortes* of this *sortes Vergilianae*, will assume the coherence of divine providence. And thus book 8 begins with Augustine having finally chosen the appropriate text for the Christian reader: he has made the transition from Platonist writings to the Holy Scriptures. "Inhaeserant praecordiis meis verba tua, et undique circumvallabar abs te"–the words of God have already stuck fast in his heart, and he is already surrounded, beleaguered by God. But even so, even though God's words are implicated in him, he has yet to be implicated in them: "In truth, all things of my temporal life were still undecided [*nutabant*]" (8.1). Augustine has reached an impasse. He is reading the right book, but not yet leading the right life. And the use of the imperfect tense here to denote both his wavering (*nutabant*) and his beleaguerment (*circumvallabar*) only underscores the sense in which this standstill is perpetual.

Significantly, what breaks the impasse is a bit of narration: the story that Augustine's friend Simplicianus tells him, after learning that Augustine has been studying Platonism. Simplicianus narrates the tale of Victorinus: onetime rhetoric professor of Rome and translator of the very same Platonist texts that Augustine has been reading. The story is one to be passed on: "And he, Simplicianus, narrated to me the story about which I will not be silent" (8.2). We learn that Victorinus, having read the Holy Scriptures most studiously and having searched through all the other Christian writings, came to Simplicianus "not openly [*palam*], but in a private and familiar way," and said: "'You should know now that I am a

Christian.'" When Simplicianus responded that he would not consider Victorinus a Christian until he saw him in a Christian church,
Victorinus, we are told, replied: "'Ergo parietes faciunt Chris-
tianos?'" Do the walls then make the Christian? (8.2)

The story, of course, ends happily. Victorinus, master both
of rhetoric and of the rhetorical question, learns to overcome
his fears of public exposure. He learns that, at least in part, the
walls *do* make the Christian, and he confesses his faith *palam*,
publicly. Augustine, for his part, is deeply affected by the narration: "As soon as your man Simplicianus had narrated Victorinus' story, I burned to imitate it: indeed, it was toward this end
that Simplicianus had narrated it" (8.5). Accepting the story as
an example to be followed, Augustine begins to find himself
within it. And indeed, what Augustine gathers from this exemplary narration is the example of Victorinus's reading. Augustine
learns the necessary public status of his own private reading: to
read figurally, to read spiritually, is not only to be personally
implicated in the text—it is to be so implicated, personally, but
only insofar as one also participates in the "us" on whose
account the text was written.

When we treat Petrarch's humanism in the next chapter, we
will further discuss the self-reflexive exemplarity of *figura*: the
ways in which the figural reader seeks, above all, to make an example of his own reading. For now it is simply worth recalling that all
the stories that Augustine hears in book 8 are tales of reading,
examples of reading, and in every case their narration is occasioned by books or by the reading of books. It is reading itself that
is exemplary here: an exemplarity that conditions exegesis as conversionary act. The examples that the text unfolds "for our sake"
are perpetuated in the example our reading will present for the
sake of others. And so, book 8 suggests, the links of apostolic continuity are forged. As the convert's book is passed from one reader
to the next, the walls that make the Christian are built—not from
bricks and mortar but from scroll and codex.

Thus, finally, Augustine narrates to us the very day of his conversion: a fellow African, one Ponticianus, who had an office in the
emperor's court, comes to visit Alypius and Augustine in their
Milan retreat, and, quite by chance, "et forte," this Ponticianus
notices a copy of Paul's epistles on the table (8.6). The fortuitous
find inspires a story: "Whence he took occasion to tell how he and

three other of his fellow officers . . . went for a walk in the gardens by the city walls" (8.6). Two of the officers by chance (*forte*) are separated from the others. Again by chance, they stumble upon a house in which certain Christian hermits live. There they happen to find a book detailing the life of Anthony, the spiritual father of Christian monasticism. Reading Anthony's story, these men are converted; agents of public affairs, *Agentes in Rebus*, servants of the state, they now determine to devote their lives to the service of God.

It is this story that finally sends Augustine out into his own garden to take up his own book.

> Thus I went out into the garden with Alypius at my heels. For my solitude was no less where he was present. And how could he leave me thus affected?
>
> (8.8)

Considering his sin, torn between the flesh and the spirit, between past pleasures and future blessings, Augustine finally breaks into tears—and breaks away even from Alypius "for I imagined that solitude was more fit for the business of weeping." He flings himself under a "certain fig tree," and abandons himself to his weeping.

> And behold I heard a voice coming from a neighboring house; whether a boy's voice or a girl's voice I don't know but it was speaking in a singsong way and repeating again and again: "take up and read, take up and read" [*"tolle, lege"*]. . . . Having restrained the onslaught of my tears, I rose up, interpreting [*interpretans*] the voice as nothing other than that I was divinely bid to open a book and read the first chapter I came upon. For I had heard from the reading of the gospel in Church which he had by chance come in upon, Anthony was admonished since he took what was read to have been spoken to him. . . . Thus I quickly went back to the place where Alypius was sitting, for there I had left the Apostle's book when I had risen up. I snatched it up, opened it and read in silence that chapter which first struck my eyes.
>
> (8.12)

The voice that Augustine hears, I want to argue, is the voice of the text: it is the mediated, ventriloquized voice that truth speaks, making itself present even while inscribing the withdrawal of God. This is the voice by means of which we are called to read insofar as we are interpellated into that which we read. Unlike the game of Virgilian Lots, which this scene so resembles, when Augustine takes up the Pauline text he does not do so of his own volition, simply, but because he is so bid. The game is sacralized, justified, by this divine call. But then again, Augustine is not *simply* called; his conversion is unlike Paul's on the road to Damascus. Augustine doesn't *simply* hear God's voice. Instead he hears the ambiguous, androgynous voice, "quasi pueri an puellae, nescio"; he wonders at first whether this voice is a boy's or a girl's, or part of a child's game. He does not, at first, know what he is hearing. No subject is addressed by name; no object is described. *Take up, read.* The voice must be glossed. He rises up *interpretans*: like Anthony hearing the gospel, like the *Agentes in Rebus* chancing upon Athanasius' *Life of Anthony*, Augustine knows that these words are meant for his sake. This ambiguous *vox* is calling *him*.

The voice of the text commands us to take up the text, but we must first interpret that voice as spoken *for us*. We must also take and read the voice itself. The voice of the text is thus not simply the voice that calls us into the text, calling us to read; it is also the voice that derives from the text, the voice that we hear only because we are already reading. We have again found a version of *figura*'s circularity—a version of the paradox: "unless you have believed, you will not understand." The text speaks to us only because we have already heard its voice calling "take up and read"; but it is only because we have already started reading that we know these words, "tolle, lege," to be spoken *for us*.

If reading has the force of an event for Augustine, it is quintessentially a *public* event, no matter under what fig tree, or in what enclosed garden it takes place. Such readings are performative, one might say, borrowing Austin's famous term for those eventful utterances in which words do things. By reading we join a sacred audience and at the same time we do so both for and before that audience. Performatively our reading converts us; as performance, it converts others. And thus it is that exegesis joins narrative: our conversionary reading immediately becomes the stuff of testimony. Indeed, in the *Confessions* it would almost seem that one *reads* in order to have something to *tell*. Reading is the event about which one may not be silent. fittingly, then, book 8 closes in the present tense, with Augustine and Alypius running to Monica with their story: "We tell [*narramus*] her how everything transpired (8.12).

Nonetheless, the story is not over. In his conversion, although quite conspicuously accompanied "at the heels," by Alypius, Augustine has imagined himself quite alone. "Thus I went out into the garden with Alypius at my heels. For my solitude [*secretum*] was no less where he was present. . . ." "I imagined that solitude [*solitudo*] was more fit for the business of weeping. . . ." "I snatched it up, opened it and read in silence [*in silentio*]." It is almost as if, in insisting upon his isolation and upon the privacy of his reading, Augustine wants to keep the text and its exegesis to himself. All the same, like Alypius we are implicitly there, unacknowledged partners in the scene of reading, which after all is narrated to us, for us. For our benefit. "To whom do I narrate all this?" Augustine asks, early on in the *Confessions*. "For I do not tell this to you, my God, but before you [*apud te*] I narrate these things to my kind, to humankind" (2.3). Augustine's narration itself is structured like *figura*: like the words of the patriarchs and the prophets, these confessions may be addressed to God, but they are written on our behalf.

Unfortunately, problematically, this deflected mode of address also characterizes the structure of *performance*. Our readings are performative, Augustine will reveal, only insofar as they are, in a certain sense, *staged*. Thus, following "at the heels" of the conversion scene of book 8, we find in book 9 another scene of reading: that pivot point that I mentioned earlier, where narrative reveals its uncomfortable complicity with exegesis. Like the conversion scene, this scene is exemplary: as readers of the *Confessions* we are meant to take the example of Augustine's own reading to heart. But unlike the episode under the fig tree, this scene has built into it a critique of readerly exemplarity.

> What cries [*voces*] I gave you, my God when I read the psalms of David. . . . I was on fire to read them aloud [*eos recitare*] to the whole world, if I could. . . . With what vehement and bitter pain was I angered at the Manichees whom, on the other hand, I pitied since they knew nothing of those sacraments. . . . I wished

that they had been somewhere near me, without my
knowing it that they were there, that they might have
gazed upon my face and heard my cries [*voces*] when I
read the fourth psalm. . . . I wished that they might hear
without my knowing whether they heard me, lest they
should think I spoke it for their sake [*propter se*].

(9.4)

Reading in this scene is a matter of enunciation—a matter of *legere*,
of rehearsing the text out loud, syllable by syllable. In that sense,
reading is a matter of performance: of performing the text by reciting it in linear, narrative time. But reading here is also a matter of
performance in a second sense: as Augustine reads aloud, he imagines an audience—the Manichees—that witnesses the event. Indeed,
it is precisely the presence of such an imagined audience that renders the moment exemplary: Augustine reads "for their sake."

And yet, it is Augustine's wish to read for an audience without
knowing that he does so. He wishes to be overheard, to read as if
for their sake while still reading solely to himself. "I wished that they
might hear without my knowing whether they heard me, lest they
should think I spoke it for their sake." As he considers the scenario,
he realizes, however, that the wish is impossible; even if his audience, the Manichees, *had* overheard him, they would not have
understood him, because he was talking to himself. "Nor, had I so
spoken, would they have thus understood [*acciperent*] the way I
spoke with myself and to myself before you [*coram te*]" (9.4).

In short, Augustine's impossible wish is that he could perform
without performing. In a passage from Matthew that Augustine
cites elsewhere in the context of the same psalm, Psalm 4, Jesus
cautions us to pray behind closed doors: "And when thou prayest,
thou shalt not be as the hypocrites are: for they love to pray standing in the synagogues and in the corners of the streets, that they
may be seen of men. . . . But thou, when thou prayest, enter into
thy closet, and when thou hast shut thy door, pray to thy Father
which is in secret" (Matt. 6:5–6).[45] Typically, for Augustine, this
closeted interior space is not intramural but intrapsychic: he consistently glosses "closet" (*cubiculum*) as heart, as the place in which
our *verba* reside.

Nonetheless, it is precisely this interior space which Augustine
wants to display, that it might be an example to the unbelieving.

Unfortunately, however, the interior is what, by definition, can*not* be displayed. Augustine cannot read before the Manichees without his reading, as a sacrosanct private act, becoming a potentially hypocritical public performance. His spiritual reading runs the risk for him of spiritual death. And yet, such suspect performance is the necessary underside of Christian exegesis. To read for the Manichees is to read *propter alios*, for the sake of others, but such a reading merely serves to close *figura*'s loop. For the sake of others, Augustine translates exegesis into narrative, reading into writing; he thereby performs that very community signaled by his own act of reading: the audience for whom he reads is the *nos* in whose name he reads. "These things touched them in figure, but they were written *propter nos*, in whom the ends of the ages have come." Augustine's wish in book 9 is, then, the wish to read figurally without reading performatively. He wishes to read as if he were an example, as if on our account, without actually taking us into account. It is an impossible wish—as Augustine's most lyrical audience, Petrarch, will discover. But it won't be until Luther that the Christian West finds an authoritative—indeed *exemplary*–gloss of this impossibility.

When the absent-present *now* of Christian figurality does take place, book 9 suggests, it takes place as hypocrisy: as a performance mortal to the lector. In a certain sense, then, Augustine's recitation of the Psalm 4 exposes *figura*'s great liability. But this is a liability that must remain hidden if Christian redemption is to be possible as Augustine conceives it. Like the image of Moses breathing words into Augustine's ear, this scene of reading's performance is imagined only to be disavowed. For Augustine, the example of reading must sustain itself—but it must do so as an impossible wish.

TWO

Petrarch in the Shade of the Laurel

Nor for any new figure could I leave the first laurel, for still its sweet
shade turns away from my heart every less beautiful pleasure.

(*Rime* 23.167–69)[1]

In poem 23 ("Nel dolce tempo de la prima etade") of the *Rime
sparse*, the so-called *canzone dei metamorfosi*, Petrarch offers the
fantasy of perpetual translation, of endless turning. The fantasy's
material imagination is, of course, Ovidian: the story Petrarch
tells in this, his longest lyric poem, is a recycling of stories from
the *Metamorphoses*, beginning with the tale of Apollo and Daphne:
"ei duo [la Donna e l'Amor] mi trasformaro in quel ch'i' sono, /
facendomi d'uom vivo un lauro verde" [those two, Love and the
Lady, transformed me into what I am, making me of a living man
a green laurel] (23.38–39). Yet, as many have noted, the force
behind the *canzone*'s story is Augustinian, its final image of an
Actaeon-poet on the verge of dismemberment already an image
voiced in the *Confessions*: "I want to recall my past filthy acts. . . .
For love of your love I do this, retracing my most wicked ways . .
. and collecting myself out of that dispersion in which I was shattered into pieces" (*Conf.* 2.1).[2] It is, as we shall see, from Augustine
that Petrarch derives his sense of a junction between narration
and re-membering.

But Petrarch continually thwarts the linearity of his narratives in favor of a focus on narration itself; moreover, he does so, as I will argue below, by imagining a figural translation that gets "stuck." He imagines, that is to say, a turn that keeps turning–and thus fails to complete its turn at all. Thus, while from one perspective "Nel dolce tempo" undermines a linear narrative by means of a perpetual turning, an endless troping from one Ovidian *topos* to the next, from another perspective on the poem, Petrarch never turns at all because he never manages to close his turn's loop. He turns continuously but without ever letting his turn be taken. Thus the poem closes with a pun: "né per nova figura il primo alloro / seppi lassar" (23.167–68): "Nor could I leave the first laurel for a new figure." Petrarch's first transfiguration–"I became aware of my transfigured [*trasfigurata*] person" (23.41–42)–is his last. There can be no new figure here. The sequence of turns that we think we have just completed, from Petrarch as Daphne to Petrarch as Phaeton, to Cygnus, to Battus, to Byblis, to Actaeon, this sequence has never occurred, no narrative action has transpired, Petrarch has never turned over a new leaf, he has never left the first tree. But at the same time, this final line refers to Laura: "né per nova figura il primo alloro / seppi lassar." She, and not Petrarch, is the "primo alloro," the first laurel tree; she is the figure from which he'll never turn, just as, in all his turning, his own figure has never changed. Nor can we readers stop turning from the "lauro" of line 39 ("facendomi d'uom vivo un lauro verde") to the "alloro" of 167. The translation back and forth between the two keeps us guessing: are we barking up the wrong tree?

However we read, or fail to read, these final lines, they mark Petrarch's vexed commitment not only to a certain figure–i.e., to the laurel–but to figure itself, to *figura*. A poem like 23 thus foregrounds its own figurality, revealing the text as a site of translations: of recyclings, for instance, of old textual *topoi*, as well as of the more local negotiations between letters and words. But such foregrounding of *figura* comes at *figura's* expense, as we will see at the close of this chapter with a reading of perhaps Petrarch's most explicitly self-thematizing poem, the sestina "Giovene donna." Both "Nel dolce tempo" and "Giovene donna" are poems about *figura* and poems that expose figura: both are poems about

turning and transfiguring–retrospective poems, figural poems–
and both poems imagine, one in Ovid's terms and the other in
Dante's, the dissolution of any narrative that *figura*'s retrospection was meant to enable. Furthermore, by thematizing the very
way in which *figura* structures meaning as an exchange between
new and old, between sign and thing–by thematizing, in short,
the very structure of *figura*–both poems pull the reader into the
text as witness to a conversion that will never end nor, properly
speaking, ever begin. While Augustine marks his place in the
book only to save a place for Alypius ("Then I closed the book,
marking the spot with my finger between the pages or with some
other sign" [*Conf.* 8.12])–Petrarch passes the book on but keeps
his place in it marked. He is eager for those pitying eyes "of anyone born . . . a thousand years from now" (30.35), but he is
equally eager for his own "I" to hold sway for millennia. As a
"breve sogno," a brief dream on the way to enlightenment,
Petrarch's lyrics will fill page after page, gesturing toward a plenitude of meaning that they continually hold at bay. In this way
the lyrics emerge as the work of an eternal pilgrim–as the consummate work of an unconsummated desire. In Petrarch's
poetry, the flesh is never fulfilled.

Ultimately Petrarch's ambivalence about *figura* cannot be
resolved; it can only be, as Luther will show us, *reformed*. Such
ambivalence is, after all, central to *figura* itself, straight from its
Pauline start. We find this ambivalence literally embodied in Paul's
contorted stance toward his own "flesh"–at once his body and his
people[3]–and it does us good to remember, as we turn now to
Petrarch's own vexed turning, that Abraham is not the only biblical Jew to endure a name change: there is also that problematic
Saul of Tarsus, whose name change amounts to conversion (cf.
Acts 9:1 ff. and 13:9). Saul/Paul's ambivalence toward the Jews
serves as both the origin and the emblem of an ambivalent figurality: thus, for Augustine, who understood Pauline *figura* better even
than Paul, the figural sign marks our implication in a past that we
simultaneously efface with our present. And thus, for Petrarch, this
impossible, chiastic structure is recast in a critical vein: self-consciously, the poet-humanist remarks his commitment to a figure
that he will never leave and equally never embrace. *Né per nova
figura . . .*

Ethics and religion differ herein; that the one is the system of human duties commencing from man; the other, from God. . . . They both put nature under foot.

—Emerson, "Nature" (1836)

ETHICS OF DESIRE/ETHICS OF VOICE

When, in *On Christian Doctrine*, Augustine argues that the whole of Christian teaching can be summarized in the twin commandment to love God and our neighbor (*Doctrina* 2.26), he is invoking a Christian commonplace as old as the earliest gospel (cf. Matt. 22:37, 39–40). But at the same time he is appealing to a classical tradition of ethics that extends at least as far back as Plato's Socrates.[4] According to this tradition, ethics is a function of desire and of desire's proper expression. So defined, ethical action begins in proper object choice. That which we desire we seek, esteeming it our highest good even if it is merely one of those *infima bona*, one of those lowest, most inferior goods that Augustine associates with sin in his famous analysis of the pears he stole as a boy (*Conf.* 2.5–6). The ethical act consists, then, in the discernment and pursuit of the true *summum bonum*—and since according to this analysis action as such is inconceivable without a motivating desire, without an object in sight, wickedness emerges as a kind of epistemological error: a mistaken pursuit of the lowest object in place of the most high.

Hence Augustine's distinction between use and enjoyment in the *Doctrine*: "Some things are to be enjoyed, and some things are to be used, and some things are both to be enjoyed and used" (*Doctrina* 1.3.3). Such a distinction guides the desiring subject, orienting him (I use the pronoun advisedly) with respect to the highest good and thus disposing his world of things ethically. *Things* are transformed into *objects* desirable either for their own sake or on behalf of other objects. And thus the world is reformulated: in deference to the Trinity, the ultimate object of desire and the end of all enjoyment.

More resonant, perhaps, for the medieval texts we will be considering in this chapter are the terms that Dante's Marco Lombardo sets forth in canto 16 of *Purgatorio*.[5] For Marco Lombardo, the problem for desire is finding a proper "guida o fren" (*Purg.*

16.93), a guide or curb to aid in object choice. Without such guidance, or with "la mala condotta" imposed by a failure to separate sacred and temporal powers, the "simple little soul" (16.88) that the Lombard describes seeks only transient pleasures and immediate gratifications, "and seeks no further" (16.102). As the Lombard then concludes, addressing the political and moral crises that have torn Dante's universe: "'Well can you see that ill-guidance is what has made the world wicked, and not nature that is corrupt in you'" (16.103–5).

Whether in the stoicized terms of *On Christian Doctrine* or according to Dante's more explicitly neoplatonic framework, the basic presumption remains the same: to conduct oneself ethically is to conduct one's desire well: to lead it to its appropriate end, however that end be defined. Ethics here relates to a system of deferred references, ordered according to an economy of use: some things are to be enjoyed; some things are to be used; some things are to be both enjoyed and used. As we shall see further when we discuss the problem of free will in chapter 5 or the question of the "ab-use" of figure in chapter 4, it is *figura*'s conception of a world of signs teleologically ordered and oriented toward Meaning that enables this ethics of desire, even while it structures our narratives of conversion, telling the exemplary story of how we learned to distinguish use from enjoyment. If I use the term "ethics" in this context, it is with a nod toward Emerson's critical eye. *figura* relies upon deferral, finds its Meaning in its end; to justify our desires in figural terms is indeed to put nature "under foot" as the means we take en route to enjoyment. figurally construed, our responsibilities to created things "commence" in the Creator only from the *Creator*'s standpoint. For us, vagabond creatures of time, responsibility begins here at home—indeed, right under our feet—and desire carries no legitimating marks.

But alongside this ethics of desire, the figural tradition lays claim to a slightly different conception of ethics, an ethics of *voice*. This is the ethics implied by Genesis 22—an ethics of response and responsibility: "temptavit Deus Abraham et dixit ad eum Abraham ille respondit adsum" [God tempted Abraham and said to him, "Abraham," and he responded "here I am"] (Gen. 22:1).[6] This ethics concerns not so much our relation to things or objects as it does our self-constitution as *subjects*–subjects of discourse. This is an ethics of vocation and profession, founded in our capacity to

answer when summoned, to answer when called. Yahweh calls
and Abraham answers, even if his readiness entails the sacrifice of
a beloved son.[7]

The crucial biblical figure for an ethics of desire, on the other
hand, is found elsewhere in Genesis: "Of every tree of the garden
thou mayest freely eat: But of the tree of the knowledge of good
and evil, thou shalt not eat of it" (Gen. 2:16–17, KJV). To conduct
one's desire rightly is to choose desire's proper fruit. Significantly,
however, even an example like this one, so nakedly (as it were)
detailing the risks of desire, is enfolded within a discursive
moment: God gives a command that is broken, and the token of
man's shame is his failure to answer God's call: "I heard thy voice
in the garden, and I was afraid, because I was naked; and I hid
myself" (Gen. 3:10, KJV). When we compare this moment with
Augustine's own unhesitating response to the voice in the garden
we realize the extent to which the two systems of ethics are intertwined: *figura* structures our desire even while it commands our
response.

What Yahweh tests in Abraham or Adam is the latter's willingness to be drawn into discourse, *whatever the cost*–to be designated by a proper name[8] and to take his place within a system of
symbolic substitutions and deictical references. The temptation of
Genesis 22, then, does not consist in the binding of Isaac so much
as in the moment of call and response. "God tempted Abraham
and said to him, 'Abraham,' and he responded 'here I am.'" The
question of the episode is not "how far?" but "how near?" At issue
is not how far Abraham will go, whether he will perform a specific
action or not; rather, at issue is Abraham's capacity *not* to go, but
to stand *near* the Lord, *coram Deum*, and to take his place in discourse with Him, answering to His call; to be "thou" to the Lord's
"I" and "I" to the Lord's "thou."[9] In short, at issue here is the nature
of faith in a covenantal religion. Thus, informing Genesis 22 is
Genesis 15, which recounts the settling of Abram/Abraham's
covenant with God: "On that day God settled a covenant with
Abram saying, 'I will give this land to your seed'" (Gen. 15:18). The
act of covenanting fixes the relation between God and his chosen
in a specific time and place, in a specific moment of discourse: *in
die illo*, on that day. Both Abram's covenant and Abraham's later
response to the name that God has, in fact, given him, are governed by the same ethics of voice. It is as *tu* to Yahweh's *ego* that

the covenant is forged and as *ego* to Yahweh's *tu* that Abraham responds: "*adsum*, here I am."

Grounded in discourse, this ethics of voice, of *adsum*, is organized not in terms of desired objects but instead in terms of what Roman Jakobson called "shifters": deictical or indexical expressions like "I," "you," "today," "a minute later," which must continually refer back to a given discursive context in order to gain referential meaning.[10] Bertrand Russell called such terms and phrases "egocentric particulars" because their ultimate point of reference is the first person: i.e., the speaker, whose act of uttering defines the present instance, the here-and-now, of discourse. As Émile Benveniste writes, "*I* can only be defined in terms of 'locution,' not in terms of objects, as a nominal sign is. *I* signifies 'the person who states [*énonce*] the present instance of discourse containing *I*.' This instance is unique by definition and valid only in its uniqueness."[11]

In other words, as a function not of extra-discursive objects but rather of discourse's ever-changing "present instance," the referent of the "I" keeps shifting, reassigned with each passing moment, with each alteration of discursive context. In contrast, nominal reference is presumed to subtend any number of discursive contexts; the word "apple," for example, refers to a certain, definable signified that remains more or less constant no matter who utters the word, no matter what circumstances attend the utterance. Indeed, our acquisition and use of nouns depends upon this presumed stability of reference: it is thus that we know, for instance, when to call a spade a spade. With shifters, on the other hand, usage relies precisely upon the *flexibility* of reference.

Benveniste's term for such flexibility is "inversibilité": "'I' and 'you' are reversible [*inversible*]: the one whom 'I' defines by 'you' thinks of himself as 'I' and can be inverted into 'I,' and 'I' (me) becomes a 'you'" (1:230). Merely to speak, Benveniste suggests, is to transform a second into a first person, to shift from "you" to "I"—or, as we've already seen with Abraham, to shift, in answer to a call, from third-person name to first-person pronoun (*Abraham?—Here I am*).[12] In either event, discourse, it would seem, requires a shift of persons—an exchange of places. As Benveniste writes: "When the individual appropriates it, language [*langage*] is turned into instances of discourse, characterized by this system of internal references of which *I* is the key" (1:255).[13] To enter discourse the individual positions herself at the center of a system of deictical references—references that are "internal" to the act of uttering per se. Merely by responding, by uttering "I," the speaker organizes language around herself, becoming the reference point for a discursive framework that she has now taken up as her own. It is this conversion of *langage* into discourse that marks the ethical moment of voice. Thanks to a shift in persons, thanks to the shifter's flexibility, language is transformed into a scene of address and response—of exchange between "I," "you," and the third-person designation of the proper name.[14]

An ethics of desire positions the subject in relation to a world of things-as-signs, all referring and deferring to the *summum bonum* of enjoyment. An ethics of voice, on the other hand, positions the subject in relation to a world of *persons*. Thanks to *figura*, both of these ethical subjects come together, collated in time and within narrative, by means of that promise—that covenant—that structures time both discursively and in view of a future fulfillment: the end of desire.

Thus far we have considered an ethics of voice through the paradigm of Genesis 22: God speaks to Abraham and Abraham responds. The ethical moment here, we have maintained, consists in Abraham's ability to respond as a *person*, as an "I" to Yahweh's "you" and as a "you" to Yahweh's "I." Ethical "response-ability," we have tried to suggest, consists in the refusal to turn a deaf ear—and ethical response, we have argued, consists in the way each speaker converts a merely formal *langage* into the discourse that knits a community together. However, thus far we have taken the shifter's flexibility more or less for granted. We have noted that discourse requires a shift in person, and we have perhaps developed a vague sense that the ligaments that bind a discursive community are to be found in such deictical shifts—almost as if the shifter's purely formal exchange of places were linked to empathy or charity: to our willingness to trade places with an other, to walk a mile in her shoes. At any rate, we have up till now described the appropriability of language: if the shifter is flexible it is because certain elements of discourse are always there for the taking, or at least always available for our temporary "habitation," as it were. To make language one's own, to "enter" discourse as I have been describing, is thus to "inhabit" those elements. Accordingly, Benveniste describes deictics as "an ensemble of 'empty' signs, non-referential with respect to 'reality,' always available, and which become 'full' as soon as a speaker assumes them in each instance of his discourse" (254).

Nonetheless, as we discovered with *figura* in the previous chapter, the entrance into discourse through deixis is not always such a straightforward affair. With *figura* the ethics of voice is anchored in the written text rather than in spoken dialogue, and it is centered in the Pauline conviction that the scripture of the Jews was written *propter nos*: on our account. In Augustine's hands this conviction generates a notion of reading as *vocation*: we find ourselves and our circumstances cited in a text that is written for us, addressed to us like a letter. We are called upon to read, interpellated, just as in spoken discourse we may be called upon to respond, to take up the first person. However, the deictical flexibility of Christian figurality does not reflect a referential emptiness or an absolute and general availability of the shifter to all comers. Instead, sacred discourse is understood to be previously occupied. As we saw in chapter 1, for Christianity the sacred text already *belongs* to someone: namely, to the Jews. The signs are all already taken. Thus the appropriation of Scripture involves a transfer of property—a theft, or a vindication,[15] depending on whose ground one stands; the Hebrew Bible is repossessed as Christian Old Testament. Through figural interpretation the Christian believer quite literally takes the place of the Jew in Scripture, displacing a Jewish meaning and a Jewish reference. Furthermore, as Augustine sees it, this displacement involves a kind of discursive chiasmus in which past and future, Jew and Christian, "they" and "we" are all intertwined. Thus the patriarchs were bound to follow Mosaic law only insofar as it prefigured a future that would declare it void; thus the Holy Scriptures are written *for us* only insofar as they are written for the patriarchs, *for them*, on our behalf. For Augustine, the Christian first person positions itself in sacred discourse only chiastically, bound inextricably to its patriarchal counterpart. Hence, as Augustine sees it, *figura* complicates the smooth exchange between persons that characterizes deixis in spoken discourse. Instead of a simple shift, *figura* endows deixis with the structure of trope. In other words, the shifts involved in figural interpretation entail a substitution that is also an effacement or a displacement.

In this manner, *figura* turns on the difference—real or imagined—between speech and writing. If an ethics of spoken voice consists in the deictical shift by which an individual enters discourse, becoming a person in relation to other persons, an "I" in relation to "you"s, then the ethics of *written* voice also involves such a shift. With writing, however, the shift is necessarily disjunctive and effacing, its underlying condition consisting in the structural gap, inherent to the text, between the instance of writing and the instance of reading. To recall Benveniste's image of an essentially seamless discursivity: with each utterance the here-and-now shifts—every invocation of the "I" is unique—but even with a change in speaker, no radical break disrupts the flow of deictical reference from one instance to the next. In contrast, however, the written utterance would be inconceivable without the possibility of just such disruption: in order for a written language to exist, the linguistic sign must be understood as potentially and radically free-standing—as that which can be cited long after its initial relevance has disappeared and sustained absolutely independent of its original discursive context. In other words, our ability to produce a written text depends upon our ability to imagine our signs outliving us. We write toward the future. Continuity of reference is thus essential to spoken discourse, while written discourse cannot even be imagined without the possibility of absolute referential *dis*continuity.[16]

It is thus no accident that the deictics of Holy Scripture are already "inhabited" by the time the Christian reader comes along. The sign's unavailability is a structural feature of deixis in written discourse, a product of the referential gap between author and reader. As you read them, the deictics that announce my presence in this writing are at a distance. They belong to another time, another place (*my* time, *my* place) and are not *simply* available for your habitation. In actual fact no time need separate the moment of writing from the moment of reading: you might be reading these words over my shoulder precisely as I write them, responding right now in words of your own tapped out on this very keyboard or whispered in my ear. But such considerations are merely empirical: in actual fact, in any given instance, the moment of reading *may* be continuous with the moment of writing, but structurally the possibility for a radical discontinuity is *always* available. The possibility always exists for any written text—not simply for holy script, but for the written text per se, insofar as it is *written*. Thus, even if you are reading over my shoulder, inevitably your reading carries the potential of my absence: of a disjunction between my referential context and your own. *In potentia* your reading always announces my disappearance; to appropriate my "I," my "here," my "this" and "that" is to replace my presence in discourse with your own.

In this way what the reader always reads is the (potential) anachronism of the text's deictics—the potential pastness of deictical reference. What she reads, in short, is the possibility that these signs have outlived their original context. In Augustine's hands, in his notion of *figura*, this possibility underlying all writing is thematized, radicalized. And thus it is that Augustine makes possible an ethics of written voice: an ethics, that is, of reading. We can understand the logic of this position as follows: Since reading always announces the potential absence of the author, in a certain sense the author's absence serves as the precondition for the reader's presence. One element, then, of readerly responsibility consists in being present at another's expense: to take our place in written discourse is to *displace* the author. Every readerly shift in shifter, from author's "I" to reader's "you," thus at once marks a certain loss—and signals a kind of guilt, an ethos and pathos of remorse.

But this is not yet the whole story, because for Augustine the reader is never simply present—nor could such a one-way displacement (e.g., author replaced by reader) account for the retrospective, tropological structure of *figura*. Instead, as we've seen, Augustine's *figura* works chiastically: not only is the reader implicated in the writer's absence, so is the writer implicated in the reader's absence. The displacement cuts both ways: it is as past to the future that the patriarchal *now* is constituted, and as future to the past that the Christian *now* exists. Either end of the text's temporality, past or future, insists on the other; in shifting from author to reader, deictics endure a radical break in reference, but they are at the same time radically linked, implicated in each other's passing. Potentially, the two *now*'s—the present discursive instance of the author and the instance of the reader—are absolutely noncontiguous. At the same time, however, neither *now* is present in its own right; neither moment of the text, in other words, can stand alone, constituting a discrete and decisive discursive instance. Instead, as I suggested in the last chapter, these *now*'s are best-described as "absent-present": present only by dint of implication in what is past or yet to be, while the *now* per se, as a moment of unqualified presence, somehow slips out of count. Thus, unlike Benveniste's picture of adjacent discursive moments seamlessly succeeding one another like beads on a string, here the borders between instances are blurred and unstable: the future moment loops back upon a past that lurches forward to the future. And again, as Augustine's imagined performance before the Manichees in *Confessions* 9 suggests, even this loop itself is not self-contained but rather defined in troping deference to a *future* future: i.e., to those future readers before whom the exegete turns from reader to writer and for whom his exegesis turns to text. *Tolle, lege.*

In this way the deixis of *figura* entails a structure of discontinuous continuity: with its doctrine of *propter nos*, figural interpretation bases the possibility of a unified textual tradition upon the radical discontinuity of Old and New, Jew and Christian, us and them, author and reader. The referential gap between the instances of writing and reading becomes the basis for discursive community. The two moments of writing and reading simultaneously invoke each other's presence while proclaiming each other's absence. And reading itself, as an act anchored textually in the co-implicating shifts of figural deixis, becomes a non-arbitrary ethical affair. We read because we are already part of the text.

Now, at least as Benveniste describes it, speech "works" because the shifters are all vacant: to enter discourse is to fill those shifters with our personal presence. In contrast, however, we might say that *figura* "works" by recognizing and exploiting the fact that the shifters of a written text are *not* empty but are instead occupied and outdated, inhabited by an author who is (potentially) long gone. In this light *figura* legitimates–authorizes–the stealth by which we enter that occupied territory, implicating ourselves in the past of the text by announcing ourselves as its future. When we take our place in spoken discourse, we fill the shifters of speech with our presence. But to take one's place in a text, in written discourse, entails a different operation. With respect to the text, we no longer fill an "empty" shifter but instead, in our role as readers, we simultaneously empty and are emptied by the shifter which is already full. As living, breathing biological entities we have, of course, not changed. But as functions of or positions in discourse, as *persons* interpellated by and responding to the voice of the text, we are present only by dint of our relation to what is absent. We are "present" only insofar as we are the future of what is past. The discursive instance we inhabit as readers is not the present but the *absent-present*.

These remarks concerning absence and presence, deictical shift and readerly responsibility are at base less abstruse than they perhaps seem, for they derive from a basic Augustinian insight. Simply put, *figura* operates under the assumption that the written text is best understood as an epistle–as that which is *addressed* to a reader. Everything follows from this founding insight. Indeed we might say that in his response to Faustus, Augustine is at pains simply to work through the implications of the idea. How can it be possible for a text written in the past to be addressed to a reader from the future? How can a text written in the third person, with no mention of "I" and "you," be addressed at all? Or how can a text written with a certain audience in mind become meaningful for a different audience?

This last question is central, as becomes clear from the importance Augustine grants to Paul's dictum that Scripture was written *propter nos*. By arguing that the patriarchs wrote on our account, Augustine circumvents the text's historical audience and establishes the Christian reader as its authentic addressee. It is in this context that figural interpretation is, precisely, *figural* and not literal: the text is not *literally* meant for us, as an epistle would be, but is written for "our" sake insofar as it touches "them" in figure. The text connects with its literal destination only as figure. In this way the literal address of the text is a function of the figural destination: once again we see "us" and "them," the Old and the New, joined together chiastically.

It is the peculiarity of a chiastic, nonliteral notion of address that *figura* brings to light, makes conceivable. figurality, as a function both of language and of texts–as a matter of the tropological shift from the "proper" to the "figured" sign–thus derives from the problematic of address. How can Jewish texts address Christian readers? To answer the question is to define a uniquely Christian scriptural authority–but it is to do so at the expense of the historical author. To conceive the text's *figural* address, the Christian exegete must reject any appeal to the text's *literal* author. The insight is one that Augustine's medieval readers will codify. Just as Augustine imagines Moses whispering in his ear only to disavow that image, declaring that Moses' presence would be superfluous to the knowledge of truth–so does the medieval exegete insist upon the superfluity of the human author. Indeed, as we shall see, the monastic practice of *lectio divina*, divine reading, comes to define a notion of *auctoritas* or textual authority that precludes the human *auctor*. It is in the context of such a tradition that we will find Ser Petracco's son, Francesco. Petrarch's work in the *studia humanitatis* transforms the reading of texts, secularizing but not supplanting the notion of *figura* by (re)introducing a sense of the human author–an author who, like his reader, is *absent-present*.

DISPLACED PERSONS: AUGUSTINE AND THE PSALM

Addressivity is central to figura's view of ethics. Because the sacred text is presumed to address its reader, reading becomes a matter of call and response, its ethics grounded in voice, in discourse. As we have seen, however, the addressivity of the written text *qua* written involves a certain potential for disjunction, for a spatial or temporal gap between the call and the response. Texts are addressed to their readers across light-years: *figura* exploits this potential in the realm of the sacred, thereby developing an ethics of reading informed at once by a sense of voice and by a sense of loss; by a sense of the speaker's presence in discourse, and by intimations of silence and absence. Indeed, the voice of Scripture speaks only as a function of loss: future hangs on past, past hangs on future, old and new are bound together, mutually engaging and mutually effacing, like the two hands in the famous M. C. Escher print, drawing each other drawing. In other words, *figura* is the theory of voice for a fallen world. The voice of the text–the voice that Augustine hears in the garden–is the voice spoken by a *deus absconditus*.

Accordingly, figural address is a mediated and indirect affair. The discursive structure of *figura*, its sense of the sacred text as touching "them" in figure but written on "our" account, resembles the structure of a theatrical scene where an exchange transpires for the sake of an audience. Whence Augustine's fantasy of performance: his fantasy of a reading on behalf of the Manichees–an exemplary reading of Psalm 4. Both *figura* and theatrical performance are characterized by a deflected or triangulated mode of address: both envision words addressed to one auditor on account of others. If direct address takes place between two invertible persons, an "I" calling to a "you" who responds, in turn, as "I"[17]–then both *figura* and performance mediate that scene of address, implicating a third person and bending reversible symmetry into a less tidy scene of witness and discovery. Discourse, in this way, becomes asymmetrical: to get to "you," in some sense "I" has to pass through "he" or "she" or "they." In place of Benveniste's idealized shift between persons, discourse is triangulated through the impersonal. No longer disposed symmetrically, "I" and "you" are no longer mere inversions of each other. Instead, their relation is now a matter of translation and displacement.

As several commentators have remarked, Augustine's use of the Psalms throughout his *Confessions* is extraordinary, without precedent. His language in that text, Peter Brown notes, is "studded" with verses, fragments of verses, sometimes even single words drawn from the psalter. Suzanne Poque describes an act of "appropriation," as Augustine changes mode, time, and person, adopting the psalmist's words as his own and building a unified tone out of incorporated fragments.[18] Such a process would seem to culminate in book 9 where it achieves a kind of self-commentary and reflexivity in Augustine's recitation of the fourth psalm. And indeed, if the scene under the fig tree offers an emblem for the voice of the sacred text, then it is this second scene of reading that depicts that voice in the mouth of a reader. And thus, in a sacred, scriptural register we approach the voice of the lyric.[19]

The figural conception of the Psalms reaches back to a tradition at least as old as the first century A.D. that takes the psalter as a kind of songbook written and performed by King David, the tenth century B.C. father of Solomon.[20] Indeed, the very word "psalter" derives from the name of the stringed instrument–*psalterium*–that David was supposed to have played. For the Christian figural reader, the Book of Psalms exists both as the record of a past vocal performance and as a text to be taken up and read in the present devotional practice of the church. As A. J. Minnis notes, Augustine's treatment of the psalter in his *Enarrationes in Psalmos* was widely influential, helping to popularize the figural interpretation of David as *imago* of Christ. For the *Enarrationes* Augustine provides detailed expositions ("enarrationes") of each psalm, treating David as prophet and his psalter as prophecy of Christ's unity and of the unity of humankind in Christ.[21] Thus, in his *Enarratio* of Psalm 4 Augustine demonstrates the proper viewpoint of the Christian exegete, who should "now [*nunc*]" interpret the words of the psalm as "words of the Lord Man after the resurrection or those of man in the Church believing and hoping in Him."[22] To read the psalter is to read it figurally, as pertaining to, as *personifying* the Christian reader, or as spoken in the incarnated person of the Christian God. Later exegetes would codify these different figural possibilities according to a fourfold schema–but for Augustine the primary issue is simply recognition: the words were spoken for "our" benefit.[23]

Nonetheless, this recognition involves a shift in the psalm's context: "They are however called psalms which are sung to the stringed instrument which history [*historia*] declares David to need as prophet in the high mystery. Of which matter, *here* [*hic*] is not the place for discussion. . . . *Now* [*nunc*] we should [*debemus*] expect words of the Lord Man after the resurrection." (*En. in Ps.* 4:1, emphasis mine). Augustine invokes the legendary origin of the Psalms only to displace it: the words that we now interpret for our purposes as words of Christ or of the Christian believer used to be words sung by David to his psaltery. *Historia* has been displaced: both as that specific biblical narrative recorded in, e.g., the Book of Chronicles,[24] and, in general, as the non-figural dimension of Scripture (from the early Latin fathers on, *littera* and *historia* are taken as synonyms). *Hic et nunc*, here and now, David's practice as prophet is not to be discussed; supplanting a *historia* described in the present tense ("psalmi . . . qui *cantantur*") is a present tense of reading and discussion. A David who sings, presumably, in his own person, is replaced by the first person plural ("debemus") on whose account, in figure, that history was written.

At the same time, this shift from a Davidic *ego* to a Christian *nos* seems both to enable and to necessitate the presence of a *third* person. In truth, this third person is neither exactly "present," nor exactly a "person," since he stands outside the *hic et nunc* of discourse. Indeed, in this case, "he" even stands *behind* discourse, since the third person to whom Augustine refers is the first person *as* third person: i.e., David himself as author, whose words [*verba*] the exegete cites. "When I called, God heard me, he says, from whom is my righteousness" (*En. in Ps.* 4:2).[25]

The split between David's personal "I" and his impersonal "he" would seem to be inevitable given the psalm's written status. Essential to the structure of any written sign, we will recall, is its capacity to be cited and rehearsed long after its original context has disappeared. If we are to be able to read David's words, we need be able to cite them–quite literally, to reformulate them as quotation. "'When I called, God heard me,' he said . . . " At once a product and a precondition of such citation, the words of the psalm are split between speaker and author, between "I" and "he."

As it happens, this particular psalm, the very psalm that Augustine recites in book 9, sets these matters into sharp relief by actually enacting a deictical shift in its very first verse. In order fully to understand the impact of the psalmic, as a privileged instance of figural discourse, on Petrarchism, we'll need to examine this moment, along with Augustine's analysis of it, in some detail. Augustine's *enarratio* of Psalm 4 will illuminate the ways in which *figura* simultaneously requires and suppresses a notion of the author. In general, in a fallen world, God no longer speaks to us directly: as penman of the word of God, the human author is our necessary conduit to the divine. A later monastic tradition may reduce the role of such an author to the transparent functioning of amanuensis, but for Augustine the author is far more than secretary, for it is primarily in response to his voice that we read–even if our reading entails his absence. Just so, in the *enarratio* of Psalm 4, the shift from the psalmist's first person to the reader's "we" entails a pass through the impersonal, a distancing of the author. And as we will discover, the psalm's deflected structure of address conditions a particular notion of exemplarity–a notion crucial for Petrarchan humanism and Petrarchan lyric alike. Such a notion, as we will see, centers on the exemplary status of the "I."

"When I called, God of my righteousness heard me; in tribulation You enlarged me." The first verse of Psalm 4 conveys a shift from impersonal description to personal address. For Augustine, however, this transition from third to second person seems to defy all logic.

> The change of person however–since he passes immediately from the third, where he says "He heard me" to the second, where he says "You enlarged me"–if it is not for the sake of variety and sweetness that this was done, it is

strange that he would want first to indicate to men that he had been heard and afterwards to address the One who had heard him [*exauditorem suum*]. Unless by chance when he had indicated that he had been heard in that very enlargement of heart he preferred to speak with God so that even in this way he might show what it is to be dilated in heart; that is, to have God, already infused in his heart, with whom he might inwardly speak.

(*En. in Ps.* 4:2)

When the psalm is understood merely as spoken utterance, its temporality makes no sense: first the psalmist announces that God has heard him, then he goes on to address God. The sequence of events would seem to be backwards: as in a flashback, we hear the moment of appeal after we have already learned its outcome (*God heard me*). Furthermore, the shift in persons itself poses a kind of paradox, since it would seem to put the psalmist in two places at once: at once narrating an event and participating in it; at once standing outside and within his discourse with God. *When I called, God heard me.* A moment of call and response, of an exchange between an "I" and a "you," is shifted into the distance; the "You" becomes a "He" and so fades into the past. In the very next clause, however, the "You" returns. *You enlarged me.* Now, instead of describing dialogue as a thing of the past, the speaker describes the past from a dialogic standpoint. In converse with God's "You," David cites a past act of deliverance.

Shifting between third and second persons, the psalmist thus seeks simultaneously to establish a bond between *ego* and *tu*, and to announce that bond as accomplished fact—a fact hence relegated to the past. In other words, the psalmist wants to have his discourse and speak it too. As an utterance unfolding in linear time, such flexibility would not be possible. But despite his speculations concerning the psalm's *historia* as song, Augustine, as we have said, treats the work as a written artifact. Thus he can resolve the apparent paradox of the psalm's first verse by distinguishing between David as author and David as speaker. Moreover, Augustine suggests that this split between author and speaker entails a corresponding split in the psalm's audience. Just as we imagine David the author, a "he" standing behind words uttered in the first person by David the speaker, so we imagine an audience comparably split into interlocutor and witness, into the second person with whom the speaker speaks and the third person who observes the scene.

For Augustine, then, the psalm transpires as a performance conducted for another's benefit. Like the scene before the Manichees in book 9 of the *Confessions*, Augustine would here have the words of the psalm, as hymn and praise to God, unfold *propter alios*, for the sake of others.[26] "He preferred to speak with God so that even in this way he might show what it is to be dilated in heart," Augustine explains. The psalmist's appeal to God is calculated, designed to demonstrate what it is "to have God, already infused in his heart, with whom he might inwardly speak." A purely inward colloquy is hence enacted for an outward show. As speaker, David is entirely caught up in the linear flow of his utterance and utterly committed to the present discursive instance. But as author, he is free of such constraints and able to manipulate the text's effects as a whole.

It is perhaps not surprising that the *Enarrationes*, begun around 392, should reflect the structure of address that Augustine brings to his *Confessions*, written in 397. It is during this period that Augustine wrote his major treatises concerning *figura* and explored the performative aspect of the doctrine of *propter nos*.[27] As he asks in the *Confessions*: "To whom do I narrate all this? For I do not tell this to you, my God, but before you I narrate these things to my kind, to humankind" (*Conf.* 2.3). Nonetheless, Augustine also confesses an inverted direction of address: "It is Your mercy to which I speak, not man who is my mocker" (*Conf.* 1.6). Somehow both expressions are true; at once Augustine speaks *to* man and *before* him, *to* God and *before* God. Man is at once the *Confessions*' witness and its interpellated second person. In the *enarratio* to Psalm 4, we learn how such duality is possible. In that psalm as Augustine reads it, the relation between "I" and "you" isn't simply triangulated: more precisely, it is chiastic. The psalm has two addressees, God and man, who yield to one another, alternately standing in the place of the second person. When God is the "you" addressed, man is the distant third-person witness. And when the psalmist actually addresses his fellow humankind ("*filii hominum*, Sons of men, how long heavy in heart, why do you love vanity and seek a lie?," v. 2), it is God who is relegated to the impersonal. In this way the psalm's "you," like the psalm's "I," shades into the third person.

Where, however, are we readers in all of this? *figura* assumes that the psalm is written "for our sakes": we are the text's intended audience. But at the same time, clearly we are not *literally* the "sons of men" who witness David's discourse with God and whom the psalmist addresses. Instead we find ourselves figured, but not directly addressed, in that apostrophe. Hence, on a variety of fronts, the psalm's relation to its audience is no simple matter: simultaneously literal and figural, within and without the psalm, present and absent, affirmed and denied, the third-person witness disrupts discourse's symmetry and linearity on both sides, disturbing both the "I" and the "you."

In this manner, the psalm supports the same complexity of address that Augustine constructs in his own recitation of Psalm 4 in the *Confessions.* As we will recall, that recitation is *narrated.* The lector's impossible wish to perform without performing is articulated in the past tense. The rhetorical coup of the scene hence consists in the way it positions the reader: *we* are the Manichees. *We* are the audience for whose sake Augustine recites those words without seeming to do so. By citing himself and thus exploiting the split between author and speaker, Augustine is able to present, quite self-consciously, an un-self-conscious recitation of the psalm.[28] "I wished that they had been somewhere near me, without my knowing it . . . when I read the fourth psalm . . . : 'When I called upon you, you heard me, God of my righteousness.'" (*Conf.* 9.4).[29] His impossible wish is achieved–but with the reader and not with the Manichees, and only insofar as Augustine recounts his wish's failure. It is we who "overhear" a discourse mediated by narration, just as it is the author's critical stance that saves the speaker from hypocrisy. Like Freudian denegation, where the unconscious affirms by denying, Augustine fulfills his fantasy by disavowing it.

Slippery as this structure is–as slippery as paradox[30]–it forms the basis of *figura*'s conservatism. As Henri de Lubac argues, from the time of the fathers throughout the Middle Ages, the figural sense of Scripture is "presented as the dogmatic sense par excellence"; Gregory the Great's dictum, for instance, that allegory constructs (*aedificat*) faith becomes a medieval commonplace.[31] *Figura* builds faith and builds a Christian community by building–*edifying*–a reader. Thanks to *figura*, reading the Bible unfolds as a shift from the "I" of the prophets or patriarchs to the "we" of a Christian community. Furthermore, this shift depends upon the intervention of the third person. At first we stand outside the text, like Alypius or the Manichees, potential witness to the author's devotions, potential audience waiting to be converted. To enter sacred discourse, however, to take up the text and *read*, is to recognize the text as written *for us*. With such a recognition, we displace the text's first person with our own second person; we take the "I" as a figure enacted for our benefit. Augustine becomes an example for us as we read his *Confessions*, just as Anthony was an example for the *Agentes in Rebus*, just as, more generally, the places and persons of the Hebrew Bible are "figurae," paradigms or examples, for the new covenant.[32]

Furthermore, it is by assuming the text's exemplary status that we presuppose a distinction between the text's author and its speaker—just as Augustine presupposes the psalmist's dual function in his *enarratio* of Psalm 4. Taking possession of the speaker's words as *figurae* enacted for our benefit, we leave the author behind. As a "he," the author is drained of concrete actuality. Our conduit to God, this "he" stands behind the truth of the text. He is the source of the Christian doctrine written, "in figure," in Hebrew law. As such, however, in his own person he is entirely superfluous to the text; instead, the author's "he" serves as cipher or placeholder for any Christian truth we find. By definition, his intentions are true and holy and proper to our needs:[33] what "he" intends is a function not of the writing "I" but instead of *us*—of the reader as first person.

In this way, if the figural sense of Scripture builds faith it is because the central doctrine of *figura*—the doctrine of *propter nos*—makes an example of the text. But it does so only by passing through the impersonal. To take my place as the text's interpellated "you," I must invoke a third-person vantage point that, strictly speaking, belongs neither to reader nor to writer, neither to "I" nor to "you." Benveniste's sense of discursive "inversibilité" is disrupted on both sides by the non-person who remains ever outside of discourse. On the one side, the impersonal holds open a place for the potential convert, for the outsider or unbeliever on behalf of whom the scene transpires. On the other side, the impersonal reserves the place of the author. As an impossible, virtual place, unlocatable in real space, the place of the author is that "place" from which a figural address originates—that place from which we are called *in figure*. Without an audience, without an author, the text's figural address cannot take place. Yet unlike the positions of "I" and "you," the "he" of the author and "they" of the audience are positions that cannot be held in the here and now. As non-persons, both author and audience can *only* be placeholders.

Thanks to such placeholders, both the text itself and our response to the text become exemplary. Our reading amounts to a shift in person while that shift amounts, more or less, to a conversion performed for others. To be interpellated by Scripture is to become one of the "us" on whose account the text was written: it is to join a preexisting community. At the same time, however, this community is, precisely, a discursive community–a community defined, in fact, by its relation to Scripture. Thus the reader at once *joins* the community and *exemplifies* it. To become part of the "us" is to instantiate the community as "I," embodying it in one's individual first person. As figural interpretant I thus *figure* the community: I both take my place among the "us" and represent that "us" for the unconverted outsider. Thus, I read secure in the faith that the text was written *propter nos*, but my reading–and ultimately, perhaps, even my writing–unfold *propter eos*, on their account.

I have dwelled on Augustine's reading of Psalm 4 in order to suggest how *figura* structures an exemplary first person: the "I" of the *Confessions* or of the Davidic psalms. Indeed, it is this exemplary "I" that offers later writers an authoritative model for the lyric persona itself. As I have suggested, within a sacred tradition the normativity of the first person requires, however, that we forget the author. The "I" becomes law, a figure to follow, but only insofar as the author becomes insubstantial, a mere non-person placeholder for God's Word. In the secular tradition that Petrarch inaugurates, the situation is somewhat more complex: in becoming law, the author is forgotten but also foregrounded. His very loss is noted; his absence as such is remarked.

Imitatio AND THE LAW OF THE AUTHOR

"Petrarque sur moy / N'avoit authorité pour me donner sa loy," writes Pierre de Ronsard in 1556, concluding the *Nouvelle continuation des amours* with a playful denial of the obvious.[34] Merely by invoking Petrarch, Ronsard announces his allegiance to him.

Indeed, on closer inspection Ronsard's anti-Petrarchism works as the purest form of imitation: with his *Amours* he seeks to become the true heir to Petrarch's legacy—not a slavish imitator, not a mere *petrarchista*, but the French Petrarca, the *François Pétrarque* himself. This idea of an imitation that doesn't simply ape its exemplar would have been a humanist commonplace, one whose roots trace back at least as far as Seneca and whose medieval context—the assimilative "divine reading" or *lectio divina*, which derived from Augustinian principles—would have influenced Petrarch.[35] And indeed, the origin of a humanist *imitatio* or exemplarity, along with the sense of historical difference with which it is inspired, is usually ascribed to Petrarch.[36] It is perhaps this notion of imitation that Ronsard imitates when he denounces Petrarch's authority.

Ronsard's playful disavowal of Petrarch's law sets into relief the paradoxical structure of humanist imitation: a structure that simultaneously erases and reinscribes the exemplar's authority. For my purposes, Ronsard's Petrarchan anti-Petrarchism also suggests the ways in which such *imitatio* itself imitates the normativity of Augustinian *figura*. As we shall see, a Christian figural tradition mediates between the two sides of Petrarch's bilingual literary career, linking his authority as Latin humanist to the authoritative voice of his Italian lyrics. By refocusing discussions of Petrarchan *imitatio* around the question of his first person, both Petrarch's humanist endeavors and his lyric *rime sparse* become legible as recto and verso of the same ethics of voice.

At the same time, a focus on Petrarch's exemplary first person makes it possible to situate his work with respect not only to a tradition—Latin, for Petrarch—of patristic and psalmic utterance, but also in relation to the vernacular and secular tradition of lyric that immediately precedes Petrarch's own experiments in vernacular poetry. I refer here to the so-called clear lyric of the troubadors—that is, the lyric of a predominantly oral culture. For Judson Boyce Allen, the "I" of the troubador tradition "enacts itself only to invite plagiarization."[37] Such an "I" is indeed discursively "available" in ways that Benveniste would recognize; it marks an open discursive position that anyone might inhabit. Yet, according to Allen it is the task of this "I" task to dramatize that position not for the sake of a "you," not for the sake of an *other*, but for the sake of the *same*: the troubador ego exists in order to be *fleshed out*. Now, for Allen, since anyone can fill the position, this cipher ego serves as an exemplum:

its words are universal, gnomic, not so much defining a posture that is true for everyone as defining a posture from which everyone can be true. In this way, what clear lyric reveals is a place rather than a speech. Like Victorinus's walls in Augustine's *Confessions*, the walls that make the church and without which his confession of faith is ineffectual, the clear lyric delimits the public stance from which a speaker may speak Truth. In this manner, Allen's account suggests one way to conceive the lyric first person's exemplarity. Because the troubador lyric enacts a position in discourse from which any individual can speak normatively or truly, the position is itself, in a sense, normative. By taking our place in such discourse we conform ourselves to certain social roles and rules, engaging, like Victorinus before the congregation, in a certain ritual stance. In a word, we *perform*.[38]

In rough and dirty terms, I'd like to suggest that—both formally and historically—the Petrarchan lyric falls somewhere between this medieval conception of performance and the much later conception of the Romantics, especially as the latter gets refined by the New Critics. In 1833 John Stuart Mill writes, in a formulation that proves wildly appealing, that "eloquence is *heard*, poetry is *overheard.* . . . Poetry is feeling confessing itself to itself, in moments of solitude."[39] What for Mill is an appreciative declaration of poetry's spontaneity and authenticity, for certain New Critics serves almost as prescription, identifying the genre and guiding the reader's response. According to this approach, the lyric poem is best read as a kind of soliloquy—as a representation of a personal utterance, or, as Barbara Herrnstein Smith more problematically puts it: as a "fictive utterance."[40] Interpretation then begins by presuming the poem's unity as speech-act and thus inferring the complex set of concerns, intentions, and circumstance that would inform such an utterance. Hence the reader frames the poem in a fictional context, placing it between quotation marks, as it were, in order to reconstruct the attitude of the speaker to whom such words might be ascribed. In this manner, a fictional persona and the narrative that defines him or her is construed. The fictional scene is set.

This treatment of the lyric seems irreducibly theatrical, conceiving the poem along the analogy of a soliloquized moment in a play. As readers, we are the audience, unrecognized by the players and seated, as it were, at a respectful distance from the proscenium. The contrast between this approach to the lyric and Allen's couldn't be more pronounced. Where Allen's performative lyric left the first person transparent and generic, absolutely lacking in substance, the New Criticism imagines the lyric "I" as a *dramatis persona*, as a more or less fully conceived and realized stage character. Furthermore, where the lyric "I" of the troubador tradition enacted itself for the generalized occupancy of its audience, the Romantic "I" described by the New Criticism precludes such readerly appropriation. Instead, we watch at a remove while its persona declares itself. In sum, the performativity of the medieval lyric is that of the purely present and the transparently generic, while the performance of the Romantic lyric, understood to be equally present, nonetheless is opaque in its particularity. One invites occupation, the other resists it, but both do so in present time.

Between a generic performativity and a performed particularity falls the exemplarity of the Petrarchan lyric. Petrarch's "I" is not exemplary because it enacts a generalized space in discourse for us to inhabit; nor does the "I" affect us as fiction, articulating a particularized space and personality while we look on with more or less sympathy and interest. Our connection to Petrarch's "I" is based neither in the availability of an empty shifter nor in the psychological mechanisms according to which we identify as subject to other subjects. Instead, as a thing of discourse, Petrarch's "I" enacts its very rootedness in discourse, its deictic contextualization. It enacts the fullness, and not the emptiness, of the shifter. The inertia and not the flexibility. Yet it enacts itself rooted in discourse for our sake–for the sake of an absent *posteritas*–and in so doing, it enacts its commitment to the here-and-now as anachronism, as a commitment to the there-and-then from the standpoint of the yet-to-be. Petrarch's "I" draws us neither into a fiction nor into a vacant shifter. Instead it draws us into a complex net of deictic references, into a discourse shot through with glissades, absences, overlaps; in short, into a deixis that has been opened up to absence and to the non-person, a deixis constructed around the passage of time.

The "I" of Petrarch's *Penitential Psalms* is not quite exemplary in the way described above but for precisely that reason the psalms provide our discussion with an indispensable transition point. As a distinct lyric sequence, the group of seven "penitential" psalms (nos. 6, 31, 37, 50, 101, 129, and 142 in the Vulgate) is recognized as early as Cassiodorus in the sixth century; in all likelihood, however, the sequence found liturgical use long before then. By the twelfth century, monasteries across Europe were daily reciting these seven psalms in their worship, and from at least the thirteenth century the penitential psalms came increasingly to play a role in lay devotions and public masses.[41] As Stephen Greenblatt has pointed out in his treatment of Thomas Wyatt's paraphrase of the sequence, the psalms taken together express a paradigmatic movement "at once repetitive and linear," filled with remissions and relapses, from moral sickness to moral health. Furthermore, in developing its system of penitence, the Church institutionalizes the seven psalms and the movement they describe. The pattern becomes prescriptive, Greenblatt suggests: a mold for individual experience.[42] In this way, in their medieval devotional use the psalms reflect the same generic transparency we've already examined with respect to the troubador "I." Suitable for any man, the penitential psalms thus provide a template for everyman.

Such is not, however, Petrarch's view of the psalms, nor are his *Penitential Psalms* a paraphrase of David's. Instead, they are a loose imitation, written in metered Latin verses and more closely approximating the lyrical prose of the *Confessions* than the clunky Latin psalter of Jerome.[43] In Petrarch's own day his *Psalms* were among his most influential and admired works, copies of them held in secular as well as monastic libraries.[44] Even though their date remains uncertain (1342/3 or 1348 being the most likely contenders), it is thought that Petrarch wrote the *Psalms* during the decade of spiritual crisis that surrounded his brother Gherardo's 1343 decision to enter a Carthusian monastery.[45] It is in fact around this time that Petrarch writes Gherardo in defense of poetry, arguing "theologiam poeticam esse de Deo," theology is the poetry of God.[46] "Even the Fathers of the Old Testament used heroic and other kinds of poetry," he tells his brother.

> And David's psalter itself, which you sing day and night, for the Hebrews consisted in meter. Hence it is neither undeservedly nor inelegantly that I dare call him the poet of the Christians.
>
> (*Familiari* 10.4)

The title "poet of the Christians" would indeed be a surprising one–"inelegant," no less–for a king of the Hebrews were it not that Petrarch, like Augustine, reads the Psalms figurally. As he reminds Gherardo in the same letter, the Psalms sing "the birth, death, descent into Hell, resurrection and return of a blessed man–namely Christ." In imitating the Psalms, then, Petrarch is imitating a figural rather than a generic structure. The Psalms are to be read in view of history and not merely, like a troubador lyric, performed in an eternal present. Furthermore, Petrarch's response itself follows a figural rather than a generic paradigm: Petrarch doesn't merely take David's place in the Psalms; rather, in writing psalms of his own, he displaces David from the Psalms. A translation has occurred–the very *translatio* that, according to Augustine, defines the figural sign.

Even so, the *Penitential Psalms* are a failure. In them Petrarch's first person achieves neither the luminous anonymity of the "clear" lyric nor the discursive authority of his vernacular *rime*. This is why the work is so useful for our purposes: in the collection of psalms we see a transitional piece; we see Petrarch working his way out of a medieval troubador context, even as he works his way from theology to poetry–from a sacred to a secular sense of discourse. In the context of intellectual history, the *Penitential Psalms* clarify the role of *figura* in both Petrarch's humanism and his poetics; in the context of the lyric, the *Psalms* help explain the transition from a psalmic, confessional, and Latin first person to the restless "io" of Petrarch's Italian lyrics.

Key to this transition is the particular way in which the *Penitential Psalms* "fail." Their "failure" consists in a thematization of *figura*. As we have seen it operate so far, *figura* has been tricky, stealthy, the terms it displaces or "converts" having been doubly effaced, since their displacement itself is erased, forgotten. In the *Penitential Psalms*, however, Petrarch presents a kind of resistance to *figura*; moreover, this resistance consists simply in foregrounding *figura*'s activity, in rendering its shifts and slides and turnings visible *as such*. In the universe of Petrarch's *Psalms* nothing moves because everything is turning: *figura* no longer works, having been revealed as trope.

It is not just that the *Psalms* are repetitive. The biblical sequence of seven is also repetitive, and yet it manages to convey a salutary movement forward. The difference is that, from the very start, Petrarch's *Psalms* thematize their repetition. The prevailing image is that of a journey that keeps turning back upon itself, of a traveler going in circles, precisely when he most thinks to be moving ahead.

> Heu michi misero, quia iratum adversus me constitui Redemptorem meum, et legem suam contumaciter neglexi.
> Iter rectum sponte deserui; et per invia longe lateque circumactus sum.
> Aspera quelibet et inaccessa penetravi; et ubique labor et angustie.
> Unus aut alter ex gregibus brutorum; et inter lustra ferarum habitatio mea.
> In anxietatibus cum voluptate versatus sum; et in sentibus cubile meum stravi.

[Woe to me miserable one, because I have made my Redeemer angry against me; and I have stubbornly neglected his law. Of my own accord I have abandoned the right way; and without a way I have been driven about far and wide. I have penetrated in every harsh and inaccessible place; and gone everywhere with toil and shortness of breath. I have become one beast or another; and among the dens of wild beasts I make my dwelling place. I have turned with pleasure amidst anguish; and I have made my bed among thorns.]

(1.1–5)[47]

Petrarch's problems begin with a metaphor so common, so ubiquitous that at first we miss it. "Iter rectum . . . deserui": I abandoned the right way. The path is *deserted*; literally, the image of a "way," of a "path" is imprecise, empty. It scarcely even counts as an *image* because it gives us so little to envision. But over the course of the next three verses Petrarch renders it precise and concrete; the metaphor thickens as the landscape does, charting a movement toward density and specificity that sparks the faded image of life's "iter" and drives us forward. We move from the vague and indefinite adjectival nouns of verse 3–"aspera" and "inaccessa," harsh and inaccessible places–to the more specific designation, "inter lustra ferarum," among the dens of beasts (4), to the precision of a bed laid "in sentibus," in thorns (5). The psalm is getting somewhere, as is the wanderer, although he is most certainly headed in the wrong direction, plunging ahead through a dense wilderness, settling down in the brambles.

However, this thrust into the thicket soon turns back upon itself; at the journey's moment of greatest concreteness, we return to a dim spatial abstraction: "In anxietatibus cum voluptate *versatus sum.*" *Versatus sum* can mean "I have lingered," although literally it means "I was turned about": Petrarch has lingered in mortal pleasures, turning round to make his home in anguish just as a dog will circle to make his bed. In this way, the phrase glosses the entire spatial movement, the penetration of the forest, that has come before. Without a way, the wanderer has gotten nowhere, although driven "longe lateque," far and wide. He has only run round in circles, just as the verses' specificity has only led us back to where we started, to a faded spatial metaphor.

At stake in these lines is the psalm's figurality at its most basic level—as a matter of the exchange between *signs* and *things*. As we will recall from our discussion of *On Christian Doctrine* in the previous chapter, for Augustine a "figure" is a thing taken as a sign. His example is the ox in Deuteronomy 25:4, which, as, precisely, an *ox*, a *res* and not a *signum*, comes to signify a Christian preacher (cf. 1 Cor. 9:9–10). At the same time, however, the exchange must work in reverse if it is going to work: these signs must, in turn, again be translated into things. Once revealed as figure, Old Testament oxen are exchanged for New Testament preachers. Christian liberty thus reads things as signs in order to transform signs into a higher order of thing, "elevating them to the things which they represented" (*Doctrina* 3.8.9). Revelation, then, consists in a translation between the two orders.

In this first psalm the circuit drawn from initial abstraction, an abandoned *iter rectum*, to the final turn *in anxietatibus cum voluptate*, is itself a kind of movement from sign to thing and back again, a translation aimed at revelation. The *iter* is a sign which the psalm reads as a thing, i.e, as an actual path, in order to elucidate its meaning as sign. Indeed, this is the movement that we usually associate with narrative allegory: an abstraction is embodied in specific and concrete terms in order that, in turn, those terms can be glossed and so explicate the abstraction. With such a schema, language seems to find a way out of itself, a path, as it were, to meaning, even while it remains self-referential: at the level of the allegorical narrative–that is to say, at a thematic level–signs turn into things that, in turn, explicate the signs. In this way, narrative allegory thematizes *figura*'s translational power.

But in the instance of Petrarch's first psalm, we do not simply find ourselves turning between signs and things; instead, we are turning toward *the language of turning* itself. And indeed, the psalm's pivotal point is that moment of glossing in the fifth verse: "With pleasure amidst anguish *versatus sum*; and I have made my bed among thorns." The fulcrum of the verse is a verb that can neither be read as a sign nor be taken as a thing: *versatus sum*. As the phrase "I have lingered," *versatus sum* leaves Petrarch in abstraction, but as the phrase "I was turned," the verb places him in the midst of *things*, rolling about on a bed of brambles. Both sign and thing, and neither sign nor thing, *versatus sum* must be read at least twice. The turning point of the psalm's opening movement thus turns upon itself. At the same time, however, this turn of phrase is already a phrase of turning: *versatus sum* from *versare*, to turn. Turning between the language of signs and the language of things, our eyes are drawn to the word "turning" itself. We are thus forced to note language itself in its materiality, language as a *thing* that, precisely, mediates between signs and things. Instead of recounting the smooth translation between the two, the psalm thus insists on the letter or signifier that *turns* signs into things, and vice *versa*. The focus is drawn to the site of translation itself, to the materiality of the sign *qua* sign (the place where signs actually *are* things). The psalm hence alerts us not only to the way language turns; it alerts us even more radically to the turn made flesh, as it were, in the pun on *versare*: *versatus sum*. Instead of thematizing the power of *figura* to transform and translate–to make the old new and the flesh spirit–the psalm thematizes the act of translation per se.[48]

And so *figura* gets stuck in the midst of its turning. The problem is a serious one since, as the declaration of a penitent, the psalm's avowed purpose is to complete a turn toward the right path–to announce a turn toward God. In other words, presumably the psalm exists to effect Petrarch's *conversion*. But as long as the language of the psalm turns around itself, this turn toward the Other will never take place. Mired in the thicket and texture of language, the "I" of the psalm will keep pulling away from its "You," resisting its position in a shifting discourse. "What am I going to do now [*nunc*]?" Petrarch asks two lines later. "Where will I turn [*Quo me vertam*] amid such danger? The hopes of my youth have all fallen away" (1.7). Petrarch is at the verge of change, at the very moment, the *nunc*, of conversion. It is *now* that he needs to turn–and yet this very turn literally takes him back to those thorny pleasures of youth: *quo me vertam* returns us to *versatum sum*. At the level of the letter these two different turnings turn out to be mere *versions* of the same. Indeed Petrarch has nowhere to turn because with each turn he only entangles himself further: "I have gone backwards through inextricable turnings [*anfractus*]," he writes in Psalm 7 (7.7).[49]

Petrarch's only answer comes from beyond himself: if he is to turn toward God and not merely toward his own turning, he will need God's help. But here lies the catch: in order to gain God's help he needs to call Him, and yet that appeal itself would be tantamount to a conversion. The paradox here is an ancient one: to be able to invoke the aid he needs, Petrarch needs already to have received it. Otherwise, the more he tries to turn his language toward God, the more he turns it away from Him–a problem which, significantly, is already apparent in the wordplay of the first verse of the first psalm: "I have made my Redeemer angry against [*adversus*] me."[50] At once Petrarch stands against God and turned toward him, *adversus* and *ad-versus*, entrapping and indicting himself with each new verse, each *versus*, of this carefully numbered poetry. "I will call whom I have offended and I will not fear; I will call again whom I have rejected, and I will not blush" (2.1). To open his discourse to God would be to relinquish his hold on the first person, making way for the "You" to respond to his call. Petrarch won't do it. He won't allow the shifter to shift. Instead he repeats the gesture of calling just as he repeats the gesture of turning: "I will call . . . I will call again . . ."

In the final psalm, in a passage that we've already cited in part, Petrarch at last articulates the problem: "I have pursued transverse and tortuous ways of life [*secutus sum transversas et tortuosas vivendi vias*] . . . / You know since you were always my goal [*finis*]; but believing to come to you by myself, I have gone backwards through inextricable turnings [*retrocessi per inextricabiles anfractus*]" (7.6–7). Trying to reach God on his own has only foregrounded Petrarch's own efforts, turning him back upon his own turning. But in this way Petrarch has kept to himself: to relinquish those efforts seems impossible. The result would be a kind of oblivion, a total disappearance of person. "Coge me ad te," he writes in the third psalm, "Bring me to you if calling isn't enough; in short, let it be as you wish, as long as I don't perish" (3.11). His own calling might not be enough, Petrarch realizes—but nor is it enough for God's will to be done. One must also stipulate the continued presence of person: "as long as I don't perish [*modo ne peream*]." He even asks God Himself to turn, as if he can't absorb his own conversion but must, instead, keep the world turning round him, turning so that he not perish. "Respice, Domine, vide, miserere, succurre": Look back at me Lord, see me, have mercy, come to my side (3.12).

THE SECULAR AUTHOR

In the "Letter to Posterity," Petrarch writes that above all other things he has dwelt (*incubui*) on the study of antiquity because his own age has always displeased him. In this way, when he was not pulled in the other direction out of love for his dear ones, "I always wished to have been born in any other age and to forget this one, with an effort of mind always grafting [*inserere*] myself onto other ages."[51]

Petrarch's anachronistic wish to graft himself onto a previous age cannot help but recall an equally anachronistic Pauline revisionism: "For if some of the branches were broken and you being the wild olive were grafted to them . . . do not boast against the branches" (Rom. 11:17–18). It is from the hybrid logic of *figura* that Petrarch learns how to *insert* himself into history; Paul gives Petrarch the terms for thinking about the past. But how could the same tradition that does its best to annihilate the cultural specificity of the Jews and their Book be responsible for the humanist respect—even reverence—for people and texts past? I would like to argue that *figura* structures Petrarch's regard for the past; however, I am well aware that quite the opposite argument has long prevailed: the tendency in Petrarch criticism has long been to distinguish between a humanist hermeneutics and a Christian allegorical tradition.[52] Thomas Greene, to cite a typical and influential example, differentiates between what he calls "subreading"—i.e., the humanist's palimpsestic efforts to reconstruct the past—and a medieval allegoresis that sees only continuity between past and present. "This [latter] method," Greene writes, "aligned author and reader in a single universe of discourse wherein no cultural distance could exist because, with the sole exception of the Christian revelation, historical change was virtually unknown. The new 'archeological' hermeneutic, on the other hand, presupposed a considerable distance" (*Light in Troy*, 94).

It would not, however, be difficult to demonstrate the profound similarity between Petrarch's hermeneutic goals and the goals of a Pauline allegory. Isn't it precisely in order to salvage a Jewish scripture for a Christian audience that *figura* is first conceived? Doesn't *figura* exist precisely to redress "a considerable [cultural] distance"? And similarly, aren't the subreader's efforts likewise designed to "align author and reader in a single universe of discourse"? Instead of Jews and Christians, we have ancients and moderns; where the coming of Jesus bifurcates human time in the Christian world, the fall of Rome and the ensuing Dark Ages divide Petrarch's world history.[53] Indeed, as we have already seen in the *Penitential Psalms*, whenever Petrarch envisions his historical being, he does so according to the dyadic terms of a now/then, new/old retrospectivity. "What am I going to do now? . . . The hopes of my youth have all fallen away" (*Penitential Psalms* 1.7).These are the terms that *figura* has offered him–and yet, something *has* changed. At a structural level, Petrarch's sense of history is thoroughly and profoundly figural; structurally, too, his very project of inserting himself into the past is also figural and, as we shall see in the famous letter detailing his ascent of Mont Ventoux, so too is his ethics of reading, which emulates and extrapolates the *figura* of Saint Augustine. In terms of underlying structure, then, Petrarch has merely adopted the tools of the Christian exegete.

At the same time, however, the whole spirit of the enterprise has been transformed. After all, for the Christian exegete, the task of bridging the "considerable distance" between Old and New is assured in advance. The success of such exegesis is a foregone conclusion, guaranteed by the very definition of Christianity as revealed truth: these *figurae* were written for our sake. Indeed, the most egregious examples of Christian allegorizing testify to just how foregone the conclusion is: any particularity, any incongruence annulled, immediately glossed over in the name of *propter nos*. For the humanist reader, however, success is never assured in advance. No Eschaton directs his reading; instead of sacred

Advent, he reads in view of an imperial fall. Hence, if a doctrine of *propter nos* governs his exegesis, it does so only as enabling, and thus *necessary*, presupposition. The very real possibility exists that the obstacles are too great, the distance will remain unbridged. The humanist, in other words, reads without foregone conclusions. He can only read *as if*: presupposing the text's figural address, *propter nos* is for him a theorem whose proof can only lie in the reading.

The rules of the game have not changed, but the playing field has. It is not simply that Petrarch is reading the same texts differently than a Christian allegorist would or that he is reading different texts in the same way. Rather, his whole conception of textuality itself has changed. Thus the issue isn't simply what sort of books Petrarch reads–for example, pagan writings or secular poetic works in place of Scripture. After all, it was Augustine who first urged the figural plunder of pagan wealth–an argument that Petrarch cites in defense of his own reading in the treatise *De sui ipsius et multorum ignorantia*.[54] Furthermore, Petrarch does read Scripture, and, as we've seen with the *Penitential Psalms*, he even considers it worthy of imitation. The difference for Petrarch does not then emerge with the secular text, or even with a secular view of history, a focus on *imperium* rather than Eschaton. Instead, at issue is the *authority* behind both history and text. At stake is Petrarch's focus on the secular *author*.

According to Mary Carruthers, such a focus would not have been possible within the memorial culture of the Middle Ages. As Carruthers has shown, the medieval text, whether sacred or profane, functions as a communal repository of *auctoritates*, of "flowers" or *topoi* that circulate in the culture freely, reproduced and cross-referenced in the *florilegia* that readers compile and consult in the course of study. Hence the medieval reader is always composing, culling, and assimilating his own storehouse of authorities and thereby adding to the communal store.[55] In such a culture, the text is infinite and its authority is collective. Its boundaries, everexpanding, are those of the community. Accordingly, to speak of such a text's author is to engage in tautology: "an 'auctor' is simply one whose writings are full of 'authorities'" (Carruthers, 190). Indeed, in practice the words *auctor* and *auctoritas* are used almost interchangeably: to cite an "author" is to cite a text, not a person.

That Petrarch belongs to a generation already calling this notion of the transparent author into question is clear from an anecdote that he himself tells. In a letter to Pulice da Vicenza, a fellow poet, he recounts how, having once censured Cicero's character to a group of friends, an old man, a venerable scholar, responded irrationally and with outrage:

> In response he had nothing else to offer either to me or to the others [*aliis*] than to contrast everything being said with the splendor of Cicero's name, thus replacing reason with authority [*autoritas*]. Again and again with his hand outstretched he would exclaim: "Gently I beg, gently with my Cicero!" When asked whether he thought that Cicero had ever erred in anything, he would close his eyes and, as if struck by the word, he would turn his head, groaning, "Alas, are they accusing my Cicero?"—as if we were dealing not with a man but with a god.
>
> (*Fam.* 24.2)

Petrarch strives to counter *auctoritas* with reason, and his target is an easy one, its defense a feeble old man with nothing to say and only a splendid name to fall back on. And perhaps we should thus say that Petrarch strives to replace one authority with another. After relating how he defeated the old man, Petrarch asks: "What could I say? Myself the greatest admirer of Cicero's name." One generation of scholar, one type of authority has ceded to another. It is Petrarch and not the nameless *senex* who admires Cicero best and who can say, with reason, what's in a name.

Thus, as Petrarch sees it, behind the text lies a fallible and mortal human rather than an eternal source of truth. In Petrarch a secular sense of the author–a profane sense, even–finds its authoritative spokesman. What role Petrarch actually had in developing this view of the author will be impossible to assess. Certainly he himself describes his view of an errant Cicero as novel; he writes how astonished the company was by the newness and strangeness–the *novitas*–of the idea [*sententia*]. Nonetheless, in this letter the generational lines are drawn clearly: it is only the old scholar who objects while the others present, the "aliis" to whom the scholar has nothing of reason to say, seem quickly to join Petrarch's side. Astonishing or not, his novelty was in keeping with his age.

In *Medieval Theory of Authorship*, A. J. Minnis suggests that the influx of Aristotelian ideas in thirteenth-century scholasticism was responsible for a shift away from the divine-author concept. New academic prologues to the *auctores* placed emphasis upon the literal sense of the text, which was understood to express the intention of a human author. Now, whether or not Minnis's argument is sufficient to explain so great a shift in the history of letters,[56] it is important to realize that when Petrarch comes to express it, the novel idea of a secular author is neither so novel nor so secular. Instead, the human author as Petrarch embraces him, foibles and all, was there all along in Augustine—his was the voice whispering, half-heard, in Augustine's ear. To acknowledge that voice, however, indeed changes everything. Without the idea of the infinite text, without the idea of an author whose presence is doubly effaced, the structure of *figura* structures history: the gap between old and new merely begins to plumb the depths of a historical difference. Once having stripped the author of his divine office, the distance between him and the reader becomes the stuff of unredeemed time. And isn't *that* precisely the danger that Augustine is continually courting, continually avoiding in his work?

THE "ASCENT" OF THE BOOK

The astonishment that Petrarch's companions display when he voices his novel *sententia* only deepens once he brings out a box containing his own letters—two of which are actually written to Cicero. "Along with many letters written to my contemporaries [*ad coetaneos meos*], a few are addressed to illustrious ancient authors [*antiquis illustrioribus inscribuntur*] . . . and thus an unsuspecting reader would be amazed at finding such old and distinguished [*clara et tam vetusta*] names mingled with the new [*novis*]" (*Fam.* 24.2). It is from Cicero's own letters, a major collection of which Petrarch recovers in 1345, that Petrarch first gets the idea of creating his own epistolary collection. Moreover, it is also from Cicero, from these same recovered letters, that Petrarch learns enough about the orator's private life to write him a letter of censure.[57] From Cicero, then, Petrarch gets the idea of an *epistolary author*: an author *of* letters, in the complex and double sense of the genitive; an author whose discursive link to other authors, to his co-respondents, is displayed for all to read.

Nowhere is the fate of this secularized, epistolary author so vulnerable and so visible, so fixed in a given *hic et nunc* while reaching across time to the reader, nowhere is his fate more striking than in the twenty-fourth and final book of the *Rerum familiarium*. This is the book of the *Letters on Familiar Matters* that contains Petrarch's letters to "illustrious ancient authors," and in it, what we might call Petrarch's "epistolary consciousness" is starkly apparent. The sheer deictical complexity, for instance, of his farewell to Livy must give us pause:

> From the land of the living, in that part of Italy and in that city where you were born and buried, in the vestibule of Justina Virgo and before your gravestone, on February 22 in the year from the birth of Him whom you might have seen or heard born had you lived a little bit longer, 1351.
>
> (*Fam.* 24.8)

For Thomas Greene this envoi sounds a note of resignation, committing Livy and the Roman history he presents to an "inaccessible remoteness" (Greene, 29). To my ear, however, the closing instead dazzles, demonstrating the ways in which an epistle can cut across time, inserting its writer into the past and shuttling its reader into the future. Time here is very nearly chiastic, as we are tempted to imagine impossible coexistences: Livy and Petrarch, Christ and Livy, pagan and Christian Rome, the land of the quick and the dead. The effort of reconciling these deictics, the "ea" ("this," "that") of Livy's birthplace with the "ea" of his tombstone, leaves us with both Livy and Petrarch half here, half gone. Any attempt to fix this moment (which moment? whose moment?) in history—in precisely the sort of history that a Livy might have written—fails. Or rather, the envoi transforms such history into discourse, bridging the impossible gap between *then* and *now* while entirely disrupting the possibility of narrative. Thus the periphrastic closing date, "in the year from the birth of Him ... 1351," transforms even that objective marker, that ground zero of Christian history, the birth of Christ, into a kind of deictic, shifting according to the play of discourse. If you had lived a little longer, or been born a little later, you might have seen Him *here*, *then*.

But where the letter to Livy literalizes such discursive play in its use of dates and deictics, the letter for which Petrarch is best known, the so-called "Ascent of Mont Ventoux" addressed to

Dionigi da Borgo San Sepolcro, dramatizes it. Livy also figures in this letter–and here again, in the "Ascent," we find discourse somehow thwarting the narrative presentation of history. At the same time, not unlike the *Penitential Psalms*, the letter also thwarts the development of a narrative allegory. Indeed, it would seem that narrative itself, whether "allegorical" or "historical," is somehow at issue in this letter. Moreover, as we shall see, this crisis in narrative–a figural crisis, as I shall argue–undermines any effort to distinguish rigorously between allegory and history as separate discursive modes.

For most modern critics, however, the "Ascent" offers a decisive contrast between the two modes, marking allegory and history as two competing hermeneutics between which (depending on whose account you read) Petrarch vacillates, or chooses, or attempts a reconciliation, or is suspended.[58] Furthermore, just as various critics see various resolutions, and non-resolutions to the conflict, so do they define "allegory" and "history" in slightly different ways. However, all agree on the source of the conflict: namely, the contrast between the two major authorities cited– Livy's *History of Rome* and Augustine's *Confessions*. Thus: the impulse with which the letter begins, so many have argued, is a historical impulse–an impulse directed outward, toward making history, toward reading history. This first impulse, as Petrarch sees it, originates with Livy.

For many years, Petrarch tells the Augustinian canon, Dionigi, to whom he writes, for many years, he has been intending to climb Mont Ventoux. Now today, he writes, the impulse (*impetus*) to make the climb finally overcame him, "especially after, while rereading the day before things Roman in Livy, by chance [*forte*] I came upon the passage [*michi locus occurrerat*] where Philip, King of Macedonia . . . ascended Mount Hemo in Thessaly, from whose summit by rumor he believed that two seas could be seen."[59] Petrarch goes on to assert his own uncertainty about the rumor's truth: the mountain is too far away to check the story and the writers (*scriptores*) on the subject all disagree.

Petrarch introduces the second authority once he has reached the top of Mont Ventoux and is admiring the view:

> It occurred to me [*visum est michi*] to look into the gift of your charity, the book of Augustine's *Confessions*, which I

shall always keep on hand in memory of the author [*conditor*] and of the giver, a handy little work, of scant volume but of infinite sweetness. I opened it to read whatever I came across, for what could I come across but pious and devout things? By chance [*forte*] the tenth book of that work appeared. My brother, expecting to hear something from Augustine on my lips, stood by with intent ears. As God be my witness and my brother who was present, where I first cast my eyes was written: "And men go to admire the summits of mountains and the vast billows of the sea and the broadest currents of rivers and the circuits of the ocean and the revolutions of the stars–and they pass over themselves." I admit that I was astonished; and asking my brother, who was eager to hear, not to bother me, I closed the book, angry with myself that I even now admired earthly things who long ago ought to have learned from the pagan philosophers themselves that nothing is admirable besides the mind next to whose greatness nothing is great.

The letter to Dionigi is constructed such that we will place the two passages, Livy and Augustine, both hit upon by chance, *forte*, side by side. Indeed, the letter is constructed around these two passages even while it comes between them: written after the passages themselves were read, it is nonetheless the letter itself, itself a passage, a bit of text excerpted from the *Familiares*, that allows us to pass between pagan historian and Christian allegorist.

Thus while the "Ascent" opens by enunciating a desire for movement and discovery, it almost immediately reconfigures that desire in relation to textuality. The passage through space is reconsidered in terms of the passages in, and between, texts. The letter begins: "The highest mountain of the region which, not without merit, they call 'Windy' [*Ventosum*] even now *this very day* [*hodierno die*], led only by the desire to see the noteworthy [*insignem*] height of the place, I climbed." One climbs to see a place. But within a few sentences we learn that today's desire to see a place, a *locus* noteworthy or signal in its height, its loftiness [*altitudinem*], is properly speaking a desire of reading: Petrarch had long wanted to climb the peak, but was only seized with the impulse *the day before, pridie*, while rereading things Roman in Livy. There he was struck by another place, another *locus* upon which one might chance [*forte ille michi locus occurrerat*]—in this case, a textual *locus*. There, reading Livy, Petrarch came across the *locus ubi*, the place where Philip of Macedonia climbs Mount Hemo.

This lofty place, this book-place of *res romanes* and of kings like Philip, is thus the setting for another place, that signal lofty *locus* that Petrarch has just seen today. Petrarch has grown up with Mount "Windy" dominating his view—yet, in the context of this letter, the place inscribed in Livy's book is given priority: in the book we find the locus of *things*, of matters or *res* Roman, as opposed merely to the sign (*insigne*) that the actual mountain, Mont Ventoux, has always been. Paradoxically, it is the text that places us among things while the world offers us only signs. In this way, an order of things is privileged over an order of signs—even while the lofty text is privileged above and beyond the actual height of mountains. But then again, perhaps we cannot ascribe anything more than a temporal priority to the place inscribed in the book—Petrarch saw *that* place before he climbed *this* one—since for Philip in Livy's book the priority of things and signs, of books and mountains is reversed. In climbing Mount Hemo, Philip himself put mountains before books, although he did so in following the words or signs of others: what impelled his action was the report of *fama*. But then again: even for Petrarch in a certain sense mountains come first. He must have seen Mount Ventoux long before seeing the passage in Livy, since he grew up with the mountain "always in view."

In the terms Petrarch gives us, we simply cannot privilege either locus, book or mountain. The priority of *res* to *signum* remains undecidable. In this way, the letter undermines whatever historicizing impulse it asserts, challenging any discourse that would attempt to verify words with things. However, if we cannot sort out the relationship between things and signs by writing history, we nonetheless can perhaps do so by writing allegory. We can place these two places within the literary context that Petrarch so conspicuously constructs: today he climbed that place which since his early childhood has always been in sight (*ab infantia . . . semper in oculis est*) but whose notable loftiness only yesterday, having seen another place, he decided to see for himself. One place has been before his eyes since before he, as *in-fans*, could speak, much less read. But it wasn't until another place struck his readerly gaze that the first place actually came to light. The frame that at last sets one locus (Mount Ventoux) before another (Livy's text) is an allegorical one: the first *qua* first must come last; it is the book that finally makes the mountain visible. Furthermore, the end result of this allegorical revelation is Petrarch's letter itself, which offers another site of readerly sight. Written immediately on the return from the summit the letter will leave nothing of Petrarch's heart hidden from our reading eyes. As he tells Dionigi in closing, "See thus, dearest father, how I have wanted nothing in me hidden from your eyes."

But before the letter can be written and its reader can see everything for himself, the letter's author will have to see more mountains: the *alta montium*, the mountain-peaks in the *Confessions*. As he did with Mount Hemo, Petrarch orients us carefully with these summits: we are in book 10 of the *Confessions*, in the midst of Augustine's discussion of memory and the human soul. What looks like a mini-narrative, a story about the men who admire mountains and look at rivers and thereby relinquish themselves, is merely a hypothetical example in one of the *Confessions'* last, non-narrative books. Augustine's point is that the real marvels are within, in the vast complexity and wonder of the human mind. It is a point that Petrarch should have already known—a commonplace, a *locus classicus* even, which, like Windy Peak itself, has long been right before his eyes: "I ought to have learned from the pagan philosophers themselves that nothing is admirable besides the mind next to whose greatness nothing is great."

The passage from Augustine thus signals the value of introspection—of taking stock of one's mind and one's life and perhaps, like Augustine, writing one's *Confessions*. And indeed, Petrarch finds this passage just after having attempted, and having failed to complete, such an inventory: "The time will perhaps come when I will review all this in the order in which it happened, prefaced by that passage of your Augustine [*prefatus illud Augustini tui*]: 'I want to recall my past foul deeds and the carnal corruptions of my soul not because I love them but that I might love you my God.'"

This narrative never happens—which is another way of saying that Petrarch never converts. The letter's allegorical frame is never completed; the relationship it proffers between reading and telling, between signs and things, mountains and books remains as undecidable as the historicist's efforts to verify *signa* with *res*. For Augustine, the moment under the fig tree serves as a turning point, a *now* of reading, of looking into the book, of *inspicere*, around which retrospection, *respicere*, and thus narrative, become possible. Furthermore, as we have seen, from the standpoint of this *now*, exegesis also becomes possible: *figura* thus harmonizes space and time into narrative, signs and things into allegory. But such figural harmony requires an infinite text, a divine author: a third signifying dimension (if you will), through which to twist the loop of the Moebius strip. Petrarch has no such text, no such author. For him the text is *finite*— and the only order it conveys is the order of written discourse, with its time and space of reading, its time and space of writing.

Thus it is that in a letter where *loci* are equally textual excerpts and geographical spaces, and where the *passage* from one such place to another seems as much a matter of reading, or writing, as a matter of travel—thus it is that, in such a letter, what emerges as *terra firma* is the book itself. I mean, of course, the copy of Augustine's *Confessions* that is dear to Petrarch on account of both its author and its giver—on account of Dionigi, the very addressee of this letter. The description of the book is so lovely that we will want to repeat it: "the gift of your charity, which I shall always keep on hand in memory of the author and of the giver, a handy little work, of scant volume but of infinite sweetness." Literary history is filled with bibliophiles, Petrarch not least among them, yet I know of no more evocative description of a beloved book's ready-to-hand existence than this. Precisely because finite, the finite text is portable, ready at hand and thus paradoxically *infinite* in its sweetness.

Moreover, unlike the communally held infinite text of a medieval *lectio*, this little volume, this finitely infinite book, can be kept to oneself. Thus, critics have pointed out the way in which Petrarch, in contrast to Augustine, withholds the book from his companion. Petrarch's brother Gherardo, expectant and eager to hear, is left hanging. In contrast, as we have noted, Augustine's conversion is situated within a chain of similar conversions, each one instanced by the hearing or the reading of a text. And indeed, Augustine's own conversion begins and ends with Alypius, the figure of the witness and the stand-in for us, the reader—Alypius who initially safeguards the copy of Paul's epistles when Augustine runs under the fig tree, and to whom the book is returned after Augustine has read his oracle text, in order that Alypius himself might read on, and likewise be converted.

Most often critics have related Gherardo's exemption from reading to his own conversion to Carthusian monasticism in 1343. Without discounting the importance of biography we can, nonetheless, point out the profound logic that also underlies Gherardo's exclusion. Exemplarity has two moments: following an example and setting an example. Reading the book, and passing the book on. Just as Augustine follows a host of examples before him, so does he become an example to Alypius and, by extension, to us who read his text. In repeating Augustine's exemplary reading by, precisely, reading Augustine—while in the meantime withholding the book from his brother—Petrarch, it would seem, is trying to follow an example without setting one. He keeps the book to himself. As he tells Dionigi, he could not imagine that he had come upon the passage by chance; rather, he writes, "what I read there I thought to have been said to me and to no one else." But even this sense of his uniqueness as reader follows Augustine's example, as Petrarch himself notes. And it is here that Petrarch turns Augustinian exemplarity back upon itself, calling to mind that other scene of reading in Augustine's text, the recitation of Psalm 4, and the impossible wish to perform without performing.

Petrarch literalizes this impossibility—and he does so, I want finally to suggest, not only by literally failing to be an example, but by literalizing the way exemplarity passes the text from one reader to the next. In doing so he exemplifies a new kind of reader and a new kind of book. Exemplary in the failure of his exemplarity, Petrarch foregrounds the materialities of discursive exchange. The text as Petrarch knows it is no longer the infinite, exemplary text of an Augustinian conversion: it is now the finite text, the *epistle*, embodying a specific time, place, addressee, relationship. It is the *mortal* text, recording the passage of time. When, in the year before his death, Petrarch gives the copy of the *Confessions* that Dionigi had given him to the monk Luigi Marsili, we realize just how dear this dear little book is. It has become coextensive with the person, the very embodiment of the "I" and inextricable from the "you." The book Petrarch imagines and passes on is no longer the exemplary book. It is, instead, the ethical book—a book that one does not so much read as *live*. "And thus, coming and going with me it has gotten old," Petrarch writes Marsili, "even as I have gotten old. . . . Accept it as it is, and of it, take good care" (*Seniles* 15.7).

USCIR DEL BOSCO ET GIR INFRA LA GENTE . . .

In the absence of an infinite text, *figura* falters, forestalling that exemplary Augustinian narrative that would pass the book from hand to hand in silence. Petrarch, instead, holds on to his books as long as he can, grows old with them, and passes them on only after indelibly marking his place within.

Figura passes the book along, translating readers into writers into readers again as a communal text weaves its universal truths. Furthermore, *figura* translates signs into things, a past order of *signa* into a future order of *res*, organizing space and time as narrative, converting signs and things into allegory. Such translations, however, depend upon a double effacement: not only does the pursuit of infinite truth erase the text's determinate particularity, but this erasure is itself erased, forgotten. As I have said before: in its turn, the suppression of Scripture's human author is itself suppressed. It is this double suppression that Petrarchan humanism seeks to avert. Petrarch's commitment to an epistolary view of authors and readers is indeed a commitment to *figura*: a commitment, that is, to the figural sense of the text as that which is addressed to us, written *propter nos*. At the same time, however, it is precisely the acuity of his epistolary awareness that bars Petrarch from fully accepting *figura*. Instead, all too aware of the author's potential disappearance from the text, Petrarch works to prevent or, at least, to *remember* the passage from author to reader, from old to new.

Thus, for instance in the "Ascent" we are presented with two *auctoritates* but are unable to choose between them: we cannot assign priority to either passage. Instead, the letter foregrounds the passages themselves, the Livy and the Augustine as versions of one another, without allowing us simply to *pass* from one passage to the other. Hence, neither Livy nor Augustine, pagan nor Christian, is permitted the last word; rather, the latter simply reveals the failed lessons of the former: "I ought to have learned from the pagan philosophers themselves that nothing is admirable besides the mind next to whose greatness nothing is great."

One outcome, then, of the "Ascent" is the dissolution of a certain medieval, a Dantesque even, syncretism when it is pushed toward a greater insistence on historical difference. For Petrarch, pagan and Christian can neither easily rest side by side nor be

resolved into hierarchy. In other words, neither of Dante's syncretic strategies in the *Commedia* succeeds here. But this syncretic
failure is only symptomatic of the more general failure of an exemplary narrative order. The Dantesque subtext for the climb up the
mountain only signals Petrarch's inability to collate spatial hierarchy with temporal progress in a unified narrative of conversion
and ascent. "The time will perhaps come," Petrarch writes, "when
I will review all this in the order in which it happened, prefaced by
that passage of your Augustine: 'I want to recall . . .'" That time has
been held off–and with it the exemplary use of Augustine's text.
Instead, like the passage from *Confessions* 10 ("And men go to
admire . . ."), the text is cited and held in place, captured at the very
moment when an exemplary reading would force it out of view.
Just as Petrarch wants to follow an example without setting one, so
does he want to invoke Augustine without eclipsing him.

The result of Petrarch's forestalled narrative, at the levels both
of theme and of form, is a new centrality of the book itself–the
book as meeting place for past, present, and future: as that medium
in which absence and presence coexist. In the "Ascent of Mont
Ventoux," the little copy of the *Confessions*, marking and marked by
the exchange between persons, dear on account of its author and
its giver, emblematizes this new vision of the book. But Petrarch's
letter itself offers a concrete example of the ethical text–of the text
that renders visible an ethics of reading. In such a text the absent-
ing of the author is made present, just as the presenting of the
reader–of Dionigi, for instance, or of *us*, for that matter–is held in
abeyance. More specifically, Petrarch's elaborate use of deixis and
other formal features (e.g., proper names and dates) establishes the
text as an epistle written at a particular time for a particular audience.[60] In this way, at a sheerly formal level, the "Ascent" is riven
with traces of the first person's absent-presence in discourse, while
at a thematic level such traces exist in terms of an incomplete reading and a thwarted conversion–in Petrarch's very failure to make
an example of himself. Furthermore, this conjunction of form and
theme is no accident. Indeed, the new visibility of the book, its
newfound centrality as embodiment of discursive exchange, constitutes a newfound textual self-reflexivity: form becomes visible as
theme; theme becomes visible as form. And thus it is, as a formal
and thematic principle of resistance to narrative that Petrarch's "I"
manages, after all, to set an example.

Teodolinda Barolini has described this same resistance to narrative in the broad structural terms of the genre that Petrarch
invented: the lyric sequence. Simultaneously continuous and discrete, the modern lyric sequence is paradoxical by nature. Thus, at
once pulling toward narrative and pulling away from it, strung into
a linear order even as each autonomous lyric represents a fragmentation of that order, the *Rime*, Barolini argues, presents "the
paradox of mobile fixity."[61] The inevitable linearity of the text–of
legere, we might say, in order to recall the Augustinian terms of our
argument–is thus foregrounded only to dissolve into stasis. For
Barolini, the various formal and thematic strategies that Petrarch
employs in the *Rime* are thus "strategies for defeating time"
(Barolini, 11).

Traditionally the collection of songs and sonnets that Petrarch
reworked over the course of much of his adult life has been called
the *Canzoniere*–i.e., a songbook analogous to the *chansonniers* of
troubador poets like Raimon de Miraval. Barolini, however, points
out the assumption of unity and integration behind such a title–an
assumption that the more recently adopted title, *Rime sparse* ("scattered verse"), a phrase borrowed from poem 1, neatly avoids
(Barolini, 2). Petrarch's own title for the collection was *Rerum vulgarium fragmenta*, *Fragments of Vernacular Things*. In its paradoxically Latinate way, the title attests to the poet's own sense of his
work's plurality and incompleteness.

> Instead of following in the wake of Dante's lyrics, which
> are in fact *rime sparse*, connected by no internal principles
> of construction, Petrarch followed in the wake of Dante's
> *Vita nuova*, the first modern collection of lyrics to be delib-
> erately arranged according to a predetermined sequential
> order, an order that is invested with a narrative burden.
>
> (Barolini, 4–5)

But, significantly, Dante adopts a prosi-metrum style, using prose
passages to elucidate his poetry, while Petrarch, as has often been
noted, writes his lyric sequence without prose.[62] Following a troubador *vida/razo* tradition, the *Vita nuova* contains explanatory
glosses alongside a running autobiographical narrative; the
glosses analyze the form and meaning of the poems, while the
autobiography serves to contextualize the lyrics in a lived narra-

tive.[63] In this way the history of Dante's "New Life" emerges indistinguishable from the literary analysis of his poems. In the *Vita nuova*, as in the *Commedia* with its figural progress from one canticle to the next, meaning and narrative are conjoined. One supports the other.

But for Petrarch the two are ever at odds. Keenly attuned to the stakes of *figura*, Petrarch recognizes its status as trope, the structure of its meaning as chiastic. He steadfastly refuses a narrative resolution that would amount to his own disappearance from the text. Thus, instead of yielding a completed narrative order, the signs of the *Rime sparse* seem to turn ceaselessly, their famous "unilinguismo"[64] witness to a recycling of language as dramatic as the collection's endless thematic recycling of image and motif. In this way, meaning seems to come at the expense of narrative; or, to put the matter another way, the formal structure that would align meaning with narrative is instead mirrored at the level of theme: the tenor of this poetry's figural turns is the act of *turning* itself. Nonetheless, if this ceaseless troping about ceaseless troping ultimately gets us nowhere, it does manage to tell a *kind* of story: a narrative (of sorts) of indefatigable weariness:

> Io mi rivolgo indietro a ciascun passo
> col corpo stanco ch' a gran pena porto.

[I turn back at each step with my weary body which with great effort I carry forward.]

(15.1–2)

> Io son già stanco di pensar sì come
> i miei pensier in voi stanchi non sono

[I am already weary of thinking how my thoughts of you are weariless.]

(74.1–2)

> Omai son stanco, et mia vita reprendo
> di tanto error

[Now I am weary and I reproach my life for so much error]

(364.5–6)

In this last example from poem 364 we are approaching the end of the *Rime*, where the renunciatory prayer "Alla Vergine" (poem 366) provides a certain narrative fullness to the sequence by offering a final, conversionary perspective. But even in these final poems the terms of Petrarch's conversion invoke, curiously enough, the empty repetition of his error; thus, in 364, his attitude of reproach, of *reprendere*, may easily be confused with RI*prendere*, with the mere resumption of his error. As Barolini argues in a different context, "resistance to forward motion is so ingrained in Petrarch that even conversion is figured as a turning back" (11 n. 23).

As lucid and suggestive as Barolini's account of the *Rime* is, however, I find it misleading in several aspects. For Barolini, Petrarch's resistance to narrative is a resistance, above all, to time (and thus to mortality). In this way Barolini conflates narrativity with sheer linearity–with experience as it is lived, one moment at a time, step by step. As Barolini sees it, then, Petrarch's allergy to conversion, his confusion between the *resumption* of a life unchanged, "mia vita riprendo / di error" [I resume my life of error] and the *reproach* for a life repented, can be understood in psychological, subjective terms: "in making his lyric sequence . . . Petrarch was above all concerned with what always concerned him most–the experience of the passing of time, the fact that he was dying with every word he wrote" (Barolini, 1). However much this argument may appeal intuitively, nonetheless, given our consideration of *figura* and its impact on Petrarchism, it ultimately does not satisfy. Barolini quotes *Familiari* 24.1:

> Having reached this point in the letter, I was wondering what more to say or not to say, and meanwhile, as is my custom, I was tapping the blank paper with my pen. This action provided me with a subject, for I considered how, during the briefest of intervals, time rushes onward, and I along with it, slipping away, failing, and, to speak honestly, dying. We all are constantly dying, I while writing these words, you while reading them, others while hearing or not hearing them; I too shall be dying while you read this, you are dying while I write this, we both are dying, we all are dying, we are always dying.
>
> (Quoted in Barolini, 1–2)

The passage is characteristic for Petrarch, flattening the distance between textuality and life. The material physicality of the writing, the very act of tapping pen to paper, serves Petrarch equally well as a source of truisms about life and as subject matter for his text. Writing in its most material existence feeds both life and books.

Barolini, however, presumes the primacy of life: "Petrarch was *above all* concerned with . . . the experience of the passing of time." For Barolini, Petrarch's experience of the text derives from his experience of life: animating the literary endeavor is an extraliterary concern with finitude and mortality. In contrast, I'd like to suggest the exact opposite: in the *Familiari,* as in the *Rime sparse,* Petrarch's sense of time derives from his sense of the text. Indeed, his very discussion in the letter above "de inextimabili fuga temporis," of the inestimable flight of time, is occasioned by the rereading of a much earlier letter on the same subject (cf. *Fam.* 1.3). "Thirty years ago–how time does fly! . . . I wrote to that venerable and worthy elder, Raimondo Subirani. . . . I even then confessed to a dawning recognition about the flight and swiftness of my young life" (*Fam.* 24.1). Even when Petrarch's sense of the text derives from lived experience, that experience itself is the experience of the text. The passage of time is understood by means of a rereading that gauges and bridges the gap between two texts, two letters, old and new. Thus, while Barolini posits a psychological basis for Petrarchan poetics, I would maintain the priority of Petrarch's interest in his own *person*–in his positionality in discourse–rather than in his psyche or his selfhood. In this way Petrarch's discourse does not so much reflect a lived reality; rather, it is discourse that above all structures such reality. Time interests him because discourse does.

Accordingly, Barolini's conflation of temporality and narrative is highly misleading. As our previous discussion has suggested, within a figural framework narrative order is never simply a linear matter. Instead, *figura* structures narrative as that which proceeds forward only insofar as it advances toward that point from which it may be told *in retrospect.* Such a narrative, thus, is not time itself but time recounted from a particular standpoint taken as final; in this way figural narrative (and is there any other kind?) involves the co-articulation of the linear and the recursive. The narration moves forward because the narrator keeps looking back: "The time will perhaps come when I will review all this in the order in which it happened," as Petrarch says. Of course, in an Augustinian universe, that time comes at the moment of one's conversion. To defer that moment is to evade the vantage point from which the recursive circling back to origins yields a linear momentum forward.

Hence, in a Petrarchan universe where conversion is perpetually deferred, recursion and linearity do not work together; instead, as we shall see in a moment, each fails as a version of the other. On closer inspection, circular structures turn out to be linear and linear structures precisely *turn out* to be circles. In this way Petrarch continually evokes the terms of a figural textuality, only, just as continually, to deconstruct them. When we examine the famous sestina "Giovene donna sotto un verde lauro," poem 30, we shall see this strategy working on three distinct levels: formal, thematic, and semantic. Indeed, that poem is a splendid instance of the way that Petrarch makes failure *work*, harmonizing various levels of his poetry to present a unified picture of *figura*'s defeat. But Petrarch is equally comfortable pitting one level of his poetry—e.g., formal, thematic, or semantic—against another and allowing their contestation to undermine figurality. Thus, for example, where he uses the retrospective deictical structure of *figura* to organize the sequence in general, he pulls the structure apart locally through thematic and semantic contrasts.

For instance, two poems like 125 ("Se 'l pensier che mi strugge") and 126 ("Chiare fresche et dolci acque") look back on the *innamoramento* and strive, as Thomas Greene would say, to "subread" Laura's absent-presence in the *now*. "Ovunque gli occhi volgo / trovo un dolce sereno / pensando: 'Qui percosse il vago lume'" [Wherever I turn my eyes, I find a sweet brightness, thinking: 'Here fell the bright light of her eyes'] (125.66–68). But even within these two so similar poems, retrospection pulls in opposite directions. In 125 Petrarch's act of remembrance constitutes a *florilegium* of sorts, a literal gathering of flowers, while in 126, precisely what Petrarch remembers, what the memory itself consists in, is the orgasmic scattering of those same flowers, their petals tumbling into Laura's lap: "qual fior cadea sul lembo, / qual su le treccie bionde" [this flower was falling on her skirt, this one on her blond braids] (126.46–47). Thus, while both poems look back on Petrarch's enamorment, in 126 we encounter just that sort of dissemination, that drift of flowers, which would preclude the root-

edness upon which 125 relies: "Qualunque erba o fior colgo, /
credo che nel terreno / aggia radice ov'ella ebbe in costume /
gir" [Whatever grass or flower I gather, I believe that it is rooted in the
ground where she was wont to walk] (125.69–72). Recollection
becomes impossible because that which is to be collected is the
very *stuff* of dispersion.

But even if such retrospection were possible in Petrarch's world,
this version of a turning back would conflict with those poems that
also envision Laura's absent-presence–but from the standpoint of
her death: "Quinci vedea 'l mio bene, et per queste orme /
torno a vedere ond' al Ciel nuda è gita" [From here I used to see my love,
and with these steps I come back to see the place whence she went
naked to Heaven] (301.12–13). And again, how distant this distinction between Laura *in morte* and *in vita* is from the retrospectivity
established firmly in the sequence's close: "Medusa et l'error mio
m'àn fatto un sasso / d'umor vano stillante" [Medusa and my error
have made me a stone dripping vain moisture] (366.111–12).
Petrarch's *rime* strive to reconcile the poet's here-and-now with a
distant past, yet the varied referents of Petrarch's deictics ("*Qui* percosse il vago lume," "*Quinci* vedea 'l mio bene'") disrupt those
palimpsestic efforts: how can his *qui*'s and *or*'s coincide with the
past, when they fail even to coincide with each other?

Furthermore, if Petrarch's retrospectivity is called into question across the sequence, it is even more directly challenged within
individual *rime* where Petrarch pits retrospection's two deictical
poles, *then* and *now*, past and present, against each other, so that
the revisionary gesture itself, and any narrative it might enable, is
compromised.[65] "Voi ch'ascoltate"–the very first sonnet in the
sequence–offers the paradigm case of such compromise:

> Voi ch' ascoltate in rime sparse il suono
> di quei sospiri ond'io nudriva 'l core
> in sul mio primo giovenile errore,
> quand' era in parte altr' uom da quel ch' i' sono:

> [You who hear in scattered rhymes the sound of those
> sighs with which I nourished my heart during my first
> youthful error, when I was in part another man from what
> I am now:]

(1.1–4)

first and foremost, the sonnet raises the question of sound and of audience: of a *you* who hears the *suono* of sighs. It's as if we were in the *hinc-et-nunc* world of a troubador *jongleur* who performs his sighs in our presence, every *suono* invoking the first-person immediacy of *sono*. Yet quickly that stance is unraveled: these sighs aren't unfolding in present time; instead they are sighs with which Petrarch *nourished, nudriva*, imperfect tense, his heart in the past of a youthful error. They are *past* sighs, which we somehow "hear" in the present. But that hearing-present is itself strangely disrupted: we hear these sighs in *scattered* rhyme. "The time will perhaps come when I will review all this in the order in which it happened." That time still hasn't come. Scattered like the cascading petals in *Rime* 126, these rhymes do not unfold in order—which is as much as to say that they do not *unfold*. The time of our hearing, like the time of Petrarch's sighing, is not the simple present; it is instead a time of *reading*.

Indeed, the first quatrain of the sonnet establishes a kind of paradox that renders its temporality irreducibly *non*-simple. You who hear the sighs with which I nourished my heart when I was a different man from the one I am now. . . . As witness to these sighs, the reader is only indirectly present in the poems, merely a figural and oblique addressee: a third-person audience to the past. And yet, Petrarch does address his audience directly: *you* who hear . . . In order to address his reader in the present, Petrarch must position the *suoni di quei sospiri* in the past; he must, in other words, exploit the disjunction between speaker and poet. He must imagine himself in the third person—as the *altr' uom* whose sighs the reader "hears." Yet even as he so positions himself, Petrarch belies the position by producing another poem: namely, this very poem itself, which cannot take place in the present if it takes place before a reader who only "hears" the poems of the past. In this way, the poem holds open the gap between reader and writer, even as it works toward closure. The more Petrarch seeks to bring himself eye-to-eye and I-to-I (to borrow a pun from Shakespeare) with his reader, the greater the distance between them grows.[66]

Nor is the dilemma mitigated in the second quatrain, where Petrarch transposes his past poetic productions into the present:

> del vario stile in ch' io piango et ragiono
> fra le vane speranze e 'l van dolore,
> ove sia chi per prova intenda amore
> spero trovar pietà, non che perdono.

[for the varied style in which I weep and speak between vain hopes and vain sorrow, where there is anyone who understands love through experience, I hope to find pity, not only pardon.]

(1.5–8)

The stanza encompasses two incompatible present moments: the *now* of tears and of discourse ("io piango et ragiono") and the *now* of hope ("spero trovar pietà"). To reconcile these two moments, Petrarch would need to segregate and dispose them according to that retrospective structure that disjoins poet from speaker: *for the varied style in which I then wept and spoke, I hope now to find pity.* Instead, however, by conflating the two moments into one *now,* Petrarch tries to keep himself present as both poet *and* speaker. This effort is accentuated by the contrast with line 4, where Petrarch sharply distinguishes between the two, differentiating the man he once was, *era,* from the man he now is, *ch' i' sono.* Furthermore, in the wake of line 4's distinction between past and present tense, the inverted syntax of the second quatrain inevitably gives us pause. Initially we read line 5 as an extension of the previous four lines, aligning the present tense of weeping and discoursing with the *io chi sono* of line 4. But we are forced to reread the second quatrain once we get to its end and realize that the varied style "in ch' io piango et ragiono" is a style relegated now to the *past,* its "vain hopes" sharply contrasted by the hope for pity that animates the *present.* In this way, in rereading we impose a temporal order on these two moments that matches their disposition in space (thanks to the inverted syntax, *piangere* and *ragionare* literally precede *sperare* on the page), but we do so, precisely, by backing up and thus negating the linearity of that order.

Thanks to our rereading, we endow "Voi ch' ascoltate" with a certain temporal coherence and unity. At the same time, however, our rereading also reveals the decisive limits of that unity. Instead of linking *voi* to *io* in a single and coherent discursive gesture, our rereading disassembles the poem. Where we expect to find something like an appeal to the reader—as pitying witness to both the past sighs and the present changed man—we find that the octave instead splits into two temporally incompatible pieces: the vocative address to a reader who hears scattered rhymes in the present and the poet's appeal for pity on account of rhymes now past. The *voi* of line 1, and the *io* of line 8 now seem worlds apart. Indeed, thanks to the full stop at the end of line 4, it is not even clear that it is from "you" that ultimately the poet seeks his pardon. *You who hear in scattered rhymes. . . . For the varied style in which I weep . . . I hope to find pity.*

In its very first eight lines the *Rime sparse* thus undermines its own retrospectivity, establishing itself as a kind of intermediate locution, hovering between past and present without coherently conjoining the two. In the sonnet's last six lines this ambiguous middle ground between past and present is identified with a sustained figural moment.

> Ma ben veggio or sì come al popol tutto
> favola fui gran tempo, onde sovente
> di me medesmo meco mi vergogno;
> et del mio vaneggiar vergogna è 'l frutto,
> e 'l pentersi, e 'l conoscer chiaramente
> che quanto piace al mondo è breve sogno.

[But now I see well how for a long time I was the talk of the crowd, for which often I am ashamed of myself within; and of my raving, shame is the fruit, and repentance, and the clear knowledge that whatever pleases in the world is a brief dream.]

The "or(a)" of clarity and renunciation is not the simple present. Instead, it is revealed in lines 10 and 11 as a perpetual present tense, a sustained and "often" repeated looking-back that never manages completion: "onde sovente / di me medesmo meco mi vergogno." This *now* is a figural *now*: not the present itself but the present as it looks back on and is implicated in, by, the past. Furthermore, because perpetual, the *now* cannot be identified by or with a unique utterance; inherently plural, the moment cannot then mark the singular presence of the poet. Indeed, the exaggerated reflexivity of this moment, the repetition of the *me* of which and with which Petrarch is ashamed, serves to mark the moment's multiplicity—a lapse of singularity that corresponds to Petrarch's failure either to choose or not to choose, between past and present, between speaker and poet, in the first two quatrains. Instead, Petrarch sustains a gesture of self-splitting and juxtaposes it to a "popol" that is similarly, sustainedly split: the audience to whom

Petrarch *speaks* is also that body by which he is *spoken*, since he has been *favola*, matter for talk, on account of his own talking, his "raving," for a long time.

Hence it is that the moralistic and gnomic turn of the last tercet fails to represent the achieved vantage of the convert. Rather it is, precisely, a *turn*–that moment which becomes so central to the history of the sonnet: the moment of closing where finality is paradoxically induced by a revolution; where the poem comes to rest precisely by refusing to rest. We end this first sonnet then and start the sequence as a whole with a *sententia* whose sententiousness scarcely conceals its ambiguity: "quanto piace al mondo è breve sogno." What does this "clear knowledge" entail? What is Petrarch's "brief dream"? Presumably, with the authority of hindsight, the poet here rejects the "giovenile errore" of loving Laura–and yet this poem itself serves, also in hindsight, as introduction to the lyric sequence. Does this last line also operate as a last judgment on the *rime* that will follow? But if this sonnet refers to the sequence of poems to follow, how does it account for its own existence? Is it too a brief dream, pleasing to the world? Or, as in the first stanza, does Petrarch's utterance once again fail to take itself into account?

Once again we see a retrospective stance collapsing. If the *Rime*, like the Laura of Petrarch's youthful error, are "brief dreams" that please the world, then they cannot also provide that vantage point from which the statement "quanto piace al mondo è breve sogno" might be spoken. Instead, the poems become an extension of Petrarch's error–and the error itself can no longer be distinguished from the sighs with which it was nourished. Any further sigh, any further poem, even a poem of introduction, will continue to feed the lover's sin. Alternatively, if the *rime*, unlike Laura, consist of that which *endures*, what relation do they establish with the *you* who listen? According to the terms of this poem, the durable poem is that which fails to please the world. To whom, then, is the poem spoken? Who is the *voi* outside the world who "hears" these *rime sparse*? We might posit a divine audience–the Virgin, perhaps–and yet if this first poem pleases Her, we already know that the following 364 will not: "del vario stile . . . spero trovar pietà, non che perdono."

As an introduction to the sequence, this first poem adopts the most starkly retrospective stance imaginable: coming first, it nonetheless was written last. Yet the poem stages nothing so much as the impossibility of introduction. Instead, in this first poem we see the poles of a retrospective construction, *then* and *now*, fold together even as the poet insists on their distinctness. The poem draws us as readers into a linear process, a process of *legere*, only to have that process double back as *intellegere*, and vice versa. As a pronouncement of conversion the sonnet fails to take its own utterance into account—and at the very moment when the convert might give it to us straight, speaking from a stance of "clear knowl-edge," clarity doubles back as paradox. Once turning back, the poem keeps turning: its error and its errancy know no end. In this way, at odds with itself, "Voi ch' ascoltate" promotes the absent-present *now* of *figura*—even while depicting the failure of a figural narrative, of a passage *from* past *to* present.

In "Giovene donna sotto un verde lauro," the same picture is constructed, but even more dramatically. In "Giovene donna," instead of fighting against itself the poem establishes a powerful unity of form and theme. Such unity, and the self-reflexive stance toward the text that it denotes, is Petrarch's great innovation in the lyric. Where Augustine's *signa figurata* denoted the in-forming of language by the retrospective folds of meaning, Petrarch's retro-spection yields finally figures that shape meaning of themselves. In Petrarch's *Rime*—and especially in the paradigmatically self-con-scious "Giovene donna"—we read form *as* meaning. "Giovene donna" thus reveals how a critical attitude toward *figura* develops into the thoroughly self-reflexive, form-conscious secular lyric.

"Giovene donna" is a sestina—an instance of that poetic form of cycled and recycled ends invented by Arnaut and used by Dante in his *Rime petrose*. At the same time it is the first of the *Can-zoniere*'s anniversary poems, one of those fifteen poems sprinkled throughout the sequence whose retrospective structure marks the cycling of time itself, the turning of the years (anni-versary) back to April 6, the *innamoramento*. For Barolini, "Giovene donna" con-stitutes "an impasse between form and content" (20) since, given her loose equation of time and narrativity, she defines the mission of the anniversary poems as a matter of recording the passage of time, while the *Canzoniere*'s collection of sestinas would seem by dint of their circular form precisely to resist time. But as at least one critic has noted,[67] perhaps the most powerful of all the anniversary poems, "Padre del Ciel," literally *turns* on the irony that, in 1338,[68] April 6 is Good Friday: "reduci i pensier vaghi a miglior luogo, / rammenta lor come oggi fusti in croce" [lead my wandering thoughts back to a better place, remind them that today you were on the cross] (62.13–14). As the word *anniversary* itself suggests, the retrospective viewpoint from which we mark our distance from one day to the next is possible in the first place because, each year, the year turns back upon itself; each year Christ dies again, just as each year He rises, just as each year Laura is sighted all over again.

For those who would see the *Rime sparse* as a kind of secular breviary, this suggestion of an erotic year emulating, striving against the liturgical one, is inevitable. And it is a suggestion that Petrarch himself can hardly refrain from making, slyly contrasting his Laura to Beatrice, and both mortal women to the Virgin, the "vera beatrice," mediatrix and bearer of happiness (366.52).[69] An entire school of Petrarch criticism, a school grounded in the perception of Petrarch as quintessential desiring subject, takes off from this contrast between cult of the Virgin and idolatrous *eros*. For such critics, Petrarch's secularism—and with it his pivotal role in literary history—emerges from an errant object choice: as Dante's Lombardo would put it, what generates Petrarch's poetics is the "mala condotta" of desire. Nonetheless, while the shift from "vera beatrice" to mortal idol may be crucial, it is, I would like to suggest, a trivial instance of secularization—one that fails to account for the more fundamental innovation in Petrarch's work. At stake with the swerve from *vergine* to *donna* is a mere shift in devotional content while, formally, devotion itself remains constant. In contrast, the secularization with which I am concerned is not the fairly straightforward substitution of one content, one object of desire for another; rather, I mean to consider the secularization of discourse itself. At issue most radically is the ethics of Petrarch's discourse, not the *condotta* of his desire.

At stake, in other words, is the move, anything but straightforward, that I began to chart in the "Ascent": the transition from an infinite to a finite text. A form, as well as a content, is at stake here; indeed, it is form itself that is at stake—form in its complicity with content, a question that the divine text never poses for its reader. Instead, it is only for the reader of the secular text that form can be understood as that which structures a content, since now, precisely, content is understood to be finite (and hence, *structured*). With the text understood as sacred, whatever form exists is incidental: it stands merely as accident to that transcendent substance that is truth. In other words, for the divinely inspired, infinite text, the form is always transparent—the content always, precisely, infinite.

In "Giovene donna" form and content are not at an impasse, *pace* Barolini; instead, the poem exploits a radically new poetic possibility: the concerted effort of form and content to produce meaning. For Dante, such work would still scarcely have been conceivable; meaning would not have been constructed or constrained by form, but rather *conveyed* within it insofar as form is in-formed by it. As vehicle or vessel, for Dante the text would have enacted meaning by the grace of God, enabling within its confines a figural passage of infinite scope. The architecture of the *Commedia*, for instance, is meant to enable such passage, thereby enabling meaning as that which literally *takes place*. In this way, *figura* serves Dante as that "shaping" (the very word derives from the Latin "fingo," to shape) of language, that in-forming of the sign by meaning, that calls us into meaning. For Dante, we are *edified* by structure, perhaps; brought into the fold and embraced within communal truth, just as Augustine understands the walls of the Church to make the Christian. But meaning itself is understood on the sacred model as, precisely, *un*-structured, *in*-finite. It is only with Petrarch where *figura* is blocked and figural passage is foreclosed, that meaning begins to be understood as that which structure *structures*.

Thus, in "Giovene donna" where, since *anni* is one of the repeated end-words, the years literally turn from one stanza to the next, we find a form particularly well suited to content, to the idea of anni-versary.

> Giovene donna sotto un verde lauro
> vidi più bianca et più fredda che neve
> non percossa dal sol molti et molt'anni;
> e' l suo parlare e' l bel viso et le chiome
> mi piacquen sì ch' i' l' ò dinanzi agli occhi
> ed avrò sempre ov' io sia in poggio o 'n riva.
>
> Allor saranno i miei pensieri a riva
> che foglia verde non si trovi in lauro;
> quando avrò queto il cor, asciutti gli occhi,
> vedrem ghiacciare il foco, arder la neve;
> non ò tanti capelli in queste chiome
> quanti vorrei quel giorno attender anni.

[A youthful lady under a green laurel I saw, whiter and
colder than snow not touched by the sun many and many
years, and her speech and her lovely face and her locks
pleased me so that I have her before my eyes and will
always have wherever I am, on slope or shore. Then my
thoughts will have come to shore when green leaves are
not to be found on a laurel; when I have a quiet heart and
dry eyes we will see the fire freeze, and burning snow; I
have not so many hairs in these locks as I would be willing, in order to see that day, to wait years.]

(30.1–12)

What we come upon first: a tableau, young woman under a green
tree, no article or verb for this *donna*, nothing to position us in any
way with respect to the scene. Our only orientations in this first
line are the singularity of the tree (*un lauro*) and the preposition
"sotto," which positions *giovene donna* with respect to that tree, but
the tree itself stands as if in a vacuum, nothing placing it in time
or in space—even its color serving as a useless detail, since the laurel, as Petrarch will tell us again and again, is *always* green. With
the second line, however, this suspension of time and space is
shattered: the first person erupts into the scene—*vidi*—and with it
comes a certain perspective, a certain basis for comparisons and
comparative judgments. "Vidi *più* bianca et *più* fredda *che* neve /
non percossa dal sol." This moment is in the first person's past, this
woman is part of, and comparable to a world shaped by cyclical
events—a world shaped by the change in seasons, by the revolutions of the sun.

But: she is not just colder than snow; she is, instead, colder
than snow that has gone untouched by the sun for many years. She
is, in other words, more unchanging than a part of nature apart
from nature: a part of nature where the snows don't simply freeze
and thaw, where suns don't simply rise and set. She is less mutable
than perpetual snow lying under perpetual shadow. It is natural for
the years to turn, but even in nature there are places where the
years come and go without change—without snows melting, without shades lightening. Perhaps this is how the world looks on top
of Mont Ventoux: endlessly cold, snowy, shady. From the vantage
of such a high mountain, the world would be visible in all its ceaseless change. At the same time, around us, in the thin, trans-alpine

air, all would be endless winter. The world would turn below us, but we would remain still.

In these first three lines, seasonal, cyclical change is introduced only to be denied: literally we are frozen, caught in a tableau in the simple past. In the next three lines, however, this changelessness changes: the poem explodes into a textbook example of the sequencing of tenses. It's almost as if the past seeds, and flowers into, all of time. What starts off simple, the simple past, bursts into three new tenses. The *io* of the poem is so pleased by Laura's words and her looks and her hair–*mi piaquen*, they pleased me (we are still in the simple past)–that he has her now and will always have her wherever he might be on slope or shore. Past is followed by present, which in turn is followed by future, in turn to be followed by the present subjunctive.

In this first stanza, then, the initial tableau, which defies time in its cyclical, seasonal returns, emerges as the source for linear time in all its complex, sequential syntax. In other words, the time-less, almost dimensionless *giovene donna sotto un verde lauro* emerges as that beacon ever before Petrarch's eyes that marks time, and space, as he moves forward through both, even while this youthful lady and her laurel stand still in time and in space, immune to the seasons as the years roll by–and as the years return to the same point. In this way the *giovene donna* marks that alle-gorical high point from which space and time can be brought together into narrative; wherever Petrarch goes, there she is, was, will be, might be. She organizes time into sequence, space into journey. Even so, she herself withstands time and space: an ever snowy evergreen, planted outside of any context.

The paradox is a familiar one, and for those readers who see secularization in terms of substitution–i.e., as the topical shift from sacred to profane–we can point out how *lauro/Laura* replaces the Word, which was in the beginning, is now and ever shall be, and yet is spoken outside of time. This substitutive gesture, however, is not the final resolution of the sestina but merely the first move that the poet makes–a move achieved, moreover, in the very first stanza, before any of the sestina's repetitions have unfolded. In fact, lines 6–8 with their repetition of *riva*, immediately threaten this initial high allegory: "ed avrò sempre ov' io sia in poggio o 'n riva. // Allor saranno i miei pensieri a riva/ che foglia verde non si trovi in lauro . . ." [And I will have (her always before my eyes) wherever I might be on slope or shore. // Then will my thoughts be on shore when green leaves might not be found on a laurel . . .]. Where stanza 1 ended with a sense of Laura, like the Word, like an endless beacon, allegorically centering all journeys, stanza 2 begins with an image of endless wandering–an errancy, not a journey, extending without an end in sight. The shore of line 6 has thus receded. With it, the present subjunctive *sia*, a tense that allowed for the infinite expansion of meaning–*wherever I might go, there she will be*–has been transformed into the *si trovi* of line 8. Here the present subjunctive marks the shrinking of meaning to the most finite of points: *never–I will never get anywhere near her since laurels will never lack green leaves*. Similarly, the future tense, *avrò*, signifying the certitude of possession, has turned around into the future *saranno* whose certainty lies in *non*-possession: *I will never be at peace, my thoughts will never reach the shore, because I will never have her.*

Thus, with the poem's first turn, with its repetition at the semantic level of *riva* and its repetition at the structural level of verb tense (*avrò* and *sia*; *saranno* and *si trovi*), the situation of stanza 1 has itself been turned. No longer can we locate the *giovene donna* and her laurel as that point, origin and terminus, thanks to which a linear journey may be defined and from the standpoint of which all journeys are circles. Instead such a retrospective construction has faltered. The *then* by which Petrarch's *now* might take its bearings has been displaced; instead, as meeting place between *allora* ("then") and *alloro* ("laurel"), the "allor" of line 7 marks a time and a place that will *never* take place. "Allor saranno i miei pensieri a riva." Furthermore, this failure of retrospection emerges only when the poet considers the timeless laurel: *My thoughts will reach their end, then, when the laurel comes to an end, its leaves no longer green.* A figural space and time, a world without end where omega is recycled into alpha, that world collapses not because the laurel itself comes to an end, but precisely because it *doesn't*.[70]

We have replaced the familiar paradox of the Word with the unfamiliar paradox of the laurel. Instead of orienting the poet in space and time, instead of structuring his life as journey and quest, somehow the self-sameness of the tree contracts time into a point: into a finitude, a *never* or a death at which the poet soon arrives.

Ma perché vola il tempo et fuggon gli anni
sì ch' a la morte in un punto s'arriva
o colle brune o colle bianche chiome,
seguirò l'ombra di quel dolce lauro
per lo più ardente sole et per la neve,
fin che l'ultimo dì chiuda quest'occhi.

[But because time flies and the years flee and one arrives
quickly ("in a point") at death either with dark or with
white locks, I will follow the shadow of that sweet laurel
in the most ardent sun and through the snow until the last
day should close these eyes.]

(30.13–18)

In "The Fig Tree and the Laurel," John Freccero reminds us that
to follow a tree's shadow is to walk in circles (Freccero, 28): it is
to orbit the tree as the sun seems to do, rising in the east and setting in the west in any given day, moving from north to south
over the course of the year. I, however, am struck by the relation
between this image of a circular pathway and the stanza's suggestion of a life contracted into a point, *in un punto*: it is, after all,
because time flies and death arrives of a sudden that, instead of
waiting years to reach his terminus (30.12) Petrarch ends up
walking in circles. He is following the shadow or figure–remember, *umbra* is another word for *figura*–that the laurel casts. Presumably he is following the *donna* and not the tree, Laura and
not the *lauro*. But the woman is not herself the tree's shadow–
she is, after all, seated *beneath* the tree; she is herself *in* shadow.
To pursue the shadow in hopes of catching up with the tree is
doubly to miss the point: in the first place, the tree, being a tree,
isn't going anywhere; in the second place, if we're standing in the
tree's shadow we are standing with Laura herself. We needn't go
any further.

Thus the circular journey of stanza 1 has turned into the irresistible march toward death–but, in turn, that linearity has itself
been contracted into a point, into the *punto*, the end-stop at which
we quickly arrive. Further, we have learned that this point is itself
a circle, a path around a tree, but such a circular path, we have
come to realize, curiously lacks a point: we never really needed to
go anywhere since the shadow in which we stand is precisely the

point, the *punto*, of our search. In the fourth stanza, however, the sestina takes another major turn, a revolution in the poem's very perspective.

> Non fur giamai veduti sì begli occhi
> o ne la nostra etade o né prim' anni
> che mi struggon così come 'l sol neve,
> onde procede lagrimosa riva
> ch' Amor conduce a pie' del duro lauro
> ch' à i rami di diamante et d'or le chiome.

> [There never have been seen such lovely eyes, either in our age or in the first years; they melt me as the sun does the snow: whence there comes forth a river of tears that Love leads to the foot of the harsh laurel that has branches of diamond and golden locks.]

> (30.19–24)

Signaled initially in the shift from Petrarch's *occhi* in line 18 to Laura's in line 19, we might say that now we are seeing everything through a different set of eyes. If in stanza 1 the *giovene donna* under her laurel was stationary, an immobile point by virtue of which the poet measured his steps, now the poet has gained the vantage. From his new perspective Petrarch is able to pronounce on all of time: "non fur giamai veduti sì begli occhi" [there never have been seen such lovely eyes]. Where in stanza 1 the young lady was whiter and colder than snow, here the poet is himself snow–and yet he is snow that melts, touched by the sun and the change of seasons. He is snow that flows into water–into a stream of tears that gathers at the base of the laurel. We have come back, full circle, the poet's momentary vantage lost, the laurel's immobility all the more adamantine for our departure from it.

Yet this return to the stationary laurel has brought with it a dissolution of the sestina's opening image: *giovene donna sotto un verde lauro*. There is now no distance between *lauro* and *Laura*–the two have melted together and thus the unchanging tree has, for the first time in the poem, been transformed: its green leaves have become golden locks. By the logic of the second stanza, Petrarch's search should be over, just as it should have ended in the third stanza, as he stood in the shadow of the tree and in reach of his

lady. After all, here in stanza 4 we have finally achieved that supposedly never-to-be moment "when green leaves are not to be
found on a laurel." Halfway through the sestina the poem's logic suggests an ending. Nonetheless, both the poem and the poet continue.

> I' temo di cangiar pria volto et chiome
> che con vera pietà mi mostri gli occhi
> l'idolo mio scolpito in vivo lauro,
> ché s' al contar non erro oggi à sett' anni
> che sospirando vo di riva in riva
> le notte e 'l giorno, al caldo ed a la neve.
>
> Dentro pur foco et for candida neve,
> sol con questi pensier, con altre chiome,
> sempre piangendo andrò per ogni riva,
> per far forse pietà venir ne gli occhi
> di tal che nascerà dopo mill' anni,
> se tanto viver po ben colto lauro.

[I fear I shall change my face and my locks before she with
true pity will show me her eyes, my idol carved in living
laurel; for, if I do not err, today it is seven years that I go
sighing from shore to shore night and day, in heat and in
snow. Inwardly fire, though outwardly white snow, alone
with these thoughts, with changed locks, always weeping
I shall go along every shore, to make pity perhaps come
into the eyes of someone who will be born a thousand
years from now—if a well-tended laurel can live so long.]

(30.25–36)

At this juncture, instead of the poem's theme guiding its form,
the form leads the theme. By all accounts we should have reached
the end: the evergreen is no longer green and so the poet's
thoughts should have arrived at their final *riva*. But the sestina is
only half done; the poet's thoughts will need to keep turning for a
little while longer, finding a motive for their turning in the very fact
of turning. The sestina's very form will force the poet's hand. In
this way, just as in the *Familiari* 24.1, Petrarch found a theme for
writing in the very need to find a theme for writing, or as in the

canzoni degli occhi (poems 71–73), where the desire to write end-lessly produces the writing of endless desire, here, in stanza 5, counting the years since falling in love yields the very theme of cir-cular repetition–of years that cycle from night to day, from heat to snow. In other words, to commemorate the anniversary is to pro-duce the poem, and vice versa. The counting of years leads, as if inevitably, to the *anni*, which keep turning from stanza to stanza–but those *anni* themselves force the poet to keep counting the years. "S' al contar non erro oggi à sett' anni / che sospirando vo di riva in riva."

In the last stanza before the significantly named *tornada*, Petrarch turns from Laura's eyes to the eyes of the distant future: "sempre piangendo andrò per ogni riva, / per far forse pietà venir ne gli occhi/ di tal che nascerà dopo mill' anni." These eyes to which he finally turns are, of course, the eyes that read: the pity-ing eyes of a distant audience. Characteristically, he aligns his own future with his future reader, identifying his fate with the fate of the text–that well-tended laurel that may, perhaps, endure: *I will go weeping along every shore to make pity come into the eyes of someone who will be born after a thousand years, if a well-tended laurel can live so long.* It's as if the sestina's turn inward, *dentro*, toward its own formal reality has reoriented the poet. A shift toward form has apparently turned Petrarch away from his lady and toward his reader. Similar moments abound in the *Rime*. In "Chiare fresche et dolci acque," for instance, Petrarch will turn away from the flow-ers tumbling into Laura's lap, which "girando parea dir: 'Qui regna Amore'" [turning seemed to say, "Here Love reigns"] (126.52). Thus he turns away from that immensely coded space of shade where, as Dante puts it in the source poem for "Giovene donna," "Suoi panni fanno ombra," her skirts make a shadow.[71] And thus "Chiare fresche" closes by turning away from the turns of love–by turning away, that is, from Laura and her own "cortese giro" [gra-cious turning] (108.11). Instead, Petrarch turns toward his poem and toward his reader: "uscir del boscò," *Leave the wood,* he tells the canzone, "et gir infra la gente" *and turn among the people* (126.68).

But "Giovene donna" doesn't simply end with this turn toward the audience. Instead, it invokes a final reversal: from the *lauro* of line 36 to the *l'auro* of line 37.

L'auro e i topacii al sol sopra la neve
vincon le bionde chiome presso a gli occhi
che menan gli anni miei sì tosto a riva.

[Gold and topaz in the sun above the snow are vanquished by the golden locks next to the eyes that lead my
years so quickly to shore.]

(30.37–39)

In its last glittering moment, the sestina has taken us from the singular, verdant integrity with which we began—*sotto un verde lauro*—
to a beauty fragmented, disassembled into its jewellike parts:
golden locks, eyes, white skin. Certainly, the laurel's fragmentation
attests to the fetishism inherent in Petrarch's idolatry: a fetishism
that, as more than one critic has argued, transforms the lady's
absence into the sign of the poet's presence.[72] Yet the laurel's dis-
integration can only yield *ambiguous* signs; these signs are translated out of context. *Neve, chiome, occhi*: utterly deracinated and
subject to so many revolving repetitions, are we any longer certain
to whom these signs belong?

We must at the least concede the possibility that these eyes
that lead the poet to death are not necessarily, or perhaps not
solely, *Laura's* eyes. Instead it seems at least possible that these are
the same *occhi* that Petrarch has just imagined: the eyes of the
reader who, perhaps a thousand years from now, will arrive on the
scene only to mark the disappearance (and precisely not the presence) of the poet. In this way the transformation from *lauro* to
l'auro and from Laura to gold not only represents the kind of
alchemy that Robert Durling associates with the fetishizing
lover;[73] even more significantly, the moment also marks the poet's
dissolution into discourse: into the very discourse that names his
desire. If so, it is a dissolution that occurs *for our eyes only*, since it
is only to us as readers that Petrarch bequeaths his words. In this
way, "Giovene donna" stands with those poems like "Quando io
movo i sospiri a chiamar voi" (poem 5) or the sestina 239 which
takes *L'aura* as one of its end-words, or even the collection of
poems whose starting word is *l'aura*, invoking the play on *l'aura* as
breeze and *Laura* as name (see poems 194, 196–98, 246, 327, 356).
Such poems remind us that, above all, the sighs which we are
called upon to "hear" are sighs—breaths—breezes which call a *name*.

More dramatically than the coupling of *Laura* and *lauro*, the homonymic pair *Laura/l'aura*, like the pair *lauro/l'auro* in "Giovene donna," invokes the reader's presence as witness. Because Laura-as-name and *l'aura*-as-breeze are phonetically identical, their difference can only be imagined via a written text: in a strictly oral culture the two words could scarcely exist as separate. Homonyms, after all, are the luxury of a written culture. Of a figural culture, even: a culture that knows how to punctuate, how to distinguish *legere* from *intellegere*. *figura* provides us with the knowledge that a gap might separate the breeze from the name and the *aura* from its article even if, as would have been the medieval practice, *la* and *aura* are elided into one apostrophe-less word.

And so the reader is called upon–to hear a difference that, in the end, can only be *seen*. It is then toward the reader's absent-present eye and toward his own disappearance that Petrarch's "I" finally turns.

THREE

Luther Disfiguring the Word

Thou shalt have no other gods before me. Thou shalt not make unto thee any graven image, or any likeness *of any thing* that *is* in heaven above, or that *is* in the water under the earth: Thou shalt not bow down thyself to them, nor serve them: for I the Lord thy God *am* a jealous God, visiting the iniquity of the fathers upon the children unto the third and fourth generation of them that hate me; And shewing mercy unto thousands of them that love me, and keep my commandments.

–Exod. 20:3–6 (KJV)

You shall not have other gods. . . . To have a god is then nothing other than to trust and believe in him with all one's heart, as I've often said that it is alone the heart's trusting and believing which makes both God and idol [*beide Gott und abeGott*].

–"The First Commandment," *Grosser Katechismus* (1529)[1]

THE LAW OF LAWS

At the center of Martin Luther's Reformation is the First Commandment: the impossible commandment *to love*. The commandment, moreover, to love an absolute being, absolutely. Luther's Yahweh does not simply demand that we put Him before all others; He demands that we have *no* others: *Du sollt nicht andere Gotter haben–You shall not have other gods.*[2] Luther's Yahweh demands that which, by definition, it is impossible to give on demand: a devotion that proceeds not from mere obedience but, as Luther will say, *von hertzen*, from the heart–from our freely given desire. The desire that is freely given is what God first and foremost requires from us. *Love me*. It is an imperative that, strictly speaking, cannot be obeyed, since obedience implies just that tension or distance between the One who asks and the one who gives–just that sense of resistance that belies any act of love.[3]

Or so Luther feared throughout his career, buying his insights dear from his own experience–from his own early (and recurring) hatred, of self and of Lord, in the face of a deity who demands the impossible.[4] In his 1535 Commentary on Galatians Luther recalls his early despair as an Augustinian monk:

> When I was a monk, I used to think that my salvation was undone when I felt any desires of the flesh. . . . I tried many methods. I made confession every day, etc. But none of this did any good, because the desires of the flesh kept coming back. . . . The flesh prevents us from keeping the commandments of God, from loving our neighbors as ourselves, and especially from loving God with all our heart, etc. Therefore it is impossible for us to be justified by works of the Law. The good will [*voluntas bona*] is present, as it should be–it is, of course, the Spirit Himself resisting the flesh–and it would rather do good, fulfill the Law, love God and the neighbor, etc. But the flesh does not obey this will [*voluntas*] but resists it.[5]

For Luther, the First Commandment reveals the absolute rift between our works and our salvation, our flesh and the spirit. Our recalcitrant flesh prevents us from loving God with all our heart, and yet any effort to quell the unruliness of this flesh not only fails: it produces more of the very resistance it had sought to overcome. "The will [*voluntas*]," as Luther would formulate in his 1525 response to Erasmus' *Diatribe seu collatio de libero arbitrio*, " . . . is the more provoked to crave the more it is opposed."[6] At stake for Luther in the First Commandment–in the commandment of all commandments–is the thorniest of all religious paradoxes: the requirement that we love God ensures that we will hate him. It is the Commandment, the impossible Law to love, that produces that very spirit of opposition it legislates against. The more we are compelled to give, the more we will find ourselves guilty of holding back. Our recalcitrance only increases when opposed. Simply put, no "gift" can be free when offered in response to a command and it is the oxymoronic par-adox of a *mandatory gift* that condemns us.[7]

In the decade or so surrounding his break with Rome, this par-adoxical vision of the Law leads Luther to a series of seemingly disparate formulations and doctrines–formulations that distin-guish him from other reformers, no less than from the "papists." From his view of justification by faith alone to his polemics on the use of images in worship, to his treatment of the Eucharist and his debate with Erasmus on the status of the human will, Luther's writings of the 1520s explore positions that, however disparate they appear, all share a fundamental point of departure. Underly-ing each of the stances Luther takes in these polemics is his abso-lutist vision of the First Commandment and the challenge that vision poses for a traditional figural perspective.

As we have already seen, this orthodox figural perspective encompasses more than mere allegoresis–more than the "figural interpretation" that Auerbach delineates–and Luther's impact on the tradition will be felt in equally encompassing and complex terms. When Tertullian argues in *De Baptismo* that the flesh comes first as the figure of spirit,[8] he suggests the ways in which Christ-ian figurality both articulates, and resolves, a dualist worldview. "For the flesh lusteth against the Spirit, and the Spirit against the flesh: and these are contrary the one to the other: so that ye can-not do the things that ye would" (Gal. 5:17, KJV). As we've already seen with Augustine–for whom figure's *translatio* bridges the gap between old and new, first and last, now and then–and with Petrarch's forestalled translations, the resolution that *figura* pro-vides is a temporal one: what joins spirit to antagonistic flesh is a narrative of fulfillment. In the fullness of time, flesh and spirit are reconciled. In the fullness of time, the promise of the flesh is redeemed: *as it turns out*, the flesh "came first" as figure of the spirit. At its most basic, then, Christian figurality defines the reconcilia-tion of flesh and spirit over time.

Yet, as our discussions of Augustine and Petrarch have already suggested, this basic vision of temporal fulfillment covers a vast terrain: *figura* braids together at least five overlapping but nonethe-less distinct lines of thought. (1) *History*. First and foremost, Chris-tian figurality concerns the logic of historical succession. The old, fleshly reality is succeeded by and fulfilled in the new. In world-his-torical terms, a Jewish dispensation cedes to Christianity. In personal terms, figurality governs the narrative of conversion: the sinner's life prefigures the life of the saved man, the *vetus homo* is fulfilled in his *nova vita*. (2) *Authority*. The Christian West defines the relation of its Gospel to a prior Jewish Law in figural terms, and in so doing elaborates a theory of *auctoritas*–of the authority and authorship that makes a text binding or compelling. (3) *Signs*. Figurality outlines a theory of signs, and especially of trope, by reconciling the dead letter of the Law to the vivifying spirit of Christian Gospel. (4) *Readers*. Figurality also governs Christianity's confrontation with the Hebrew Scriptures by defining an imitative ethics of discourse. We read the text *propter nos*, as if it were written on our account, retroactively imagining ourselves as its addressee. (5) *Will*. Finally, and as we shall see in greater detail when we turn, at last, to *Will* himself, the figural tradition provides a language for understanding intention and desire. In the first place, because *figura* envisions human history as the embodiment of divine promise, it offers a notion of divine will in terms of testament or covenant. God's will is done in accordance with His Word. However, unlike God, man seldom manages to keep his promises. Accordingly, *figura* also offers a vision of a flawed, human will. Galatians 5 tells us that the flesh and the spirit are at odds: accordingly, we cannot do what we *would* do. But *figura* reconciles flesh and spirit, allowing us to make sense of our failure and to preserve a notion of free will in the process.

Radiating outward from his reading of the First Commandment, Martin Luther's thought will challenge and transform *figura* on each of these five levels, replacing a thematics of reconciliation with the unsettling oscillations of ambivalence. In place of a dualism resolved over time, Luther will argue for an unending and irresolvable tension between flesh and spirit. His dualism is absolute. In the next three chapters, first in the context of Luther's own work and then in the context of Shakespeare, we will consider Luther's dualistic viewpoint, and his challenge to each strand of *figura* in turn. History, Authority, Signs, Readers, Will. By examining the way Luther recasts each aspect of *figura*, I will demonstrate not only his devastating impact on the tradition but also the shaping role that *figura* itself plays in the development of his thought.

Luther rethinks the figural tradition, I will argue, from the ground up, analyzing and resynthesizing its component elements. As we shall see, in contrast both to the moderate reform of an

Erasmus and to the men whom Luther called "Schwärmer" (fanatics)–the more "radical" reformers like the first-generation Swiss
reformers Huldreich Zwingli and Johannes Oecolampadius (his
primary opponents in the Eucharist debates of the 1520s) or his
fellow Wittenberger, the iconoclast reformer Andreas Bodenstein
von Karlstadt–it is Luther's version of reform that alone entails a
sustained and rigorous critique of *figura*.[9] Indeed, it is this sustained critique that unifies the apparently disparate or inconsistent
aspects of his thought. While other reformers also assert the irreconcilability of flesh and spirit, only Luther pursues the idea to its
logical conclusions, radically undermining any notion of the flesh's
temporal, figural fulfillment. Where other reformers seem to pre-
scribe a more decisive rift between flesh and spirit than Luther, in
truth it is he, not they, who maintains in absolute terms the incommensurability of flesh and spirit. In the end, it is Martin Luther and
not Karlstadt, Zwingli, or even a second-generation reformer like
Calvin, who decisively reinvents the figural tradition–and it is his
transformed vision of *figura* that will resonate in the transformed
vision of Petrarchism we find, with Shakespeare, at the century's
end.

HISTORY: SUCCESSION AND THE GRAFT OF FAITH

As far as the Christian West is concerned, Luther devastates the
Christian notion of succession. He devastates, that is to say, the
"hybrid" logic of inheritance and fulfillment according to which
the spirit is heir to the flesh, and the flesh is prefiguration of the
spirit. At its source, we have seen, such logic girds Pauline Christianity's spiritual claim to a "carnal" Jewish revelation. Just as the
cultivated olive tree flourishes by means of its wild graft, so too
does God's promise to the Jews bear fruit in, and as, Christian revelation. Here time is itself defined as a function of flesh and spirit.
Temporality is organized, teleologically, as that which brings flesh
and spirit together while keeping them apart. Thus is Pauline time
simultaneously linear and circular–or rather, it is linear *because* it is
circular: the spiritual *telos* which gives time its arrow exists both at
the end and at the beginning of time. It is the *verbum*, the intention, underlying the sentence–or, as Augustine says, the *poem*–of
human history, allowing meaning to unfold in individual words,

voces, voices that take their turn in proper order and sequence. Such voices make the Word flesh, and thus deliver it, as it were, to our ear–while at the same time, these voices are themselves delivered, redeemed and brought to life, in the Word that inspires, inspirits them. Without the spiritual *verbum* to inhabit it, to in-form it, fleshly *vox* is dead and meaningless–but without *vox* to carry it, to give it body, the *verbum* of spirit will never make its way to us. To paraphrase a formalist almost as totalizing as Paul: flesh without spirit is empty; spirit without flesh is blind.[10]

Such is the teaching about succession that Luther inherits–but in proclaiming himself as Paul's true heir, Luther, no less than Paul with relation to the Hebrews, cracks the very backbone of the bequest. Like Augustine, Luther is "converted" by his reading of Paul's Epistle to the Romans–in this case the pivotal verse is Romans 1:17: *Iustus ex fide vivit.* The just man lives by faith. For Augustine, the confrontation with Paul opened up the very possibility of succession, knitting flesh and spirit, old and new into figural unity. Stepping into the chain of exemplary conversions from Paul to Anthony to the *Agentes in Rebus*, the sinner's carnal life becomes a prefiguration of the saint's spiritual calling–and the reader, like Alypius, is next in line. In such a way Augustine's conversion opens the chain of history to us, fulfilling a communal text, a common story with private revelation.

For Luther, however, Paul's text leads to the very doctrine that will snap the spine of succession-thinking: the doctrine of *justification by faith alone.* For Augustine, the flesh contended with the spirit up until conversion–up until the moment of grace brought flesh and spirit, sinner and saint, into figural alignment. Luther, on the other hand, will rule out any such reconciliation.[11] The strife between flesh and spirit knows no end in this life: even the saints must reckon with it. As long as there is flesh, there will be sin. Indeed, Luther's doctrine of *justification by faith alone* means just this: our salvation does not rely on our holiness; it does not depend upon the eradication of sin. "The remnants of sin [*reliquae peccati*] cling to our flesh, which, as long as it lives, does not stop having desires against the Spirit"–and yet "the believer knows that his sin is forgiven him on account of Christ" (LW 27, 78, 76).

For Augustine, the remnants of sin were the traces and fragments of a past sinful life: the *figurae*, imprinted in memory, that need be collected if we are to be saved. But for Luther, there is no *accounting* for our sins—no way to add them up once and for all, to countervail them, to set them off, flesh against spirit, old against new, in a system of order and meaning. Instead, these remnants are what remains after we have done our best to collect ourselves—to confess, to squelch our desire, to conquer our flesh, to follow our good will. The remnants are that necessary, ineradicable left-over that remains with us as long as we live, trapped between the absolute demands of spirit and the limited resources of flesh. Where a Pauline tradition dichotomizes flesh and spirit only in view of their future reconciliation in the fullness of time, Luther, in contrast, redefines the two, insisting upon an infinite, irreconcilable gap between them: a gap that time fails to *flesh out* but instead only renews, reiterates. In his revision of Paul, Luther argues that the flesh is not simply the corporeal self but the human as creature in distinction from the Creator. Carnality in this light goes far beyond concupiscence, far beyond the corporeal, to include intangibles like our reason, our intentions, and our desires.[12] In contrast, as Luther suggests in the 1535 Commentary on Galatians, the spirit includes only whatever pertains to faith; he cites Romans 14:23: "Whatever does not proceed from faith is sin" (LW 27, 76). In this way, for Luther the opposition between flesh and spirit is absolute: it is the opposition of Creator to creature and of infinite commandment to finite capacity.[13]

    We need, then, to read Luther's *reliquae peccati*, the remnants of sin that cling to our flesh, as an objective genitive: at stake here is that very remainder which *constitutes* sin.[14] For, in this light, sin emerges in absolute terms as the constitutive, ineradicable inadequacy of the flesh to the spirit. "Sin" names, in other words, our definitive inability to fulfill the command of Exodus 20:3: "You shall not have other gods." The work of salvation can never be completed, the fragments can never be collected together. No matter how hard we try, there will always remain something more, something yet to be done or undone: a *reliquus* holding us back from holiness—from wholeness. Thus the just live, must live, can only live, by faith.

    And so, when Martin Luther returns to the Pauline trope of the olive tree in his crucial early lectures on Romans, he rejects Paul's teleological hybridity. Instead of highlighting the difference of Jew and Christian in order to establish the two poles of a figural narrative, Luther collapses the distinction, renouncing any essential difference between the cultivated olive of a Jewish past and the wild olive of a Christian legacy. Even the cultivated olive (*olea*), Luther tells us, is not tame by nature, for "from the tame olive nothing is produced by nature except the wild olive [*oleaster*]." The seeds of the cultivated plant will only produce wild olives. "And yet," he tells us, "the branch of the wild olive through grafting becomes the branch of the tame olive, which the tame could not have done by nature" (LW 25, 101 n. 20).[15] In Luther's terms, the wild graft does not disrupt the natural generation of the cultivated olive. Instead there is *no* "natural" or genetic transmission of tame olives. Without the unnatural act of grafting, all olives are wild.

Luther's formulation undermines the Pauline distinctions between natural and unnatural, tame and wild, Jew and Gentile. For Luther, "ingrafting grace" (*gratia inserens*) serves as the difference between *olea* and *oleaster*, but this is now not the difference that divides Jew and Christian; it is, rather, the difference that unites them. Where Paul distinguished between two religions and two inheritances, linked together as flesh to spirit, natural root to grafted branch, Luther underscores the singular importance of grace. "Just as the wild olive does not by nature but by the art of ingrafting become the branch of the tame olive tree, so the Gentiles become the people of God through the ingrafting grace, and not through the righteousness or virtue of their own nature" (101 n. 22). Paul's hybrid figure—the wild olive that only "by the art of ingrafting" yields tame branches—now signifies both a Jewish and a Christian dispensation. Both are wild olives made tame; both rely alike upon the graft of faith.

Yet, if all olive trees are wild "by nature," then the Jews no longer serve as a privileged point of origin in a Christian story of succession. They, too, became the people of God through ingrafting grace; they too could not rely on the righteousness of their own nature. Paul's tree offered a figure of figural narrative, a figure of origins and ends. Luther's tree, however, figures precisely the impossibility of any such narrative. For him, the link between root and branch is always already severed by the graft of righteousness; his tree offers the image of a temporal rupture that is primary, irreconcilable, in play already at the root of things. For Luther, there is no original and ungrafted tame olive tree since righteousness per se is never natural. The tree of Romans 11 is split from the start.

Written in 1515–1516, Luther's lectures on Romans reflect the breakthrough insight of the years just preceding his schism with Rome. In these lectures Luther developed his doctrine of justification. *Iustitia*, righteousness, Luther argues, must not be understood as the justice with which God judges man's actions, but rather in terms of the mercy by means of which man is justified in God's eyes through faith.[16] There is no righteousness for Luther that does without the "ingrafting grace" of God–a grace without which we lack even the capacity for faith. Luther's true olive tree, always already a hybrid, thus bespeaks the constant, ineradicable tension between the works of man–which can never achieve salvation–and the justifying faith freely given by God.

Iustus vivit ex fide: so Luther reads the letter of Paul and defines himself as Paul's successor. But at the same time, by leveling the difference between *olea* and *oleaster*, Luther cuts down Christianity's family tree, radically undermining the logic of succession itself.[17] In this way, Luther simultaneously insists upon and denies a principle of succession: he declares himself the next Paul while nonetheless preaching the doctrine that renders any such claim invalid. But, as we shall see, far from weakening Luther's stance, this paradoxical claim to authority reinvents the idea of authority itself. And therein lies the devastating force of Luther's reading of Paul. As Paul's successor, Luther shatters the Christian West's sense of ecclesiastical continuity and tradition. The very doctrine of apostolic succession is shaken from the ground up. And we all know what comes next. Splintered into ever further splintering bits, Christianity in the West can no longer unambivalently support the idea of the visible church, of the one true church as Christ's embodiment on earth, as His most palpable body.[18] The comfort of a visible church, of a Word made institutionally flesh, is now no longer the Christian birthright.

AUTHORITY: THE BESHITTED AUTHOR

In his 1527 polemic against the Eucharistic views of his two Swiss rivals, Zwingli and Oecolampadius, Luther bemoans the vulnerable status of the secular author. He reports that "the best book I ever wrote, the [1522] *Postil*, which even pleases the papists," has been corrupted in its Latin translation by the Strassburg reformer

Martin Bucer.[19] Ultimately Bucer would become convinced of the possibility of a "concord" between the opposed Protestant visions of the Lord's Supper–a reconciliation, that is, between the Swiss view of the bread and wine as mere representations and commemorations of Christ's body, and Luther's insistence on the Real Presence of Christ in the sacrament.[20] But in 1527 no such concord was yet imaginable, and in his preface to the translation of Luther's *Postil*, Bucer commended the Swiss reformers' views, seeking to correct Luther's Eucharistic teachings.[21]

For Luther, characteristically, this experience of having his own words turned against him, his "favorite book" "disfigured" (LW 37, 148) and his authority countermanded, amounted to a confrontation with the devil and with his filth.

> Under my name, this blasphemous, shameful teaching has been spread and disseminated more widely, perhaps, than by all your books. . . . The devil saw clearly that this book was being disseminated everywhere. Therefore he seized it, and loaded and smeared it with his dung. So I, an innocent man, must now be the wagon driver of the devil's manure, whether I will or not.
>
> (LW 37, 147–48)

There is much to be said about Luther's interest in shit–and most of it has already been said.[22] For our purposes, however, this vision of the author's vulnerable public face–a face so easily defaced, disfigured, and smeared with dung–quickly encapsulates Luther's departure from the conceptions of authorship we have examined thus far. Certainly, the prefatory complaint of prior textual corruption is a long-lived *topos*.[23] But what seems novel, and characteristic, here is how Luther ups the ante on the traditional plaint, intensifying not only the nature of the contamination but also its deadly source. At issue is no longer merely the contingent fact of corruption, but a structural necessity: the inevitable risk we sinners run each and every time we author word or deed. The devil is always out there, ready to yoke his foul burden to our necks. Satan, as Luther reminds us, "takes no vacation" (LW 37, 17).

Luther's remarks here recall his uniquely ambivalent dependence upon the printing press. As has often been noted, the Reformation exploited the innovation of print in unprecedented ways;

the success of the movement, no less than the heightened role it accorded "scripture alone" as the pathway to salvation, is inconceivable without the ready dissemination and popularization of texts afforded by print culture. Luther's beshitted author is in large measure a product of his times, a product of the new technology by means of which the reformer wrests God's Word from the devil's hands only to render it more vulnerable than it has ever been before. The double edge of the situation becomes explicit in the opening passages of Luther's polemic here against the Swiss reformers, when he controversially remarks that the devil is the cause of all scriptural controversies. The devil, Luther reminds us, wants to steal Scripture from us, and has succeeded admirably: in 1229 the Council of Toulouse declared the Bible a heretic's book, forbidding its possession by laymen (LW 37, 14). Unfortunately, however, to free the text from its Babylonian captivity at the hands of the devil is nonetheless to render it available to all, opening the door to controversy.

In this double bind we see Luther's departure from an Augustinian notion of textual authority. For Augustine, and the medieval tradition he influences, the text–paradigmatically the sacred text– is as communal as the truth itself. It is only falsehood, Augustine teaches, that I possess of my own in private. The voice of the human, secular author–seductive and fleshly–is the private *vox* that must be erased in view of the *Verbum* or Wisdom of God. "Those who love your works instead of yourself," Augustine writes in his treatise *De Libero Arbitrio*, addressing God's Wisdom, "are like those who hear a wise and eloquent speaker, who listen too eagerly to the pleasant voice and the carefully uttered syllables, but lose that which matters most, the meaning of the speaker, whose words are spoken only as signs."[24]

Luther's text is also a public text, freed from the devil only insofar as it is made common and accessible to all. Yet its availability leads for Luther to its vulnerability: for Luther, the authority of the text no longer resides at a transcendent remove from its "carefully uttered syllables." The commonality that liberates the text from the clutches of Satan emerges, in this light, equivocally as the threat of widespread contamination. Hence, Luther's condemnation of the Swiss "fanatics," or *Schwärmer*, runs deeper than it first appears: not only have the *Schwärmer* fouled Luther's teaching in the very process of disseminating it, but they have created a following eager to deface any text: "Just now a story against the sacrament is circulating among the masses who have been misled by the teaching of the fanatics, that one should rather die than write and send out a sermon among them, for when they hear that it is all nonsense, they immediately want to do a mess on it and wipe their behinds on it" (LW 37, 67). The mass dissemination of doctrine that print culture affords leads to a potential defilement by the masses. For Luther, more than anything else, the *Schwärmer* represent the danger of the Word made common.

Most important, this is a danger that Luther takes *personally*. In his awareness of the risks of publication, Luther implies that the text bears a singular human face, ever vulnerable to public deface-ment. Like Petrarch, and against Augustine, Luther refuses to erase the personal, human author of the text in the name of a common, transcendent truth. In this measure, Luther's sense of textual authority is a humanist one, deriving ultimately from his university days at Erfurt, where the *via moderna* of nominalism, with its atten-tion to the context and usage of a given author's words, merged with newer humanist views.[25] But unlike Petrarch, for Luther the risk that the human author runs is not simply erasure—not simply a disappearance, in the fullness of time at the hands of posterity, once the *now* of writing has slipped into the past. More pro-foundly, the risk Luther faces as writer amounts to a captivity in the *present* moment: a captivity even *now*, as, yoked to the devil, we drive the wagon of his dung.

The shift that Luther marks from a humanist sense of the sec-ular author is a profound one; to clarify the stakes of the matter, it will be useful here to rehearse, in part, the discussion of chapters 1 and 2. The vision of a secular author underlying both Petrarch's humanism and his lyric derives, as we have seen, from the pathos of Augustine's occulted Moses. As we will recall, for Augustine that powerful, sensuous moment of fantasy in book 11 of the *Con-fessions*—a fantasy of direct contact with the human author of Scripture—dissolves immediately into a recognition that the pass-ing of time, the passing away of the author, is the precondition for the apprehension of truth. "Behold these things [of the world] give way [*ecce illa discedunt*]," Augustine also writes in the *Confes-sions*, "so that other things may take their places [*ut alia succedant*] and the whole be preserved in all its lowest parts" (4.11). In a world governed by *figura*, our sensuous attachment to the present, to the beauty of the world or the sounds bursting from our neighbor's mouth, can only sinfully distract us from the necessary unfolding of meaning.

"Thus Moses wrote; he wrote and he passed away, he passed over hence from you toward you, and he is not now before me" (*Conf.* 11.3). It is this very passing away that preoccupies Petrarch—and that he resists, striving to maintain that impossible moment of Augustine's fantasy, pressing his lips to the imagined ear of the reader and straining to catch the last whispers from a dead author's mouth. In his deictical play within the *Familiari* or the *Rime* we have seen Petrarch positioning the living, aging text as that intermediary between past and present, author and reader. Petrarch's texts thematize and hence foreground the very translational work of Christian *figura*. It is thus not simply, as we have seen, that Petrarch rejects figural meaning as conveyed by the arc of time; rather he uncovers its bittersweet erotics, its promise of plenitude carried in the movement of loss. Indeed, the erotic investment of the *Familiari*, no less than the *Rime*, consists in this attention to loss: an attention to that effacement of the past that *figura* always further effaces.

Ultimately, such attention to loss conditions a specifically Petrarchan *imitatio*. For Augustine, the figural relation between author and reader is necessarily an imitative one: taking the past as his example, his "figure," the reader steps into exemplarity's chain, trumping what has come before and inviting his own future erasure. Petrarch, on the other hand, wants seemingly to follow an example without setting one; he strives consistently, as we have said, to keep the moment of conversion present, self-conscious: to keep turning without ever *having turned*.[26] The figural translation between past and present becomes then the very theme of Petrarch's imitations. In this way, both as humanist and as poet, Petrarch remains committed to the logic of *figura*, but nonetheless resists the very loss—the loss, ultimately, of the *now* of writing—that *figura* demands.

In the end, however, no matter how obsessively he foregrounds the present moment of writing, Petrarch never escapes the logic of a tradition that defines plenitude, meaning, and presence in terms of the troping relation between beginnings and ends. Indeed, the *now* that he defines in his *Rime* consists in just this turning between past error and future reading, between the *altr' uom* of his youthful wandering, and the *voi* who listen. Petrarch's lyric presence stands thus as the briefest of "brevi sogni," continually elided in the translation between a past from which it differs and a future with which it cannot coincide. In this way, the poet's presence as an author is imagined in terms of absence: in terms of a projected future that looks ever backward to an ever forward-looking past.

Hence, despite the extent to which a humanist hermeneutic seems opposed to all allegories, Petrarch's authorial voice rehearses a figural dilemma, recapitulating in its brief dreams the problem of Moses and the Law. Within the tradition that Augustine helps define, the question of authorial presence cannot be separated from the question of how the Law binds: the question, that is, of the Old Testament's authority for its reader. In his treatise against Faustus we've seen Augustine define this authority, arguing that the Jewish patriarchs' "present performance" (*praesens functio*) of the Law relied upon their prophetic understanding of the Law's future meaning. "For by revelation to them of the spirit of God they understood . . . in what manner God determined the future by all those acts and sayings to be figured and predicted" (*Contra Faustum* 4.2). Moses and the patriarchs constructed their present "functio" as a function of, and in full view of, their future obsolescence. The authority of the Law–already available to the Jews– cannot be separated from the passage of time whereby that Law is abrogated, the Old fulfilled in the New. Small wonder, then, that as Christian exemplar for the human author–the very author of the authoritative Law–Moses appears for Augustine only in that brief dream of *Confessions* 11: the dream that heralds his disappearance.

But, as it turns out, Martin Luther will also dream of Moses. For Luther, no less than for Augustine or Petrarch, Moses serves as exemplar of the human author. And yet, Luther's Moses is an author whose authority exists not in view of its fulfillment–an annulment that also preserves–but only insofar as it is utterly negated. In this way, once again, Luther splits open the smooth narrative of Christian dialectic; Luther envisions a negation without reserve.[27] For Luther, Moses is that paradoxical author whose words carry most weight when they are carried against him. We see Luther's Moses in a fragment of the theologian's table-talk–an early fragment (before 1531) that imagines the juridical moment of the Last Judgment. It is a spare account, lacking the sensuous detail that distinguishes Augustine's fantasy; instead, Luther emphasizes a stark dichotomy of judgment and forgiveness.

> I won't tolerate Moses because he is an enemy of Christ. If he appears with me before the judgment I'll turn him away in the name of the devil and say "Here stands Christ." In the last judgment Moses will look at me and say, "You have known and understood me correctly," and he will be favorably disposed to me.
>
> (WAT 2, no. 1242)[28]

For Luther, Moses stands as the authority who simultaneously condemns and approves; indeed, Moses is the author who approves insofar as he is himself condemned–repudiated in the name of the devil. As Heinrich Bornkamm writes: "Moses, the father of Jewish customs and man of the law, and Moses, the Christian and prophet of Christ, are deadly enemies [for Luther] in one and the same figure" (165). The patriarch's two-sidedness is immediate and irresolvable: insofar as he stands for Law, Moses cannot stand for Christ–but to stand for Christ amounts to the very recognition that one stands condemned before the Law.

Moses's double nature here is part and parcel of the "office" (*Amt*) of the Law, as Luther conceives it–an office that is defined not in figural terms as the *functio* prophesying Christian salvation, but rather as the scourge that reveals our unworthiness for such salvation. As Luther explains in his 1545 "Preface to the Old Testament," "the true intention of Moses is through the law to reveal sin and put to shame all presumption as to human ability" (LW 35, 242).

> He [Moses] does this ... when he teaches that men ought to fear, trust, believe, and love God; and that, besides, they ought to have or bear no evil desire or hatred for any man. When human nature, then, catches on to this, it must be frightened, for it certainly finds neither trust nor faith, neither fear nor love to God, and neither love nor purity toward one's neighbor. Human nature finds rather only unbelief, doubt, contempt, and hatred to God; and toward one's neighbor only evil will and evil desire. But when

human nature finds these things, then death is instantly
before its eyes, ready to devour such a sinner and to swallow him up in hell.

(LW 35, 243)

It is in this manner that Luther glosses 1 Corinthians 15:56: "The
sting of death is sin, and the power of sin is the law." The Law, by
teaching us what we ought to do, only teaches us the extent of our
sin. The more we are exhorted in the name of the Law, the more
we are stung by the recognition of our inability to fulfill our duty.
Nonetheless, "this office [*Amt*] of sin and death is good and very
necessary. For where there is no law of God, there all human reason is so blind that it cannot recognize sin" (LW 35, 241). In place
of a Law that binds only insofar as it prefigures its future
fulfillment, its Christian abrogation, Luther presents the unsettling
ambivalence of a Law that knows no end. The Law, as Luther
conceives it, maintains its hold on us, binding us even now as it
bound the Jews, but with this difference: for the Christian such
bondage inevitably bespeaks the presence of Christ. *Hie stet Chris-
tus*: Here stands Christ.

   "You have understood me well," Moses says in Luther's fantasy–his voice no longer a whisper, no longer destined to fade
away with the sublation of the Old in the New. For Luther there
can be no such final passage from Old to New: we cannot dispense
with the Lawgiver's office. To hear the truth that Moses offers, the
necessity of faith that he teaches, the Christian must also hear the
sentence of the Law. Luther's Moses thus speaks simultaneously
for Christ and against Him; with his "true intention" he reveals
himself as promulgator of Satan's lies. *The power of sin is the law*.
To put it still another way: the Christian freedom that Moses,
despite himself, uncovers–a freedom from the burden of Law–
cannot be separated from the bondage of our will: from our inability to satisfy the Law, to merit salvation, even to the slightest
degree, through our works. We are freed of the Law's sentence
precisely because we realize our incapacity to satisfy its demands.
Irrevocably double-sided, Luther's Moses articulates in one and
the same figure freedom and bondage: both the consolation of
Gospel and the damnation of the Law.

   In Luther's fantasy, Moses is not degraded like the befouled
author of the 1522 *Postil*, but he too experiences his words turned

against himself. He too finds himself driving the devil's dung. Like Luther's beshitted author, Moses stands for the sting of fleshly failure—for the putting to shame of human presumption. Such shame, such failure is what Moses both reveals and also endures in his own person, finding himself repudiated (as Luther imagines it) "in the name of the devil." In short, Moses stands for the office of the Law: for the damning voice that, damned in its own right, reveals our salvation by faith alone. What underlies Luther's ambivalent vision of the human author, then, is ultimately this vision of the Law's ambivalent office. As that giver of laws who judges only insofar as he himself is judged, Moses stands as the exemplary human authority; his greatest triumph is at once his greatest shame.

"Here stands Christ," Luther responds to Moses, turning the authoritative sentence on its head and transforming the judgment of the Law into the proclamation of faith. Is it any accident that Luther's vision here of an encounter before the ultimate worldly authority—Moses himself—repeats the terms of Luther's own founding moment of self-authorship? I refer here to Luther's confrontation with Eck at the 1521 Diet of Worms—the confrontation that followed his excommunication and preceded his imperial censure. When asked to recant, Luther affirmed simultaneously his strength and his weakness. "Hier steh ich," Luther announced at Worms. "Ich kann nit anders." *Here stand I. I cannot do otherwise.*[29]

SIGNS: THE OFFICE OF THE LAW

"The sting of death is sin, and the power of sin is the law." In book 6 of the *Confessions*, Augustine recounts how Ambrose, then Bishop of Milan, removed a major stumbling block in the path of conversion by teaching Augustine the principle of figural exegesis: "Ambrose would commend most diligently as a rule . . . : The letter kills, but the spirit gives life [2 Cor. 3:6], when, having removed the mystic veil of the text, he would lay open spiritually those things which taken literally [*ad literam*] seemed to teach perversity" (6.4). From Origen on, the 2 Corinthians verse had become the commonplace justification not only, of course, for allegorical readings but for the whole familiar lineup of Platonist dichotomies: form/content, inner/outer, material/spiritual.[30]

When Luther himself turns to the spirit and the letter in his 1519 Commentary on Galatians, he does not condemn allegorical readings per se; after all, he began his own career as exegete by applying the fourfold allegorical method in his 1513–1515 lectures on the Psalms.[31] But neither does he accept allegory's traditional justification in the 2 Corinthians distinction. Allegorical readings are, for Luther, a "game"; ornamental and extrinsic to the sense of Scripture, they bear no theological weight.

> This kind of game may, of course, be permitted to those who want it, provided they do not accustom themselves to the rashness of some, who tear the Scriptures to pieces as they please and make them uncertain. On the contrary, these interpretations add extra ornamentation, so to speak, to the main and legitimate sense. . . . But these interpretations should not be brought forward with a view to establishing a doctrine of faith.
>
> (LW 27, 311)

Analogous to Jesus' parables in the Gospels, allegorical readings can be useful—especially, Luther says, for those who are "not very well instructed" (LW 27, 310)—but "that four-horse team," the fourfold method of exegesis, "is not sufficiently supported by the authority of Scripture, by the custom of the fathers, or by grammatical principles" (311) to support authoritative readings.

In these deceptively mild terms Luther rejects more than a millennium of the figural practice that has, precisely, grounded the authority of the text in the use of trope.[32] Instead, Luther argues that, while allegories are permissible, the patristic distinction between letter and spirit is entirely misguided. The early Church fathers,[33] Luther writes, "take the outward form and historical account to be the 'letter.' But the mystical and allegorical interpretation they call 'spiritual.' And they call that man 'spiritual' who understands everything in a lofty sense, and, as they say, allows nothing of the Jewish tradition" (LW 27, 312). The Church fathers, Luther argues, wrongly conflate the allegorical search for mystical, hidden doctrine with the verse from 2 Corinthians ("the letter kills, but the spirit gives life"). Such a reading not only stultifies the spirit, identifying it with the search for esoterica; more important, it threatens the very fabric of Christian faith. To understand everything "in a lofty sense" entails the total rejection of the history and tradition of the Jews. The reading that equates "spirit" with mystical doctrine shears the Gospel from the Law and thereby divorces faith from the history of God's revealed Word.[34]

For Luther, this dangerous patristic conception errs in one crucial particular: it identifies the Law with the "letter."

> Nevertheless, these two words, "letter" and "spirit," as also the "literal" and the "spiritual" understanding, have to be separated and kept in their own proper meaning. . . . Spiritual understanding does not mean what is mystical and anagogical (in which the ungodly also excel); but in the strict sense it means life itself and the Law as it is put into actual practice. . . . In short, it means that complete fulfillment which the Law commands and requires. . . . We conclude, therefore, that in itself the Law is always spiritual; that is, it signifies the spirit which is its fulfillment. For others, however, though never for itself, it is a "letter."
>
> (LW 27, 312–13)

For Luther, no less than for the figural tradition he here rejects, the distinction between letter and spirit is fundamental to the authoritative exegesis of Scripture. However, in place of the troping mentality that sees the Old Testament as the fleshly letter of the Law, a letter trumped in its figurative or spiritual New Testament reading, Luther asserts that *in itself, the Law is always spiritual.* To read the letter of Scripture rightly, justly, we must recognize that the Law is a letter for others, but never for itself.

Luther's point here is a subtle one, for although he follows Paul in declaring that the Law is spiritual (cf. Rom. 7:14), he interprets Paul's dictum in a new light. For Luther, whether we are considering the First Commandment or the rest of the Decalog, ceremonial laws of worship or prescriptions regarding oxen and harvest, the literal terms of Mosaic Law are in and of themselves beyond fulfillment. The problem here is not one of sheer contingency; for Luther the issue is not simply that we happen to be too weak for the Law—that the deeds it requires just happen to be beyond our strength.[35] Rather the problem is a logical one: even the smallest article of the Law is beyond us, because what the Law requires is not simply that we do certain things but that we *obey.* It is obedience, and not the performance of specific acts, that, strictly speaking, satisfies the Law—and obedience demands not a slavish response to commands but rather that, as free men, we *accept* those commands.[36] Obedience, in other words, requires that we respond "gladly and willingly" to the dictates set before us. But, as Luther teaches: "No work of law is done gladly and willingly; it is all forced and compelled" (LW 35, 241). Even when we do what the Law requires of us, we fail, according to Luther, to satisfy its command: a command, at its base, to *love*. "Since no work is done well without love . . . it is clear that every law that commands a good work signifies and requires a good work, that is, a work of love" (LW 27, 313). Without our loving consent, our performance can be neither complete nor good. The Law, Luther teaches repeatedly, can only be fulfilled by love, and it is this love that we are constitutively unable to offer.

Again, our failure to love the Law is not merely an empirical failure; the problem here is not to be understood in terms of some fact about us, as if some men, more loving than others, would consequently have more success in obeying the Law. Rather, our failure is to be understood as *absolute*. All men fail equally, absolutely, to obey the Law, since to obey requires that we subject our will to an external constraint—that we act heteronomously rather than as self-willed, autonomous creatures.[37] Luther's insight, at once a psychological and a philosophical one, concerns the lack of consent that such heteronomy implies. As he writes in his 1521 "Preface to Romans":

> The work of the law is everything that one does, or can do, toward keeping the law of his own free will or by his own powers. But since in the midst of all these works and along with them there remains in the heart a dislike of the law and compulsion with respect to it, these works are all wasted and have no value.
>
> (LW 35, 367)

Our empirical circumstances alone determine whether we are able to "do the law"—to keep it by acting in accordance with its strictures. But true fulfillment requires that we obey without being compelled to do so; that we act as we "ought" to act, but without the sense of compulsion that such "ought" judgments imply.

Such fulfillment is logically impossible. To fulfill the Law we would have to live in effortless accordance with it; we would have to live as we *ought* to live, but without that sense, however slight, of dissonance between the legislated world of morality and the brute facts of empirical contingency. To fulfill the Law, as Luther sees it, would be to live in a world where there is no distinction between what is and what ought to be. But in such a world there would also be no such thing as law.

Here we return to Luther's conception of the office or function of the Law. Without the grace of God, it is impossible to fulfill the Law because our response to it will always be colored by compulsion. Furthermore, as Luther knew from his own experience as a compulsive monk, the more obedient we strive to be, the more we hate the Law that compels us and, even more devastatingly, the more we hate the very God Who has commanded that we love. Consent to the Law flees from us the more we enjoin ourselves to achieve it. Nonetheless, this very abyss of hatred and sin, this very damnation that the Law not only reveals but even creates, is necessary for our salvation. We must mistake the Law for a letter in order to realize the deeply spiritual nature of its command. To be saved is not to live in a world without the Law nor to interpret its dictates in mystical terms; rather, it is to recognize the Law's true office. Our salvation, in this measure, requires the Law, for it is only by means of the Law—as it exists *for itself,* as spirit—that we recognize that even our best efforts fall short: we can never merit salvation. Indeed, the better our efforts, Luther suggests, the more sinful we become.[38]

In this way, Luther reinterprets the notion of Christian freedom.

> To be without the law is not the same thing as to have no laws and to be able to do what one pleases. Rather we are under the law when, without grace, we occupy ourselves with the works of the law. Then sin certainly rules [us] through the law, for no one loves the law by nature; and that is great sin. Grace, however, makes the law dear to us; then sin is no longer present, and the law is no longer against us but one with us. This is the true freedom from sin and from the law.
>
> (LW 35, 375–76)

Christian freedom is not an escape or release from the Law in a conventional sense; it is rather a release from our hatred of the Law; a release from these paradoxes of an "obedience" that only incurs further resistance. Yet such a release comes only provisionally in this lifetime, and only through the grace of God. As Luther often suggests, through grace we "werden ohne Sünde": we become without sin, insofar as we come to love the Law. The dissonance that marks moral action lessens, although it never disappears since "the whole man is himself both spirit and flesh, and he fights with himself until he becomes wholly spiritual" (LW 35, 377)–that is, he fights until the day he dies. We *become* without sin, but we are never free from it; as long as we live, the spiritual Law will demand what the whole man, both flesh *and* spirit, can never wholly give.[39]

In this way Luther rejects the figural definition of Christian freedom as the utter abrogation of the Law. As he writes in his 1537–1540 tract "Against the Antinomians": "These true disciples of Satan seem to consider the law as something finite, which ended under Christ, just like circumcision" (WA 39$^\text{I}$, 350; quoted in Bornkamm 135). What the Antinomians wrongly infer is that, because the finite demands of specific laws–e.g., the law of circumcision–are no longer required, the Law itself must be at an end. Luther's teaching on the Law reveals, however, that in itself the Law is *infinite* and without end, requiring not the finite fulfillment of specific actions but the absolute fulfillment, which is love. Certainly the Law's office of condemnation is dead for Christians, since through Christ we are saved and not damned, our sins forgiven (LW 35, 244). Nonetheless, that office is still essential to our faith, since it reveals the crucial truth about us: even at our best moments, we are the worst of sinners. Indeed, at times Luther suggests that faith consists precisely in the recognition of sin that the Law enables: "By faith alone it must be believed that we are sinners, and indeed more often than not we seem to know nothing against ourselves" (WA 56, 231).[40] As Heinrich Bornkamm puts it: "The forgiveness of sin abrogates the law and yet at the same time irrevocably presupposes it. Otherwise man would never know what sin is" (136). Somewhat paradoxically, then, the Law is abrogated only because its office has finally become apparent as such; the Law has not ceased to judge us, but we now recognize that under such judgment we stand, inevitably, condemned.

Indeed, just as a view of the Law as letter—whether Antinomian or Origenist—wrongly assumes that the Law is finite, so too does it mistake the nature of human sin. As Luther explains in his treatment of Moses, the patriarch promulgated so many and various laws "that sins might simply become numerous and be heaped up beyond measure. The purpose was to burden the conscience so that the hardened blindness would have to recognize itself, and feel its own inability and nothingness in the achieving of good" (LW 35, 244). Heaped up beyond measure, the infinite laws of Moses burden the conscience so completely, eliciting our resistance so absolutely, in order to reveal the immeasurable, infinite nature of sin.

> The main knowledge and true wisdom of Christians, then, is this: to regard as very serious and true these words of Paul, that Christ was given over to death, not for our righteousness or holiness but for our sins, which are real sins—great, many, in fact, infinite and invincible. Therefore you must not think of them as minor or suppose that your own works can remove them. Nor must you despair on account of their gravity if you feel them oppressing you either in life or in death. But you must learn from Paul here to believe that Christ was given, not for sham or counterfeit sins, nor yet for small sins . . . ; not for sins that have been overcome—for neither man nor angel is able to overcome even the tiniest sin—but for invincible sins.
>
> (LW 26, 35)

Invincible faith—true assurance that Christ was given for our sins—demands a recognition of invincible sin. Our works cannot justify us: since our efforts to be holy only yield our further recalcitrance, even the "tiniest" sin cannot be overcome. Even a "small" sin is infinite, bespeaking our absolute non-consent to, and damnation under, the Law. Nonetheless, even if the Law cannot save us, it still plays a role in the life of every Christian by revealing the infinite nature of our sin. In this way, by linking the office of the Law to the assurance of our salvation, Luther reconsiders the nature of spiritual distress itself. The fits of despair he was himself prone to throughout his life—his *Anfechtungen*, or tribulations, as he called them, when he felt himself to be an abandoned sinner—were merely preludes to his exultant joy in being saved. For Luther, despair and faith are the lub-dub of the Christian heart, just as the Law and Gospel together compose an irrevocably double-edged Word of God. As Heiko Oberman puts it, for Luther "tribulations are not a disease, so there can be no cure for them. They are a characteristic condition of Christian life" (1982:178). Without the spiritual Law, as Luther sees it, there can be no Christian life; the despair it produces serves, in this manner, as the indispensable companion to our experience of the good news.[41] "We cannot reach heaven until we first descend into hell," he writes in his *Grosser Katechismus.* "We cannot be God's children unless first we are the Devil's children. Again before the world can be seen to be a lie it must first appear to be the truth" (WA 31^1, 1:249).[42] Law and Gospel, damnation and salvation, are the two sides of the same story of justifying faith–the two sides of the same word of God–and as such, they reside together not only in the historical relation between two testaments, but in the ongoing life of Christians.

In this manner, Luther's vision of an infinite, spiritual Law points toward a deepening of dualistic thinking. Instead of a temporal trajectory announcing the end of the Law in the triumph of the Gospel, for Luther the two remain forever conjoined as the twin pulses of God's Word. The Law is no more extinguished by the Gospel than the flesh is defeated by the spirit. Instead, in itself the Law *is* spirit and its office is to make our blindness visible as such. Ultimately, what the Law reveals in place of a teleological narrative from Judaism to Christianity and from dead letter to living spirit, is an essential and ceaseless ambivalence–a restless shuttling back and forth between mutually exclusive alternatives: flesh/spirit, law/gospel, damnation/salvation, slavery/freedom. This ambivalence, Luther teaches, is at play not only within the history of the Church, but also within the lives of the just.

READERS: THE FLESH IS OF NO AVAIL

It has become a commonplace in Luther studies to argue that Luther rejects a Platonic dualism since he teaches a doctrine of the "the whole man": of man as a total moral entity, neither his sin nor his salvation existing piecemeal. "'Flesh' means man through and through as he lives in this life," Luther writes in 1523 (WA 12, 373, quoted in Pelikan, *Luther the Expositor*, 147): it is not a mere outer wrapping—an extraneous shell—to be stripped away on the road to salvation.[43] We are saved in our entirety, and yet, since our salvation is imputed to us by an all-merciful God and not earned by our works, we remain the greatest of sinners. *Totus homo peccator, totus homo justus*: the whole man is both sinner and saint.[44]

Along these lines, critics have understood Luther's divergence not only from the medieval Church (with, as I see it, its deeply "figural" standpoint), but also from the other reformers of his day. Thus Roland Bainton argues that the chief distinction between Zwingli and Luther lies in their differing interpretations of the word *sarx* (flesh, *Fleisch*) in the New Testament: the Swiss reformer conceives the flesh in the mere neoplatonic sense of "body" while Luther reads it in a "Hebraic" sense as "the evil heart which may or may not be physical" (266). Heiko Oberman, for his part, argues that Luther abolishes the "arbitrary" distinction between "higher" and "lower" instincts in man and envisions the flesh as the entirety of man as creature (*Luther the Expositor*, 272–76). For Carl Christensen, Luther replaces a mind/body dualism with the essential polarities between "faith and unbelief, the 'new man' and the old," striving to define a spirituality that is not divorced from the material world.[45] And Jaroslav Pelikan describes at length the manner in which Luther seeks to "de-platonize" the New Testament opposition of flesh and spirit (*Luther the Expositor*, 122 ff.).

For critics like those cited above, Luther's redefinition of flesh and spirit is central to his vision of a fully embodied, instead of dualistically riven, Christian life. Luther, it is argued, thus combats a tradition of spiritualism that encompasses both the moderate neoplatonic reforms of an Erasmus and the iconoclastic asceticism of radical Protestant reform.[46] Both types of reform begin with the strictest of Johannine dualisms—"It is the spirit that gives life, the flesh is of no avail" (John 6:63), a phrase that is a favorite with reformers of all stamps[47]—and such reformers accordingly emphasize the dangers of a religion caught up in the "mere externals"[48] of ritual and icon. Salvation, for these theologians, requires that we transcend the flesh—while Luther's doctrine of the whole man, it is argued, promotes a "cheerful integration" of matter and spirit.[49] In this reading, Luther's critique of a traditional dualism amounts not only to a rejection of the flesh/spirit antagonism per se, but also to the rehabilitation of a material world denigrated by centuries of ascetic spiritualism.

This reading of Luther's divergence from other reformers, however, mistakes the consequences of his reform. Luther, it is true, does define flesh and spirit in absolute terms and thus rejects a Platonic tradition that thinks in terms of the flesh as *parts* of a spiritual *whole*[50]. For such a tradition, the visible, material world is at best incomplete; to linger on any one aspect of it–to become too attached to the parts–is to lose sight of the immaterial whole. By insisting on the *total* man, however, Luther rejects both the notion of the flesh as partial and the attitude of ascetic detachment that that notion fosters. However, rather than banish dualism or promote a more integrated worldview, Luther's vision instead entails a still sharper–indeed a *total*–sense of the rift between flesh and spirit. In his view, the two are utter incommensurables. "Flesh and spirit," Luther writes in his preface to Romans,

> you must not understand as though flesh is only that which has to do with unchastity and spirit is only that which has to do with what is inwardly in the heart. Rather, like Christ in John 3[:6], Paul calls everything "flesh" that is born of the flesh–the whole man, with body and soul, mind and sense–because everything about him longs for the flesh. . . . "The spirit" is the man who lives and works, inwardly and outwardly, in the service of the Spirit and of the future life.
>
> (LW 35, 371–72)

That which is born of the flesh is flesh; the spirit alone comes from and works toward God. *Totus homo peccator, totus homo justus*: the totalization of man's nature means that there is no way to overcome our sin by degrees, no way to purchase our salvation in pieces. In rejecting the flesh as partial, Luther also rejects the possibility of compromise. There can be no mediation between flesh and spirit–no way "to get from" sinner to saved, from flesh to spirit. In its entirety, its totality, the flesh "longs for the flesh" and fails utterly in the service of the spirit.

In the first place, then, readings that celebrate Luther's triumph over dualism misinterpret the reformer's views: Luther's "whole man" is anything *but* whole, anything but undivided; to be all sinner, all saint, all at once, is to be profoundly cleft. At the same time, these readings err on the other side of the analysis: they miss the complexity of Christian figurality, and thereby they misrepresent the tradition against which Luther defines himself. Certainly a spiritualist emphasis pervades this tradition, privileging an immaterial spirit over the material world or the carnal letter and bemoaning the "judaizing" attitude that worships idols and externals rather than the one true God. Nonetheless, at stake in such spiritualism is not ultimately the denigration of the carnal but rather its elevation in the very name of transcendence.

"What I utterly condemn," Erasmus writes in his 1503 *Enchiridion militis christiani,* in the context of the veneration of saints, "is the fact that they [i.e., saint-worshipers] esteem the indifferent in place of the highest, the nonessentials to complete neglect of what is essential. What is of smallest value spiritually they make the greatest."[51] This language of hierarchies–of high and low, indifferent and essential–reveals Erasmus' commitment to a Platonist, figural tradition. His spiritualism entails an ascent from the mundane to the most high, from the physical to the abstract, but it is an ascent that is impossible unless we "push off," as it were, from that which we would leave behind. Transcendence thus entails a dependence on the very materiality it would overcome. Indeed, ultimately this problem of idolatry–of venerating the low in the place of the most high–leads Erasmus back, this time in specifically Christian and figural terms, to Diotima's logic in Plato's *Symposium*: a logic whereby the material world provides the leverage for a spiritual ascent. "Raise yourself," he urges in his 1503 *Enchiridion,* "as on the steps of Jacob's ladder from the body to the spirit, from the visible to the invisible, from the letter to the mystery, from sensible things to intelligible things."[52]

Where Diotima urged an ascent to the eternal forms, Erasmus envisions the ladder of Jacob's dream (Gen. 28:12), which joined the earth to the heavens. And yet, the rungs that join heaven to earth are themselves composed of earth; they are the fleshly distractions from which we gradually tear ourselves away and on which we gradually raise ourselves up.[53] All the while arguing against a doctrine of works, against the externalization of religion, Erasmus nonetheless treats the flesh as the very vehicle–the Jacob's ladder, no less–by means of which we scale the heavens. His nonessential flesh avails, it would seem, a great deal.

For a Karlstadt or a Zwingli, on the other hand, transcendence is less a matter of weaning than of an outright renunciation. No Jacob's ladder joins flesh to spirit for these writers, but like Erasmus they too will end up elevating the inessential flesh–albeit in purely negative terms. For them, as we shall see in a moment, the prohibited, unavailing flesh becomes a fetish object, granted a supreme importance, as Luther points out, in its very denial. Indeed, from Luther's standpoint, both the radical reform of the Swiss and the moderate reform of Erasmus' Christian humanism turn the flesh into fetish–paradoxically elevated in importance by the very attempt to transcend it. Such reform seeks to overcome the carnality of a doctrine of works, and yet, as Luther will argue, in truth it differs not at all from the "papist" doctrines it abhors. Papist, iconoclast, and humanist alike end up, as Luther puts it, "drowning in the flesh." They, and not Luther, are the non-dualistic thinkers, for ultimately their spirituality becomes indistinguishable from the flesh it denies.

Nowhere does Luther argue more persuasively for this strange collapse of dualism than in his response to Andreas Bodenstein von Karlstadt and the Wittenberg iconoclast movement. Karlstadt had been in Luther's camp since the beginning; it was he who challenged Johann Eck, sharp critic of Luther's Ninety-five Theses, to a public disputation in 1519 on Luther's behalf (the so-called Leipzig Disputation), and it was he who led the reform in Wittenberg when Luther went into hiding following the Diet of Worms. During Luther's year-and-a-half absence, students and townspeople–agitated by radical members of Luther's monastic order–engaged in a number of small riots against the use of images, culminating in late January 1522 when the Wittenberg city council decided to remove images from all houses of worship. Three days after the council's decision, Karlstadt's pamphlet *Concerning the Abolition of Images and that No Beggar shall be among Christians*, hit the streets, initiating the Reformation's first significant discussion of iconoclasm. In February townspeople took the matter into their own hands and broke into a parish church. When Luther returned from hiding a month later, the terms of the debate had already been established.[54]

Karlstadt's main contention against images returned to a concern that the Church had officially resolved as early as 787, at the Second Nicene Council: the problem of the image as *idol*. "That we have images in churches," Karlstadt declared in the opening thesis of *Concerning the Abolition of Images*, "is wrong and contrary to the first commandment: 'Thou shalt not have strange gods'" (quoted in Christensen, 28). For the early Church, however, idolatry had not been an issue; instead, as John Phillips has noted, the need to assimilate pagan artifacts had harmonized with a strongly incarnationist perspective: God had already shown that the earthly world was a fit vessel to embody the sacred. At Nicaea, this view became settled doctrine: the ecumenical council of bishops ruled that, although true worship belongs to God alone, the veneration of images is acceptable since such honor is immediately passed on to its archetype. As likenesses of corporeal things, images could allow man to reach higher, incorporeal truths. For the Second Nicene Council, in other words, the image functioned as a *figure*, its materiality become transparent in the ascent to the realm of spirit.[55]

For Karlstadt, however, this figural defense of images mistook the relationship between flesh and spirit. Drawing heavily on John 6, Karlstadt argued a strict doctrine of the unavailing flesh. The Word of God, he maintained, is spiritual, and it alone profits the believer. No image of Christ could bring us close to Christ, Karlstadt argued, since, as Christ Himself said, such was the work of God alone: "no man can come unto me, except it were given unto him of my Father" (John 6:65, KJV). Indeed, the flesh could only teach us about the flesh, about how Christ looked, how He died, and not at all about *why* He died: "all those who worship God in images, worship in lies, and think of God in semblances and external reports" (quoted in Christensen, 33).

In his own treatise, however, Luther counters Karlstadt by reminding him that the crucial step lies not in outlawing images but in teaching their insignificance: "one pleases God alone through faith" (LW 40, 84). Karlstadt, of course, had also based his position on the doctrine of justification by faith alone: it is thus not Karlstadt's point of departure that Luther will reject. Indeed, in general, Luther's strategy in this debate is not so much to dismiss the iconoclasts as too extreme in their assumptions as it is to chastise them for not being extreme *enough*. In certain ways, of course, Karlstadt and his followers were plenty extreme; the rioting they encouraged horrified Luther, and he feared that their violent measures would only accustom the masses to rebellion, as was already the case with Thomas Münzer's followers in Allstedt (cf. LW 40, 88–90, 104). "Mr. Everybody is not to be toyed with," Luther intoned (LW 40, 105).[56] Nonetheless, while their practical measures might be extreme, their theology, Luther argues, simply revisits a papist doctrine of works, promoting a new type of mortification, "eyne new weyse mortificationis," that entails seeking its own worldly death of the flesh (LW 40, 81; WA 18, 63). In their zeal to implement a doctrine of solafideism, of justification by faith alone, the iconoclasts paradoxically end up replicating the self-mortifying asceticism of the medieval Church. "The flesh is of no avail," Karlstadt and his followers argue, imagining that they have taken solafideism to its logical limit, while indeed their supposedly strict dualism of flesh and spirit has only reproduced the papist error. To strive for the death of the flesh in this life only "means teaching works and the free will all over again" (LW 40, 89).

The problem, Luther argues, lies not with iconoclasm *per se* but rather with its legislation. Insofar as iconoclasm finds its impetus in the First Commandment, the injunction against images must be understood not as a law in itself but as adjunct to the Law of laws: *Thou shalt have no other gods*. Here Luther follows medieval and Roman Catholic practice, listing the prohibition against images (Exod. 20:4) as an integral part of the First Commandment (Exod. 20:1–6).[57] In interpreting the prohibition, Luther argues that context is everything: "'You shall have no [other] gods,' is the key phrase, the standard and the point [*zil*]" of the Commandment. In context it becomes clear that at issue is not idolatry per se, but rather that *Ziel* of the Law itself. At stake with the prohibition against images is our failure to love God *von hertzen* (WA 18, 69).

As Luther points out, by outlawing the use of images, Karlstadt establishes a new legalism to be followed without a "freyem gewissen," without the free conscience that alone heralds our loving fulfillment of God's Law. Not only are his followers then disobedient in the very name of the law, but they are more idolatrous than ever. In devoting themselves to these works, the iconoclasts follow a new Lord, adopting a false assurance or faith, a "falsch vertrawen" in their salvation.[58] Karlstadt's followers, Luther argues, "eusserlich bilde ab thun und das hertz vol goetzen da gegen setzen": outwardly the iconoclasts put away images, but inwardly they put their trust in a new icon—in the work of law itself (WA 18, 68). Karlstadt's iconoclasm is thus dangerously superficial, stripping away external problems while it fills the very heart with idols. In contrast, the real iconoclasm, Luther suggests, would be to destroy those idols in the heart—a task that, by definition, no human work can achieve without the grace of God, since the only way to abolish all false gods is through faith.

Ultimately Karlstadt's teaching reveals the impossible bind of solafideism. If only faith can save us, then, it is true, the flesh is of no avail. And yet, to imagine that one can dispense with this unavailing flesh is only to adopt a false trust, a *falsch vertrawen*, which mires us ever more deeply in sin. The flesh cannot save us, but seeking to renounce it will surely damn us.

> This Karlstadtian abomination is no less effective in destroying the kingdom of Christ and a good conscience, than the papacy has become with its prohibitions regarding food and marriage, and all else that was free and without sin. For eating and drinking are also minor, external things [*gering eusserlich ding*]. Yet to ensnare the conscience with laws in these matters is death for the soul.
>
> (LW 40, 90–91; WA 18, 73)

What Karlstadt's "abomination" shares with the papacy is not simply a doctrine of works but a strategy of fetishization. By prohibiting matters of indifference—those unavailing matters of the flesh like eating, drinking, looking at pictures—both the iconoclasts and the papists transform the *gering eusserlich ding* into an absolute threat: an idol of the heart. To deny the flesh is only to make its hold on us absolute; it is to turn the dead letter into a spiritual law. It is to transform the merely flesh into the deadly fetish.

Images, Luther writes elsewhere, are "neither here nor there, neither evil nor good, we may have them or not, as we please" (LW 51, 81–82; quoted in Christensen, 47). As with all matters of the flesh—indeed, I would argue, as with the flesh itself, as Luther conceives it—the trouble arises not merely when, like the papists, we imagine using these "minor, external things" to our spiritual advantage. Equally problematic is any insistence that such things work to our spiritual *detriment*. Whether prescribed or prohibited, the flesh becomes our idol. As such, it is no longer an external, minor thing, but instead the absolute and inward fetish that defines us.

"The emperor," Luther writes, discussing the iconoclastic controversy of the eighth century, "held that he had the authority to banish the images, but the pope insisted that they should remain, and both were wrong. . . . They wished to make a 'must' out of that which is free. This God cannot tolerate" (quoted in Christensen, 47). Both sides, iconoclast and papist, seek to resolve that Pauline strife of flesh and spirit—the one side through ascetic renunciation and the other by surmounting the flesh on the way to spirit. The two sides fail equally, delivering themselves to a flesh whose claims are the more insistent, the more intractable for the effort. Both sides, iconophobic and iconophilic, *Schwärmer* and papist, drown in a flesh that has taken the place of God. Instead of promoting a sharper reliance on faith, the effort to renounce the flesh proves to be the greatest of all works.

The same paradox of a spiritualism that mires one in the flesh emerges in Luther's Eucharist debates with Swiss reformers Zwingli and Oecolampadius. In the early 1520s, both Zwingli and Oecolampadius adopt a spiritualizing interpretation of the sacrament, viewing the Lord's Supper as a merely symbolic reminder of Christ's new covenant. The words with which Christ instituted the sacrament—"This is my body which is given for you: this do in remembrance of me" and "This cup *is* the new testament in my blood, which is shed for you" (Luke 22:19–20, KJV)—these words, Zwingli and Oecolampadius argue, are to be taken figuratively and not literally. "Tunc corpus Christi editur, cum pro nobis caesum esse creditur," Zwingli writes. The body of Christ is eaten when we believe that it was killed for us.[59] No actual, bodily consumption of Christ's actual, bodily flesh takes place in the sacrament of the Lord's Supper; instead, our *edere* is a mere representation of our *credere*. The "est" of "Hoc est corpus meum" thus designates a trope and not an identity. This bread *signifies* my body, Christ told His disciples. The true consumption of such "bread" is a matter of, and for, faith.[60]

Luther, in response, upholds the doctrine of the Real Presence, insisting that Christ is truly, *leiblich* (bodily or physically) present in the bread and wine of Holy Communion. The Swiss reformers call him a papist and a "Capernaite," or "flesh-eater" for this doctrine; nonetheless, as Luther's analysis shows, it is they and not he who are the real flesh-eaters.[61] Like Karlstadt, Zwingli and Oecolampadius rely upon John 6:63 ("It is the spirit that gives life, the flesh is of no avail"); indeed, for Oecolampadius, John 6:63 is the "iron wall" that no doctrine of the Real Presence can break or scale. But, as Luther argues, the ascetic piety of the Swiss reformers derives from and devolves into a carnal-mindedness from which they never escape.[62] Like Karlstadt–who indeed shared similar Eucharistic views–these reformers reject any doctrine or practice that suggests the magical efficacy of merely outward or fleshly rituals; like Karlstadt, Zwingli and Oecolampadius renounce the profitless flesh in the name of spirituality. But in the process–and once again like Karlstadt–these reformers create more idols than they smash.

The *Schwärmer*, Luther writes in his 1527 Eucharistic treatise ("That These Words of Christ, 'This Is My Body,' etc., Still Stand Firm Against the Fanatics"),

> simply gape and stare at the physical eating, thinking that the divine Word must set forth nothing but spiritual things and have nothing to do with outward, material things. But this is the seed of Münzer's and Karlstadt's spirit, who also wanted to tolerate nothing outward, until they were utterly drowned in flesh.
>
> (LW 37, 135)[63]

To reject the Real Presence is not to escape the flesh but rather to drown in it. Or, alternatively, it is to drown in the *spirit*. "They [i.e., the *Schwärmer*] want nothing but spirit; and indeed, this is what they do have: the devil, who has neither flesh nor bone" (LW 37, 136). To hold fast to a strict assertion that "the flesh is of no avail" is to deny Christ's passion and sacrifice altogether in the name of spirituality. The arguments of the Swiss, Luther points out, take "Christ right out of the garden, the cross and his whole passion, saying that none of these things happened bodily, because of course he had to be bodily present in them all and yet his flesh is of no avail if it is bodily there" (LW 37, 83). Or, as Herman Sasse puts it: "If 'This is my body,' 'this is my blood,' were understood figuratively, then there would be no assurance that 'given for you,' 'shed for you' were to be taken literally" (*This Is My Body*, 329). To deny the Real Presence is equivalently to suffocate in the flesh as deadly fetish *and* to deliver oneself to the fleshless, boneless devil. Either way we look at it, the Swiss views erode the very difference between flesh and spirit. They leave us trapped in a world that is equivocally all flesh or all spirit–a world ultimately, Luther argues, without the Word of God.

Indeed, what Luther–seemingly alone among his contemporaries–posits is a connection between sacrament and Incarnation: at stake with both is the revelation of God's Word. "And the Word was made flesh, and dwelt among us" (John 1:14, KJV). Most fundamentally, Luther's doctrine of the Real Presence drives toward a reconsideration of the Word Made Flesh, and with it a renewed understanding not only of flesh and spirit but also of the covenant that bilaterally binds God to man in the Word of His promise, and man to God through man's faith in that promise. "For where there is the word of a promise-keeping God [*verbum promittentis dei*], there is needed the faith of a man who accepts it [*fides acceptantis hominis*]" (WA 6, 514).[64] For Luther, the sacramental sign–e.g., the water of baptism or the bread and wine of communion–is the sign of God's promise. As such, the sacrament recapitulates the miracle of Incarnation: the sacramental sign is also God's Word Made Flesh. Like Noah's rainbow (Gen. 9:12–17) or Abraham's circumcision (Gen. 17:11), the sacrament is a visible sign of God's covenant; it is an embodiment of God's Word–a palpable token or *Zeichen* of God's faith with us, to be grasped according to our faith in Him. Thus, as early as 1520, Luther argues that God's promises comprise two elements: both a *verbum* and a *signum*, both a word and a sign. The verbal element of God's promise, Luther argues, is the *testament* that appoints us as heirs to His blessing; the sign-element of the promise is the *sacrament* that bears witness to the testament itself, like the "seal" (*Sigill*) or "pledge" (*Pfandt*) that makes a legal document binding. Any sacrament–e.g., the bread and wine of the Lord's Supper–thus confirms our status as the appointed heirs of Christ's sacrifice: the benefactors of his crucified flesh.[65]

> This is what Christ has done in this testament. He has affixed to the words a most precious seal and sign [*sigill und zeychen*]: his own true flesh and blood under the bread and wine. For we poor men, living as we do in our five senses, must always have along with the words at least one outward sign to which we may cling [*daran wir uns halten*] and around which we may gather–in such a way, however, that this sign may be a sacrament, that is, that it

may be external and yet contain [*hab*] and signify [*bedeut*] something spiritual; in order that through the external we may be drawn into the spiritual, comprehending the external with the eyes of the body and the spiritual or inward with the eyes of the heart.

(LW 35, 86; WA 6, 359)

As "eusserlich zeychen," as external sign, the sacrament doesn't so much refer us to a spiritual reality that exists *elsewhere* as it allows us instead to find and hold fast to God's word right in front of us. *Daran wir uns halten*: we cling to the sacramental sign in the way one is said to keep one's promise (*sich an sein Versprechen halten*) or to stick to the facts (*sich an die Tatsachen halten*). We keep to the sign and in so doing the sign allows us to keep the faith.

With this early language of sign and testament, Luther critiques the twelfth-century definition of sacrament as "the efficacious sign of grace" (*efficata signa gratiae*). As he elaborates in his momentous attack on traditional sacramental theology, the 1520 *De Captivate Babylonica*, the problem with the canonical definition is that it forgets about faith, focusing attention on the mere "materia et forma" of the sacrament, and presuming that efficacy lies in the "mortua et occidens litera," in the dead and lethal sign, rather than in the "spiritus" of divine promise and of our faith in that promise (WA 6, 530).[66] Replicating the letter/spirit, form/content language of Origenist allegory, this early critique seems at first glance to promote what Ralph Quere terms a "significationist" approach to sacrament: that is, to assert the merely symbolic aspect of, for instance, the bread and wine of Holy Communion.[67] If the sacrament is only a *sign*–material and external to the spirit–surely it is superfluous to faith, and even dangerous if we rely upon it. From the significationist standpoint, the sacrament as fleshly, *eusserlich* sign merely points to a spiritual content that exists ever elsewhere and with which it cannot coincide. And indeed, thus it is that spiritualist reformers like Zwingli interpret the sacrament of the Lord's Supper: the Eucharist offers a *remembrance* of Christ's sacrifice and not (as the "papists" presumably maintain) a magical reenactment of it.[68] Nothing, Zwingli will argue, *gets done* in the sacrament of the Eucharist; the public fleshly ritual is itself of no avail since it is only the personal, internal movement of God-given faith that can save us. As the merely outward sign of Christ's sacrifice, the Lord's Supper *represents* God's forgiveness but cannot instantiate it. The deeds of man, in other words, can in no manner compel the saving grace of God.[69]

For Zwingli and the Reformed Church he comes to represent, the Eucharistic controversy covers the same ground and works through the same issues as the iconoclastic debate. At stake is the nature and efficacy of the "flesh" in the wake of solafideism. If faith alone saves, then our reliance on the physical eating of physical bread–no less than our reliance on images–runs the risk of idolatry. And to Zwingli, Luther's insistence on the Real Presence can only perversely double the requirements of faith. Luther, Zwingli charges, posits *two* faiths for salvation: "one that is trust in Christ and another which requires belief that the bread is flesh" (Quere, 62).

However, Zwingli most profoundly misses the point of Luther's sacramental theology: for Luther, to have faith in Christ is, first and foremost, to take Him at His Word. The doctrine of Real Presence doesn't require an *additional* faith; it is instead a doctrine necessitated by our acceptance of the Word of a promise-keeping God to begin with.

> Faith in God's Word is necessary for us, because it has been spoken in order that we should believe it, and God wills and demands of us to have faith where his Word is. Now, there stand God's words, which embrace and comprehend the body of Christ, saying that he is present.
>
> (LW 37, 140)

How God's bodily presence in the Supper takes place is not for us to know, Luther argues; instead, we are simply to *believe* it: to take Christ simply at His word, the way we hold fast to a promise (cf. LW 37, 64). Or, as Luther puts it in *De Captivate Babylonica*, we are not to ask *how* Christ is in the bread, but instead simply to believe *that* He is in the bread–and in so doing, we cling simply to His words in themselves: "'Hoc est corpus meum, das ist meyn leyb'" (cf. WA 6, 511). Breaking into German vernacular ("das ist meyn leyb") in the middle of his erudite, clergy-directed Latin, Luther reminds his readers that they *do*, in fact, understand the words of institution–that this is not some scholastic formula, *hoc est corpus meum*, but the intimate words of a promise-keeping Lord. "This is my body." Christ is talking to *us*.

In this way, underlying Luther's doctrine of the Real Presence is not—as Zwingli imagines—the invocation of a second order of faith requisite for our salvation, but rather Luther's redefinition of faith *tout court*. Faith, Luther suggests, is not propositional but *performative*; at issue, in other words, is not that we accept a given state of affairs as fact—that, for instance, we believe *that* the bread is flesh, or even *that* Christ died for our sins—but rather a matter of our performative stance within discourse: in faith, we accept God's Word as a promise, spoken to us. Spiritual faith, Luther argues, is then faith not in the content of God's Word, but in its *form*. It is faith in God's Word *as covenant*.[70] At stake in our response to the Word is hence nothing less than the First Commandment. In accepting God's covenant with us, we commit ourselves to the one true God. In this way, our faith yokes us to God just as His promise binds Him to us.

> Promise and faith, are necessarily yoked together [*sunt simul necessaria*]. No one can believe if there is no promise. If there is no faith, a promise is useless, because faith is its counterpart and completion [*cum per fidem stabiliatur et impleatur*].
> ("Pagan Servitude," 277; WA 6, 517)

Faith is not a belief in the fulfillment of God's promise but rather, Luther argues, such faith is itself the fulfillment of promising. "Where there is the word of a promise-keeping God, there is needed the faith of a man who accepts it." It is in this sense that our faith is *performative*: our faith consists in our assent to a vow, rather than in our mental pictures about a present or future state of affairs. Love "clings more to his [i.e., the beloved's, Christ's] words than to that which the words say" (LW 37, 76). Faith does not rest on propositions; to the believer, as to the lover, it is the beloved's *act of saying* that alone matters. To recall Benveniste's terms from chapter 2, it is the *énonciation*, the utterance, and not the *énoncé* or statement, to which we cling when we cling to the Word of God. Like a bride who responds to the vow of the bridegroom, our faith, our *fidelity* consists in our acceptance of God's pledge.[71] And also like a bride, this acceptance is never performed once and for all, but requires instead a daily and constant renewal—a reaffirmation as long as we live.

Whence Luther's emphasis throughout his career on the need for daily prayer, for continual reading and practice in the articles of the Catechism "so that, through such reading, speaking and thinking, the Holy Spirit is present [*gegen wertig*]" (WA 30, 1, 127). Through our constant clinging to God's Word, the Spirit remains constantly present. Our faith and God's Word counterbalance and complete each other—neither, it would seem, can exist without the other. "Belief is impossible without a promise to believe in, and a promise is void when it is not believed" ("Pagan Servitude," 301). The formulation knits a beautiful symmetry between accepting man and promise-keeping God, invoking the intimacy of a dialogue. And yet, this picture of mutual fulfillment, of faith and promise intertwined, is curiously absolute and self-enclosed. Just what, for instance, is being promised here? And in accepting God's promise, just what is it that man holds fast? The dialogue of faith and promise as Luther imagines it is tautological, defining a self-referential loop between vow and belief without allusion either to content or to context. Sheer, absolute form, the speech-acts are as balanced as they are empty: "I promise you"–"I believe you."

Indeed, Luther's formulation radicalizes the promissory logic of Christian *figura*. For Paul, Tertullian, and of course for Augustine, it is time that circumscribes both our faith and God's promise. It is time that offers a context for God's Word, time that fleshes out our faith. Legible in past and present figures, God's promise is fulfilled in the fullness of time. Or perhaps we should say that God's promise makes time itself legible, for if it is accurate to say that divine promises are fulfilled in time, it is equally accurate to say that such promises reveal time itself as full–as unified, completed, significant. Governed by the telos of God's will, in a figural cosmos each transient *now* tropes between an expectant past and a consummated future–and thus human time borrows the structure of promising even while promising finds its meaning in time.

But for Luther, promising finds its meaning only in faith, and human history is the history of that faith–a history of clinging to the Word.

> God never has dealt, and never does deal, with mankind
> at any time otherwise than by the word of promise. Nei-
> ther can we, on our part, ever have to do with God other-
> wise than through faith in His word and promise.
>
> ("Pagan Servitude," 277)

God's promise is singular, eternal and absolute; it is the Word itself, unbounded and unchanged by past or future and yet visible throughout the history of man's faith. But such history remains in an important sense uneventful, since it tells the same story over and over again. This is not a prophetic history–not a history where promises are first made and later kept (i.e., fulfilled). Or, rather, Luther redefines the idea of prophecy, arguing that the prophet's task is not to reveal God's plan so much as it is "to hold the people in faith in the coming Christ; and so they clung to Christ with the Word, they believed in him as well as we now believe in and cling to him" (WA 19, 388; quoted in Bornkamm, 109). The Advent is foretold, to be sure, and yet Luther refuses to define prophecy in figural terms–or to imagine the faith it inspires as the anticipation of future events. The emphasis for Luther's prophet lies not on an anticipated fulfillment but rather on the present moment of faith. The people clung to Christ just as we do now– they held to God's Word as we do today. Thus, where Augustine surveyed the faith of the Jews in figural terms, arguing that the patriarchs defined themselves in light of their future obsolescence, Luther sees Old Testament faith as an end in itself. He describes Adam, for instance, as one who waited patiently for the woman who would bruise the serpent's heel; Adam, Luther tells us, "died in this faith and expectation" ("Pagan Servitude," 274). Unlike Augustine's Old Testament patriarchs, who play their present role in light of a future fulfillment, Adam's life is unconsummated– fulfilled only in holding fast to the promise of God.[72] And yet, we who come after Adam, after Mary, live and die no differently if we are to live in faith.

"Faith rests upon history," writes Luther in his 1527–1530 Lectures on Isaiah, urging us to "beware of allegories" that might obscure the Word of God (WA 31[II], 242–43; quoted in Bornkamm, 91–92). What would have happened, Luther elsewhere asks, if Abraham had not attended to the "simple word" of God's command when he was asked to sacrifice Isaac? "Had he proceeded to dispute with God, like our fanatics . . . or had he tried to invert God's words, what sort of blessing would he have obtained? Just the same as Lucifer merited in heaven!" (LW 37, 129). To read allegorically, Luther suggests, is potentially to dispute with God–to put personal inclination over the commandment of His Word. The counterexample to Abraham is of course Eve, who is tempted by the serpent's question "'Why has God commanded this?'" (LW 37, 129). Where Abraham hearkens without question, Eve fails, unable simply to take the Lord at His word. In her desire for reason, for a meaning and context behind the Word, she seeks a fulfillment that lies beyond the sheer movement of faith. "God wills and demands of us to have faith where his Word is" (LW 37, 140). As we've already seen, for Luther God's Word is irrevocably double-sided. We have now come to the core of that teaching: if God's word of salvation simultaneously bespeaks our sentence as sinners, if His promises are all commandments, it is because the Word of God requires our faith. To hold fast in faith is to recognize God's claim on us. As the promise that commands our belief, as the command-ment that performs His promise, the Word of God in every sense binds us. It binds us *to Him*.

And thus it is that *faith rests upon history*. Luther becomes increasingly distrustful of allegory in his debates of the 1520s when he sees men like Zwingli transform divine promise into human trope.[73] Figural interpretations put human reason before God-given faith. They allow us to avoid God's Word altogether. "With this rancor [of reason] . . . my dear fanatics prepare the way for the vir-tual denial of Christ, God, and everything. In part, already, they have made a start at believing nothing at all" (LW 37, 53).

How far we've come from Augustine. For Augustine and the figural tradition he helped define, there could be no faith without allegory. Without allegory, the Word of God was trapped in the past–made irrelevant, inaccessible to the present moment of faith. To *take it and read* was to read allegorically, to gloss over the cir-cumstances of history, the confines of the original context, and to hold the text in one's own hands, as one's personal possession, written for one's own sake. But for Luther, who approaches Scrip-ture as a humanist, confident in his ability to forge a link with the past, the transparency that allegory achieves for the text has become a problem in its own right. Luther's battle is not to render the text transparent, but to reveal once again the *alien* Word of God: the Word that comes from beyond ourselves, as promise and as law.[74] This is the Word revealed, in particular places and things and moments–the Word Made Flesh and thus made available to our grasp. Faith rests upon history because it relies on the external presence of God's Word in a particular sacrament, in a particular *signum*. Without this particularity, without this presence within

reach and yet outside ourselves, the Word would not exist for us—
it would have no tangible, *leiblich* reality upon which we could rely.
Thus the very particularity that Augustine's *figura* elides, glosses
over in the name of essential truth, is for Luther the *sine qua non* of
our faith.

> See, the bright rays of the sun are so near you that they
> pierce into your eyes or your skin so that you feel it, yet
> you are unable to grasp them and put them into a box,
> even if you should try forever. . . . So too with Christ:
> although he is everywhere, he does not permit himself to
> be so caught and grasped; he can easily shell himself, so
> that you get the shell and not the kernel. Why? Because it
> is one thing if God is present, and another if he is present
> for you. He is there for you when he adds his Word and
> binds himself, saying, "Here you are to find me."
>
> (LW 37, 68)

Christ is everywhere, and nowhere. He fills all creation, and
yet He can only be reached through faith. He is everywhere present, but only present *for us* in His revealed Word. And yet,
although bound up in particular signs, although revealed in particular places and moments, the Word remains absolute. In this way,
the history upon which Luther's faith rests is, as we've already suggested, curiously contentless and lacking in detail. It is a spare history, telling the same revolving story of promise and faith, of law
and works, over and over again. The particulars of this history are
in this sense meaningless; the signs to which God's Word is bound
are arbitrary. In this sense Zwingli and Karlstadt are right: the flesh
is of no avail. And yet, meaningless and trivial as they are, such
fleshly details are indispensable. Anything—Isaac who was mere
flesh but was promised through God's word, or a side of beef—anything at all is useful, Luther tells us, if it is "embraced and presented
in God's Word":

> Even the devil, death, sin, hell, and all kinds of trouble
> would be nothing but benefit and advantage if they were
> presented to us as embraced in God's Word, and were
> believed by us.
>
> (LW 37, 134–35)

Truly the *Schwärmer* are right; faith is all that matters. And yet, there is no faith without promise–and, for us, there is no promise without the *Sigill*, the sacrament that seals our faith.

By insisting on particularity, Luther reveals the limitations of the radical view of an unavailing flesh. At the same time, Luther strikes down the presumptions of traditional *figura* where the Christian relationship to the Word requires the troping effacement of context. The *propter nos* of Pauline allegory is replaced, by Luther, with the idea of a Word made present in a particular place at a particular time *for us*. But by the same token, although he insists on the Word's particularity, Luther refuses to domesticate it or cut it down to size; God's promise remains absolute, its claim on our faith remains infinite. Through his translations, sermons, catechisms, pamphlets, Bible illustrations, and the like, Luther certainly brings the Word of God closer to his coreligionists, rendering it an intimate part of daily life. But he brings the Word close in all of its strangeness, in all its unreasonable and alienating demand. "Hoc est corpus meum, das ist meyn leyb." Through the vernacular, Luther reminds us that we *do* understand Christ's words–and yet at the same time he also chides the scholar who would make sense of these words, rationalizing and allegorizing them into something human-sized. In this way, the "simple sense" of Scripture upon which Luther insists that we rest is hardly the most reasonable or comfortable sense of Scripture. At its most simple, indeed, the Word of God is the hardest to swallow.

And here we finally return to Luther's doctrine of the Eucharist. By insisting on the Real Presence, as we have said, Luther insists that we take Christ at His word: to cling to the words of institution is not to believe in some second-order reality alongside our faith in Christ; instead, it is the requirement for our faith in Christ to begin with. But even further, at stake with the Real Presence is that sacramental unity of *verbum* and *signum* thanks to which we "poor men, living in our five senses" are able, literally, to swallow God's Word: to take in and accept His promise.[75] For men like Zwingli, faith in Christ may be likened to eating–but it is a consumption that remains "mere" figure; a consumption that is purely metaphorical, spiritual, as in the central Zwinglian text, John 6: "I am the living bread which came down from heaven: if any man eat of this bread, he shall live for ever: and that bread that I will give is my flesh, which I will give for the life of the world" (John 6:51, KJV). The physical eating of sacrament is not to be confused with this spiritual "eating" that constitutes faith. The Lord's Supper can symbolize the movement of faith, but it cannot take its place. For Zwingli, to assert otherwise is either to insist upon a doctrine of works or to mistake metaphor for literal meaning and to join the Capernaites in a literal cannibalism of Christ.

But it is the *Schwärmer* who are the real flesh-eaters, Luther reveals, because it is they who sever the sacramental sign from the Word of God.

> The fanatics are the real Capernaites, for the Capernaites also divided the work from the Word and fastened on the physical eating of flesh, just as our fanatics do. They excise and set aside the words in which the spiritual eating consists and meanwhile gape and gawk at the physical eating, like fools who look someone in the face and stare with fixed eyes, so that they cannot perceive the words clearly confronting them, "Take, eat, this is my body."
>
> (LW 37, 93)

The Swiss distinguish between literal, physical eating and the figurative, spiritual eating of faith, and they strive in the name of righteousness to keep the two distinct. But, once again, their efforts to establish a purely spiritual sphere of action leave them on par with the worst of flesh-eaters. Luther, on the other hand, agrees with the Swiss that faith consists in a spiritual eating–but this eating, he argues, is in no sense merely figurative. Instead, faith, he argues, is quite literally the consumption of the Word of God. Or rather, if the very notion of a "spiritual eating" is not exactly a literal term, nor is it exactly a figure. To call faith a spiritual eating is to speak precisely, but by way of *catachresis*, where the "literal" name of a thing is irrevocably "figural."[76] In his characteristic manner Luther thus rejects any clean separation between the "leiblich" and the "geistlich." Instead, he argues for an intensification of dualism; embraced within the sacrament, defining its not-so-simple "unity," is the twin pulse of God's historical word: letter and figure, flesh and spirit, *signum* and *verbum*. Thanks to such dialectical, double-sided unity, "the mouth eats physically for the heart and the heart eats spiritually for the mouth,

and thus both are satisfied and saved by one and the same food"
(LW 37, 93). In this way, the sacrament offers in *one and the same
food*, a food/"food" that is at once literal and metaphorical. The
flesh does the work of the spirit and vice versa. The mouth takes
in the physical sign of God's Word, but it needs the heart to recognize this sign *as* sign. And yet, the heart cannot lay hold of the
sign by itself. Without the heart, the mouth eats only flesh–but
without the mouth, the heart "eats" nothing at all.

> This word of God is the beginning, the foundation, the
> rock upon which afterward all works, words, and
> thoughts of man must build. This word man must grate-
> fully accept. He must faithfully believe the divine promise.
> . . . This trust and faith is the beginning, middle, and end
> of all works and righteousness.
>
> (LW 35, 82)

In the Eucharist Luther offers an instance of our best-case
response to the Word of God–the best-case instance of our obedience to and acceptance of the divine promise. In the Supper we
reveal ourselves in our entirety: we are both strong and weak,
saints and sinners, our flesh and spirit mutually reliant but mutually helpless, each bespeaking the frailty of the other, both bound
together indissolubly while yet the tension between them remains
unresolved. The heart cannot absorb food any more than the
mouth can take in a promise, but the true fulfillment of God's
Commandment would require that we do both: that we reconcile
that strife between flesh and spirit so that our works might satisfy
God's Law. This we cannot do. In the Eucharist, however, we
accomplish the next best thing. Our physical eating cannot
embody our faith, but nor does it merely symbolize a faith that
would remain forever distant and elsewhere. Its relation to that
odd catachresis–the spiritual eating that is faith–will remain tanta-
lizingly, frustratingly indeterminate. And yet, thanks to the Word
Made Flesh, our physical eating of the sacrament at least gives us
something to chew on: food for thought indeed.

FOUR

Willful Abuse: The Canker and the Rose

Take all these similes to your owne command.
                    –Shakespeare, *A Lover's Complaint*[1]

As figures be the instruments of ornament in euery language, so be they also in a sorte abuses or rather trespasses in speach, because they passe the ordinary limits of common vtterance, and be occupied of purpose to deceiue the eare and also the minde, drawing it from plainnesse and simplicitie to a certaine doublenesse, whereby our talke is the more guilefull & abusing.
                    –Puttenham, *The Arte of English Poesie*[2]

THE ABUSE OF FIGURE

For Luther, the flesh is no figure; its opposition to spirit is absolute. Here Luther's views are strikingly original–distinguishing him from other reformers no less than from the Roman Catholic Church. For other Protestants–like the Swiss reformers Zwingli and Oecolampadius, and the second-generation reformers like Calvin whom they inspire–the doctrine of justification by faith entails a critique of any effort to embody divinity in "flesh": in, that is to say, the material world, be it bread, or wine, or icon. Such Protestants indeed insist upon a radical doctrine of figurality: for them the flesh is "mere" figure; it can at best only symbolize a spiritual world from which it is forever foreclosed. But Luther's rejection of iconoclasm and insistence on Christ's Real Presence in the bread and wine of the Lord's Supper signal a subtler and more difficult stance. For Luther spirit cannot be reconciled to the flesh[3]–but nor can it be divorced from it. We must precisely *live* the irreconcilability of flesh and spirit. We cannot stand above the strife that defines us and denounce the flesh's inadequacy–we must, instead, *embody* that inadequacy. The flesh is no figure of spirit; it does not, as the "papists" maintain, instantiate spirit–but nor does it merely symbolize it, as the Puritans will argue. Instead: indissoluble, irreconcilable, the claims of flesh and spirit permeate the whole of human life.

By decisively rejecting the language of flesh-as-figure, Luther's theology forces open the poetic problem that defines Shake-speare's Sonnets:[4] the problem of *catachresis*–or, the *figure of Abuse*, as Puttenham calls it.[5] While, as we shall see, for Puttenham (who follows Quintilian in this point), catachresis is a necessary function of language–a seeming ornament that we seemingly cannot do without–modern readers have tended to characterize the figure as an extravagant linguistic vice. Such readers have tended to invert and qualify Puttenham's terminology: for these readers, catachre-sis is not the *figure* of abuse in general, but the *abuse* of a given figure in particular.[6] Thus, the OED defines the term as an "abuse or perversion of a trope or metaphor"–an abuse that entails a mis-application of names or an improper use of words. Catachresis, according to one influential modern handbook, "improperly" applies a term to that thing "which it does not properly denote." Its terms violently "wrenched from common usage,"[7] catachresis is often glossed as a "mixed" or "implied" metaphor; its language is "extravagant," "far-fetched." The emphasis here lies on the vio-lence, extremism, and torsion entailed by the figure, although such vices can become virtues within a masculinist aesthetic of genius. Accordingly, Sr. Miriam Joseph commends the figure's use in Shakespeare's powerful hands; indeed, the trope "forges sudden concentrations of meaning" and becomes a mark of the poet's sublimity, securing the "compression, energy, and intensity which characterize great poetry."[8]

Understood simply as a mixed or excessive metaphor, cat-achresis constitutes an unwarranted and entirely avoidable breach in propriety.[9] It is in such terms that the author of the first-century treatise *Rhetorica ad Herennium*, distinguishes catachresis as wrong-ful abuse (*abusio*) from the appropriate appropriations of metaphor (*translatio*). "Metaphor occurs when a word applying to one thing is transferred to another, because the similarity seems to justify this transference." Catachresis on the other hand entails a transfer based not on justifiable similitude, but on mere proximity. "Catachresis is the inexact use of a like and kindred word in place of the precise and proper one" (*Ad Herennium* 4.34.45, 4.33.45).[10] Quintilian's definition, however, distinguishes this abuse from *acyron*–"impropriety"–characterizing catachresis as a *necessary* abuse: "These facts [e.g., that many neologisms and onomatopoeia are impermissible in Latin] make *catachresis*, which we rightly call 'abuse,' all the more necessary. By this term is meant the practice of adapting the nearest available term to describe something for which no actual term exists" (*Institutio Oratoria* 8.6.34).[11] Quintilian's definition of catachresis as *necessaria* deeply complicates the distinction between abuse and metaphor; indeed, at one point in his discussion he seems to include catachresis within metaphor, while at other points he suggests that catachresis entails a closer relation to things than metaphor does.[12] It is small wonder that Quintilian's terms here, as one modern scholar writes, are "inconsistent"; the problem is less a fault of his exposition than it is a symptom of the oxymoronic nature of the figure he describes.[13] As that contradiction in terms–a *necessary* abuse–Quintilian's *abusio* destabilizes the notion of propriety itself, suggesting the ultimate untenability of any hard and fast distinction between abuse and translation.

The stakes of the problem become even clearer when we examine Puttenham's text:

> But if for lacke of naturall and proper terme or worde we take another, neither naturall nor proper and do vntruly applie it to the thing which we would seeme to expresse, and without any iust inconuenience, it is not then spoken by this figure *Metaphore* or of *inuersion* as before, but by plaine abuse, as he that bad his man go into his library and set him his bowe and arrowes, for in deede there was neuer a booke there to be found, or as one should in reproch say to a poore man, thou raskall knaue, where *raskall* is properlly the hunters terme giuen to young deere, leane & and out of season, and not to people: or as one said very pretily in this verse.
>
> *I lent my loue to losse, and gaged my life in vaine.*
>
> Whereas this worde *lent* is properly of mony or some such other thing, as men do commonly borrow, for vse to be repayed againe, and being applied to loue is vtterly

> abused, and yet very commendably spoken by vertue of this
> figure. For he that loueth and is not beloued againe, hath no
> lesse wrong, than he that lendeth and is neuer repayde.
>
> (3.17.9–10 [150])

The catachrestic word, as Puttenham defines it, is "utterly abused
and yet commendably spoken." Marking an improper use of language, catachresis nonetheless intervenes where propriety itself is
lacking: where "for lacke of naturall and proper terme or worde we
take another." Catachresis thus compensates for an original lack in
the proper order of nature; a lack that compromises the very
notion of origin itself. "Signs are called proper [*propria*]," Augustine tells us, "when they are used to signify those things on account
of which they were instituted. . . . Signs are translated [*translata*,
i.e., figurative] when the things themselves which we signify with
proper words are taken up [*usurpantur*] to signify something else"
(*De Doctrina Christiana* 2.10.15). The translation or "transport" of
figure, as Puttenham calls it ("what els is your *Metaphor* but an
inuersion of sence by transport," 3.7.1 [128]), implies a narrative
of sorts: a linear succession from original institution to secondary
use.[14] Figure, as we've already seen in our discussion of Augustine
in chapter 1, *follows* sign: figures are logically dependent upon, pos-
terior to signs, since the act of translation that defines them presupposes an initially "proper" act of naming. Language, according
to this view, thus begins in those originary moments of institution—those moments of naming—that bind signs to things. Before
a name can be "translated" from one use to the next, it must then
first sustain a *proper* usage; names, in other words, are *properties* of
things—and figuration consists in the appropriation of such property. Or rather—to adopt Augustine's precise terminology—figures
entail a "usurpation," a transfer of power and function. It is not the
name that is appropriated, but the signifying power associated
with the name; what is transferred or transported is the agency of
the letter. In this way, the *res* originally designated by a name now
becomes a *signum* of its own. A figure, then, is a second-order sign.

Catachresis, however, entails a transfer and an appropriation
where no proper name exists; in this way it calls the secondariness
of figure into question. In catachresis, translation is not a secondary effect of naming, but rather its primary and originary source.
Furthermore, the same secondariness of figure that sustains a lin-

ear narrative of translation also vouchsafes that ethics of use/enjoyment (Augustine's *uti/frui* distinction from *Doctrina* 1.3.3) so crucial in defining, as Luther would put it, the difference between *Gott* and *Abgott*: between a life built on the certainties of faith and a life grounded in idolatry. As misuse–ab-use–catachresis upsets the economic calculations that organize, defer, and ultimately overcome the pleasures of the flesh.[15] Some things are to be enjoyed and some things are to be used, as Augustine tells us; and where there is usage, there are signs, referring and deferring us to the end (both terminus and telos) of all use: the End that alone signifies, and satisfies, in and of itself.[16] Augustine's figural universe is hierarchically structured around what Derrida has called the "teleology of meaning" ("White Mythology," 270): signs refer to things, and taken as or "translated" into figure, those things refer to other things, and so forth, until at last we arrive at the ground of all figure: the *Verbum* of God. Catachresis, however, is an abuse that can never be set right since it collapses any such teleology. It names a translation, as Puttenham points out, that can never be translated back to a proper name.[17]

As the figure of abuse, of misappropriation, catachresis thus names that "figure" that confounds the distinction between proper and translated uses of language. In this way, Puttenham's figure of abuse announces an abuse at the very heart of figure itself: an abuse *of* figure that upsets the order of language, disrupting the distinction between vehicle and tenor, between the letter and the spirit. To return to the theological terms with which we began: for Luther it is, we might say, as an ab-use of figure, of *figura*, that the Word of God binds us; it is, we might say, as a *catachresis* that God's Word commands us, committing us to an impossible promise and judging us under an infinite law. In short, just as *figura* defines the poetics implicit in Augustine's Christian doctrine, so does *catachresis* name the master trope at the heart of Luther's reformation. If Luther's critique of Roman Catholic piety constitutes a critique of *figura*, it does so by revealing in figure's place a far more disquieting theology of catachresis. Where Augustine's figural world satisfyingly distinguished between letter and spirit, Jew and Christian, sinner and saint, Luther's world collapses the narrative order that allows such distinctions. And with this collapse, all certitude vanishes. Am I saved? Am I damned? Sinner and saint, flesh and spirit, all at once: time in Luther's world is not full, for it does not answer all questions, nor heal the divide between flesh and spirit. If Augustine's world was a figural one, Luther's world is catachrestic, continually invoking undecidable and yet unavoidable oppositions.

The shift in perspective, from a figural worldview to a catachrestic one, enables an equally decisive shift in poetics. Hovering on the brink of conversion, Petrarch transforms the theology of figure into a poetics of deferred meaning. What animates his poetic figures is his refusal to decide between flesh and spirit. As we shall see, Shakespeare's poetic stance is, however, somewhat different: he *cannot* decide between flesh and spirit. Indeed, that is the poetic problem that the sixteenth century inherits from Luther–although few writers confront the legacy in terms as precise and thoroughgoing as Shakespeare, who, as many readers have recognized, writes his sonnets belatedly, as if to sum up an entire poetic tradition. It is Shakespeare, after all, whose Christian name itself prompts a consideration not only of Luther's legacy but of the very idea of legacy–of a *will* that outlives its author. The onomastic and deictic play so crucial to Petrarch (and so readily imitated by the sonneteers who pick up his book and follow his example) offers a medium, as we've seen, for a highly self-conscious figurality. But for Shakespeare such verbal self-consciousness tends instead to unravel figurality, forcing our eyes not to the turnings of trope so much as to the catachrestic improprieties of the proper name. *Will.*

It is possible that Shakespeare read Luther–after 1585 increasingly few of Luther's texts were translated and published in England, but they were by no means rare. Even so, my argument does not require that Shakespeare did read Luther, nor (as I've already argued) does it entail any assumptions about the poet's own religious faith or upbringing beyond the fact of his texts emerging within a culture marked by the history of figure.[18] It is a Lutheran universe that Shakespeare's sonnets invoke–or rather it is a Lutheran universe that the book called *Shakespeare's Sonnets* taken as a whole invokes. Read as a whole, the book deploys a theology of catachresis in order to establish a poetics of collapsed ideals in place of Petrarch's poetics of deferred meaning. Indeed, the text's much-cited aura of retrospective authority–of a lyric voice that speaks at the end and expense of an entire sonneteering tradition– that voice of disillusioned and belated authority, I would argue, presupposes a sustained and pervasive critique of the theology of *figura*; presupposes, that is to say, a culture that has come to distrust figures. Central to the poetic imagination of *Shakespeare's Sonnets*, then, is just this critique and this distrust. Figure is on trial throughout the text, as the poems portray the impossibility of telling the tenor from the vehicle, the original from the copy, the true from the counterfeit, and the stirrings of the spirit from the bawdy prickings of the flesh.

As we shall see, from the very start of his sequence Shakespeare links the collapse of ideals to a world in which flesh is no longer reconciled to spirit and time is no longer full. Niggardly prodigal, the young man addressed in these initial poems withholds himself from propagation and thus consumes himself to death, destroying himself by failing to produce others like him. "From fairest creatures we desire increase, / That thereby beauties *Rose* might neuer die,/ But as the riper should by time decease, / His tender heire might beare his memory" (1:1–4).[19] Through the young man, Shakespeare envisions a world of sheer mortality: the "rose of beauty" itself–the very ideal of ideals–has become curiously mortal, its spiritual "memory" coterminous with the bloom that was merely meant to convey it. Like a just-so story, the young man's failure to produce an heir explains a more general breakdown in the tenor/vehicle logic of figure. In this world the flesh no longer bears the spirit. Instead, time threatens to bury both.

The rose of beauty that Shakespeare's poetry depicts is, I argue, best understood not as a poetic figure but rather as the "abuse" of figure that calls into question the difference between a fallen world of flesh and a transcendent world of spirit. As we shall see, in several crucial sonnets Shakespeare explores the catachrestic relationship between the rose and the canker. In addition to naming a type of rose–the dog rose or brier rose (*rosa canina*), the most common rose in the south of England and one that flowers only in June and July–in Elizabethan English "canker" also denotes two types of parasites: both the chancre or gangrenous sore of cancer, and the larva that invades blossoms and foliage, consuming the bud slowly and secretly from the inside out. On the one hand, then, the canker is that dog rose that counterfeits the rose. Its beauty is, literally, *inessential* since the canker lacks that sweet perfume or essence that makes the rose, whatever its name, truly beautiful. The beauty of the canker blossom is, Shakespeare tells us, only show. But the canker is also that cancer or worm hidden *within* the rose, whose presence we may fear but cannot necessarily confirm: the canker is that hidden blemish that falsifies beauty, invisibly tainting its essence. Ultimately these poems suggest that the difference between rose and canker, between a true beauty and a dog, is undecidable.

In the so-called dark lady sonnets,[20] Shakespeare pushes this undecidability to the extreme, declaring the ultimate loss of ideals: "Sweet beauty hath no name" (127:7). At this extreme of disillusionment, Shakespeare's figures collapse inward, into almost unreadable amphibology. In such puns Shakespeare's poetics achieves a kind of zero-degree of maximum density: low and high, false and true, flesh and spirit are all pressured into a single word. Yet such pressure forces us, literally, to read Shakespeare's *will*: a word that simultaneously conveys rational volition, irrational desire, vagina, penis, future auxiliary, female "common place" (the dark lady's vagina is that "baye where all men ride," 137:10), common male proper name (the poet's name, his friend's name?, the dark lady's husband's name?) and, of course, testament.[21] To read Shakespeare's *will* is to read the implosion of flesh into spirit, of spirit into flesh.

And yet, *will* is not Shakespeare's last word. The chapter concludes with a reading of *A Lover's Complaint*, the poem that closes *Shakespeare's Sonnets* and whose doubled voice, exploded narrative frame, and corrupt authority finally acknowledge the impossible task of laying beauty's carcass to rest.

AUTHORIZING ORIGINS: *"a Booke called Shakespeares sonnettes"*

Virtually all we know about the origins of the book called *Shakespeare's Sonnets* derives from a slim notation in the Stationers' Register: "20 Maij Thomas Thorpe Entred for his copie vnder thandes of master Wilson and master Lownes Warden a Booke called Shakespeares sonnettes."[22] On May 20, 1609, the publisher Thomas Thorpe registered his copy of the book called *Shakespeare's Sonnets* with the Stationers' Company–the printers guild. The license he thereby obtained certified his sole "copy right": before 1709 the only literary property rights protected in England were the rights of the bookseller who intended to reproduce a text and not those of the author who first had penned it.[23] Thorpe exercised his prerogative by having the shop of George Eld print some number of the ephemeral, unbound quartos. Thirteen of these volumes are extant.[24] It has proved impossible to trace any one of these surviving volumes definitively back to the hand of William Shakespeare: we know who published the book, where it was printed, whose name is on its title page, and where it was sold. We know that two of the poems (138 and 144) appeared in slightly different form in the 1599 anthology *The Passionate Pilgrim*. This volume, published by William Jaggard (the future publisher of the First Folio), also bears William Shakespeare's name on the title page, although most of its content—including a version of Marlowe and Raleigh's exchange "The Passionate Shepherd" and "The Nymph's Reply"—is thought to belong to other poets.[25] We know that, in 1598, Francis Meres described a "mellifluous & hony-tongued *Shakespeare*" whose "sugred Sonnets" apparently circulated "among his priuate friends."[26] And we also know that it was a full century before the poems of the 1609 quarto (Q) were reprinted.[27] Ambiguous and circumstantial, the available evidence has convincingly supported diametrically opposed interpretations. Date(s) of composition, authenticity, arrangement, addressees, historical references, and autobiographical contexts: these are all matters that serious critics have continued seriously to debate.

Given the ambiguity of the available facts, it is not surprising that critics have been unable to resolve their questions about the book called *Shakespeare's Sonnets*. What *is* surprising, however, is the considerable interest that such questions still hold even for critics profoundly opposed to biographical criticism. Why has the question of origins—of the author behind these poems and the circumstances, real or fictive, that begat them—continued to animate debate? Even critics who would reject the logocentric metaphysics implied by a sonnet like 76—"euery word doth almost fel [tell] my name, / Shewing their birth, and where they did proceed" (76:7–8)—struggle with the question of these poems' paternity.[28] Even after the Death of the Author, we cannot seem to let daddy go.[29]

The question of authorization is a paradigm case in point. The debate over whether Shakespeare authorized the publication of Q reveals the strange persistence of biography in our consideration of the sonnets. At the center of the debate is the place of the author in our reading of these poems. It is thus a debate we will need to consider at length before we can justify our own readings of the sonnets, generalizing about "Shakespeare's" meaning or about "his" text's place in literary tradition. But furthermore, at issue here is the very authority inscribed in our reading practices; this is the authority a figural tradition seeks to define, authorizing the reader's own appropriation of textual forms and meanings. As we shall see, to consider Q's authorization is, then, to consider the role of *figura* in the book called *Shakespeare's Sonnets*.

At stake with the authorization controversy is precisely our ability to trace the book called *Shakespeare's Sonnets* back to its putative origin. But unlike debates about canonicity, the concern with authorization addresses the question of origin only obliquely. If the manuscript that Thorpe acquired was published without authorial consent we can have no guarantee that the publication reflects any single or coherent authorial design. Like the 1599 *Passionate Pilgrim*, the book called *Shakespeare's Sonnets* could well be a random collection of poems transcribed not from autograph manuscripts but rather from commonplace books and from memory—poems that not only were composed originally by different authors but that have been reshaped by the processes of memorial transcription.[30] But significantly, no modern reader asks whether *The Passionate Pilgrim* was an authorized text. External evidence, decisive in this case (unlike the ambiguous evidence for Q), tells us that Shakespeare could not have written all of the poems, and even that one of the authors was furious that his work had been published under Shakespeare's name.[31] With *The Passionate Pilgrim*, instead of authorization, the critical question becomes whether to admit the text, in whole or in part, into the Shakespearean canon. In contrast, to wonder about Q's authorization is already to assume, *more or less*, that Shakespeare authored the poems—but it is to assume such authorship tentatively and skeptically, without a clear sense of what we are thereby entitled as readers.

To be sure, both questions—the question of a text's canonicity and the question of its authorized publication—address the problem of ascribing authorship, but they do so in different ways. We might view this difference in terms of the distinction between lower- and uppercase notions of authorship; between the empiri-

cal author of a text–the living, breathing human who, at a particular moment in time, penned its words–and the transcendent
Author to whom we readers, after the fact, attribute meanings
unlimited by biography. For Augustine, this distinction was the difference between Moses and God as the sources of biblical truth–
between human scriptor and divine authority. Or again, between
the impersonal "he" of the Davidic lyricist who stands, thanks to
the prophetic structure of *figura*, behind his discourse, and the personal "I" cited by the discourse.[32] In a secular context, the distinction becomes harder to define, but the role of the New Criticism
within the contemporary development of literary studies would
suggest that a modern, professionalized readership confronts the
issue through the doctrine of the intentional fallacy. For a modern
critic, to question a text's canonicity is to question Shakespeare as
little *a* author; it is to wonder whether a particular glover's son
born in 1564 actually put quill to parchment and composed a particular sequence of words. Claims made about the empirical
author are, ultimately, empirical claims; they are claims to be supported by means of historical proof and physical evidence. But, as
Wimsatt and Beardsley were first to point out systematically, such
claims will not help us prove the presence of an intention within
the text. "One must ask how a critic expects to get an answer to
the question about intention," Wimsatt and Beardsley write. "How
is he to find out what the poet tried to do? If the poet succeeded
in doing it, then the poem itself shows what he was trying to do.
And if the poet did not succeed, then the poem is not adequate
evidence, and the critic must go outside the poem–for evidence of
an intention that did not become effective in the poem."[33] The
intentional fallacy consists in the belief that we can prove our
claims about textual meanings empirically–that empirical knowledge about a text's origin will *authorize* our readings. But our
claims about the big Author behind the text–our claims, conven-
tionally written in the literary present, about what Shakespeare or
"the poet" "means"–these are not biographical claims. These are
interpretive claims that can never finally be proved empirically.

And yet, in our most mundane reading practices the two types
of author, big *A* and little *a*, seem to support each other. True, any
particular knowledge about the empirical author fails to help us
prove the validity of any particular reading, but in general such
knowledge seems to authorize our *efforts* to interpret the text–

legitimating the act itself, if not the substance of the act. It becomes suddenly both possible and valid to read design, clarity, coherence within the text. The text falls open to us, for us, like the book of Paul's epistles under the fig tree, falling open in Augustine's lap.[34] Little *a* undergirds the arguments we ascribe to the big *A* Author, although those arguments will never be reducible for us to an empirical origin and moment of writing. From *a*uthor to *A*uthor: we manage to make the leap for all the works in Shakespeare's canon–with the crucial exception, I'd argue, of Q. Thus, for example, our attitude toward textual variants shifts sharply when we move from the plays to the Sonnets. The existence of multiple versions of most of the plays that we ascribe to Shakespeare has, from the eighteenth century on, forced us to think carefully about the way we construe Shakespeare's canon and the extent to which we can declare the poet's authorship for this or that "bad" quarto. In contrast, there are *no* bad quartos for the book called *Shakespeare's Sonnets*–there is only Q–and yet even for the majority of readers who have, since George Steevens's 1766 edition, accepted Q into the canon, the question of authorization lingers, troubling our reception of the book.[35] Similarly, it is of little concern to critics that many of the canonical plays were entered in the Stationers' Register without mentioning Shakespeare at all; however, at least one modern scholar was so disturbed by the mere absence of Shakespeare's *Christian* name from the May 20, 1609, Register entry–"a booke called Shakespeares sonnettes"–that she uses the fact to argue against authorization. "Had the poet endorsed the publication, the registration would have appeared with his full name."[36]

The problem with Q's registration, of course, is not that Shakespeare's first name goes unmentioned, but rather that his name in general is cited as part of the book's *title*. In this sense, indeed, the problem with Q is the lack of Shakespeare's will–if not his "Will." Shakespeare is not entered as the authority *behind* the book but rather as the author anthologized *within* the book. For skeptical readers (and we are all perforce, I'd like to suggest, skeptical readers of the Sonnets), the very title of the book announces a gap between the author of the individual poems and the author of the book. To what extent can we assert continuity between an anthologized Shakespeare who wrote the poems, and an authorizing Shakespeare who compiled the book called *Shakespeare's Son-*

nets? To question authorization is to accept Shakespeare's author-ship–again, *more* or *less*–of the poems contained in Q, while remaining skeptical about his authorship of the book called *Shake-speare's Sonnets*. It is, ultimately, to call into question the link between an empirical and a transcendental *a/A*uthor.

The most influential recent argument in favor of authorization implicitly revolves around this very point. For Katherine Duncan-Jones, to support the idea of an authorized quarto is to offer a "more direct and simple approach to the text." An authorized Q allows us to read the book called *Shakespeare's Sonnets* in its integrity, as a for-mal unity, a sense-making whole. In contrast to such integrated vision, however, modern editors of the Sonnets "have often given the impression that what these poems need is not so much editing as fundamental rewriting; or, failing that, the provision of a volumi-nous accompanying text of commentary and explication" (151). With its reordering of individual poems or its "voluminous" work of explanation, such editorial efforts seek to apologize or compensate for an incoherent text. But instead of yielding a more coherent read-ing, Duncan-Jones suggests, the work of modern editors only fur-ther undermines, further dis-integrates our sense of the book as a whole. In contrast, once authorized, Q lies open to our "direct and simple" approach. Not only is our sense of the work's empirical author assured, but even more important, we are ourselves author-ized in our attempts to interpret the book as a whole: to ascribe to it a unified meaning, positing an Author behind its words. Indeed, once Duncan-Jones feels she has established Q's authorization, she treats the book's coherence as axiomatic; in point of fact, for her the claim that Q is "authorial" is synonymous with the claim that its poems "make very good sense," composing a "formal whole" (165). For Duncan-Jones, to argue for Q's authorization is to argue for the text's "substantial integrity" (154).

Tellingly, however, Duncan-Jones's argument is marred by its circularity–a fact that, as far as I know, none of its critics has com-mented upon. Her argument rests on two primary grounds: the reli-ability of Thorpe as publisher and the evidence of intelligent design within Q. She convincingly paints a portrait of Thorpe as "a pub-lisher of some deserved status and prestige" (154–55), arguing against the still popular image of him as unscrupulous opportunist. Yet, as Arthur Marotti has argued, Thorpe's respectability has "little to do with the possibility that he followed a quite ordinary practice of printers" in publishing a manuscript without authorial consent (171 n). We cannot judge Thorpe's practice by modern standards, Marotti insists. Pirating unauthorized manuscripts does not make him the "predatory" blackguard that Sir Sidney Lee described in 1905,[37] nor does his high regard among his contemporaries translate, as Duncan-Jones would have it, into modern publishing standards. Furthermore, as Heather Dubrow has recently pointed out, in order to maintain her view of Thorpe's reliability, Duncan-Jones strives to dismiss the one clear case of his publishing an unauthorized text as a "deliberate prank" (Duncan-Jones, 155). Not only does Duncan-Jones fail to present her evidence for this claim, but, as Dubrow notes, the picture of Thorpe as "something of a prankster" (Duncan-Jones, 155) compromises Duncan-Jones's very efforts to portray the publisher as eminently respected and respectable.[38]

But ultimately even Duncan-Jones herself admits that rehabilitating Thorpe alone cannot prove Shakespeare's authorization of Q; it can only remove some of the obstacles preventing such a proof. "I see no real reason why Shakespeare could not himself have sold the manuscript . . . to Thorpe, unless it is clear that the texts as they stand cannot be authorial" (164–65). In the end, it is the formal integrity of the text–its structural cohesion–that will serve to establish authorization. Indeed, even the arguments in favor of Thorpe's respectability rest, finally, on his tendency to produce "authoritative" volumes (155)–volumes, that is, that offer evidence of the shaping hand of an Author. In the final analysis, Duncan-Jones's reasoning is circular: her arguments in favor of authorization serve as the rationale for asserting the unity of the text (i.e., if Shakespeare authorized the edition then we are justified in reading it as a coherent whole), at the same time that arguments about the coherence of the text justify the claim that it was authorized.[39]

For Duncan-Jones, authorization secures the link between little *a* author and big *A* Author. But it is telling that Duncan-Jones can only assert this link in circular terms: claims about the big *A* Author (about the meaning or structure of the sequence as a whole), support claims about the little *a* author (about the biographical agent behind the poems), that in turn support claims about the big *A*. Her arguments about the structural unity of the Sonnets help bolster her reading of Thorpe's respectability and tendency to produce "authoritative" texts, while the faith in his respectability supports the claim that the book's title page is accurate: these

Sonnets are indeed *Shakespeare's*. Furthermore, a belief in Shakespeare's authorship reinforces assertions of the structural, "authorial" integrity of the sonnet sequence as a whole. Nonetheless, Duncan-Jones's article–which, it should be noted, is one of the most often-cited recent essays on the Sonnets–is certainly not alone in its circularity. Similarly recursive arguments pervade the literature on Q's authorization. Even a writer like Joseph Pequigney, who maintains the authorization of Q but, unlike Duncan-Jones, refuses to rule out the biographical reference of these poems–the possibility, that is, that "Shakespeare sonnetized his own amorous experiences"[40]–builds his argument in terms of the circular reasoning from integrated structure to authoritative origin. "The arrangement of the Sonnets in Q," he writes toward the close of his book *Such Is My Love*, "is so intelligible, coherent, and aesthetically satisfying as to be indubitably and conclusively that of Shakespeare himself" (209).[41]

As Pequigney and other critics have suggested, however, arguments asserting the biographical reference of Q have more often than not *denied* authorization. "A purely literal interpretation of the impassioned protestations of affection for a 'lovely boy,'" Sidney Lee writes in 1905, ". . . casts a slur on the dignity of the poet's name which scarcely bears discussion."[42] The same anxieties about sexuality or propriety that have led readers since Malone to reject a literal or biographical reference for these poems have led other writers, presuming a literal reference, to deny the text's authority.[43] One of the best recent forays into biographical criticism–Robert Giroux's *Book Known as Q*–exemplifies this line of reasoning in its arguments against authorization. Giroux's reading reveals little hint of sexual anxiety,[44] yet nonetheless seems eager to preserve a sense of propriety, of tidy separation between private life and public text. "The publication of these highly personal sonnets probably disturbed their author profoundly," Giroux writes. "The sonnets to my mind . . . were not even written as a book, nor were they intended for many other eyes" (12). For Giroux, Q lacks the structural integrity ascribed to it by readers like Duncan-Jones. Instead, Giroux maintains that Q's numerous errors and lack of internal coherence support the view that its publication was unauthorized: "Q was not a book prepared by its author," he asserts (13). And yet, this lack of textual unity and structural integrity serve to support Giroux's insistence on biography. The less evidence Q reveals of an author's shaping hand, the more likely it is that the poems contained were entirely personal documents, never meant for public view. Furthermore, the more personal these poems are understood to be, the more license Giroux assumes in reading biographical reference back into the text. A narrative sequence is assigned to the poems and aligned with the events of Shakespeare's life. The date of composition is thereby established (1592–1595). The beautiful youth addressed in poems 1–126 is Henry Wriothesley, the Earl of Southampton. The poet's love for Southampton is real, intense and ultimately nonsexual. The rival poet described in sonnets 78–86 is Christopher Marlowe. The assumption of a haphazard, unauthorized publication thus supports the very biographical criticism that grants the book both its unity and its narrative–while the narrative, with its highly personal details, supports the assertion of an unauthorized text.

Taking diametrically opposed positions, Duncan-Jones and Giroux trace out the same circular path. Giroux vehemently criticizes what he calls "the antibiographical fallacy": "To maintain that poems, a product of the prosodic gifts, imagination, and verbal resources of an author (craftsmanship), cannot have any connection with actual events in his life (biography) is as fallacious as maintaining that they must have a connection" (Giroux, 52).[45] Duncan-Jones, for her part, discourages drawing any biographical conclusions: "Shakespeare nowhere asserts his presence in the plays, either as a writer or a personality. We should therefore be wary of making assumptions about what he was like when approaching the *Sonnets*" (Duncan-Jones, 154). Her Shakespeare is very much the Shakespeare of Keats:[46] the poet of no character, of negative capability, whose gift lies in his very transcendence of biography. Yet despite their opposing views on biography and authorization, the two critics encounter the same problem in reading the book called *Shakespeare's Sonnets*: the problem, that is, of reconciling the contingencies of a private life with the demand for coherence, meaning, and unity evoked by the public text. On the one hand, to argue, like Duncan-Jones, in favor of authorization is simultaneously to base claims about the text's structural unity upon the assumption of an authoritative volume, *and* to use arguments about such unity to justify the claim that the text was authorized. On the other hand, arguments *against* authorization can also help justify textual unity. As Giroux argues, if *Shakespeare's*

Sonnets was *not* authorized, it is all the more likely that its poems refer directly to lived experience—its details are too intimate to be made public. At the same time, the assumption of biographical reference supports a structured reading of the book: unified by its reference to an individual life, the text now reveals a coherent narrative. Indeed, it reveals the very narrative that Shakespeare would have wanted to keep secret from a reading public.

From opposite sides of the question of authorization, both Duncan-Jones and Giroux face the same problem: the problem of reading a first person who is neither clearly private nor securely public. To possess in certain terms a story about authorization would be to possess the narrative linking manuscript to published book, linking the coterie "intimacies of 'I' and 'you,'" as John Kerrigan puts it, with the impersonal "form and ordering of the quarto."[47] But every modern reader of Q is instead haunted on the one hand by Francis Meres's words in 1598 about "sugred sonnets" circulating "among priuate friends"—and on the other hand by the 1609 words of Thomas Thorpe's epigraph[48] that publicly invoke the ensuing sonnets' "ONLIE.BEGETTER." Tantalized by such clear, and yet utterly indirect, vestiges of textual origins, we remain suspended between the intimate and the impersonal, unable to bridge the gap between a private act and a published acknowledgment.

For Donald Foster, it is Thorpe's epigraph—the inscription that follows the title page of Q—that most decisively illuminates our problems with Shakespeare's first-person:

TO.THE.ONLIE.BEGETTER.OF.
THESE.INSVING.SONNETS.
M[r].W.H. ALL.HAPPINESSE.
AND.THAT.ETERNITIE.
PROMISED.
BY.
OVR.EVER-LIVING.POET.
WISHETH.
THE.WELL-WISHING.
ADVENTVRER.IN.
SETTING.FORTH.
T.T.

For the past two centuries of critics, the epigraph has proved almost irresistible, since its language of begetting, along with its double reference to an eternity both promised and experienced by "OVR.EVER-LIVING.POET" suggests a genealogy that would link empirical origins to public or transcendent meanings.[49] Once we know where such fancy is bred, how begot and nourishèd, we could, it is hoped, moor private experience to public authority.[50] At the same time, this genealogy has remained notoriously unstable, collapsing under ambiguous syntax and epithets. In this way, as Foster suggests, our experience of Thorpe's epigraph performs in little our relation to the book called *Shakespeare's Sonnets* as a whole. "The poems tease us with what appear to be references to real persons," but remain inaccessible to biographical research; instead, the "text dwells, as it were, in the twilight of both autobiography and fiction, with metrical feet in both worlds.... The sonnets are in large measure defined for us by their very ambiguity" (Foster, 51). For Foster, however, such ambiguity is not essential to the text: he argues that there is nothing inherently mysterious about either the epigraph or the ensuing poems. Instead any mystery is mere accident, the simple result of the way in which these poems, long ago "cut loose from their moorings in a specific life" (52), now hover undecidably between private and public stances, between autobiography and fiction. Shakespeare's words, Foster writes, "exist now as a symbolic structure in search of a thing signified" (52).

To discern the identity of Thorpe's Master W.H., Foster suggests, would be to recover the Sonnets' moorings; to discover their "ONLIE.BEGETTER" would be to trace that symbolic structure back to a thing signified. Yet, as countless readers of Thorpe's epigraph have realized, origins have a way of recessing infinitely into the distance. How can we locate the "begetter" of these poems when we don't even know what "beget" means in this context? Is the "begetter" the sonnet's author in the sense of their writer—or is he, as a quick glance at the very first of the "insving sonnets," the seventeen procreation sonnets, would suggest, not "OVR.EVER-LIVING.POET" but rather the poet's friend? Is the "begetter," in other words, the fair young man described in those seventeen poems who, resisting marriage and thus failing to beget biological children of his own, nonetheless exists instead as the sole inspiration, the only begetter of *Shakespeare's Sonnets*? But then, if the "begetter" W.H. is the patron/muse and not the poet, can we be sure that "OVR.EVER-LIVING.POET" is Shakespeare? After all, the phrase "ever-living" is the kind of epithet one grants *in memoriam*, and in 1609 Shakespeare was still very much alive.

Perhaps, however, the "begetter" of the *Sonnets* denotes not so much the source (inspirational or scribal) of the poetry, as the source of the *manuscript*. Indeed, since 1799 critics have argued that "begetter" can also mean "getter" or "procurer." The begetter of the ensuing sonnets would then have been the gentleman who brought them to their publisher—the latter whose identity readers have, almost entirely without hesitation, been able to discern in the "WELL-WISHING.ADVENTVRER" and "T.T." of the paragraph's last lines.[51] In fact, despite the promise of genealogical clarity, it is almost as if the only authority that the epigraph makes apparent is its own: knowing nothing of authorial origins, all we can really surmise is that Thomas Thorpe—whose initials appear on Q's title page as well—published this edition and wrote its inscription. But further complications have called even this modest claim into question. With its full stops and capitals throughout, the lapidary inscription has proved almost oracular in its ambiguity. Apposition and syntax have proved impossible to assert with certainty.[52] Thus while the epigraph holds forth the promise of defining origins, referring us to W.H. and T.T.–as well as to a begetter, a poet, and a well-wishing adventurer–with its elliptical initials and slippery syntax, it has only occasioned, in the words of Hyder Rollins's oft-cited lament, "the spilling of more ink, the utterance of more futile words, than almost any other personage or problem of Q" (*Variorum Sonnets*, 2:166).

Donald Foster, however, takes to task both Rollins's lament and, with it, the history of this spilled ink, arguing that there is nothing ambiguous nor particularly remarkable in Thorpe's language. Drawing examples of comparable usage and phrasing from contemporary documents, Foster argues that the inscription deploys conventional epithets and metaphors; neither its syntax nor its phrasing would have been misunderstood by contemporary audiences. "Begetter" can only mean the author-father who penned the manuscript; "ever-living poet," on the other hand, is a phrase that contemporaries would have unerringly associated not with the human author of these poems but with God, the divine author of creation; finally, "Mr. W.H.," established by clear apposition as the

"onlie" writer of these poems, may very well be "the most well-hon-
ored typographical error in the history of world literature" (Foster,
49): a misprint for **Mr. W**[illiam] [S]**H**[akespeare].[53]

Foster's analysis is a search for signifieds designed to end all
searches. In decoding Thorpe's references and detangling his syntax, Foster wants to demonstrate that there is nothing to decode,
nothing to detangle. He wants to lay Master W.H., the only begetter of these ensuing sonnets, to rest. Thorpe's epigraph, he seeks
to demonstrate, is not a "private message" dedicated to Shakespeare's young friend or to the procurer of the pirated manuscript.
It is instead a public proclamation of Shakespeare's sole authorship of the ensuing poems. The epigraph, in short, puts to an end
the authorization debate. In the first place, the inscription offers
proof of the text's authority. It is black-and-white evidence that
Shakespeare authorized the publication of these poems; it is nothing more, and nothing less than an "ordinary advertisement to the
reader that all the ensuing sonnets belong to Master William
Shakespeare and that they were printed with his consent or at his
request" (Foster, 50). But furthermore, read as an "ordinary advertisement," the inscription puts an end to debate simply by refusing
us the tantalizing vestiges of a private life or a secret communiqué.
Read as advertisement, the epigraph ushers us into a purely public
text, leaving no purchase for any detective work.

By reading W.H. as a typographical chimera and Thorpe's
inscription as a mere advert, Foster both satisfies and defies our
search for origins. He identifies W.H. but in a manner that forecloses the very possibility urged by those initials: the possibility
that we might exhume an empirical, biographical context for the
poems. If, as Wimsatt and Beardsley will tell us, all biographical
criticism fails in the end to "prove" anything about meaning, Foster pushes that failure to its logical extreme: he concludes his
empirical research and forecloses any further research with an
assertion that patently *defies* empirical proof. How, after all, can
one *prove* the "existence" of an absence, the presence of missing
letters? This is biographical criticism reduced to the absurd, the
search for empirical origins having dead-ended in the conjuration
of the missing name. **W***[illiam]* *[S]***H***[akespeare]*. Where Duncan-
Jones and Giroux reveal the futility of efforts to anchor meaning in
an account of empirical origins, Foster seeks by similar means to
pull up that anchor, using empirical research to negate the lure of

origins itself. But as he notes, "Master W.H. dies hard. . . . We keep him breathing so as to preserve the illusion that we know what these sonnets mean. In fact, we know nothing of the sort. . . . Here are 19,083 words[54] . . . that have long since been cut loose from their moorings in a specific life" (50, 51–52). Foster argues that it is *we* who keep W.H. alive; it is our critical need that keeps renewing the debate over origins. It is *our* need to locate, or imagine that we *can* locate meaning that keeps us returning to questions like the authorization issue. Moreover, Foster suggests that this need marks our weakness and even, perhaps, our folly: we are unable to endure the loss of the "signified," as he calls it. (Empirical *referent* would, perhaps, be the better term, since the one thing we readers never come up short with, never manage to lack for, is meaning. We seem always to have signifieds aplenty, unmoored though they may be.)

Foster's remarks are compelling, and he is certainly correct to argue that our reading habits demand, in some sense, the search for origins–even so paradoxical and self-swallowing a search as the one he ventures upon. As I have tried to suggest throughout this study, the readerly practice that Augustine invents for the Christian West entails precisely the sense of connection to the past, at the same time that it entails the effacement of that past in all of its presence. However, it is not, as Foster would suggest, that our readings strive to fill in the loss of the past. It is, rather, the other way around: in order to read, we construct the past as lost. We invoke Moses in order to reject him, that we might have a divine authority for the Book. Nor is this construction of the past a failing or an error on our part, as Foster implies, unless we are to say that reading itself consists in failure and error since its folly is to take any text at all as one written *for our sakes*.

At the same time, this general folly of our reading does seem to meet with unique difficulties when it comes to the book called *Shakespeare's Sonnets*. Now, for Foster, these difficulties are extrinsic to the text itself–contingent artifacts of literary history. Yet even he notes that such contingency can acquire a certain necessary force. "If we were someday to discover the 'facts' concerning Shakespeare's relationship with the persons alluded to in this work," he writes, "what we have always known as Shakespeare's *Sonnets* would, in a sense, cease to exist, to be replaced by another book of the same title" (51). The absence of historical data, the irretrievability of its lost empirical context, have come to define our sense of Q. For Foster, it is entirely possible that this defining ambiguity could disappear–it just *happens* to be the case that we know nothing about Q's origins–but with the ambiguity, the book we know would also disappear.

I both agree and disagree with Foster here. I agree that it is entirely possible, however unlikely after so many years and so many sleuths, that new "facts" about Q could emerge that could transform the text as we know it. But to suggest that Q's ambiguities are essentially, as it were, *accidental* to the text–matters of brute historical contingency, effected and affected by chance alone–is both to yield too much power to the historical record, and to let ourselves off the hook as readers. There is always more to learn about the origins of a text, of *any* text; there is always more to learn, because there exists no way in advance to determine what counts as origin. No measure exists by which we could say that we have finally learned all there is to learn about that originary moment of writing; our efforts to contextualize the text within its historical moment will never be complete. Instead, what counts as context, as pertinent "fact," will be continually shaped and reshaped by our reading. Certainly our knowledge of contexts also shapes and reshapes our reading, but it does not do so exhaustively–it does not, in other words, *put an end* to reading. As readers, to learn about the origin of a text is to learn about the origin of its meaning–and this is the sort of origin that keeps shifting as we learn. The crucial point here is that there will always, necessarily, be a gap in our knowledge about texts; once again, Wimsatt and Beardsley hold sway: our arguments about meaning will never be reducible to historical proof.

The difficulties Foster notes in *Shakespeare's Sonnets* are thus not merely accidental features of our reading. Nor are they reducible to general deconstructive "truths" applicable to all texts. Instead, I'd like to suggest that such difficulties are also peculiarly Shakespearean: they are intrinsic to the text itself. It is true that we know little about the "facts" surrounding Q's composition. But it is also true that such ignorance is a leitmotif in discussions of Shakespeare, playing a decisive role in our conception of him as Author. I am reminded here of the perennial contentions that we know "nothing" about Shakespeare's life, or of the deathless zeal with which writers seek to fill in supposed gaps in the historical record, offering more or less fanciful biographies–from the excesses of the Oxfordians or Baconians, out to find the "real" Shakespeare; to Marc Norman and Tom Stoppard's whimsical *Shakespeare in Love*; to Park Honan's 1998 biography, which eschews "imaginative reconstructions and elaborate psychological theories" but nonetheless, with a nod to new historicism, embellishes the documentary facts of this life through a vivid sketch of "social contexts."[55] It's as if we somehow need these historical gaps, these biographical lacunae–inventing them if we have to–in order for Shakespeare to be the kind of Author we take him to be, the Author of negative capability surrounded, as it were, by a cloud of unknowing. Our investment in our own ignorance about the author is too strong, I would maintain, to be seriously challenged by any actual broadening of historical knowledge.

And yet, even this last formulation of mine doesn't quite get to the heart of what's so odd about the book called *Shakespeare's Sonnets*. Its ambiguity is not just the result of our flawed historical knowledge, but nor is it simply the by-product or back-formation of our concept of Shakespeare the Author. Efforts to demystify the text and its ambiguity routinely fail–whether they call into question our use of history (as Foster's essay on W.H. does), or historicize and thus challenge our concept of the Author (as, for instance, Arthur Marotti does in his textual criticism, or as Margreta de Grazia and Peter Stallybrass do, when they trace editorial histories and the formation of the canon). If anything, such demystifying efforts only seem to deepen our attachment to the mystery of the text, calling forth responses as varied as Heather Dubrow's recent polemic in favor of a radically "indeterminate" sequence, and Helen Vendler's even more recent insistence on the profundity of Shakespeare's lyric genius. Ultimately such efforts fail because they do not consider seriously enough the ambiguity *intrinsic* to Q. The book called *Shakespeare's Sonnets* itself works to mobilize the gap between empirical origins and received meanings; in precise formal, rhetorical and thematic ways the text invokes a sense that authority itself is in question. Authorization, and the link it implies between private and public, author and Author, is not, in the first place, a question *we* bring to the text: it is a question that the text itself raises.

At first blush, this claim is impossibly paradoxical. The debate over Q's publication pivots on one crucial point: that we must resolve the question of authorization before we can claim coherence for the book called *Shakespeare's Sonnets*. We must trace the text back to its authorial source, one way or another, before we can ascribe it unity, meaning, purpose. How then could the book be "about" the problem of authorization? Indeed, if the very authority of the book remains in question, then how can we maintain that the book is "about" anything? But it is just such circular reasoning that we've already discussed vis-à-vis Duncan-Jones and Giroux: the coherence of meaning that would settle the question of authorization can itself be established only once we settle the question of authorization. Despite themselves, in the circularity of their arguments, Duncan-Jones and Giroux reveal not only that the question of Q's authorization cannot be resolved; even more important, they reveal the very nature of the question. The problem of authorization with which Q confronts us is not a dilemma extrinsic to our arguments about the text. It is not a historical dilemma, like the question of canonicity, to be laid to rest through empirical research before we move on to our readings of the work. It is not, in short, a problem to be resolved before we make our arguments. Instead, what distinguishes the concerns over authorization from related concerns like canonicity is that at stake is a problem we encounter in the very process of making our textual arguments. The problem of authorization, as we encounter it in our reading of Q, is that problematic aspect of our interpretive work itself. In other words, the circle Duncan-Jones and Giroux describe as they struggle to resolve the problem of authorization is itself the expression of that problem. Authorization is not, then, a problem outside, beyond, prior to (the choice of preposition is yours) our ability to construct the meaning of Q. It is instead a problem *intrinsic* to our construction of meaning. It is in this sense a problem *of* the text.

Indeed, to take the claim even further, I want to argue that authorization is *the* problem of Q, for it is insofar as the poems foreground the gap between origins and meanings that the book called *Shakespeare's Sonnets* generates a sense of its own thematic and structural unity, even while it defines that unity as problematic. In other words, it is only once we start to read the ways in which these poems question their own authority that we can resolve the problem of authorization, demonstrating the coherent terms with which the text challenges its own authorial status. *Pace* Duncan-Jones, such demonstrations of Q's coherence will not prove that Shakespeare authorized the publication of the book. Instead, such readings merely reveal that the question of authorization remains *essential* to any interpretation of the book as a whole. We cannot put an end to the question of authorization in this text, but we can demonstrate that the question is, indeed, the *end* of the text.

A curious decorum, then, yokes these individual poems together under one roof, under one name: the question of authorization that the book *qua* book raises merely recapitulates the subject matter of the poems themselves; form, as it were, follows content, for the sonnets themselves meditate obsessively on just those questions of paternity, origin, and authenticity that trouble our efforts to interpret the book. It is, finally, I would maintain, on the basis of such decorum that we are justified in interpreting Q, both its content and its form, reading each of its poems against the backdrop of the book as a whole. We are justified, that is to say, in ascribing an a/Author to the book called *Shakespeare's Sonnets*. For the sake of argument, let's name him after (and not before) his book: Shakespeare.

AUTHORIZING TRESPASS WITH COMPARE

Despite the intense interest in the question of authorization, there is one rather literal-minded question that critics have failed to ask: how would the a/Author of Q define authority, or the act of granting authority–the act, that is, of *author-izing* a thing?

As is often the case with the OED, Shakespeare is the prime author used to authorize the entry for the verb "to authorize." Under its first heading (*to authorize a thing*), the OED cites Shakespeare twice:

1. To set up as authoritative; to acknowledge as possessing final decisiveness. Obs. [. . .]
2. To give legal force to; to make legally valid. [. . .]
3. To give formal approval to; to sanction, approve, countenance. [. . .]
   c1600 Shaks. Sonn. xxxv, Authorizing thy trespas with compare. [. . .]
   b. Of things: To afford just ground for, justify. [. . .]

> 4. To vouch for the truth or reality of; to confirm by one's
> authority. Obs. [. . .]
> 1605 Shaks. Macb. iii. iv. 66 A womans story, at a Win-
> ters fire, Authoriz'd by her Grandam.

According to the OED, all five of these definitions are current–
and distinct–during Shakespeare's career. To authorize a thing is
to acknowledge its final authority, or to grant it legal force, or to
give it official approbation, or to afford it justification, or simply to
confirm its reality. But even though the word *authorize* appears
only three times in the entire Shakespearean canon, and two of
those occasions are cited with the above definitions, when taken
in context the semantic field of the word as Shakespeare uses it
seems both more fluid, and more precise, than the OED would
suggest. At stake with authorization for Shakespeare is, as we shall
see, a problem that informs all five of the definitions above: at
stake is our failing capacity to distinguish between truth and falsehood, good and ill, original and copy, innocence and guilt, legitimacy and bastardy. Remarkably consistent in his usage, what
Shakespeare calls into question with the term is nothing less than
our ability to make authoritative moral and epistemological distinctions.

> LA.   O proper stuffe:
> This is the very painting of your feare:
> This is the Ayre-drawne-Dagger which you said
> Led you to Duncan. O, these flawes and starts
> (Impostors to true feare) would well become
> A womans story, at a Winters fire
> **Authoriz'd** by her Grandam: shame it selfe,
> Why do you make such faces? When all's done
> You looke but on a stoole.
>   (*Macbeth* 3.4.76–84, emphasis added)

"To authorize" a thing, according to Lady Macbeth, is to endow it
with one's own authority, endorsing its authenticity. It is to anchor
the phenomenon in a reliable source; to vouchsafe its truth and
reality. The OED cites a related usage from 1489: "The more that
a werke is wytnessed . . . the more it is auctorysed and more
auctentyke." The authorized "werke" is credible; it is no mere

wives' tale, but sound evidence, backed by dependable witnesses. The authorized work thus acquires the force of collective truth: what is authorized becomes official, public—indeed, authoritative in its own right and capable of legitimating future action or knowledge. For Lady Macbeth, however, her husband's "flaws and starts" are entirely ungrounded—as baseless as the shivers "a womans story at a Winters fire" might stir. Macbeth has become unmanned, swayed not by an authentic and authoritative public discourse—the words, let us say, of history—but instead by the discourse of the hearth, born of woman, the merely domestic stuff of folklore. O improper stuff! What unmans her husband, Lady Macbeth suggests, is precisely that he credits such incredible, inappropriate stuff. He relies, as it were, on the unreliable testimony of women. For Lady Macbeth, who envisions herself a world-class dissembler—"looke like th'innocent flower, / But be the Serpent vnder't" (1.5.73–74)—the distinction between reality and illusion, between "impostors" and truth, can be at any moment subjected to proof. When all's done, you look but on a stool.

In short, nothing authorizes Macbeth's fears;[56] his visions lack all authority, and reduce him to the feminine passivity his wife so despises. The irony of the passage is, however, that Lady Macbeth's misogynist words are more accurate than she herself realizes: Macbeth's problem is indeed that he relies on the authority of women, from his wife to the Weïrd Sisters. Furthermore, the very appearance of the dagger or of Banquo's ghost challenges Lady Macbeth's positivist assurance: in a world of airborne daggers and walking ghosts how is it possible to tell impostor fears from true ones, private illusions from public realities? The audience, subject to Macbeth's visions, knows what Lady Macbeth has forgotten: her husband's fears have been authorized indeed, from the moment he met the witches. "This supernaturall solliciting / Cannot be ill; cannot be good / . . . / If good? why doe I yeeld to that suggestion, / Whose horrid Image doth vnfixe my Heire . . . / Present Feares / Are lesse then horrible Imaginings" (1.3.145–46, 149–50, 152–53). Macbeth's authority is undermined, but not because his groundless fears unman him; rather Macbeth's manhood feels groundless because authority, in general, has already been compromised in this play. Hailed by the witches as Thane of Cawdor, and as king that shalt be, Macbeth has been solicited into disorder, into a world where heirs/hairs are unfixed. It is thus that Macbeth succumbs to horrors that, however imaginary, yet loom larger and press harder, seem "realer," than present reality. Thanks to the equivocation of fiends who lie like truth, that authority behind the play is, from the start, neither good nor ill, fair nor foul. The very ground of clear distinctions between king and tyrant, truth and lies has given way to the tales of women.[57]

To authorize a thing, as Lady Macbeth understands it, is to avouch its truth and authenticity, distinguishing it from all impostors. Yet significantly Lady Macbeth only uses the term with reference to the inauthentic and nonauthoritative: it is the old wives' tale that is "authorized," although it is not to be believed. In this way, the very idea of a confirmed, authoritative truth only emerges for Lady Macbeth in the context of its dissembling double—the authorized tale that is, nonetheless, false. Authorization allows us to distinguish truth from falsehood, but we must first be sure that our authorizing sources are themselves true and not false. Yet on what grounds may such a judgment be made? Who will authorize the authorizers, as it were? The difficulties invoked by Lady Macbeth's usage reflect the aporetic nature of authority in the play: in Macbeth's world, it is precisely the old wives who are the final, albeit profoundly equivocal, authorities. As old wives—ambiguously gendered and bearded old wives—the Weïrd Sisters inspire fears that are not true, but are not, strictly speaking, *false*.

Lady Macbeth's difficulties with authorization are not an isolated occurrence. Indeed, strikingly enough, in Shakespeare's other two uses of the verb "authorize," the poet again calls into question the very distinction that, seemingly, authorization is meant to stabilize: the difference between true and false. Furthermore, and most stunning for our purposes, these two remaining uses both appear in Q—as if all the more to suggest that our problems with the authorization of this book arise from the book's own problems with authorization.

> No more bee greeu'd at that which thou hast done
> Roses haue thornes, and siluer fountaines mud,
> Cloudes and eclipses staine both Moone and Sunne,
> And loathsome canker liues in sweetest bud.
> All men make faults, and euen I in this,
> **Authorizing** thy trespas with compare,

My selfe corrupting saluing thy amisse,
Excusing their sins more then their sins are:
For to thy sensuall fault I bring in sence,
Thy aduerse party is thy Aduocate,
And gainst my selfe a lawfull plea commence,
Such ciuill war is in my loue and hate,
  That I an accessary needs must be,
  To that sweet theefe which sourely robs from me,
                    (Sonnet 35, emphasis added)

Sonnet 35 appears in the midst of a group of poems that address some offense–a betrayal of some kind–committed by the poet's friend. No sooner is the young man obliquely accused (Sonnet 33), than he apparently repents and is forgiven, despite the poet's lingering sense of loss: "Though thou repent, yet I haue still the losse, / ... / Ah but those teares are pearle which thy loue sheeds, / And they are ritch, and ransome all ill deeds" (34:10, 13–14). By the end of this mini-sequence, the poet has assumed the burden of the crime altogether: "So shall those blots that do with me remaine, / Without thy helpe, by me be borne alone" (36:3–4). Falling somewhere between the young man's repentance and the poet's forgiveness, sonnet 35 strives to make sense of a simultaneous experience of "losse" and richness, blot and beauty. And so the poet presents similitudes, comparing the young man's mingled beauty and shame to the natural faults of natural beauty. Roses have thorns, and every silver fountain has a muddy bottom: nothing could be more natural than the blemish–the cancerous, wormy excess–that mars a beautiful nature.

The OED cites sonnet 35 under its third definition: *to give formal approval to; to sanction, approve, countenance.* "All men make faults, and euen I in this, / Authorizing thy trespas with compare": the poet's comparisons sanction the young man's deed, exonerating him by providing a rationale for error, an inescapable logic of fault. The similes that liken the young friend's trespass to natural flaws not only ease the young man's sorrow, they entirely exculpate him by suggesting that trespass itself is only natural. All men make faults, after all. But here the poet doubles back, pointing to the surface of his own forgiving discourse: "and euen I in this ... / ... / My selfe corrupting saluing thy amisse." With this *this* the poet recognizes his own fault: his error in approving error. Even more important, however, this *this* marks a moment of discursive self-consciousness acute enough that it forces the reader to take the poet even more firmly at his word. *All men make faults*: the locution is odd, even for an Elizabethan; we *have* faults, we *make* mistakes, but in what sense do we "make" faults?[58] The poet's diction, however, is quite precise: in excusing the young man, the poet has literally *made* a fault, in the sense of a fault line: he has created a crack or split within himself. By condoning the crime and swallowing his hurt, absorbing his loss, the poet has corrupted himself by working against himself; he has introduced a cancerous blot within, becoming false to himself. He has become his own enemy by exculpating his "true" enemy: "Thy aduerse party is thy Aduocate." Divided from himself, at war with his best interest, the poet now suffers a fault or fracture of his own (a "ciuill war") and of his own making.

But the poet also *makes faults* in another sense. Puttenham, like so many Renaissance writers, will remind us that a poet is a maker–"our English name well conformes with the Greeke word: for of **poiyin** to make, they call a maker *Poeta*" (1.1.1)–and sonnet 35 offers its own etymology lesson, suggesting that first and foremost this poet is a maker of *fault*. In wrongly comparing the young man's trespass to flaws of nature, the poet has literally made flawed images; he has fashioned likenesses of the young man that are unlike the young man–likenesses that are flawed by, tarnished with, difference. The poet is at fault for making faulty similes: disanalogies that exonerate the young man only by likening him to what he is not.

Furthermore, insofar as he ascribes the young man's misdeeds to a kind of natural errancy, the poet manages not only to condone and forgive, but also to justify the young man's crime itself. In other words, beyond simply approving the trespass after the fact, the poet's similes reach backward, retroactively providing a rationale for the young man's actions–retroactively grounding the trespass in a just cause. In this way, these faulty similes–the rose's thorns, the fountain's mud, the cankerous bud–"authorize" the crime by supplying it with an authoritative cause or origin: the fault is the fault *of nature*. By authorizing the young man's trespass with compare, the poet's similitudes in some sense then precede what they describe: the flawed natural beauties the young man *resembles* now encompass and explain what the young man, *qua* beautiful, *is*. Likeness becomes, in this sense, the origin of identity: like all natural beauties, it is only natural that the young man be flawed. The similes from nature assimilate the young man and his crime to nature, and thus trespass now assumes the inescapable validity of a natural law.

Yet the ultimate authority of sonnet 35 is not nature but the poet, for it is he who has the ultimate power to make fault. It is the poet who authorizes trespass with compare, who forges similitudes that undermine the difference between right and wrong, good and ill, fair and foul. Furthermore, as we shall see, in its evocation of a poet who makes faults, corrupting himself while he salves amiss, sonnet 35 defines the self-trespassing poetic authority that unites— *authorizes*–the book called *Shakespeare's Sonnets* as a whole.

In its final words, however, the book manages so successfully to marginalize this poetic authority that, even now, almost fifteen years after John Kerrigan's New Penguin edition of the Sonnets– one of the first editions since 1609 to include *A Lover's Complaint*– the silent omission of that last, strange poem is still common editorial and critical practice.[59] "From off a hill whose concaue wombe reworded, / A plaintfull story from a sistring vale / My spirrits t'attend this doble voyce accorded, / And downe I laid to list the sad tun'd tale . . ." (*Lover's*, 1–4). Even now *A Lover's Complaint* is rarely, and only with difficulty, read as an integral part of the book called *Shakespeare's Sonnets*–and this omission is not without good reason. The poem is formally, visually, and dramatically set apart from the sonnets that precede it: written (like Daniel's "Complaint of Rosamond") in rime royal, the 329-line narrative is clearly no sonnet, and its doubled narrative frame–the first-person narrator overhears a lover confess her woes to a "reuerend" shepherd–sets us at a deliberate distance from the lyric I/eye of the sonnets. Further distance between the sonnets and the complaint is established visually through well-marked borders: recto, verso– end and beginning. Sonnet 154 is punctuated by a large white space and a well-placed "FINIS"; the narrative poem is introduced in the top margin of the following page with a centered title and an authorial byline:[60]

A Louers complaint.
BY
WILLIAM SHAKE-SPEARE.

Yet such borders prove less certain the more we examine them: the "finis" that follows sonnet 154 is belied by the sonnet's own bawdy insistence on the interminability of love.[61] Love, as the sonnet darkly jests, is an incurable disease, literally a venereal disease: a fire that no "coole Well" can quench. Furthermore, if the waters of this black well (the dark lady's "will" itself, her unfathomable vagina/eyes/desire) only propagate more desire, inflaming Cupid's brand or shaking William's spear all the more, these waters in turn spill over themselves, rippling outward, into the superfluity of *A Lover's Complaint.* There, a weeping maid casts both her tears and her faithless beloved's favors into a river that overflows its banks: "Vpon whose weeping margent she was set, / Like vsery applying wet to wet, / Or Monarches hands that lets not bounty fall, / Where want cries some; but where excesse begs all" (39–42). The narrative poem may be set apart from the sonnets that precede it, but like the usurious river of tears, or the "thousand fauours" (36) of a fickle love, or like the superfluous excess of desire–of the will–itself, the poems of Q overflow their margins, doubling and rewording any singular poetic authority.[62]

Yet, as we shall see at the close of this chapter, it is precisely the difficulties that *A Lover's Complaint* poses for the questions of authority and authorization that make reading it so crucial. We cannot read Shakespeare's will without it. For now, however, it is enough to read Shakespeare's final usage of the verb "to author-ize." Significantly, the word appears in the complaint during the maid's description of her seducer's beauty: "one by natures out-wards so commended, / That maidens eyes stucke ouer all his face" (80–81). We are, I think, meant to hear the gruesome literal-ity of the image–of these maiden eyes literally stuck all over the young man's face, like leeches or barnacles suctioned to his coun-tenance. At stake for the "fickle maid" (5) throughout the poem is precisely the problem of attraction–the suction-like *pull* of fair semblances–to which she wrongly thinks herself immune. Where others' eyes are stuck on his beautiful seeming, she sees through his "foule beguiling," sees "how deceits [are] guilded in his smiling" and knows that his vows of love have been "euer brokers to defiling" (170, 173, 174). From the very start she knows not to trust the testimony of beauty:

His qualities were beautious as his forme,
For maiden tongu'd he was and thereof free;
Yet if men mou'd him, was he such a storme
As oft twixt May and Aprill is to see,
When windes breath sweet, vnruly though they bee.
His rudeness so with his **authoriz'd** youth,
Did liuery falsenesse in a pride of truth.

(99–105, emphasis added)

In the effeminacy of his youth, the seducer is excused much; even his flaws become him, signs of frank innocence and not ungoverned immodesty. Far from mar his beauty, his imperfections only further attest to it: even his falseness looks like truth. So is his "rudeness" authorized or sanctioned by his youth, so are his "storms" granted an inexorable vernal logic: April showers bring May flowers. In this way, the young man's beauty, with its hermaphroditic mingling of May and April, fair and foul, proves as seductively unreliable as the old wives' tales in *Macbeth*, or the poet's lovely comparisons in sonnet 35: the beauty of this youth–his youth as beauty–merely sanctions trespass, confounding lies with verities. Springlike in his storminess, the seducer is sweet, not *despite* his unruliness: he is precisely fair *because* he is foul. Once again authorization entails a falsifying similitude: like the poet's similes that make fault, or the equivocating fiends who lie like truth, the youth's qualities are approved–termed "beautious"–only insofar as falseness is "liveried" like truth.

Finally it is not, perhaps, insignificant that this last example of Shakespearean authorization performs rhetorically the very inversions and confusions it describes. The rhetorical figure Shakespeare uses here is hypallage, often described as the transferred epithet.[63] *His rudeness so with his* **authorized youth** *did livery falseness in a pride of truth*. It is the rudeness that is authorized, not the youth; hypallage transfers the modifier (*authorized*) from object (*rudeness*) to subject (*youth*): the authorizing agent becomes its own authorized object. Rhetorically, then, the verse enacts in its syntax just that equivocation between cause and effect, origin and end, that grants the rude youth his authority, transforming what mars his beauty into his beauty's very proof. Even those who move him are in turn moved by him; his adverse parties become his advocates–even his unruliness feels sweet. Hypallage mirrors such inversions at the level of syntax, and in so doing offers a precise and literal figure of Shakespearean authorization. With its transfer of qualities, hypallage confounds the order of logical and grammatical succession, confusing cause and effect, root and branch, true origins and usurping counterfeits. Puttenham renames the figure of disordered, inverted authority with his usual clarity; in doing so he evokes the cultural imagination that animates the figure and explicates its threat.

> The Greekes call this figure *Hipallage* the Latins Submutatio, we in our vulgar may call him the vnderchange but I had rather haue him called the Changeling nothing at all sweruing from his originall, and much more aptly to the purpose, and pleasanter to beare in memory: specially for our Ladies and pretie mistresses in Court, for whose learning I write, because it is a terme often in their mouthes, and alluding to the opinion of Nurses, who are wont to say, that the Fayries vse to steale the fairest children out of their cradles, and put other ill fauoured in their places, which they called changelings, or Elfs, so, if ye mark, doeth our Poet, or maker play with his wordes, vsing a wrong construction for a right, and an absurd for a sensible, by manner of exchange.
>
> (3.15.7 [143–44])

As *changeling*, hypallage exchanges fairest child for foulest fairy, rightful heir for usurping bastard. Yet of course these fairy stories are merely founded on the opinion of women; they are nothing but old wives' tales. Nonetheless, with such tales Puttenham manages to capture precisely that fear of corruption and doubtful legitimacy that, I've been arguing, both besets and characterizes the authorization of *Shakespeare's Sonnets*.

THE NAME OF THE *Rose*

If we knew that the publication of the book called *Shakespeare's Sonnets* were authorized, we would feel secure in assigning the book an empirical origin/cause. We would be, indeed, authorized to say: Will Shakespeare wrote *this*. But we would also feel author-

ized in our efforts to transcend that origin in the name of Meaning. Alongside Wimsatt and Beardsley we would proclaim that
authorial intention–Shakespeare's will–is a fallacy. But the book
published in his name doesn't allow us either of these moves. We
cannot assign Q an empirical origin, nor can we ascribe to it an
Author with a capital A. Yet, it seems, we also cannot avoid invoking such a/Authority–not, that is, if we want to read the book in
its entirety. In this way, the book *qua* book–*Shakespeare's Sonnets*
read in its stitched-together entirety–is marked by a figural tradition. To read the book called *Shakespeare's Sonnets*, to read the book
qua book, we must perforce confront not only the history of *figura*,
but also Luther's historic critique of *figura*. We must do so because,
as I've been trying to suggest, it is this history and this critique that
authorizes our reading as such. To ignore this history is potentially
to presume that our reading practices require *no* authorization.
This is a presumption that we (artists, scholars, teachers, students,
humanists) make at our own peril, in a culture with increasingly little faith in "culture."

It is, after all, a figural tradition that so persuasively defines the
textual autonomy upon which we still, for all our cultural materialist, contextualist, postmodern et cetera ways, rely. *Figura* defines
the autonomous text, liberating a formally coherent and thus self-
sustaining meaning from the accidents of history and biology–and
it does so by simultaneously forging and effacing a link back to
those accidents, back to empirical origins. It is not odd, then, ultimately, that readers should keep revisiting the question of Q's
authorization; what's odd, however, is that anyone should claim
that the text is unauthorized and yet persist in trying to read it.

Whence the problems encountered, for example, by the new
textual criticism. Critics like Martha Woodmansee and Arthur
Marotti have argued that modern notions of authorship rely on
the legal protection of a writer's property rights to his words–protection that, again, did not exist in England until 1709. Before the
eighteenth century, the only defined legal rights belonged to the
printer or publisher: these were the "copy-rights," the rights to
print or reprint a particular book.[64] Given, then, the material circumstances of publication in an age of patronage and of manuscript circulation, there is "*no* text of the *Sonnets* . . . that can be
shown to represent the ideal of old-fashioned textual critics, the
'author's final intentions'" (Marotti, 165).

While new textual criticism has refocused critical debate by addressing the material conditions of authorship and publication, in the end, as Marotti's formulation suggests, such arguments often simply recapitulate the insights of New Criticism, and the figural paradoxes that underwrite those insights. Authorial intention is a fallacy, just as Moses' *vox* or Q's "W.H." is a lure we must avoid. Thankfully, however, Q allows us to dispense with "old-fashioned" ideals of intention; in place of these fallacies, Marotti suggests, the new textual critic uncovers "the kind of fascinating textual instability that appeals to a postmodern sensibility."[65] The problem is that nothing could be more "old-fashioned" than this critique of the intentional fallacy itself. We postmoderns announce our premodern legacy when we transform the parricide of the author into the guarantee of Meaning—even though we construe that Meaning in lowercase, deconstructive terms: e.g., the Meaning of the text (i.e., the moral of our Reading) is that meaning has no guarantee.

However, as I have suggested elsewhere,[66] with such arguments critics like Marotti can neither justify their own hermeneutic practice nor account for the ways in which Q itself sustains a coherent critique of that practice. If, as Marotti suggests, Elizabethan copyright law disrupts our efforts to author-ize Q, this is also a dilemma that, explicitly, Q itself thematizes. I refer here to the first seventeen or so poems of the book: the so-called procreation sonnets. These poems repeatedly, exhaustively, tediously exhort the poet's fair young friend to marry. "Let those whom nature hath not made for store, / Harsh, featurelesse, and rude, barrenly perrish, / Looke whom she best indow'd, she gaue the more; / Which bountious guift thou shouldst in bounty cherrish, / She caru'd thee for her seale, and ment therby, / **Thou shouldst print more, not let that coppy die**" (11:6–14, emphasis added).

In their consideration of the youth's refusal—a refusal, at base, to *reproduce* himself—these opening poems introduce and explicate the universe of the book as a whole: this is a world where the rite and right of copying have been cosmically compromised—and it is also a world that isn't moving forward, that is caught up instead in an increasingly exhaustive and thus exhausted repetition. These sonnets get us nowhere: the exhortations to marry neither, apparently, succeed nor does the poet precisely concede defeat. Instead, the arguments simply *stop*, and we find ourselves amid words so often reproduced, so easily anthologized, mass-marketed, imitated, packaged and processed as "poetic," that they have become almost impossible to read: *Shall I compare thee to a Summers day?* From the very start, then, with the exhaustively reiterated arguments about biological reproduction (arguments that suddenly give way to the most often-reproduced lines of Elizabethan poetry), the book called *Shakespeare's Sonnets* thus thematizes just those historical conditions that vex discussions of intentionality. From the start Q thematizes the problem of authorization in an age, as it were, of mechanical reproduction.

As it turns out, this is an age that begins with our desire for an author:

> From fairest creatures we desire increase,
> That thereby beauties *Rose* might neuer die,
> But as the riper should by time decease,
> His tender heire might beare his memory:
> But thou contracted to thine owne bright eyes,
> Feed'st thy lights flame with selfe substantiall fewell,
> Making a famine where aboundance lies,
> Thy selfe thy foe, to thy sweet selfe too cruell:
> Thou that art now the worlds fresh ornament,
> And only herauld to the gaudy spring,
> Within thine owne bud buriest thy content,
> And tender chorle makst wast in niggarding:
> > Pitty the world, or else this glutton be,
> > To eate the worlds due, by the graue and thee.
>
> (1)

Prior to the young man's duty as a *Rose* and riper–prior to his shirking of that duty, even–we find a desire of our own, commanding and constitutive: a desire for "increase" that, in the context of this sonnet at least, is the desire for an authoritative reproduction. Q's capitalization and italicizing of *Rose*–which most modern editors omit–seems here crucial. Typographically, the word signals its importance: this is no common noun; this is somebody's *name*–a *Rose* plumped out with meaning, rich in context. However, the very print medium that enables this typographic signal, has enabled and even ensured that the name's context be stripped away. We know that *Rose* refers to *someone*, but that refer-

ence is lost to us: instead of conveying specific meaning, the italics only serve to indicate the absence of that meaning. All we
know is that *Rose* means nothing to us now: it is a proper noun
without object, attached to no one and no thing. Thus, no longer
able to point out a specific referent, to refer us to a specific person,
Rose now only denotes the failure of its reference per se.

In this way, *Rose* now only points to itself–to itself as name–
and thus, like all names in their essence, this *Rose* is supremely
empty. Dealing only in specificities, names do not convey general
meaning, do not bear concepts. Unlike a common noun, we cannot ask what a proper noun *signifies*. Instead, the name's attachment to its referent is sheerly singular, contingent and contextual:
no spirit is embodied in this flesh.[67] From the moment this name
was printed, and thus pulled out of its coterie context, this *Rose* of
beauty had for all intents and purposes already died: the name
means nothing to us now.[68] No vivifying content can bring this
dead letter back to life. And so, paradoxically, the *Rose* awakens
our desire: the *Rose* is dead, long live the rose. We want reproduction because we want *figura*: we cannot remain content with the
dead and empty letter. Given that any particular *Rose* of beauty
will surely die, we desire increase that thereby the general rose of
beauty might live. The individual may be lost, but that which we
envisioned through him, the universal that inspirited his particular
flesh, the rose that animated the *Rose*, this will live on in others.
The *Rose* who enfigured beauty–who was the rose, the paradigm,
of beauty, in fact–this *Rose* will live on in later *Rose*s who carry his
name and copy his example.

The first sonnet begins, then, with our desire for reproduction
as the means to a figural fulfillment. And yet it is also reproduction–the mechanical reproduction of print, of book technology–
that strips the letter from its living context and forces the rift
between rose and *Rose* upon us. This link between the rose's reproduction and the mechanically reproduced printed book becomes
explicit a few poems later: "She ["nature"] caru'd thee for her seale,
and ment therby, / Thou shouldst print more, not let that coppy
die" (11:13–14). With no less imprimatur than that of Nature, the
Rose of beauty must exercise his copy-right. Yet, such copy-right is
implicitly, dangerously ambiguous. In Elizabethan English, "copy"
denotes both origin and end, both the original and the impression
taken from that original. Here it is the *Rose* who is the "coppy"–

and it this copy's right to copy, to "print more" copies, that can no longer be taken for granted. The authorized transmission from exemplar to imprint, and the status of the original itself, are in danger. Indeed authorization itself—as that chiastic bridge drawn from origin to end, original to imitation, copy as exemplar to copy as impression—is compromised. Instead of an authorized passage from father to son, *Rose* to *Rose*, the copy to its copy, we find the problem of an unreproduced original: the youth here addressed is a copy that refuses to make copies.[69]

What we desire, then, when we desire increase is not merely reproduction as an endless and exhaustive copying, but rather *succession*. Lines of succession are those generational constructs that, like Paul's hybrid olive, embody and sustain authority through time; a sequence is defined, linking copy to copy and yet distinguishing copy from original, thereby defining a linear temporal order—an origin and a telos. Accordingly it is small wonder that, for Shakespeare, the question of authorization seems intrinsically linked, as we have seen, to the problem of false semblances and counterfeits: without succession, what is reproduction but a kind of plagiarism, that collapses distinctions between the true and false, first and last, writer and reader? Lines of succession, on the other hand, establish a legible and legitimate order, a sequence: the lineaments of the father are legible in the child; the father's seed (L. *semen*) is transformed into legitimating sign (Gk. *semeion*). Each particular individual thus takes its particular place as part of a general whole. The individual conveys the form of the genus, which in turn informs the individual: the father is author to the child, but the child is father to the man. The flesh enfigures that spirit by means of which the flesh itself receives eternal life.

Almost from its very first words, however, Q announces the end of succession. It is a particular end that nonetheless seems to entail a cosmic disaster. A particular young man refuses to perpetuate his family line. At the same time, however, the sonnet reveals a generalized desire: alongside the particular failings of its addressee, the poem reveals a "we" whose investment in *figura*, and in its reassuring telos of authority and succession, is even more consuming than the young man's self-love. This young man's overly particular refusal to marry marks an overwhelming general longing—a universal lack that "we" all suffer. At its most literal level, this longing exists within language: at stake in our desire is a twofold problem of signification–a twofold indeterminacy of the name: the empty specificity, on the one hand, of the proper noun, and, on the other hand, the abstract ambiguity of the common noun. The *Rose* of beauty should flesh out the abstract concept of beauty's rose–indeed this *Rose* should be the rose, the very figure or example of beauty itself–but at the same time, if we want to know who *Rose* is, we should just think of beauty and imagine its rose. Yet of course this bridge between rose and *Rose* is our *fantasy*: an image of chiastic fulfillment, *Rose* in rose, rose as *Rose*. This is what we would *like*, but the very presence of our desire signals the fact of our disappointment. With the young man betrothed, as it were, to himself, the lines of succession are already broken; the temporal order reconciling *Rose* to rose, original copy to copied copy, has already been turned back upon itself, linearity has already shrunk to a self-consuming singularity–an infinitely dense, black-hole spark of light: "But thou contracted to thine owne bright eyes, / Feed'st thy lights flame with selfe substantiall fewell, / Making a famine where aboundance lies." By the time the sonnets begin, figural reconciliation is already a lost possibility.[70]

At the heart of the problem as these sonnets envision it, is the "self-abuse"–an onanism with catachrestic consequence–of the young man.

> When fortie Winters shall beseige thy brow,
> And digge deep trenches in thy beauties field,
> . . . .
> Then being askt, where all thy beautie lies,
> Where all the treasure of thy lusty daies;
> To say within thine owne deepe sunken eyes,
> Were an all-eating shame, and thriftlesse praise.
> How much more praise deseru'd thy beauties vse,
> If thou couldst answere this faire child of mine
> Shall sum my count, and make my old excuse
> Proouing his beautie by succession thine.
>
> (2.1–2, 5–12)

In obvious reference to the Parable of the Talents, the youth is exhorted to "use" his treasure–to procreate and thereby reap a profit; to gain by way of expense. "To giue away your selfe, keeps your selfe still," the poet advises later (16.13). Indeed, without such expense, nothing adds up: the very logic of succession falters–our accounts cannot be summed. Instead of bringing fulfillment, time will only bring decay: like the servant who buries his single talent ("But he that receiued that one, went and digged it in the earth, and hid his masters money.")[71] time will only "digge deep trenches" in the young man's face, burying beauty in his "deep sunken eyes." Indeed, if the young man's problem is his hoarding introversion–the fact that he *keeps (to) himself*–then time also entails a turning inward, since it buries one's talents deep inside.

In these poems we find the image of a fatal inward-turning disrupting all sense of temporal fulfillment. In keeping to himself, the young man holds that *substance* within which should be expressed as outward *show*–drawn outward to reap a profit. The sonnet recasts the logic of temporal succession in spatial terms: in order to be conserved, the precious inward substance must be expended, spent *out*. The young man's spirit–his essence as well as his semen–needs to be *distilled*.[72] Thus the images of perfume-making in sonnets 5 and 6: "flowers distil'd though they with winter meete, / Leese but their show, their substance still liues sweet" (5:13–14). Far from offering fulfillment, time will only widen the gap between substance (or, *essence*) and show, creating an ever-increasing disjunction between a spiritual inside and its fleshly exterior. Procreation, on the other hand, will close this gap, by drawing that inward treasure *out*.

Or so it at first appears; a second look at sonnets 5 and 6 suggests that, once extracted, the young man's substance–that flower or *Rose* of beauty itself–must be brought back inside. It cannot remain expressed. "Then let not winters wragged hand deface, / In thee thy summer ere thou be distil'd: / Make sweet some viall; treasure thou some place, / With beautits [*sic*] treasure ere it be self kil'd" (6.1–4). The young man's treasure is exhumed only to be buried elsewhere: from the tomb of the self to the womb of a mother (see 3.5, 7); from the mirroring "glasse" of self-love (3.1) to the "walls of glasse" in which a distillate is "pent" (5.10). In this way, these sonnets fail to imagine resolution; instead, the disjunction of inward and outward will ever remain: any efforts to seal the gap will merely reinstantiate it somewhere else.

If inward and outward could be made to coincide, then *figura*, with its sense of temporal fulfillment, could be saved. But as these sonnets imagine it, procreation can only serve to pass the problem on–reproducing the very division between inner and outer, between flesh and spirit, show and substance, that reproduction was meant to mend. Thus these sonnets record the devastating insight that temporal fulfillment itself is a timely matter: "euery thing that growes / Holds in perfection but a little moment" (15.1–2). Flesh and spirit are not reconciled *over* time: they are reconciled *in* time, and only *temporarily*–for an instant of perfection on the very way to their ultimate irreconcilability: *death*.

Thus, insofar as we take these sonnets as arguments for marriage,[73] they are doomed to fail. The sonnets urge a logic of succession, but their urgency itself is based on a sense of time that defies succession. Time as envisioned here doesn't fulfill; it only renders the outside incommensurate with the inside. Indeed, it is because time now offers "deep trenches" in place of fulfillment, that procreation is thought necessary. All the same, since procreation is itself defined by time, it cannot fill in the chinks that time leaves behind. Lines of succession cannot repair time lines. The poet's wish in sonnet 16 is thus an impossible one:

> So should the lines of life that life repaire
> Which this (Times pensel or my pupill pen)
> Neither in inward worth nor outward faire
> Can make you liue your selfe in eies of men.
>
> (16:9–12)

If "times pensel" cannot make the young man "live himself," self-adequate, self-possessing, then neither can procreation, whose "increase" will always take place in time, entailing thereby an *increase*: a wrinkling, that is, sculpted by time, as it cuts creases into outer show.[74] And so, indeed, these sonnets register a problem with copying: the very notion of *copia*–of increase and abundance–is compromised by an inward creasing.[75]

With its simultaneous increase and in-crease, procreation is hence not the solution but a part of the problem. In the face of this realization, the poet turns his hopes to the "pupill pen" of poetry: "all in war with Time for loue of you / As he takes from you, I ingraft you new" (15.13–14). The poet will unwrite the effects of time by filling in ("in-grafting") the lines that time has carved. But quickly this optimism is itself unwritten; as we've already seen, the pupil's pen is no match for, and certainly no better than, Time's pencil. Instead, the poet's desire to make the young man "new" relies on the same figural possibilities that these sonnets have already dismantled. To maintain the young man as himself, self-adequate and self-same, would be to maintain an identity between flesh and spirit, show and substance. The goal is a figural one: to reconcile inward to outward, spirit to flesh. Given this goal, poetry will fail as miserably as procreation already has, since both are tutored by time itself. Both look to the increase that time offers ("When I consider euery thing that growes . . ." [15.1]), and can only emulate the creases scored by time's pencil. Nonetheless, this inability of the "pupill pen" itself will offer the poet a solution, of sorts, to *figura*'s failure. In the *envoi* to the procreation sonnets we see a figural logic of succession replaced by–perhaps *succeeded* by– a poetics of abuse.

> Shall I compare thee to a Summers day?
> Thou art more louely and more temperate:
> Rough windes do shake the darling buds of Maie,
> And Sommers lease hath all too short a date:
> Sometime too hot the eye of heauen shines,
> And often is his gold complexion dimm'd,
> And euery faire from faire some-time declines,
> By chance, or natures changing course vntrim'd:
> But thy eternall Sommer shall not fade,
> Nor loose possession of that faire thou ow'st,
> Nor shall death brag thou wandr'st in his shade,
> When in eternall lines to time thou grow'st,
>   So long as men can breath or eyes can see,
>   So long liues this, and this giues life to thee,
>
>   (18)

Even careful readers of sonnet 18 often simply construe its familiarity as a heightened form of compliment, a compliment that narrowly avoids cliché by turning cliché back upon itself: i.e., I would compare you to a summer's day, if summer were as lovely as you are.[76] However, the poem is stranger than such readings allow–not least because it is unclear whether, in the end, the poem actually praises the friend. Instead, presumably we see here an example of the poet's efforts to "ingraft" his friend "new": in comparing the friend's youthful beauty to a summer's day, the poet "trims" it (8)–he ornaments it with rhetorical flourish, "dressing it new" (cf. sonnet 76.11). Such ingrafting is pictured ambiguously in the "eternall lines" of the poem's close: at once, as Booth suggests in his commentary, the cords that hold a grafted shoot in place, and the lines of immortal poetry itself (cf. Booth, 161–62). Bound to time by these lines of verse, the young man will grow attached *to* time, *with* time, as a shoot grows to the root stock; as time passes, the young man will flourish rather than decline.

But what sort of ornament has the poet here provided? His metaphor of the summer's day has been, precisely, faulty. If he is ingrafting the young man new, he is not doing so after the manner of procreation–he is not providing semblances or likenesses, no "painted counterfeit" (16.8) to make the young man live (like) himself. Indeed, if anything he is offering *non*-likenesses–images that assert the very failure of his own image-making. "Shall I compare thee to a Summers day? / Thou art more louely and more temperate." Nonetheless, by asserting the inadequacy of his art, the poet manages to create a poem that says what it cannot: "thy eternall Sommer shall not fade." Summer is precisely *not* eternal, and so the metaphor is a failure–yet even so, understood *as* failure the metaphor works: *unlike* summer, your "summer" is eternal. In this way the very inadequacy of the poet's figure makes it a worthy figure for the incomparable young man.

But let's go further. In what sense is the young man incomparable? In what sense is his summer "eternal"? After all, the very aspect of natural beauty that makes it inadequate for comparison *to* the young man is also true *for* the young man: "euery faire from faire some-time declines." This rule cannot help but apply to our fair young man just as fairly as it applies to a summer's day. Indeed, everything we've read in the foregoing seventeen poems will tell us that the young man is *precisely* like a summer's day. He is *not* eternal–his lease hath all too short a date–and his beauty will soon give way to winter's "wragged hand" (6.1). In fact, it is only insofar as he has been written into the poet's verse–engrafted in eternal lines–that the young man's summer will endure. "So long as men can breath or eyes can see, / So long liues this, and this giues life to thee." It is only insofar as the young man "lives" in a poetry that declares him incomparable that he will live forever. But since, in truth this young man really is not incomparable but is exactly as transient as a summer's day, this poetry lies. It does not provide a likeness of the young man—but nor does it provide an unlikeness that would be, paradoxically, like him. The young man is nothing like the inimitable nonpareil of sonnet 18. Indeed, if the goal of writing such poems is to make the young man "live himself," then this poem has failed: insofar as the young man lives, he is not himself, since as himself he is constantly inconstant, ever declining and different from himself. As himself he is not eternal.

In this way Shakespeare, like Luther, envisions a new "art of ingrafting": one that only binds flesh to spirit, inconstant youth to eternal constancy, insofar as it remarks their ineradicable difference. In-grafting here, like in-creasing, only pries open that wound which *figura*'s graft hoped to heal. Sonnet 18 has thus introduced an image of a new poetics, one grounded in a sense of *figura*'s failure: a poetry that acknowledges that the flesh, like those fair shows of nature, like the summer's day, is an inadequate vessel for spirit. This poetry has abandoned the hybrid logic of succession. But at the same time, this poetry does not eschew the flesh, does not discard it in a gesture analogous to Karlstadt's iconoclasm or Zwingli's rejection of the Real Presence. Instead, sonnet 18 introduces a poetry that recognizes the flesh's finitude and hence the imperfection of its grafts—its figures—and yet, nevertheless, manages by way of such imperfection to present the perfect figure: i.e., the figure of perfection. In the image of the young man as nonpareil, as eternally "faire, kinde, and true" (105), this poetry envisions the reconciliation of flesh and spirit. In other words, with its failed and false figures, sonnet 18 offers nonetheless an image of figure's true success. Granted, this image is a lie—and the poetry knows it as such—but it is a lie that lies like truth.

Hence the procreation sonnets, which reject notions of origin and succession, nonetheless recount for us the origin of Shakespearean poetics: a poetics founded in/as catachrestic graft. In the wake of Luther's critique of *figura*, Shakespeare demonstrates that, regardless, we cannot help ourselves: we cannot stop (re)producing figures—even if our reproductions only amount to figures of abuse.

THE CANKER AND THE ROSE

It is hard to mistake the centrality of the rose in Shakespeare's writings of the 1590s. If, as critics have traditionally argued, his

Sonnets were written in this period, their first sustained image–the rose of beauty that animates our desire in poem 1–plays upon a pervasive motif, echoing the mingled red and white of a Petrarchan Shakespeare in *Venus and Adonis* and *Rape of Lucrece*, even while the silent war of blushes and innocence, of lilies and roses emblazoned in the beloved's face in these narrative poems (cf. *Rape of Lucrece*, 71), also evokes Shakespeare's decade-long preoccupation with English history, as he chronicles the dynastic and dramatic implications of roses at war, of Lancastrian red and Yorkist white. Shakespeare's roses flourish in a context at once erotic and combative, personal and political.[77] But the figure's multivalence should not surprise us. As erotic figure for poetry's erotic figures, the rose has been conventional since the "Song of Songs," and its politics have been apparent at least since Tillyard's discussions of the "Tudor Myth" of English history.[78] Behind the damasked red/white roses of Shakespeare's Petrarchism we have long been accustomed to see that emblem of the Tudor dynasty: the double rose, white superimposed on red.

Ultimately, however, Shakespeare's roses are striking not so much for the way they foreground their own status as signs–for, e.g., the way in which they draw attention to their own activity of figuration–but rather for their simultaneous ability to insist upon themselves as *things*. When Juliet famously proposes that "a Rose, /By any other word would smell as sweete" (*Romeo and Juliet*, 2.1.87–88), she cites the flower as the consummate *thing*, the referent whose essential qualities, whose very roseness is indifferent to an order of language. The flower becomes the very figure of the world's fundamental–as Juliet would have it–independence from figures. For Juliet the rose works paradoxically as a figure that denies the import and weight of figures.

Of course, Juliet's nominalist insight is itself as traditional as it is misguided, given its context within a play that demonstrates precisely the contingent, yet nonetheless tragic force of names. As the figure of a figuration independent from the world of things, Juliet's rose wishfully invokes an Augustinian conception of language's mere conventionality. Sticks and stones may break my bones. . . . Words, on the other hand, have no worldly impact, no phenomenal weight. Their import is *merely* conventional. But at the same time that Juliet invokes this sense of the arbitrary and autonomous sign, she seeks to offer a convincing (read: *motivated*) figure for its arbitrariness. In its separation from the word that denotes it, her rose is no arbitrary sign, tied merely contingently to meaning. Instead, as the figure of figure's autonomy from the phenomenal world, Juliet's rose relies upon its own phenomenal distance from its name. This rose (let's cite it under erasure to remember its independence from its name) would smell as sweet no matter what we called it.

Juliet's rose is a trope, but a curious one. For Juliet, the word "rose" names nothing; she is citing the word in isolation from its referent: that which we call a "rose," she says, would smell as sweet no matter what name attached to it. Her "rose" is just a word, inadequate as any other. But that nothing that "rose" names, or rather that something that "rose" does *not* name–i.e., Juliet's rose in its independence from language–does itself signify a world outside language. In this way, by failing to name the rose, "rose" nonetheless transports us to a world beyond language. The name "rose," then, yields an improper figure: i.e., the rose itself, figured by a language that can only fail to name it properly. Juliet's rose–at once both vehicle and tenor, both "rose" and rose–is thus a catachresis: it is a trope that takes the place of a name.

In the *Sonnets*, we find this catachrestic rose again–and, as with the flower's catachrestic centrality in the *Henry VI* plays, where the sliding referentiality of Lancastrian red and Yorkist white seems both to reflect and to cause the problem of dynastic succession, in the *Sonnets* catachresis is also from the start tied to the question of an heir. As we have said, the young man's refusal to procreate "that thereby beauties *Rose* might neuer die," leads to poetic likenesses–likenesses that remain in a crucial sense *unlike* their subject. And as we have seen, by negating its similes, sonnet 18 fails to give a proper image of the young man–yet produces nonetheless images of perfection: likenesses that, however unlike the young man, will remain forever like themselves. In this way, the poem's failed similes survive as successful catachreses: there is no proper name for the young man's beauty because, like all beauty, it fails to remain like itself.

Indeed, the catachrestic nature of the verse inaugurated in these sonnets ultimately reveals that it is impossible to blame the young man's problem on his own thriftless self-involvement. The young man is not the origin of this catachrestic universe–not even a fanciful, just-so story origin. He is instead the universe's symptom; or, to use the poet's own word: he is this "world's ornament": he is the figure of a world where figure no longer works. He is the rose/canker ornament that needs ornament in return. *Thou that art now the worlds fresh ornament, / And only herauld to the gaudy spring / Within thine owne bud buriest thy content.*

The problem that these poems confront lies not with the prodigal young man but with a time that is itself prodigal. "Looke what an vnthrift in the world doth spend / Shifts but his place, for still the world inioyes it / But beauties waste hath in the world an end, / And kept vnvsed the vser so destroyes it" (9.9–12). In the world's economy nothing is gained, and nothing is lost. What is spent merely "shifts" places, redistributed and still enjoyed. But beauty is somehow different; its waste amounts to an actual loss, a true end, because it is itself inextricably bound to a wasteful time, achieving its perfection on the very road to decay.

> When I consider euery thing that growes
> Holds in perfection but a little moment.
> . . . .
> When I perceiue that men as plants increase,
> Cheared and checkt euen by the selfe-same skie:
> Vaunt in their youthfull sap, at height decrease,
> And were their braue state out of memory.
> Then the conceit of this inconstant stay,
> Sets you most rich in youth before my sight,
> Where wastfull time debateth with decay
> To change your day of youth to sullied night,
>   And all in war with Time for loue of you
>   As he takes from you, I ingraft you new.
>
> (15)

The ultimate prodigal, time spends but its wealth doesn't merely shift places: what it wastes is permanently lost. It is because time, as imagined in these sonnets, is itself a waste that the arguments for procreation are doomed to fail: the notion of succession that they invoke presumes that time moves toward fulfillment, the old redeemed in the new. In fact, such succession presumes precisely that time wastes nothing–that its expenditures are always recuperated, its beginnings preserved in its ends. In the *Sonnets*, however, time only ripens on the path to rotting. Beauty's rose thus can never be preserved, even when reproduced in the "liuing flowers" (16.7) of offspring, since what is reproduced will be not beauty itself but its waste: each flower will only repeat the truth of time's law that fairness cannot remain fair, that no thing can remain like itself.

It is in this context of a wasteful time that Shakespeare imagines his poetry as "ingrafting." Just like Paul's olive tree in Romans 11, Shakespeare's graft of verse means to supplant a succession based on filial generation. A spiritual procreation will replace a merely fleshly one. And yet, significantly, where Paul's vision of the grafted tree defined the very logic of time, producing an allegorical narrative of fulfillment and right succession, Shakespeare's graft works *against* time, seeking to fill in the lines drawn by time with lines of verse. Furthermore, by working against time, the poet is also working against beauty, itself a thing of time. Indeed, he is working against the young man's very identity. "O that you were your selfe, but loue you are / No longer yours, then you your selfe here liue" (13.1–2). The young man *is himself* in time; he holds in perfection but a little moment. To work against decline preserves perfection; such work holds the young man's beauty in place, but it also paradoxically belies it.

For Joel Fineman, this paradox marks the way in which Shakespeare writes in the "aftermath" of a poetics of praise (*Perjured Eye*, 51). Shakespeare, Fineman argues, plays out (and ultimately exhausts) the epideictic logic of Petrarchism; his sonnets demonstrate the ways in which an idealizing mimesis undermines itself—and necessarily so, insofar as the metaphorical articulation of sameness at the same time requires the speaking of difference. In the dark lady sonnets, Fineman argues, such ironies become fully explicit. In those final poems, the idealizing language of likeness gives way to the paradoxical language of difference: beloved *because* she lacks "the power to make loue grone" (131.6), fair *because* she is "black as hell" (147.14), the dark lady inspires a language, and a desire, that is simultaneously true and false.

For Fineman the language of the *Sonnets* verges on paradox because of the paradoxical structure of idealization: finding their poetic necessity in the young man's praiseworthiness (and their poetic undoing in the dark lady's lack thereof), the poet's true words ultimately belie both their subject and themselves. Either the praise is superfluous, in which case as "mere painting" it cheapens its subject, or the praise is needed, and thus merely flatters a beloved who fails to live up to his ideal. Indeed, in the so-called rival poet sonnets (78–86) Shakespeare suggests that these two possibilities converge: there, a purely superfluous praise ("I neuer saw that you did painting need," [83.1]) reveals the young man's one true flaw: his vanity. "You to your beautious blessings adde a curse, / Being fond on praise, which makes your praises worse" (84.13–14).

However, the problem with Shakespeare's young man lies deeper than the related questions of idealization and vanity. Certainly Shakespeare responds to the paradoxes of a tradition of epideixis when he imagines a young man who is simultaneously idealized and non-ideal, worthy of praise and vainly "fond" of it. But Shakespeare's response is more historically specific, more exacting in its terms, and more far-reaching in its consequences, than Fineman suggests. Shakespeare uncovers the very roots of idealism, exposing and questioning the temporal structure that sustains it. As we have seen, "beauty's rose"–that is, beauty's ideal paradigm, its exemplar–seems to require a world in which succession is possible. Over the fullness of time, the flesh itself is fulfilled; in the riper's "tender heire" (1.4), the spirit of beauty lives on, just as Paul's grafted branches bear fruit on behalf of the moribund native root. But in Shakespeare's post-Reformation world, time's wastes can only recount the continually renewed decline of flesh from spirit. Here the ideal–the essence of the rose–can only be disappointed by its material, fleshly embodiment. And yet, even so, such a world does not lack for beauty–although its beauty, as such, as precisely *ideal* can only fail itself.

It is in this context that we must consider the poems that seek to preserve the young man's truth.

> Oh how much more doth beautie beautious seeme,
> By that sweet ornament which truth doth giue,
> The rose looks faire, but fairer we it deeme
> For that sweet odor, which doth in it liue:
> The Canker bloomes haue full as deepe a die,
> As the perfumed tincture of the Roses,
> Hang on such thornes, and play as wantonly,
> When sommers breath their masked buds discloses:
> But for their virtue only is their show,

> They liue vnwoo'd, and vnrespected fade,
> Die to themselues. Sweet Roses doe not so,
> Of their sweet deathes, are sweetest odors made:
> And so of you, beautious and louely youth,
> When that shall vade, by verse distils your truth.
>
>   (54)

In terms of show the canker blossom is as fair as the rose, but its
"tincture" lacks that sweet ornament, that perfume, which tells the
true rose from the false. However, the poem also suggests that
such truth remains hidden as long as the rose lives; odor here is
figured as that essence (both scent and spiritual substance) that
remains tucked inside—"which doth *in* it liue"—until the flower is
blown and dead. Of course, if such essence only lives, while the
rose lives, hidden inside the bud, then the sonnet confirms Juliet's
words in a starkly unhelpful way: with its true essence hidden, that
which we call a "rose" would smell as sweet even by the name of
"canker," since it releases no scent at all. For all we can tell, both
canker and rose smell equally sweet—and equally sour, for that
matter, for both, in their life, yield no essence at all. And yet, the
difference between the two flowers—the very difference between a
flower and a weed—is, precisely, *essential.* Unlike the rose, cankers
have beauty without truth—a beauty that is not "beautious"; when
they fade, they "die to themselues." "Vnwoo'd" and "vnrespected"
the beauty of the canker is inessential, odorless and thus utterly
lost with the passage of time: mere fleshly appearance, it lacks the
durance of spirit.

The situation that the poet here ascribes to the lowly canker
echoes exactly the description of the young man's plight in the
procreation sonnets. Without an heir, the flower of youth will die
"vnlok'd [*unlooked*] on" (7.14)—will die to himself—to his own
"sweet selfe too cruell" (1.8). Like the canker, the young man's
beauty will prove untrue once it fades, unless somehow distilled in
the grafting supplements of progeny or verse. "But flowers distil'd
though they with winter meete, / Leese but their show, their substance still liues sweet" (5.13–14). Without the possibility of distil-
lation, the young man is exactly like the canker: only his death, and
not his beauty, will prove eternal. Presumably, however, the young
man is a rose and not a canker. Presumably his beauty is true—and
true precisely insofar as it withstands the test of time. Sweet roses

do not die to themselves; "Of their sweet deathes, are sweetest odors made: / And so of you, beautious and louely youth, / When that shall vade, by verse distils your truth."

What sonnet 54 reveals, however, is the ineradicable problem of beauty in a world where time itself is prodigal. Truth in this world is compromised: it is understood both as that hidden essence or scent that distinguishes between show and substance, canker and rose—and at the same time, truth is beauty's "ornament": that superadded, ingrafted supplement that beautifies beauty by maintaining its constancy—making sure that beauty remain beauteous; that beauty be *true*. "Oh how much more doth beautie beautious seeme, / By that sweet ornament which truth doth giue." How can essential truth—the sweet odor that tells the difference between the rose and the canker, between true beauty and the counterfeit—also be understood as *ornament*, as supplement? The problem of the poet's world seems to be that the difference between essence and ornament makes *no* difference. From our perspective, from our standpoint in the midst of wasteful time, essence and ornament are the same. The difference between rose and canker is essential, but it can only emerge after death, after the fact, by means of a graft that is equivocally ornament and essence, equivocally that which supplements "vaded" (i.e., departed) beauty and that which reveals essential truth. Such a graft either brings perfume to the canker or draws perfume from the rose: from our perspective (and what other perspective is available to us?), the verse that distills pure essence will be indistinguishable from the verse that tells pure lies. Indeed, the problem of beauty in these poems is that it will never be clear whether beauty exists as the rose's truth, or as the canker's lie. Roses, like cankers, do indeed die to themselves; the essential truth of their beauty is a truth that like the eternal summer's day of sonnet 18, belies their essence-less life. Every fair from fair sometime declines—and of their sweet deaths, are sweetest odors made.

The consequences of sonnet 54—of a world where the essential difference between roses and cankers is truth-as-ornament—get worked out in the sequence in poems that explore, like the rival poet sonnets, the flattering nature of praise, and in poems like 95 that consider the young man's failings. "How sweet and louely dost thou make the shame, / Which like a canker in the fragrant Rose / Doth spot the beautie of thy budding name?"

(95.1–3). Here the problem of beauty becomes internal to the rose itself; rather than being understood as that weed indistinguishably, but essentially, different from the flower, the canker here is that hidden worm that blemishes the name of beauty itself. The spatial relations have been inverted, but the dilemma remains the same: it is now not the essence that is concealed within the "fragrant Rose" but instead the cancerous shame that, hidden within, secretly corrupts essence. Yet again, the poem explores the problem of distinguishing the rose from the canker: this young man makes even shame look good. Indeed, shame becomes sweet and lovely–it *becomes* the young man, an ornament to his beauty merely by being a part of him, a part of beauty. In this way, that name that sonnet 1 has seemed to identify, through italics, as the proper name of the young man–*Rose*–seems in sonnet 95 to have become equivocally improper by "bless[ing] an ill report" (8). The young man's name seems at once to name beauty as rose and to name the canker that disrupts that beauty, turning flowers into weeds. "That tongue that tells the story of thy daies, / (Making lasciuious comments on thy sport) / Cannot dispraise, but in a kinde of praise, / Naming thy name, blesses an ill report" (5–8). The poem alludes to this ill report but does not tell us what it consists of–what precise shame or ill-mannered "sport" lascivious tongues have recounted. Instead the poem focuses upon the fact that beauty's name equivocates between rose and canker. "Beauties vaile doth couer euery blot, / And all things turnes to faire." (11–12). What the young man has done literally makes no difference since even dispraise becomes his beauty mark. The spots that mar his budding name only attest to his beauty–only serve as beauty's mark, proving his rosy essence, since "loathsome canker liues in sweetest bud" (35.4).

There can be no "ill" reports of beauty, because in this world, beauty not only has ornaments, but *requires* ornaments in order to "live like itself"–in order, that is, to remain fair. Without its adulterating marks, beauty cannot remain unblemished. Indeed, what sonnet 95 ultimately reveals is that beauty is indistinguishable from the ornament–the beauty mark–that keeps it fair, and yet renders it false. "Beauties vaile doth couer euery blot, / And all things turnes to faire": beauty's veil, both the veil that masks beauty and the veil that is beauty, simultaneously conceals beauty's fault and renders fault beautiful. Beauty, like truth, is an ornament that equivocally veils the rose's canker, and reveals the canker as rose.[79]

And yet, how can fairness be so fundamentally unfair? In its attempt to exonerate the young man by ascribing his moral failing to immutable nature, sonnet 35 ("No more bee greeu'd") depicts, as we have seen, a fault-making poet. Let's return to the paradoxes of that poem, guided now by a fuller sense of the poet's world—a world where beauty's veil both obscures blot and beautifies it, fairing the foul and adulterating the true.

> No more bee greeu'd at that which thou hast done,
> Roses haue thornes, and siluer fountaines mud,
> Cloudes and eclipses staine both Moone and Sunne,
> And loathsome canker liues in sweetest bud.
> All men make faults, and euen I in this,
> Authorizing thy trespas with compare,
> My selfe corrupting saluing thy amisse,
> Excusing their sins more then their sins are:
> For to thy sensuall fault I bring in sence,
> Thy aduerse party is thy Aduocate,
> And gainst my self a lawfull plea commence,
> Such ciuill war is in my loue and hate,
>   That I an accessary needs must be,
>   To that sweet theefe which sourely robs from me,
>
> (35)

It simply isn't easy, as the poet learns, to speak truly and fairly of those who are truly fair. The poet finds himself at fault no matter what he says. Just as the failed similes of sonnet 18 wrongly exempt the young man from the law of nature (i.e., *every fair from fair sometime declines*), so too are the similes of sonnet 35 successful—and yet at fault—by *failing* to exempt the young man from nature. The poem's metaphors follow the same logic as the similes of sonnet 18, but they proceed in the opposite direction. Here, the poet's comparisons are apt. The young man is indeed like a thorny rose, a silver fountain stained with mud, like the sweetest bud eaten by loathsome canker. Here, the likenesses the poet offers are accurate—and yet, their very truth only manages, as we have seen, to render fault itself lovely: a thing of beauty, a thing of nature. The poet corrupts himself by exculpating the young man's moral failure as if it were only natural; the poet errs, then, in mistaking natural and moral faults.

Yet, it is important to recognize the ways in which such an error–the poet's error–is itself unavoidable; as unavoidable, perhaps, as the thorns that mar the rose. After all, within the world of these poems–a world I have identified in historical terms as post-Reformation, or at least as post-Luther–within such a world, even so-called moral fault is a natural feature of the human condition. Such fault remains a moral problem, yet exists as the inevitable and unconquerable stigma of human nature, marking that schism between the flesh and the spirit–that fault line that defines and divides us.

Beauty, as it seems to be defined in these poems, defined by this fault line, is more a formal category than it is a substantive physical property. The relative absence of blazons in the young man poems should alert us to this fact.[80] In place of a specific catalogue of the young man's features,[81] the poet offers us only three adjectives: "faire, kinde, and true."[82] The young man is beautiful because he remains constant, self-identical, equal to himself. His beauty is indeed his *fairness–nothing* but fairness, in the brutest sense of the word's meaning as *equality* or *parity*. "O that you were yourself!" as the poet exclaims in his arguments for procreation. To be fair is to be one's self, simply, perfectly, eternally. "Who is it that sayes most, which can say more, / Then this rich praise, that you alone, are you [?]" (84.1–2). The height of praise is to assert a person's self-identity. In these terms, beauty becomes for Shakespeare the self-sufficiency, the independence–literally, the perfection–of the sovereign subject: *I am that I am*, as the poet says, echoing the King of Kings himself.[83] Yet, for us growing creatures, who hold in perfection but a little moment, beauty is our birthright only insofar as time both makes us and mars us. In short, for Shakespeare "beauty" would seem to be something like the name of our particular temporal bind.

Thus, in the poem above, fault does seem to be the inevitable concomitant of beauty–the unavoidable spoilage of the ideal in a world ravaged by time. Such fault is also unavoidable for the poet, whose comparisons only idealize the very nature of sin itself by rendering it the universal property of man. In this light we might approach a reading of the notoriously opaque line 8: "All men make faults, and euen I in this . . . / *Excusing their sins more then their sins are.*"[84] In making figures, comparisons for fault, the poet has made fault beautiful, a thing pertaining to all beauty–and further, a thing of all flesh, as if flesh itself were beautiful precisely insofar as it fails to live up to the ideals of spirit. He has excused the sins of all men (*"Excusing* THEIR *sins"*) too extensively (*"more than* THERE *sins are"*); he has excused too much, too many. He has excused away sin itself. The risk the poet runs here is the same risk of complacency that the doctrine, Lutheran at its core, of the will's bondage is always at risk of running. Because the schism between flesh and spirit is decisive, sins of the flesh are inherent, natural; given such unavoidable fault, to what extent can beauty ever be said to fail–or can failure ever fail to be beautiful? "Oh in what sweets doest thou thy sinnes inclose!" (95.4) With such assumptions about beauty, how can sin as such be thought even to exist?

Erasmus argued in similar terms against Luther in the 1524 diatribe *On Free Will*: if we conclude that man's will is bound, that by nature man is sinful, then we can no longer hold him responsible for his errors. But as we shall see more fully in the next chapter, Luther's vision of the will's bondage, like Shakespeare's vision of our temporal bind, complicates simple distinctions between guilt and innocence, between sweetness and sin. For Luther, our enslaved will does not preclude free action; indeed, it is precisely because we are willful creatures, capable of acting freely according to our desires, that we are entirely responsible for our actions. When we sin, we do so willingly–but it is just such willingness that demonstrates our enslavement. Indeed, as Luther argues, we are bound by our will itself, for we are incapable of acting freely *unless* in accordance with our desires–and our desires are the one thing we cannot control. We cannot will what we will; our desire cannot command itself.

In poem 35, the poet seems to articulate a similar insight. His fault consists in his willful love of fault itself. His fault is his idealization–his idolatry, even–of sin: "For to thy sensuall fault I bring in sence," he writes, acknowledging the rationalizing work of poetry, although many readers have also smelt out the worshipful *incense* behind this claim. Once again the poet distills sweet odors from the flower, masking the difference–or the fact that there is *no* difference–between canker and rose. To remain in love with beauty in this prodigal world is to forgive beauty its fault–but one is then in the position of loving fault as if it were beautiful: to love fault *in place* of beauty. The position seems untenable: to love a faulty beauty *as* beauty is to love what in fact we hate, to want what we do not want. It is, indeed, to love and beautify fault. Such is the poet's civil war: a will torn between love and hate, freedom and bondage. "Such civill war is in my loue and hate, / That I an accessary needs must be, / To that sweet theefe which sourely robs from me" (12–14).

In the dark lady sonnets this ambivalent will comes entirely to the fore in terms of a poet who loves against his conscience, making fault beautiful because he loves. Like the young man sonnets, these poems also begin by invoking the question of succession–indeed by claiming to offer a successor to now-disappointed idealism itself. As we shall see, however, the mistress's blackness is no more successful as "beauties successiue heire" than the poet's faulty like-nesses were.

> In the ould age blacke was not counted faire,
> Or if it weare it bore not beauties name:
> But now is blacke beauties successiue heire,
> And Beautie slanderd with a bastard shame,
> For since each hand hath put on Natures power,
> Fairing the foule with Arts faulse borrow'd face,
> Sweet beauty hath no name no holy boure,
> But is prophan'd, if not liues in disgrace.
> Therefore my Mistersse [*sic*] eyes are Rauen blacke,
> Her eyes so suted, and they mourners seeme,
> At such who not borne faire no beauty lack,
> Slandring Creation with a false esteeme,
>   Yet so they mourne becomming of their woe,
>   That euery toung saies beauty should looke so.
>
>   (127)

The poem claims to offer a new start, a new poetics. For Fineman the sonnet heralds the "after" image of a homoerotic poetics of praise: the dark lady sonnets render explicit the ironies of epi-deixis, not merely exploring the limits of idealization but pushing those limits into paradox, and "inventing," in the process, a poet-ics of difference and desire. In place of a poetry geared toward image, procreation, fullness, likeness–the dark lady sonnets introduce an invaginating poetry of difference, lack, and self-hating heterosexual desire. Where the young man sonnets idealize, seeking to produce perfect likenesses of a phallic self-identity–the "faire, kinde, and true" young man–the dark lady sonnets, Fineman argues, emphasize not the ideality of the poet's vision but the "languageness" of his language: a self-belying verbality that forswears itself through paradox and pun. For Fineman, then, sonnet 127 articulates the division between new and "ould," language and vision, difference and sameness, paradox and praise, black and fair, the *nothing* of woman and the *one thing* of man,[85] fiend and angel, hell and heaven. . . .

At the same time, however, for Fineman this dividing line is not absolute; instead, both in precise formal ways and in large thematic/narrative structures, the sequence charts the crisscrossed contagion of such antitheses. It does so most *dramatically* in the image of the dark lady and young man's double betrayal of the poet, an image of heaven fallen into hell, of an angel "turned" fiend: "And whether that my angel be turn'd finde, / Suspect I may, yet not directly tell, / But being both from me both to each friend, / I gesse one angel in an others hel" (144.9–12). In this way, chiasmus–or what Fineman calls the "cross-coupler" (following Puttenham's term for the related figure, *syneciosis*)–is the master trope of *Shakespeare's Perjured Eye.* In its formal operations, chiasmus bespeaks the "way that language manages noticeably to redouble with a difference the complementary similarities of a figurality based on likeness" (37). It bespeaks, in other words, the ways in which likeness can only be articulated by means of a simultaneous act of differentiation; the ways in which every iteration is also an alteration. As a rhetorical figure, chiasmus mirrors syntactically the very dilemma that, according to Fineman, transforms praise into paradox. And, most crucially, the trope serves to enfigure the structure of a Shakespearean desiring, poetic subjectivity; chiasmus is central to Fineman's account because it offers the figure of Shakespeare's *Will*–and links that figure to a specifically linguistic problem: the problem of articulating identity.

Chiasmus is, then, the linchpin of Fineman's argument inasmuch as it neatly collates sexuality, subjectivity, and language. But the trope is also crucial because it allows Fineman to track the play of difference within the sonnets while still maintaining that unifying narrative that quilts together the sequence as a whole. With its

ABBA pattern of inversion, chiasmus bridges difference through repetition, and yet suspends resolution: meaning is generated through chiastic crossing, but answers are deferred. *Ask not what your country can do for you, but what you can do for your country.* And yet, as I tried to suggest in my reading of Augustinian chiasmus, this sense of suspension is, ultimately, an illusion–if only because of language's temporal dimension: AB comes before BA. Indeed, chiasmus relies upon the fact of this temporality, for it is only insofar as chiasmus enforces a revision–as we play back, in retrospect, the first difference in light of its inverted repetition–that the trope avoids tautology, yielding instead a sense of development: we feel that we have *gotten somewhere.* In this way, chiasmus, we might argue, is the trope built out of that recursive movement essential to construing linear syntax: its repetitions enforce rereadings–we double back and thus move forward.

Chiasmus thus engenders what Fineman elsewhere calls "the structure of allegorical desire"[86]–it does so not only in Fineman's account of allegory but also in Augustine's. It is, once again, a chiasmus that yokes the two Testaments in Augustine's famous formulation: "In the Old Testament there is a concealment of the New, in the New Testament there is a revelation of the Old." Here chiasmus reconciles the disjunction of Jew and Christian by opposing the two dispensations across a temporal span. Chiasmus thus describes, as I've already argued, the temporality of a figural rhetoric, cross-coupling flesh and spirit with old and new. And in the process, a seemingly symmetrical structure actually defines a linear narrative: from old to new, concealment to revelation. Chiasmus defines the narrative of *figura*–just as it defines the narrative that Fineman reads into the Sonnets, where the implicit paradoxes of the young man sonnets are later revealed, explicitly unfolded, in the self-belying verbality of the dark lady. For Fineman, then, sonnet 127 succeeds chiastically on the ideality of the young man poems, enabling the articulation of a new poetic subjectivity, one founded upon–quite literally, for Fineman–the structure of allegorical desire.[87]

> For Shakespearean "Will" . . . is the name of a linguistic desire, the name of a desire *of* language. . . . As *double* double entendre "Will" denominates both the "prick" (sonnet 20) which is the mark of homogenous sameness as well as

the "cut" (Elizabethan slang for "cunt") which is the mark
of heterogeneous difference, joining these together in the
verbal intercourse of heterosexual "whole" and "hole."

(26)

The poetic subject Fineman defines is, ultimately, *Will* as chiasmus—a will that is structured as allegory, as *figura*.

Fineman's *Will* "invents" poetic subjectivity; his *Will* is the ultimate proper name that authorizes—serving as occulted, transcendent origin/cause—the allegorical literary history that Fineman,
quite knowingly, constructs. With his allegory of the "invention"
of poetic subjectivity, Fineman challenges his reader to tell a story,
any story, that does not simply repeat the (Shakespearean) structure of allegorical desire. "This is the subjectivity that is willed to
literary history by Shakespeare's sonnets," he writes in his final
characterization of *Will*. "Whatever might be different from
Shakespeare's poetry of verbal difference, would therefore have to
find, outside language, another name. Excessive to language, such
a hypothetical successor to the Shakespearean would not only be
extraliterary, but, in addition, outside history" (296).

On the outrageous basis of claims such as this, Fineman is
often faulted for being ahistorical—as if allegory and history were
at odds. But as we know from Petrarch, historical thinking requires
a tremendous allegorical commitment, for it is through allegory
that the span of time can be constructed and read. The commitment to allegory allows one to conceive of a historical other, to
comprehend historical difference itself. Allegory does so insofar as
it allows us to span time—to construct a sense of time as that
closed, chiastic system that we create, even as it creates us. Allegory, in other words, allows us to write history by allowing us to
write ourselves *into* history, imagining history as something written *for us*. In his rigor to think through the consequences of history, Fineman is forced to confront the consequences of allegorical structure as a closed system of meaning. Fineman pushes us,
has no choice but to push us, toward the limits of that structure—
and then dares us to imagine what lies "outside" those limits. Fineman pushes back—like Lacan in this respect—as far as he can, to the
very origins of structure: to the structuration of structure itself.
What he finds as he pushes, again like Lacan, is that classic logical
paradox: the paradox entailed in the very effort to think the *limits*

of structure—a paradox often summed up in the terms of the Cretan Liar ("I am lying") or in the mathematical language known as Russell's paradox that invokes the "class of all classes that does not classify itself" (see *Perjured Eye*, 294). In other words, in more ways than one Fineman pushes his discussion to paradox, in order to think his way rigorously through a history that, indeed, is thinking him. So Fineman turns to *Will* as the very name of the hole that enables the whole of allegory. We should not be amazed that Shakespeare is the origin of literary history according to Fineman, for it is *Will* who authorizes the very story Fineman has to tell.

What happens, however, when we read Shakespeare's *Will* without such authorization? If our story finds its anchor, its alpha and omega, not in the terra firma of the proper name, but insists instead on its own impropriety, picking its way gingerly, knowing that every unauthorized move carries its risk of trespass? What happens, in other words, if having called a figural logic into question, we read *Will* not as chiasmus, but instead as catachresis?

Figural narrative chiastically spans the chasm between authoritative, yet effaced, origins—and fulfilled, yet deferred, meanings. In this way, it elides the present moment, plumping out the lyric *now* with a pathos of loss and longing. As we've seen, the present moment literally disappears from Augustinian chiasmus[88]—a disappearance that Petrarch strives, impossibly, to forestall by keeping the turns turning. But if figural narrative entails this elision of the *now*, history as Luther envisions it never manages to move past the *now*. At every moment the same tensions are present, the same dualistic strife emerges—and yet, how can such repetition, moment by moment, even be measured as such? From within such a history, there is strictly speaking no story (and in this measure, Fineman is absolutely right). There is no external perspective from which to compare tensions and moments—no capacity (the ability would require the turns of trope) to define *this* tension as the "same" as *that* one. Indeed, time has no *span* in this model of history, no bridge across which difference might be reconciled. In such a world time is indistinguishable from decay, for it consists in an endless articulation of difference—the endless decline from identity.

It is just such a sense of an irreconcilably divided present that informs the *now* of sonnet 127: "But now is blacke beauties successiue heire." Sonnet 127 does declare a new beginning—but it is the same old beginning. Sonnet 127 begins again with the problem of the canker and the rose. Here beauty is understood as slandered–as falsified by the hand that has faired the foul. This is the hand that paints–at once the makeup artist, and the poet, whose comparisons falsify beauty in the very process of preserving it. This beauty has no name; equally canker and rose, a beauty understood as fairness has only an improper, catachrestic place in the world of *Shakespeare's Sonnets*. Nonetheless, in this world filled with time's waste, such slander constitutes the only words of truth. In these terms the sonnet re-invokes the problem of succession with which the sequence began. There the ideal of beauty–beauty's rose–was endangered by a fairness that was turning foul and needed to find compensating likenesses to sustain itself. Here the problem is also the foulness of the fair, but the compensations themselves–the grafts and painting that would fair the foul–are now imagined not as solution but as the dilemma itself. And, in consequence, the spiritual, poetic succession that the procreation poems provisionally announced as solution for time's waste, is here declared as nothing but bastardy.[89] "Therefore my Mistersse eyes are Rauen blacke": as heir to a slandered beauty, the dark lady's blackness would stand, presumably, as beauty's legitimate heir, but as such it succeeds beauty not by supplanting it nor, still less, by fulfilling it. Rather such blackness succeeds the fair by mourning its loss. Like the canker that *becomes* the rose, that mourning that marks beauty's loss is, however, ultimately indistinguishable from beauty's ornament. By the poem's end we realize that this mourning of the fair has been the precondition for our desire all along. We are back where we started: at a loss. "Yet so they [her eyes] mourne becomming of their woe, / That euery toung saies beauty should look so." From the start our desire for beauty has been predicated on its loss.

What is presumably a compositor's error will confuse "black" with "blank" in an earlier sonnet: "Looke what thy memorie cannot containe, / Commit to these *waste blacks*," the poet tells his friend as he makes him a gift of a book (77.9–10, 4, 3, emphasis added). In Q, blackness and blankness are seemingly joined through the logic of waste, a logic that only allows us to "fill" in the blanks of our desire with the black hole of desire itself. It is tempting to take the poet at his deictical word in sonnet 77 and to imagine that "*this* booke" (77.4) he gives his friend is *this* book, the book called *Shakespeare's Sonnets*: a gift meant to save what time wastes—what the memory cannot contain—yet in the end a book whose "vacant leaues" (3) are merely "filled" with the blank blackness of waste itself. There is no way to recover what time has spent. The mind cannot remember what it has lost, nor recognize its paternity in such orphans. "What thy memorie cannot containe, / Commit to these waste blacks, and thou shalt finde, / Those children nurst, deliuerd from thy braine, / To take a new acquaintance of thy minde." Such a book cannot repair the waste of time for us; at best, it can only produce waste blacks that tell our loss.

The universe of the sonnets, then, is a world continually telling loss: a world of repetition without sameness, reproduction without succession. It is a world *in decline*. Thus when the poet asks why his verse is so barren of new pride, the problem he confronts is not, ultimately, a lack of "variation" but instead a lack of "quicke change" (76.2): variation he writes without cease, but the changes he inscribes with his lines of verse, like the changes scored by time's pencil, are not *quick* or living changes, but instead the pits and pocks of decay. If the poet's verse is barren, then, it is not because he succeeds at writing "still all one, euer the same" (76.5). The procreation sonnets have already defined fertility for us in just such terms; *increase* we learn in sonnet 1, consists precisely in the reproduction of the same. To be able *always* to say the *same thing* would be no problem at all.[90] The wit of poems like 76 or 105 precisely turns on this point:

> Let not my loue be cal'd Idolatrie,
> Nor my beloued as an Idoll show,
> Since all alike my songs and praises be
> To one, of one, still such, and euer so.
> Kinde is my loue to day, to morrow kinde,
> Still constant in a wondrous excellence,
> Therefore my verse to constancie confin'de,
> One thing expressing, leaues out difference.
> Faire, kinde, and true, is all my argument
> Faire, kinde and true, varrying to other words,
> And in this change is my inuention spent.
>
> (105.1–11)

The poet is bound to be as faithful to his beloved in verse as the beloved is in life—a situation that either convicts or acquits the poet of idolatry, depending on how we read the ambiguous "since" of line 3. The ambiguity is, of course, symptomatic of the broader problem disclosed in the poem: the problem of linguistic polysemy. This is a language that refuses, precisely, to be "still constant" (6), if only because words—like the word *still*, meaning "always," "repeatedly," "continuously," "up till now," "without movement"—will not themselves remain still or constant. The perfect likeness of a subject who remains perfectly kind, perfectly *like* himself, would be perfect monotony indeed. But it is a monotony the poet is unable to produce.

Instead of idolatrous monotony, the problem the poet faces is, once again, the still constant decline from sameness. "Why write I still all one, euer the same, / And keepe inuention in a noted weed, / That euery word doth almost fel [*tell*] my name, / Shewing their birth, and where they did proceed? / . . . / So all my best is dressing old words new, / Spending againe what is already spent: / For as the Sun is daily new and old, / So is my loue still telling what is told" (76.5–8, 11–14). Every word is *almost* proper, *almost* authorized. Instead of the order of succession, paternity, likeness, identity, the sonnet depicts an exhausting series of near misses. Sameness over time would require just that exchange of trope, coordinating like with unlike, that structures allegory. But if sonnet 76 evokes the chiasmus of *figura* in its final lines—in the crisscross movement of old and new, new and old—it does so only in order to flatten (or perhaps in order to "still") the exchange in its last line. The cyclical movement from old to new, new to old that gives time both its arrow and its fullness becomes a series that will never add up: an endless, deadly counting of what is nonetheless a finite sum. So is my love still, telling what is told.

The conventionality of the sun as the trope of tropes is well known, as is the Petrarchan familiarity of the beloved's eye as sun; that is, as fixed source of poetic illumination.[91] The sun rises and sets, tracing out its arc from new to old, old to new with circular constancy and daily regularity. "Seguirò l'ombra di quel dolce lauro / per lo più ardente sole et per la neve, / fin che l'ultimo dì chiuda quest' occhi" (*Rime* 30.16–18): it is, for instance, the turning sun, tracing out an endless circle through the moving "shadow of that sweet laurel," against which Petrarch tropes his own passage in the sestina "Giovene donna." In its endless revolutions the petrarchan sun grants the poet a stable reference point—what Shakespeare refers to as the "selfe-same skie" (15.6)—by which the lover-poet may plot his own turning course. Yet in Shakespeare's world these solar turns fail to keep us on track. Instead, each "reuo-lution" (cf. 59.12) serves less to trace a circle than to mark time. For if the sun is daily new and old, the time it tells—the time it tells *on us* —is nonetheless constantly waning: "When I doe count the clock that tels the time, / And see the braue day sunck in hidious night, / . . . / Then of thy beauty do I question make / That thou among the wastes of time must goe" (12.1–2, 9–10). Indeed, as time's marker, the sun within Shakespeare's world serves less as the privileged trope of trope around which all meaning, all iden-tity revolves, and instead, finds its own selfsame identity under question.

Thus, strikingly, in its first appearance within the sonnets, the sun is not named as such, nor cited as time's marker, but is itself marked *by* time.

> Loe in the Orient when the gracious light,
> Lifts vp his burning head, each vnder eye
> Doth homage to his new appearing sight,
> Seruing with lookes his sacred maiesty,
> And hauing climb'd the steepe vp heauenly hill,
> Resembling strong youth in his middle age,
> Yet mortall lookes adore his beauty still.
>
> (7.1–7)

The burden of the sonnet is to remind the youth that he is like the sun, the gracious source of light in whose thanks, and thanks to whom, each "vnder eye" looks; and yet, also, like the sun, he too will wane, no longer the source and target of every gaze. Yet it is, in fact, the sun that is likened to the youth; the sun who is made in the beloved's image, "resembling strong youth in his middle age" as it mounts the skies. In this way, insofar as it is like the aging youth, the sun is like the *son* invoked in the sonnet's final couplet: its path from new to old merely shadows the course set by youth. But by shadowing the youth the sun becomes unlike itself; no longer chiastically constant in its rise and fall, this *Sunne* must get a *sonne*. "So thou, thy selfe out-going in thy noon: / Vnlok'd on diest vnlesse thou get a sonne" (7.13–14). Itself "out-going," the sun no longer describes a closed circuit, daily new and old, old and new. The sun/son of *Shakespeare's Sonnets* no longer offers the trope of tropes, the chiasmus around which all likeness revolves. Instead, at once vehicle and tenor, both like the young man and that which the young man is like, the center of the poet's world is not only catachrestic: it is a *pun*.

Here at last we return to Shakespeare's *Will*, and its oddly unreadable inscription in sonnets 135 and 136.[92] I say "oddly" unreadable because, despite almost universal critical agreement that Shakespeare's puns here are explicit, compulsive, unsubtle, excessive and obvious[93]–either Johnson's "fatal Cleopatra" to detractors or Booth's "festivals of verbal ingenuity" (Booth, 466) to celebrators–it is almost impossible to find a reader ready to offer a satisfying paraphrase of the poems. Fineman presents, perhaps, the most extreme example of this resistance to paraphrase. It is not that he fails to interpret the poems; on the contrary, the very climax of his argument consists in his stunning discussion of the *Will* sonnets, and especially in his claim that, through speaking out his name, the poet of the dark lady sonnets renders the paradoxes and aporias of an idealizing poetics of praise utterly explicit.[94] "When the dark lady's poet gives voice to his name, he thereby gives expression to the original verbal difference that the sameness of a visionary language is committed to leave out. . . . As a result . . . the poet experiences at the level of his person the illogic of the *Logos*" (295–96). Logical aporias unfold (become ex-plicit) in the name itself, enabling the poet to embody such paradox in his own person, in his own *psyche*. He lives out the paradox of Logos, Fineman argues, in the eros of psychology. In speaking out the "heretofore unspeakable paradox" at the center of an "orthodox phenomenology, ontology, cosmology, theology," the dark lady's poet is, in other words, constituted as a desiring subject: as a *will* (296).

Let's put it bluntly. For Fineman, Shakespeare "invents" subjectivity by deconstructing the Western metaphysics of presence. Since such a deconstruction is, by definition, implicit within the tradition itself, Shakespeare's "invention" can only consist in thematizing–embodying in representation–what the tradition already, in some sense, "knows." In this way, for Fineman's argument to work, the paradoxes of Logos must be spoken by, and not merely bespoken in, Shakespeare's *Will*. Any paraphrase of the

Will sonnets, any deconstructive readings we might ourselves provide, should be, by this account, superfluous. If Fineman is right,
the name says, and does, it all. And so Fineman coyly informs us
that, although "it would be possible to follow out in detail the ways
in which these various binary oppositions . . . systematically extract
from their play on 'Will' a set of personal paradoxes . . . there is
really no need to do so, and this precisely because [with his name]
the poet now is able clearly to say about himself what before he
only mutely implies" (294).

Few close readings are as ingenious or elegant as this *refusal*
to give a close reading. And yet, more than anything else, Fineman's refusal to explicate Shakespeare's puns reflects the problem
such wordplay presents for any reader relying on a figural
hermeneutic. *Figura*, we must recall from book 3 of *On Christian
Doctrine*, emerges within the context of linguistic ambiguity: "The
God-fearing man seeks God's will diligently in the holy scriptures.
. . . And that he may not be deceived by ambiguous signs . . . let
him know that the ambiguity of Scripture rests either in proper or
in translated [i.e., figurative] words" (*Doctrina* 3.1.1). For Augustine, figurality resolves even the most resistant and deceptive
ambiguities of the text, freeing God's Word from the bondage of
the Jews and thereby revealing God's will (*voluntas*). Whether we,
like the righteous Christian exegete, unravel ambiguity according
to a fourfold scheme or instead, in the wake of New Criticism, celebrate and unpack ambiguity in its manifold "types," as readers we
alike authorize our efforts in essentially figural terms. Nonetheless,
those oppositions so central to *figura*'s chiastic and disambiguating
operations–implicit versus explicit, letter versus spirit, figure versus
fulfillment–will give us little purchase on the ambiguities of *pun*.
The polysemy of puns renders the spatial and temporal imperatives of our reading strategies (*reveal what is hidden, fulfill what has
been promised*) meaningless. At once too flat and "frankly" explicit
to be significant (i.e., "deep"), *and* too polysemous to be transparent, it is not quite clear how precisely one should "unpack" or *ex*-
plicate a pun. Whence that hint of dead-end fatigue one senses in
Fineman's coy obliquity. And whence, too, the tendency for explication of the *Will* sonnets to begin, and end, with a simple enumeration of the by now canonical "six senses of 'will' . . . [that]
have been distinguished" (Evans, 253). A list of implausibly discrete and distinct definitions takes the place of paraphrase.

We can count types of ambiguity–Empson gave us seven–and we can assert aporetic themes, but with a pun is it possible to connect the one to the other in the narrativized form of an *explication du texte*? I'm asking whether, literally, we can read Shakespeare's will–and whether we can do so by reading his *Will* literally. As with the question of Q's authorization, the only way we can resolve such questions is by taking quite seriously the problems we encounter when we make the attempt. The first dilemma readers face is a visual one: eleven of the twenty-one (twenty-two, if you count the *wil* in "wilt" of 135.5) *will*s in the *Will* sonnets are italicized and capitalized. What, exactly, are we to make of *Will*'s typography? The four most recent editions (Kerrigan, Evans, Duncan-Jones, and Vendler) of the Sonnets reveal a consensus in critical practice: in their modernized editions, capitalization is retained, but not italics– ostensibly to avoid rendering Shakespeare's *Will* more archly self-referential or typographically significant than an Elizabethan would have found it.[95] At the same time, however, all four editors silently strike to lowercase the single capitalized "Will" appearing in the young man sonnets: "So true a foole is loue, that in your Will, / (Though you doe any thing) he thinkes no ill" (57.13–14). Duncan-Jones's practice is perhaps the most problematic of the four above-cited editors, given her commitment to Q's authorization and her decision to follow the quarto "more closely than . . . any previous modernized edition" (103). In her headnote to sonnet 135 she points out the selectivity of Will's typography and writes, "Since there is probably a designed distinction between the two forms [e.g., roman lowercase and capitalized italic], capitalization has been retained" (304). Yet similar concerns apparently do not arise with sonnet 57, or with the other instances of italics and capitals throughout the sequence, all of which Duncan-Jones emends, and without comment–save for the "Boy" in 126, which she retains (although the same poem's *Audite* and *Quietus* are not spared).

Ostensibly by eliminating most of the typographical emphases in the text, such emendations preserve the textual indeterminacy that would otherwise be lost for the modern reader whose "susceptibility to orthographical signals" is so much more "acute" than the Elizabethan reader's (Booth, 466). Yet, I would maintain, the exact opposite effect is achieved. If the fear is that modern readers will anachronistically try to "dredge meaning," as Booth puts it (466), from relatively arbitrary orthographical distinctions, that fear is not well-served by simply eliminating most of those distinctions. Given our "orthographical susceptibility," an editor cannot restore orthographic indeterminacy by eliminating most orthographic distinctions, but instead, in doing so, s/he will merely render all the more determinate, all the less ambiguous those distinctions that remain. Thus by choosing to retain Q's capitalization only once in the *Will* sonnets–"And then thou louest me for my name is **Will**" (136.14, boldface mine)–Booth forces us to read the orthography of "will" more decisively than ever. We *know* that "Will" in the final line of 136 refers primarily–if not entirely unambiguously–to the proper name, while the use of lowercase *will*'s throughout must by contrast indicate the word's primary usage as a common noun. Limiting the text's orthographic clues, in other words, limits–rather than expands–our interpretive options by *fixing* orthographic standards in general. Somewhat paradoxically, then, the effort of modern editors to avoid typographic cues renders Shakespeare's *Will* less ambiguous, its usage less fluid.

Indeed, even if one eliminated *all* typographic cues, our orthography could not capture the indeterminacy and fluidity that the book called *Shakespeare's Sonnets* seems so ready to exploit. What makes the typography of Q so difficult is precisely the relatively arbitrary nature of its distinctions. And what makes the *Will* sonnets in particular so difficult is the manner in which polysemy is compounded by what we might call typographical *play*–i.e., by the flexibility or stretch in the system, the *slack* structured into its seeming rigidity (as when we speak of the "play" in a fishing line). Furthermore, this confluence of wordplay and typographical play dovetails within these poems with a language that keeps insisting upon, but is unable to mark in any consistent and clear way, the distinction between original and citation–between, that is, the proper and the cited, second-order, translated sign.

> Who euer hath her wish, thou hast thy *Will*,
> And *Will* too boote, and *Will* in ouer-plus,
> More then enough am I that vexe thee still,
> To thy sweete will making addition thus.
> Wilt thou whose will is large and spatious,
> Not once vouchsafe to hide my will in thine,
> Shall will in others seeme right gracious,
> And in my will no faire acceptance shine:

> The sea all water, yet receiues raine still,
> And in aboundance addeth to his store,
> So thou beeing rich in *Will* adde to thy *Will*,
> One will of mine to make thy large *Will* more.
>   Let no vnkinde, no faire beseechers kill,
>   Thinke all but one, and me in that one *Will*.
>
> (135)

Any attempt to paraphrase a sonnet such as this must first sort out the distinction, crucial to the poem, between translated and proper discourse. When is the language of this poem being presented as citation—as, that is, removed from its proper context and mediated instead by the poem itself—and when is that language presented as *im*mediate, as words proper to the speaker of the poem? Who is speaking in this poem, and whom is the language of the poem bespeaking (or interpellating)?

"Let no vnkinde, no faire beseechers kill": for an index of Shakespeare's complexity here, let us compare his no-no to Sidney's famous double negative in *Astrophil and Stella* (an intertext for this poem that, incidentally, offers yet another dimension of citational play):

> Oh Grammer rules, oh now your vertues showe,
> So Children still read you with awfull eyes,
> As my younge Dove may in your precepts wise,
> Her graunt to me by her owne vertue knowe.
> For late with hart most hie, with eyes most lowe;
> I crav'd the thing which ever she denies.
> Shee lightening Love, displaying *Venus* skyes,
> Least one should not be heard twise, said no no.
> [Sing then my Muse, now I do Paean sing.]
> Harken Envy not at my high triumphing:
> But Grammers force with sweete successe confirme,
> For Grammer sayes ah (this deere Stella way)
> For Grammer sayes (to Grammer who sayes nay)
> That in one speech, two negatives affirme.
>
> (*Astrophil and Stella* 63)[96]

Fearing (not without good cause) that Astrophil will not hear her denial, Stella rejects him twice. But the rules of grammar teach us that a double negative negates its own negation; for Astrophil, the quintessential and incorrigible Petrarchan lover, even rejection confirms success; even Stella's "no no" spells *yes.*

The wit of Sidney's poem relies upon not only a presumed univocity of speech ("in one *speech,* two negatives affirm") but also, and more importantly, upon the clarity of syntax: the linear progression of Stella's two *no*'s makes possible the troping movement of Astrophil's reading of her words. In this way, Astrophil's reading revises Stella's presumed intention in the same recursive manner that *figura* employs when it transforms *legere* into *intellegere.*[97] Shakespeare's double negative, however, uses repetition not to turn syntax chiastically back upon itself but instead to render syntax entirely undecidable. The line coaxes an initial reading that cannot be sustained: *let no unkind or fair beseechers kill.* The first impulse will be to read "no vnkinde, no faire" as parallel constructions; but there we immediately stumble on a non-sensical object-less killing: don't let **any** beseecher, whether fair or foul, kind or unkind, **kill**. Kill what? Without an object, the reading falters; "kill" will not function as an intransitive verb. Furthermore, beseechers presumably ply their suits in hope of success and from positions of weakness. They are liable not to kill but instead to *be killed,* shot down by those that have power to hurt (cf. sonnet 94). Yet once properly sorted out with "beseechers" as the grammatical object, and not the subject, of "kill," what becomes of Shakespeare's "no . . . no"?[98]

Grammar no longer rules in the world of Shakespeare's lover, no longer transforms ambiguities into certainties nor offers the consoling sublations of *figura,* where negation is transformed into affirmation, loss becomes gain. The matter becomes most problematic, of course, when we turn to the ambiguities generated by the repetitions of *will.* The flatness of puns—their tendency to elicit world-weary groans—is a function of their sheerly enumerative linearity: their duplicity of meaning unfolds sequentially, like the "bu-dum-bum" of the nightclub snare drum that mimes the double take of the double entendre. In other words, the classic "groaner" depends on our ability to sort the proper from the improper, to "hear" the pun one meaning at a time.[99] The *Will* puns, however, defy even that kind of flat enumeration. We cannot assign priority or propriety to one meaning over another.

Who euer hath her wish, thou hast thy *Will*,
And *Will* too boote, and *Will* in ouer-plus,
More then enough am I that vexe thee still,
To thy sweete will making addition thus.

(135.1–4)

Modern readers have generally approached these first four lines in one of two ways, depending on whether or not they have "dredged" meaning from the sonnet's orthography. Either they have tried to make sense of the first three italicized *Will*'s by constructing a slim narrative for the poem based upon Will as proper name (e.g., the three *Will*'s refer to three different men: the dark lady's husband–the *Will* to whom she is wedded[100]–the poet's friend, and the poet himself); or having rejected such distinctions they find (and sometimes fault) the babble of a poet whose empty repetitions offer a kind of reflection of the "large and spatious" emptiness, the yawning and insatiable no-thing of the dark lady's "will": both her desire and her vagina.[101]

Neither approach offers much help, however, when it comes to the ambiguities of the following sonnet.

If thy soule check thee that I come so neere,
Sweare to thy blind soule that I was thy *Will*,
And will thy soule knowes is admitted there,
Thus farre for loue, my loue-sute sweet fullfill.
Will, will fulfill the treasure of thy loue,
I fill it full with wils, and my will one,
In things of great receit with ease we prooue.
Among a number one is reckon'd none.
Then in the number let me passe vntold,
Though in thy stores account I one must be,
For nothing hold me, so it please thee hold,
That nothing me, a some-thing sweet to thee.
　Make but my name thy loue, and loue that still,
　And then thou louest me for my name is *Will*.

(136)

For those who decide to dismiss orthographic cues, the poem admits of no finely tuned paraphrase. Furthermore, in the absence of orthographical distinctions the final couplet yields little sense, since it seems to rely on such distinctions in order to single out one *Will* from all the others: *Will* as the proper name that alone may be admitted into that treasure of the lady's love ("make *but* my name thy love"). Instead of detailed exposition, the reader who ignores orthography will tend to reduce the dense polysemy of the poem to a general paradox about language and desire: e.g., the "great receit" of the dark lady's will is like an ocean that can always absorb one more drop, but that nonetheless shall finally be filled to capacity with the copious will of the poet, whose name is simultaneously full of meaning (i.e., the unitary some-thing of the phallus) and yet emptied by the babble of repetition (i.e., the invaginated no-thing of meaning's deferral).

Those inclined, in contrast, to read the italicized *Will*'s of these sonnets as a proper name fare somewhat better in deciphering the poem without sacrificing its linguistic density. For such readers, lines 1–6 offer a threefold and entirely readable pun. The dark lady's soul is "blind"; it is, in other words, as easily duped as blind Isaac was when his son Jacob passed for Esau and stole the paternal blessing (Gen. 27). Similarly Will wants to "passe vntold," usurping not the birthright but the bed-right of a husband–or even of the lover, the young friend, on whose account the lady's matrimonial "bed-vow" (151.3) was broken–also named *Will*. Moreover, as an attribute of the soul itself, as volition and desire, "will" in line 3 does literally belong inside the lady's soul. Hence, neither Will nor will should be chided for or prevented from speaking bluntly and approaching closely. The poet's love suit should therefore be granted. One man could never be enough for the deep "treasure" of this lady's "will." But "*Will*"–three men in one name, the super-abundant proper *Will* denoting poet, husband, and young man all at once–this *Will* will fulfill the dark lady's insatiable desire as no single *Will* or will (person, penis, desire) could.

However, with the very next line, even a reading anchored in *Will* as proper name reaches its impasse: "I fill it full with wils, and my will one." What are we to make of orthography here? We've been following the poem's italicized cues but now the ambiguity of another kind of name–the first-person pronoun "I"–undermines our efforts. We will not be able to assign priority to any of our interpretations of the line; instead, its polysemy will refuse to be ordered sequentially, according to bu-dum-bum of the double entendre. Instead our readings overlap, compete, and conflict.

"Yes, *Will* (the three men in one name) will fill you up with penises—and my penis will be one of these ." OR: "I, me, Will Himself, will fill you with as many wills (penises?) as I can, my will (penis?) being one." OR: "*I*, the Roman numeral for the number *one*, will fulfill you; one man, one desire, one penis only, that one will be enough—and that *I* or *one* is me/mine."

Neither approach, neither one that accepts nor one that rejects orthographical distinctions, will yield a satisfying and consistent interpretation of this most dense *Will* sonnet. Instead we need to find a tertium quid—and we do so as soon as we recognize the centrality of orthographical play within the poem. Orthographic distinctions, as Booth quite rightly points out, are *not* secure or consistent in early modern texts, but these poems even so do not take orthography for granted. Instead, the very absence of such secure and consistent signals becomes one more linguistic resource to be deployed. Indeed, with its shades of typographical variation, Shakespeare's *will* in these poems continually tempts us to differentiate between name and noun, literal and figurative, proper use and translation, original and citation, singularity and plurality.[102] But instead of differentiation, the very inconsistency of these typographical markings herald only the collapse of *figura* and with it the collapse of a narrative of fulfillment. It is, accordingly, precisely this figural notion of fulfillment that Shakespeare's *Will* challenges: will will fulfill the treasure of thy love. . . . Instead of a polysemy that can be neatly ex-plicated in narrative, paraphrase, and close reading, the polysemy of the *Will* sonnets serves primarily to reveal our dependence on *figura*'s unfoldings. Without *figura*, language gets us nowhere and will remains unsatisfied; with *figura*, on the other hand, we are able to transform loss into gain, absence into presence, negation into affirmation, and the dark lady's nothing into a willful something.

Finally and perhaps most important, *Will*'s indeterminacy allows us, in a manner, to fill the linguistic void left by the loss of *sweet beauty*'s name. In place of the proper name of beauty, the poet offers that superfluity that stands, undecidably, both as the cause and as the effect of such loss—as both cause and effect of *time's waste*. Sonnet 129 glosses this superfluity in its flattest terms: "Th'expence of Spirit in a waste of shame, / Is lust in action." (1–2). The ideal of spiritual procreation yields, as we learn once again, nothing but the most fleshly expense of spirit, wasting us in

the *waist* of a woman's shame or pudendum. But in the *Will* sonnets this overflowing expense and expanse–this full/empty waist
and waste of time–receives its improper name: *Will*

> Who euer hath her wish, thou hast thy Will,
> And *Will* too boote, and *Will* in ouer-plus,
> More then enough am I that vexe thee still.

Will–triply superfluous, like the beloved's fair, kind, and true
("Faire, kinde, and true, haue often liu'd alone, / Which three till
now, neuer kept seate in one" [105.13–14])–is *more than enough*.
And it is so not because the name denotes three different men, and
not (simply) because it signals the poet's copious and overflowing
pen/penis. Rather *will* is more than enough because *will* names
(provides? constitutes?) that supplement, that ingrafting ornament
that allows us to know what suffices by exceeding sufficiency.
Shakespeare's *Will* names, in other words, the ornament that
allows the fair, kind and true to remain *like* itself: to remain (as Shylock would say) a good man, all in all sufficient. Yet, in this world
of waste and ceaseless decline, simply in order to remain sufficient,
we need to keep adding *more*, and still more. More than enough
am I that vex thee *still*. What we add is thus simultaneously inadequate–we can never add enough to do the job completely–and
yet it is also excessive, a continually superadded superfluity. As
that more-than-enough ornament, Shakespeare's *Will* seems,
indeed, to take its cue from the *flesh* as Luther defines it: no mere
figure, Luther's *Fleisch* is simultaneously too little and too much–
both inadequate vessel and absolute fetish.

   Will, like Luther's catachrestic flesh, is a supplement, but it
departs significantly from the (post-)structuralist logic of supplement that Fineman employs. As supplement, *Will* is not merely
that extra thing that both enables the whole and reveals its hole. It
does not simply articulate the static paradoxes of structure, of
Russell's paradox with its self-belying "class of all classes." Instead,
this ornament unsettles the very relationship between "whole" and
"hole" by revealing a temporal confusion where we have been
accustomed to the settled stasis of paradox. As ornament, *Will*
compensates continually for the continual erosion of time; in this
way, because *Will* is an ornament that must keep ornamenting, falsifying and restoring in the very same gesture, *Will* is also that

ornament that signals our inability to distinguish ornament from ornamented, cankerous hole from rosy whole. Accordingly, instead of the (w)hole of chiasmus—the signatory X that circulates around a rupture—Shakespeare's *Will* marks the endless reiteration of difference. As catachrestic ornament *Will* catachrestically names the abuse of ornament itself.

This *Will* makes its mark on *A Lover's Complaint*—most literally in the ways in which the seducer's "craft of will" (126) finds both its copy and its original in the anticipatory wills of others who grant his desires before he has even articulated them: "al passions" (126) "dialogu'd for him what he would say, / Askt their own wils and made their wils obey" (132–33). Yet ultimately *A Lover's Complaint* washes away this catachrestic name of the author, depositing in its wake a superfluity that is as anonymous as it is, in the end, indestructible. It is this superfluity that I've mentioned before in terms of the tears and "thousand fauours" (36) that usuriously apply wet to wet, spilling over into the poem's overflowing "margent[s]" (39). Such usury seems impervious to the wastes of desire, unlike the lady whose visage reveals the holey wholeness of beauty in this time-ravaged, sunburnt world:

> Vpon her head a plattid hiue of straw,
> Which fortified her visage from the Sunne,
> Whereon the thought might thinke sometime it saw
> The carkas of a beauty spent and donne,
> Time had not sithed all that youth begun,
> Nor youth all quit, but spight of heauens fell rage,
> Some beauty peept, through lettice of fear'd age.
>
> (8–14)

The lover's beauty peeps through the holes that mar it, lattice-like; a beauty that is plaited and reticulated not only by the lines of age but also by that "hiue of straw"—the ornament that veils beauty from a "Sunne" whose burning turns only mark time. In contrast to this ruined beauty, however, are those teardrop favors—what the poem later identifies as *similes*, or similitudes—that somehow resist all ruin, emerging from a seemingly bottomless "maund" or wicker basket (yet another plaited object), continuously new, fresh and whole despite the lady's continual efforts at their destruction.

Of folded schedulls had she many a one,
Which she perus'd, sigh'd, tore and gaue the flud,
Crackt many a ring of Posied gold and bone,
Bidding them find their Sepulchers in mud,
Found yet mo letters sadly pend in blood,
With sleided silke, feate and affectedly
Enswath'd and seald to curious secrecy.

(43–49)

Try as she does, the lady cannot seem to get rid of these similitudes, these ornaments. She bids them to their graves–their
muddy sepulchers–but like revenants they refuse burial; instead
the flood continues with "mo letters" and more usurious tears.
"Bath'd . . . in her fluxiue eies" (50)–in tears–all these trophies resist
being torn. Instead, as the very *figures* of the wills held captive by
this fair young man, such trophies remain deathless. "Looke heare
what tributes wounded fancies sent me," the young man report-
edly declares, "Of palyd pearles and rubies red as blood: / Figuring that they their passions likewise lent me" (197–99). The will is
subject to time, marked by those exchanges, by that *intercourse*,
which belies it. But the similes of will are not wasted; instead they
recall the usurious economy dismissed by the procreation sonnets:
"Looke what an vnthrift in the world doth spend / Shifts but his
place, for still the world inioyes it / But beauties waste hath in the
world an end, / And kept vnvsed the vser so destroyes it" (9.9–12).
The similes are merely–the young man stresses this fact–*loaned*;
they merely shift places like a prodigal's funds, like a usurer's capital. If, in doing so, they mark the passage of time, transforming
sweet beauty into a carcass, the similes themselves remain intact,
incur no loss.

Given the indestructibility of such similes, they are easily
recycled, their allure remaining untarnished no matter how
many times they pass from hand to hand. "Take all these similes
to your owne command": despite her better judgment, the
seducer's command is easily followed. Knowing his falseness she
is nonetheless swayed by the very emblems of his past betrayals.
These trophies that were themselves lent to seduce him, even as
he seduced their lenders, are now redeployed to seduce again.
"Oh then aduance (of yours) that phraseless hand," the young
man tells our lover,

> Whose white weighes downe the airy scale of praise,
> Take all these similes to your owne command,
> Hollowed with sighes that burning lunges did raise:
> What me your minister for you obaies
> Workes vnder you, and to your audit comes
> Their distract parcells, in combined summes.
>
> (225–31)

The fantasy of beauty's ornament refuses to remain buried for long. Those engrafting *similes* that strived in sonnet 18 to immortalize a time-blighted beauty were catachrestic lies. Beauty, like *Will*, lives only insofar as it continually dies; there is no eternal summer, just as it is impossible to counter loss via the "combined summes"–the fulfilled whole–of dispersed parts.[103] Yet, if the similitudes cannot immortalize beauty they are nonetheless *themselves* immortal. Like the voice of beauty's carcass–the undying Echo with which the poem begins–these ornaments themselves shall never fade. And thus, *A Lover's Complaint* "ends"–offering Q's last word–by insisting on the impossibilty of ending. The final words are the lover's; the frame of the poem's narrative remains unclosed, just as she herself remains open to renewed seductions, renewed betrayals by beauty's ornament : "O that infected moysture of his eye / . . . / O all that borrowed motion seeming owed, / Would yet again betray the fore-betrayed, / And new peruert a reconciled Maide" (323, 327–29).

We have returned to the very insight that inconclusively concluded the opening gesture of the book called *Shakespeare's Sonnets*: an eternal summer shall not fade only insofar as it is supplemented by those abuses of figure that lie like truth. What is immortal, in the end, is not beauty, nor the figure of beauty, but the abuse of beauty's figure: beauty's in-creasing catachresis. It is beauty's carcass, its echoing and endlessly recycled voice, that death shall never claim.

Take all these similes to your own command. In the voice of the seducer with his craft of *Will*, we find Shakespeare's *tolle, lege* moment. The last word of Q is this verdict: ultimately indestructible, poetic language nonetheless only achieves its immortality at the cost of our ideals and against our will. Such immortality can only come at beauty's expense.

FIVE

Will's Bondage: Anti-Semitism and The Merchant of Venice

An ideology really succeeds when even the facts which at first sight contradict it start to function as arguments in its favour.
—Slavoj Žižek, *The Sublime Object of Ideology*

"so is the wil of a liuing daughter curb'd by the will of a dead father."
—*The Merchant of Venice* (1.2.24–25)[1]

As early as 1949, Nevill Coghill formulated what was to become one of the standard post-Holocaust responses to *The Merchant of Venice*. The play, he argued, offers an allegorical presentation of religious themes—of, in particular, the conflict between justice and mercy, between the Old Law and the New.

> Seen thus it puts an entirely different complexion upon the opposition of Jew and Gentile. The two principles for which, in Shakespeare's play, respectively they stand are both *inherently right*, and they are only in conflict because, whereas God is absolutely just as He is absolutely merciful, mortal and finite man can only be relatively so.[2]

Viewed from the proper perspective, there is no real opposition between Jew and Gentile, nor between the justice and mercy they respectively represent. Instead, the Old Law finds its completion in the New and justice is not abolished—it is, rather, fulfilled in the mercy of redemption, in the forgiveness bought on the Cross. Here Christ's words on the Mount hold sway: "Thinke not that I

238 ANTI-SEMITISM AND *The Merchant of Venice*

am come to destroy the Lawe, or the Prophets. I am not come to destroy them, but to fulfill them" (Matt. 5:17, Geneva Bible). Read from this standpoint, *The Merchant of Venice* offers nothing less than an allegory of Christian allegory per se. There is, then, no true opposition of Jew to Christian in *Merchant* insofar as the play represents Christianity as the true destiny of the Jew.

For Coghill, such an allegorical reading demonstrates that the play's fundamental themes reside "far above and beyond race feeling" (20). Indeed, read allegorically the play even offers a potential critique of racism, driving a wedge between social labels and actual practice in the name of our common humanity. "Jew" and "Christian" are not absolute markers of identity; they are instead roles—allegorical functions—that may or may not be fulfilled by the real men and women of the play, who contain "equally . . . such faults and virtues as human beings commonly have" (23). At stake for Coghill in such allegory is nothing less than the very autonomy of the play. Thanks to its archaic ("medieval," even) outlook, *Merchant* remains at an exculpating distance from modern politics. It remains utterly independent of and unresponsible for the political uses to which it has been put. Operating "above and beyond race feeling," the play has nothing to say on the modern *Judenfrage*; it is neither, as Coghill puts it, "pro-Jew [n]or anti-Jew" (18).

Implicit in Coghill's account is the absolute distinction between religious faith and race. For Coghill, modern anti-Semitism relies upon the concept of race, and is thus completely distinct from the medieval theological tradition informing Shakespeare's play. Writing some fifteen years later on "The Theology of Marlowe's *The Jew of Malta*," G. K. Hunter is even more explicit:

> It is understandable that most of those who have written on the subject [of Jews in Elizabethan literature] have had the modern "Jewish question" in mind; but this has had an unfortunate effect on scholarship, for it has tended to push modern reactions to modern anti-Semitism into a past where they do not apply. . . . The Elizabethan word "Jew" . . . was dependent on a theological rather than an ethnographical framework.[3]

James Shapiro has recently demonstrated the ways in which Hunter's thesis has, in effect, dominated modern literary criticism,

even among critics–like the new historicists and cultural material-
ists–who, Shapiro suggests, should know better.[4] But it is important to recognize the pervasiveness of the view in other disciplines
as well. The distinction between a theological tradition *adversos
Judaeos* and a racialized anti-Semitism has proved surprisingly
tenacious even among historians. Daniel Jonah Goldhagen's
much-debated recent book, *Hitler's Willing Executioners*, is an interesting case in point. Arguing that broad popular sentiment within
Nazi Germany supported even the most virulent, eliminationist
anti-Semitism, Goldhagen's book generated great controversy.
Despite the controversy, however, Goldhagen's view of the origin
and history of anti-Semitism is itself unsurprising. Anti-Semitism
begins as "a corollary of Christianity" (49), he writes, and no matter how extreme the medieval hatred of Jews would become, it
retained its theological focus: "Ultimately, the Church wanted not
to kill the Jews, for they were redeemable, but to convert them.
This would reaffirm the supremacy of Christianity" (53). For
Goldhagen, so absolute is the difference between this conversionist, theological paradigm and the racist, paranoid culture of a modern eliminationist anti-Semitism that his narrative cannot span the
gap between the two views. Instead, a white space bisects his
account, typographically dividing his discussion into a brief
description of patristic and medieval attitudes and a much longer
discussion of the nineteenth and early twentieth centuries. (The
eliminationist climate of Nazi Germany receives lengthy discussion in a separate chapter.) Typographically, Goldhagen thus represents an absolute gulf between the medieval view and the bur-
geoning race theories of the nineteenth century. An unnarratable
gap, a white hole in history, divides the story of anti-Semitism into
two distinct paradigms. In this way, Goldhagen doesn't so much
recount the gradual "evolution" of modern anti-Semitism[5] as he
describes the utter epistemic break that produced it: "German
antisemitism in the latter part of the [nineteenth] century coa-
lesced around a new master concept: race. Race, an immutable
quality, dictated that a Jew could never become a German" (65).

What makes Goldhagen's argument particularly interesting
for our purposes is the author's commitment to the idea of a
specifically German anti-Semitism–a long-standing tradition that,
Goldhagen argues, pre-dates the Nazis and helps explain their rise
to power. One would think then that Goldhagen, more than any

recent historian of the Holocaust perhaps, would have a stake in linking the early modern anti-Semitism of Martin Luther to a later eliminationist policy. And yet, his account emphasizes instead the break rather than the continuity between the two paradigms, thereby demonstrating the tremendous difficulty that any history of anti-Semitism based on the theology/race dichotomy faces. Simply put: how can we write the pre-nineteenth-century history of anti-Semitism if what defines the phenomenon itself is a concept that did not exist *before* the nineteenth century? Reformation theologian Heiko Oberman responds to this problem in his important monograph, *The Roots of Anti-Semitism*. Although Oberman offers a detailed and nuanced reading of early modern attitudes toward Jews, he stumbles upon the same problem as Goldhagen does: "Strictly speaking, 'anti-Semitism' did not exist prior to the race theory of the nineteenth century. Nevertheless, there are events, attitudes, or statements which long before the rise of the concept come very close to the reality of anti-Semitism."[6] From the very start, Oberman's project is vexed by anachronism. If anti-Semitism is, by definition, a modern phenomenon, then *strictly speaking* it has no roots. The transhistorical "reality" Oberman invokes in order to define the legacy of race hatred remains an empty concept. Like Goldhagen, Oberman has in fact limited this "reality" to the present; he has denied the historical existence of the very phenomenon whose roots he wants to trace. Oberman's account no less than Goldhagen's is doomed to ahistoricity.

In concluding this study of Shakespeare and the figural tradition with a discussion of *The Merchant of Venice*, it is my hope to begin, in some small measure, to narrate this gap in the mainstream account of anti-Semitism. In so doing I will not try to unearth the *roots* or early modern origins of modern anti-Semitism; that task presumes an essential "reality" of anti-Semitism and, not coincidentally, identifies that "reality" with an essentialist picture of the Jew. Instead, I offer merely a *reading* of anti-Semitism, one deployed through the history of its central figures. Like my "reading" of Shakespeare's *Will* more generally, and implicit in that reading by way of the patristic equation of Jewish flesh with Christian *figura*, my reading of Shakespeare's Jew is a figural one: one that locates the Jew within and as culmination of a history that calls figure itself into question. If within the sphere of Shakespeare's poetics, the improper name of this questioned *figura* is

Will, then in the politicized sphere of Shakespeare's drama, the catachresis of note is the Jew.[7]

To narrate the gap in the story of anti-Semitism, I would argue, we must first reconsider the essentialized Jew who figures so prominently in mainstream histories of the topic. The mainstream view radically distinguishes between a pre-modern and a modern anti-Semitism on the basis of a concept that becomes available only in the nineteenth century.[8] The underlying assumption here is that an essentialist notion of Jews—ultimately available only through the scientific discourse of race—is the *sine qua non* of the modern ideology. Slavoj Žižek, however, offers a decisive challenge to this viewpoint in the passage I've taken as my epigraph: "An ideology really succeeds when even the facts which at first sight contradict it start to function as arguments in its favour" (*Sublime Object*, 49).[9] The paranoid belief systems of the nineteenth and twentieth centuries, I would maintain, are *not* best understood in terms of race—in terms, that is, of the way positivist discourses (like the biology of race or the ethnography of *Volk*) offer a basis for essentialism. To understand anti-Semitism in such terms is to presume that its virulence lies in the belief that there is an "objective" basis of Jewishness. The progressive response to a racism so construed often points out the fallacy of such "objectivity," questioning the so-called facts or science taken to support the essentialism. And such a response routinely fails—because it fails to recognize the ways in which such science constructs its object (and its objectivity) hysterically, precisely starting from the dread that there is *no* objective correlative to the Jewishness of Jews. Within such a paranoid system, indeed, the very lack of evidence becomes a *proof* of one's convictions—proof, potentially, that Jews must be eliminated if only because one cannot stabilize their identity, fix their essence, and so distinguish them from the rest of us.[10]

Essentialism is not the problem—or at least it is not the decisive factor in the history of anti-Semitism. The religion/race dichotomy common both to histories of anti-Semitism and to post-Holocaust readings of *Merchant*, bespeaks conventional wisdom about the secularity of modernity. But one crucial problem attends this conventional view: the very dichotomy by means of which we distinguish between a pre-modern theological perspective and a modern secular and essentializing one is itself a construction of theology. After all, the essentialist indictment of the

Jews as an alien race distinguished by their particularity and unas-similiability dates back to that great Jewish convert himself: the apostle Paul. "There is neither Iew nor Grecian: there is neither bond nor free: there is neither male nor female: for ye are all one in Christ Iesus" (Geneva Bible, Gal. 3:28). Writing to his "brothers" in Galatia, Paul celebrates Christianity's universalism, with its abil-ity to overcome the merely fleshly distinctions of tribe, nation, sta-tus, sex. Faith in Christ overrides the dictates of birth and clan; Spirit supersedes the claims of the flesh. And, ultimately for Paul–and for the figural tradition he inaugurates–this distinction between flesh and Spirit, between race and faith, amounts to the very distinction between Jew and Christian. In this way, the dichotomy used to distinguish a theological anti-Judaism from a modern anti-Semitism, the dichotomy of religious faith versus race, is ultimately a theological dichotomy: the very dichotomy by means of which Christianity from the start determines its differ-ence from–and its supersession of–the Jews.

We need then to think beyond the dichotomization of religion and race.[11] We cannot understand either the dynamic of modern anti-Semitism or its continuity with early modern attitudes if we perceive the development of race theory as a radical paradigm shift away from a theological framework. Race theory does not so much enable the articulation of a modern Jewish question as it attempts to *fix* (in at least two senses of the word) that question. In other words, nineteenth-century positivism works to reassure a hysteria that finds its first articulation elsewhere–in the sixteenth century, and in the realm of *theology*, in fact. As we've already seen, Luther's Reformation forces a reconsideration of the nature of Mosaic Law, reconceiving and reconfiguring the relationship between Jew and Christian in the process. Returning to Shake-speare, it is this allegorical crisis, I will argue, that unsettles the rela-tion of Jew to Christian in *The Merchant of Venice*, enabling a deci-sive early modern instance of what Žižek would call a truly suc-cessful ideology.

The question of conversion–defined within a figural tradition as the supersession of the flesh–will be central to my account. The flesh is easily defined within the allegorical tradition that Luther rejects. It is, as we shall see more clearly in a moment, the material veil that separates us from the Spirit–and at the same time, under-stood rightly, it is the signifying vehicle that leads us *to* the Spirit.

But for Luther the flesh is no longer a veil–indeed it is no longer even necessarily material. As we've already seen, Luther cites Romans 14:23 ("Whatever does not proceed from faith is sin") and argues that the flesh is not just the body, but is everything not born of faith: "the whole man, with body and soul, mind and senses–because everything about him longs for the flesh" (LW 27, 76; LW 35, 371). The flesh is what cannot save us, but since it is no longer the veil-signifier that points us toward God, it cannot be stripped away either. The flesh is not the Spirit, but since we cannot peel it away from the Spirit, how exactly can we delimit and supersede it? Defining the flesh is, one might say, the central ideological task for sixteenth-century Europe; it animates all of the crucial religious debates–free will, iconoclasm, infant baptism, the nature of the Eucharist, and so forth–and resonates sharply with other emergent discourses of exploration, economy, nation. And in *Merchant of Venice*, as we shall see, it is not only in terms of Shylock's "merrie bond" (1.3.178) that the play addresses this difficulty of defining, delimiting, and thus overcoming the flesh. "This bond doth giue thee heere no iot of bloud. . ." (4.1.320). Even more broadly speaking, the problem of defining the flesh lies at the very heart of the play, connecting all its veins of discourse: law, market, will, love, marriage, family, religion, state. . . . And at the heart of that heart is the Jew: the very figure–albeit, an abused, catachrestic one–of the illimitable flesh and the locus of its peculiar bond. Ultimately the Jew in Shakespeare's play reveals the impossibility of conversion. It is, further, because Shakespeare's Jew exceeds all fleshly determination, that he thus remains ever a threat, ever an alibi for the further, paranoid reach of the Law. "Tarry Iew, / The Law hath yet another hold on you." (4.1.363–64).

THE MESH AND THE VEIL

For Augustine, conversion requires the overcoming of the flesh. Like a man struggling to awake, unable to shake the dead weight of sleep, the *gravis torpor in membris* (*Conf.* 8.5), Augustine struggles in book 8 of the *Confessions* to overcome the inertia of carnality. Such inertia is itself sin as Augustine understands it: a sin into which the body has settled against the will of the mind, even if the sinful ways began willingly enough. It is in such terms that Augustine interprets the *lex peccati,* the "law of sin" of Romans 7: "For the law of sin is the force of habit, by which the mind is held and betrayed against its will [*invitus*], yet deservedly so, since it fell into sin willingly [*volens*]" (*Conf.* 8.5). Imprisoned by the torpor of the flesh, a flesh that has become deadly habit, the "inward man" (*interior homo*) wants what he hasn't the strength to pursue. To reach God, Augustine realizes, no chariot or ship is required; no bodily distance need be traversed. All that is necessary is an act of will—but it must be a strong and complete willing, *sed velle fortiter et integre*: it must be a willing that overcomes the momentum of sin. The predicament is a Pauline one: the will itself must first be converted before the penitent is free to turn toward God. And yet, what is conversion itself if not this very transformation of the will, marking an end to the strife of flesh and spirit and breaking through the chains of habit? Conversion, it would seem, is the very condition that makes conversion possible.

Conversion must precede conversion; conversion makes conversion possible. What resolves this paradox for Augustine is nothing less than the retroactive, teleological structure of *figura.* In its impossible, recursive temporality, conversion is for Augustine already an allegorical act: an act that reconciles flesh to spirit according to a narrative of fulfillment. It is thus, as we've seen, no accident that the precise moment of Augustine's conversion consists in an allegorizing reading, as he takes Paul's text upon himself, as if its words were written just for him. "Not in rioting and drunkenness, not in chambering and wantonness, not in strife and envying. But put ye on the Lord Jesus Christ, and make not provision for the flesh, to fulfil the lusts thereof" (Rom. 13:13–14, KJV). The verse that converts provides no answers; it only rephrases the question, giving voice to the very *lex spiritus* that Augustine has been struggling to fulfill on his own. Yet, by taking up the letter of the text—by converting its dead letter into a spiritual command addressed uniquely to him—Augustine is able to put on a godly life. The allegorical reading that strips away a literal context in the name of a life-giving spiritual message is in this way coextensive with the act of overcoming a life of the flesh. To read allegorically is to overcome the flesh.

Augustine's conversion overcomes the law of the members in the name of the totality of spirit, marking a triumph of will—a will that is free, *delivered from the body of death*, as Paul puts it in Romans

7; a will that, thanks to the grace of God, can finally do what it wants. The parts will fall into line with the whole: "Behold [the things of the world] give way, that others may succeed them, and the whole be preserved in all its lowest parts" (*Conf.* 4.11). As we've seen in our discussion of Luther, however, the Reformation discovery calls into question just such parts/whole logic and the structure of temporal fulfillment that underwrites it. Furthermore, for Luther, who questions the system of Christian figurality more deeply and more thoroughly than any other sixteenth-century theologian, the critique of *figura* also entails a critique of the notion of free will and animates his early polemic with Erasmus.[12] At stake for Erasmus in the debate, as with Augustine not only in his *Confessions* but also in the roughly contemporaneous treatise *On Free Will* (written 388-397),[13] is the issue of our capacity to choose: to choose good over evil–life instead of death. Erasmus, like Augustine, sees human volition in Platonist terms as essentially rational: we are always able to choose the good once we see it and know it for what it is. Defined by rational self-interest, the will inevitably pursues what it takes to be good. Hence the law of the spirit, Augustine points out, is also the *lex mentis*, the law of the rational mind. However, we are not always able to follow that law: we may be capable of *choosing* the good, but living in consonance with that choice is another matter. For Erasmus, as for Augustine, such failure amounts to a kind of friction: to the dead and deadly weight of the flesh resisting the spirit. A spiritual whole is thwarted by the inert sum of its parts.

When he rejects the parts/whole logic of Christian *figura*, Luther also redefines the bondage of human will. For Luther, our failure lies not in the body's irrational resistance to the rational commands of the will, but rather in the inherent irrationality of the will itself. In this way, once again, Luther redefines a Christian universe, rejecting the easy Platonic divide between flesh and spirit and radicalizing the dualism that plagues fallen man.

Alongside his little children's Catechism, Luther considered the 1525 treatise *De Servo Arbitrio–Concerning the Enslaved Will*–to be his finest, most correct work. Written in response to Erasmus' *Diatribe on Free Will* (*de libero arbitrio*), Luther defines *man's* will in the context of an utterly sovereign *divine* will. At issue here is not the psychology of action, but, again, the question of justification. If God is to be God–sovereign, foreknowing and willing all things not by mere caprice or contingency but necessarily and immutably–then we must accept that nothing that man does is sufficient for salvation. Let God be God, Luther claimed, and let man be man: if man by his actions could earn his salvation, then God would become beholden to man–owing man eternal life in exchange for good deeds–and not vice versa.

For Erasmus, however, weak as man is and clouded as his will may be owing to the effects of his sin, he nonetheless contributes *something* to his salvation. Like the child whose father raises him up, sets before him an apple, helps him walk toward it, and finally places it in his little, weak hand, so too can we do nothing without God but, Erasmus says, *with* him *all* things are possible.[14] For Erasmus, at the heart of the matter is the question of man's choice in the face of divine judgment. In maintaining that the will is free, Erasmus does not claim that man, of his own powers, can do good; rather he is claiming that man can know the difference, and can choose between, good and evil. His will is free not because he is omnipotent–still less is he sinless–but because despite such obstacles, "man can apply himself to the things which lead to eternal salvation, or turn away from them" (*On Free Will*, 47). Thus Erasmus defines man's free will not as an absolute capacity but as the ability to arbitrate–to make a choice, a judgment between– opposing options. *Liberum arbitrium*, i.e., free will, connotes just such power of choice, just such discretionary judgment. Indeed, without such power, Erasmus reasons, man can no longer be held responsible for making the *wrong* choice: for choosing sin and evil in place of the will of God.

From Luther's perspective, however, the whole of Erasmus's argument is deeply flawed, because it rests on the false assumption that the opposite of *free* will is that which is *involuntary*. In arguing that our will is enslaved, Luther is explicitly *not* arguing that man's actions are involuntary. Man does not act, Luther tells us, by compulsion. In no sense when he sins does he do so involuntarily; instead, when man does ill he acts "spontaneously" and of his own accord.[15] Furthermore, Luther tells us, it is precisely this willingness to sin–this consent to do evil–that man cannot alter. The will–and the word Luther uses here is *voluntas* (that is, our will in the sense of *volition*)–this will cannot change itself, nor be vanquished with restraint, mortified, or sublimated into submission. Rather, Luther writes, our *voluntas* itself, our willingness to act, "is the more provoked to crave the more it is opposed" (*Bondage*, 102–3). In Luther's formulation, our will is that which we cannot change, as it were, *at will*.

In this way, from Luther's perspective, Erasmus's doctrine is wrong as much for what it argues as for what it argues against. Erasmus has deeply misconstrued the nature and import of the free-will debate. His opponent doesn't claim that man *lacks* free will—nor does he claim that man is incapable of doing what he wants. Rather, Luther argues that as willing creatures, we can *only* do what we want: our desires are the one thing about which we are unwilling. At the very heart of us as willing creatures, our will, *as such*, is unwilling. We don't *lack* free will; instead, what will we have, Luther tells us, is *unfree*. No simple dichotomy then obtains between our willingness and our unwillingness. Every act of will, precisely by dint of being willful, contains that about which we are unwilling: the volition or inclination that we do not choose, nor cannot change.

One biblical text proves critical for Erasmus's argument about the freedom of our will—Deuteronomy 30:19: "I have set before you life and death, blessing and cursing: therefore choose life, that both thou and thy seed may live" (KJV). For Erasmus, the verse points to the defining capacity of the human will: the power to choose the good that is set before us. Luther's reply, in contrast, reveals his uncompromising vision of the Law: "The words quoted are imperatives, and only say what ought to be done; for Moses does not say, 'Thou hast the strength or power to choose,' but, 'Choose, keep, do!' He issues commandments about doing, but does not describe man's ability to do."[16] Moses' imperative—*choose, keep, do!*—serves for Luther as a kind of meta-law: a law that commands us to keep the Law. And as such it offers no reassuring vision of our capacity either to choose or to do. Quite the contrary: like the Law in general, the injunction in Deuteronomy 30 works "to reveal sin and put to shame all presumption to human ability."[17] It too fulfills the office of the Law as Luther defines it.

"I have set before you life and death, blessing and cursing: there-fore choose life, that both thou and thy seed may live": it is with this verse of contention that we come closest, perhaps, to a point of direct contact between Luther and Shakespeare. As critics have

noted since the early 1960s, an explicit reference to the Deuteronomic injunction occurs in what was almost certainly a source for
the casket subplot in Shakespeare's *Merchant of Venice*: the story of
the three vessels in the *Gesta Romanorum*. In that story, a princess
is made to choose between a gold vessel filled with dead men's
bones, a silver vessel filled with earth and worms, and a lead vessel filled with precious stones. If she chooses rightly—and of course
she does—she proves herself a bride worthy of the son of the
Roman emperor. The "Morall" of the story reveals precisely the
biblical significance of her choice:

> The Emperour sheweth this Mayden three vessells, that is
> to say, God putteth before man life & death, good and
> euill, & which of these that he chooseth hee shall obtaine.
> Therefore saith *Sampson: Ante hominem mors & vita*. Death
> and lyfe is sette before man, choose which him lyst. And
> yet man is vncertaine whether he bee worthy to choose
> lyfe beefore death.[18]

For Barbara Lewalski, the first critic to note the connection to
Deuteronomy, the casket plot thus alludes to "the great choices of
spiritual life and death," helping establish the play's function as
Christian allegory.[19] As Lewalski reads it, the decision facing Portia's suitors refers to the choice that God set before the Israelites.
In a more recent essay, Douglas Anderson builds on Lewalski's
work, arguing that the Deuteronomic allusion demonstrates the
ways in which the very doctrine of forgiveness that the play
invokes against Shylock is itself of Mosaic origin.[20] According to
Anderson, such allusions to Mosaic law serve to complicate the
play's treatment of Judaism by demonstrating "the beauty and pertinence" of central Jewish tenets (Anderson, 122). Unlike Lewalski, Anderson is attuned to the potential ironies of a Christian allegory that invokes the necessity of Jewish Law.

However, in their treatment of the play's "moral vision"
(Anderson, 123), neither Anderson nor Lewalski notes that the
casket plot, with its link to Deuteronomy 30, nests within another
story of choosing: the story not of the suitor but of the daughter.
At the end of act 1.2, we learn that Portia's current suitors have all
decided to give up their suit rather than risk and hazard all in her
father's game of caskets. "They haue acquainted me with their

determinations," Nerissa informs Portia at the end of the scene, "which is indeede to returne to their home, and to trouble you with no more suite" (97–99). But quite unlike these suitors who are free to avoid the dilemma of choice altogether, Portia is–paradoxically enough–*bound to choose*. She has no choice in the matter.

Quite literally, Portia's will is embedded in another will–her will is not her own; her will has already been willed. Like the ancient Israelites, Portia too is bound by the law of the father; in the precise terms of Shakespeare's dramatic imagination, the dying "imposition" (1.2.100) of Portia's father–his last will and testament dictating the game of gold, silver, and lead caskets–binds her living will, her living desire. Like Luther's unregenerate man laboring under the office of the Law, Portia knows only a double bind: she is commanded to choose according to her Father's will, but at the same time she lacks the capacity of choice: she may neither "choose one, nor refuse none" (1.2.26).

Thus, at the very start of the play, Shakespeare offers us a dramatic image not of Erasmian free choice but rather of Lutheran bound will: *Choose, keep, do!* Portia's will, curbed as it is by the law of the father, is a will that has no choice in its willing, that is unfree insofar as it is bound to choose. The passage in which Portia refers to her father's will is striking, and deserves to be quoted at length. As we shall see, in its evocation of an enslaved will, the passage proves indispensable to an understanding of the play. It ushers us into the worlds of Belmont and Venice–worlds seemingly far apart, yet joined by a single Lutheran logic–just as the procreation sonnets ushered us into a reading of the 1609 Quarto's universe.

Responding to Nerissa's efforts to rouse her from her melancholy ("By my troth *Nerrissa*, my little body is a wearie of this great world" 1.2.2–3), Portia notes that it is easier to give good advice than to follow it:

> If to doe were as easie as to know what were good to doe,
> Chappels had been Churches, and poore mens cottages
> Princes Pallaces: it is a good Diuine that followes his owne
> instructions; I can easier teach twentie what were good to
> be done, than be one of the twentie to follow mine owne
> teaching: the braine may deuise lawes for the blood, but a
> hot temper leapes ore a colde decree, such a hare is mad-

> ness the youth, to skip ore the meshes of good counsaile
> the cripple; but this reason is not in fashion to choose me
> a husband: O mee, the word choose, I may neither choose
> whom I would, nor refuse whom I dislike, so is the wil of
> a liuing daughter curb'd by the will of a dead father: [is it]
> not hard *Nerissa*, that I cannot choose one, nor refuse none.
>
> (1.2.13–26)

At first glance, Portia articulates a conventional Platonic division between mind and body, between the "madness" of "hot" desire and the sane counsel of "the braine." Blood and brain, hot and cold, temper and decree oppose each other in a relatively straightforward dualism; thanks to the resistance of the flesh, it becomes difficult to do what we know is "good to doe." At first glance, Portia would seem then to articulate an Erasmian or Augustinian vision of a human will that is free in its ability to choose the good, but nonetheless thwarted by the irrational flesh. Impassive and dispassionate, the cold decree of reason is easily overleaped, easily overlooked in the heat of passion.

Portia's terms here are self-consciously sententious; in her string of truisms about practicing what one preaches, she tells us, and knows that she tells us, nothing that we don't already know. Indeed, in this manner she responds to the "good sentences" Nerissa has herself just "well pronounc'd": chiding Portia for failing to weigh her miseries against the abundance of her good fortune, Nerissa has sententiously concluded that "it is no [mean] happinesse . . . to bee seated in the meane" (1.2.11; 7–8).[21] The happy life is the temperate life, the life balanced between surfeit and starvation (5–6), where desire has been overruled by reason. But in terms no less conventional than Nerissa's, Portia manages to counter Nerissa's counsel: the "cold decree" Portia describes refers at once to the possibility of temperance–the possibility of overruling desire with the laws of reason–and to Nerissa's "good sentences" themselves, as cold instances of the mind's legislative capacity. Just as the mind in general cannot legislate the passions, neither can Nerissa's good words decree an end to Portia's melancholy.

Nonetheless, in her sententious response to Nerissa's sentences, Portia invokes her own "cold decree," instantiating that very legislative capacity of the mind whose efficacy she calls into question. In order to pronounce the limits of reason, Portia must transcend those limits; the paradox she thus puts into play is as old as Plato and as orthodox as book 8 of the *Confessions*: from what vantage point can the self articulate its own self-division? How can the self speak from beyond its own limits of language and thought? Again, for Augustine no less than Plato, it is the retroactive structure of *figura* that resolves the paradox: whether one speaks with the authority of a Diotima or with the piety of the Bishop of Hippo, it is from the standpoint of the convert that such metalanguage is possible. Standing on the triumphant side of reason, the self speaks in unitary terms, confronting its division between flesh and spirit as a function of time and not of space: the old man versus the new. Cast into (and *as*) the past, the flesh is that which may be discarded in the name of the spirit and yet nonetheless preserved in the present as figure.

But for Portia the bondage of human will is not simply a general condition of fallen man's life: it is a very specific condition of her own life. "O mee, the word choose, I may neither choose whom I would, nor refuse whom I dislike, so is the wil of a liuing daughter curb'd by the will of a dead father." From what standpoint does Portia judge our failure to do as we decree when, as she herself admits, her own *liberum arbitrium*, her own capacity to judge and decree, is "curbed"? Unlike Augustine in his celebrated account of the will's triumph over the flesh, Portia is no convert— at least not here in the beginning of the play. She lacks the retrospective standpoint that resolves the split in human nature— between spirit and flesh, between decree and desire—within a narrative of the flesh's overcoming. From what vantage point, then, does she survey that split in human nature between what the law commands and what the flesh may do, when she herself is most unhappily subject to just such a split?

The very question presumes that the split may indeed be overcome. It presumes the kind of "clean" dualism that Augustine renders orthodox: a dualism where flesh and spirit, desire and law, are tidily dissevered the one from the other, their mutual strife resulting only from their brute incompatibility. Such tidy dualist terms presume a will that is unitary and rational, bound only by its imprisonment within, its shackling by, the flesh. Once the heavy torpor of *sarx* or *caro* is, with the grace of God, shrugged off— peeled back like bark or stripped away like a veil—this fleshly husk reveals the spirit. But like Martin Luther, Portia's terms in 1.2 call such revelation into question. When Portia speaks about the will's bondage, she does so not from the side of unitary and autonomous reason but rather from the standpoint of a will that is irrevocably irrational: a will that is of its own nature heteronomous and complex. The split Portia describes between desire and decree is primary, originary; in dramatic terms, it is the very precondition of the play. *So is the wil of a liuing daughter curb'd by the will of a dead father.* This is a will that chooses spontaneously but yet has no choice over what it wills. Its failure cannot be extricated from its success; its freedom is also its unfreedom. For after all, if Portia's *arbitrium*–her will as a faculty of choice–is unfree, it is not because Portia cannot choose: indeed, constrained simultaneously by her own affections and by the dictates of her father's will, she cannot *help* but choose, for she can refuse none. It is just this tension between constraint and volition (between *decree* and *desire*) that the scene as a whole, with its survey of each miserable suitor, demonstrates: "I pray thee ouer-name them [i.e., the suitors], and as thou namest them, I will describe them, and according to my description leuell at my affection" (1.2.35–37). Portia can choose, but yet her choice is constrained by the pre-given will of her father: she must choose in accordance with his will.

   The braine may deuise lawes for the blood, but a hot temper leapes ore a colde decree, such a hare is madness the youth, to skip ore the meshes of good counsaile the cripple. In the final analysis, far from articulating a traditional "clean" dualism of desire versus reason, Portia's terms disclose a reason or "braine" that is from the start, constitutionally, already divided by the very laws it may devise. In her metaphor of mad youth the hare, Portia articulates an almost Looney Tunes logic; Elmer Fudd meets Bugs Bunny or Wile E. Coyote tracks the Roadrunner: an inept yet devious reason sets traps for its nimble prey. Like a mesh laid over a pit, or a net meant to spring on its prey, the decrees of reason amount to wily (if ineffective) guile. Instead of a unitary reason that is shackled from without by the dead weight of the flesh, reason as Portia describes it is inherently "crippled": the impediments that "good counsaile" encounters are not, as Portia envisions it, obstacles in reason's path but infirmities in its nature–the very infirmities that reduce it to trickery. Seeking to enmesh rather than to advise, reason is no longer that which is self-evident, singular, straightforward, aboveboard; rather it is hidden, devious, cunning.

And what are we to make of reason's mesh itself? *Such a hare is madness the youth, to skip ore the meshes of good counsaile the cripple.* This thin, porous covering is meant to mediate between desire and reason—meant to perform the office of the Law, even as it deforms, through its entrapping deception, the very notion of justice. True, the mesh Portia describes here in 1.2 fails in its office: either because it is too obvious or because it is too unobtrusive, it is missed by its mark. The successful trap must be just evident enough to be noticed—we must, after all, *fall for it*—but it cannot be so obvious that we avoid it. In order to be caught in the snare, we have to see the mesh, but not see it *as* mesh. The mesh does not perform its office by being invisible: it performs its office by being visibly other than itself. What renders good counsel effective is, then, not its self-evident rightness, but rather its self-othering disguise. And thus, when such meshes of reason are most successful it seems least clear that justice has been served: the brain's decrees seem then most unlike themselves. As we shall see, this paradox of a law that doesn't play fair and only works by dissembling, the paradox of a law that only works as *trick*, lies at the melancholy core of the play, underwriting Portia's triumph in the courtroom no less than Bassanio's triumph in Belmont. Portia's mesh overhangs this play, emblem of a command that succeeds—and a will that is free—only because it belies itself.

In an important sense, Portia's mesh takes the place of the notion, central to Pauline *figura*, of the Law as veil: that fleshly, external material that obscures an inner immaterial truth; that thin integument which must be peeled back in order to reveal the precious kernel inside.

For the letter killeth, but the Spirit giueth life. If then the ministration of death *written* with letters and ingrauen in stones, was glorious, so that the children of Israel could not behold the face of Moses, for the glory of his countenance. . . . How shall not the ministration of the Spirit be more glorious? . . . For if that which should bee abolished, *was* glorious, much more shall that which remaineth, be glorious. . . . And *we are* not as Moses, *which* put a vaile vpon his face, that the children of Israel should not looke vnto the end of that which should be abolished. Therefore their minds are hardened: for vntill this day remaineth the

same couering vntaken away in the reading of the old Testament, which *vaile* in Christ is put away. But euen vnto
this day, when Moses is read the vaile is layd ouer their
hearts. Neuerthelesse, when their *heart* shall be turned to
the Lord, the vaile shal be taken away.

(2 Cor. 3:6–16, Geneva Bible)

For Paul, the veil with which Moses covered his radiant face as he
came down from Mount Sinai to deliver the Law (Exod.
34:33–35), itself serves as an allegory *for* the Law. The veil hides
even God's reflected glory from the Israelites, just as the Law in its
written letters and engraved stones mediates the covenant that
itself mediates a relation to God. The Israelites are at two removes
from the Lord. The veil/Law keeps the children of Israel from
seeing the image of God; they are blind to "the end [*telos*] of that
which should be abolished"–blind, that is, both to the Law's completion and its purpose in Christ. Instead, they take the Law as an
end in itself, failing to see even that their vision is obscured. What
the Hebrews miss is that the Law, like the veil, cannot be taken at
face value.

For Paul, the Jews fail to *see through* the Law. In failing to recognize the Law as veil, they fail not only to see that which it
obscures but to recognize its instrumental, referential function.
The veil not only hides the truth, it also points to the truth *as hidden*. As Augustine argues, in their blindness the Jews mistake *signs*
for *things*: they mistake transparency for opacity, trade depth for
surface. Portia's mesh, however, is simultaneously transparent *and*
opaque: the knotted strings that construct the mesh construct it as
a system of holes. The veil hides and reveals (indeed, it hides in
order to reveal), but the mesh hides *nothing*. Unlike the veil whose
presence announces an absence, whose surface *re*-veals (both
unveils and veils over) a depth, the mesh is simultaneously present
and absent; it is a surface that refuses to signal/obscure a depth:
the mesh, in a sense, is all surface or pure surface because it is *full
of holes*.[22] Unlike the veil, the mesh refuses to turn absence into a
presence; it refuses to serve as a figure, refuses to act as the material fetish that points to (and thus supplants) what is absent.
Instead, unlike the veil, in its very materiality the mesh depends
upon, is constructed out of, absence as such. The mesh "is" nothing but holes. Indeed, early modern linguistic usage even reflects

this paradoxical formulation; according to the OED, the word (which emerged from unknown sources in the sixteenth century) signified both "the open spaces or interstices of a net, the size of which is determined by the distance of adjacent knots from one another" and the "threads or cords which bound the[se] interstices" (OED, "mesh" sb. 1a, 1b).[23] The mesh, in other words, is both the *knot* that defines the open spaces, and the *not*–the emptiness–that partitions the fabric into adjacent squares.

If, however, Portia's mesh with its ambivalent (k)nots reconfigures the logic of the Pauline veil, it does so in terms already well rehearsed–by Martin Luther. As we've seen, Luther rejects the patristic reading that conflates the *letter* of 2 Corinthians 3:6–*the letter killeth, but the spirit giveth life*–with Mosaic Law. "For others," Luther argues, "however, though never for itself, [the Law] is a 'letter' " (LW 27, 313). Luther's vision of the Law as spirit transforms the very concept of Christian revelation, redefining the Christian relevance of the Hebrew Bible. The patristic logic of veiling and unveiling no longer holds sway. For Luther the Law is no diaphanous veil, no mystic letter obscuring and revealing an underlying truth. Indeed, quite the opposite: the Law is *itself* veiled, its true infinitude hidden from our eyes when we imagine that we can satisfy it–when we delude ourselves that our performance of specific deeds constitutes true obedience to the Word of God. It is then that we mistake the Law as letter, failing to recognize the infinite command bespoken in every concrete and finite decree. We may perform individual deeds in the name of the Law, but we miss the Law in its performativity: we fail to demonstrate our obedience to the Law *as such*.

In a certain sense, the Law for Luther is unveiled *only* when we take it at face value–i.e., *as* Law. It is only once we face the Law in its sheerest, performative dimension as a commandment–*choose, keep, do!*–that we can confront the utter inadequacy of our works and recognize the extent of our sin. It is only then that we can recognize what the Law really and impossibly demands: namely, our *faith. Du sollt nicht andere Gotter haben. You shall not have other gods.* To take the Law at face value is to embrace the sheer blast of God's Word. For Luther, then, Christian revelation consists not in negating the surface of the Law in the name of a higher, or deeper, or hidden meaning, but rather in reading its formal surface *as such*, in its naked and intolerable essence as brute command.

It is indeed the nakedness of surface–the Law taken at face value–that, according to Luther, the Israelites could not endure. Significantly, then, Luther interprets the radiance of Moses' face not as reflected divine glory but instead as an intolerable glare, an unbearable knowledge: the "glare of the knowledge of our wickedness and nothingness" (LW 35, 244–45). Such glaring truth proves too much for the Israelites; it is for this reason that Moses wears a veil as he descends with the tablets of the Law. In this manner, the Israelites of Exodus 34 represent

> those who attempt to fulfil the law by their own power, without grace. . . . The law comes to them but they cannot endure it. They therefore put a veil over it and lead a life of hypocrisy, doing outward works of the law. Yet the law makes it all to be sin where the veil is taken off. For the law shows that our ability counts for nothing without Christ's grace. . . . Those who see Moses clearly, without a veil . . . understand the intention of the law and how it demands impossible things.
>
> (LW 35, 245)

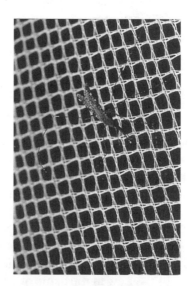

"Female Anopheles mosquito resting on a mosquito net."
© Copyright Siamdutch Mosquito Netting Co., Ltd.

Christian revelation means not a turning away from the Law but instead a turning toward it, as toward a mirror that reflects not God but rather our own sinful natures. Indeed, the very intensity of this turn toward the Law amounts in some sense not to a rejection of the Pauline metaphor of the veil, but rather—if you will—to a new sort of vision, a kind of zooming in to the very surface of the veil itself. If the Law becomes something like a mesh in Luther's eyes, it is because Luther gives us the veil at magnification 20x, as it were; he gives us nothing short of a mosquito's eye view. The warp and woof of the veil now become recognizable, and the fabric's surface area grows fractally more immense, tending toward infinity. To a mosquito, the veil is a mesh—albeit solid enough. Push the focus further, however, and the whole dissolves into a sequence of holes.

To "unveil" the Law as Luther sees it—the Law as mesh—is to examine its surface unwaveringly. It is to recognize the Law in its infinitude and to recognize that it is also a trick of sorts: it is our lure and our trial. To unveil the Law is to reveal the futility of our efforts to fulfill the Law. Such unveiling exposes not hidden depth and mystical content but rather the loopholes and lacunae that sig-

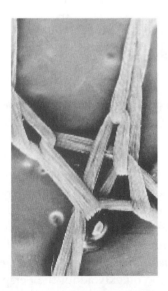

"Multi-filament polyester yarn used for mosquito nets."
© Copyright Siamdutch Mosquito Netting Co., Ltd.

nal the trapper's intent.[24] However, as we've already seen in our consideration of Luther's own spiritual crises–his *Anfechtungen*– there may be no end to such unveiling. In arguing that the Law is a trial, meant to push us to despair, Luther opens up a second-guessing hermeneutics–a hermeneutics of suspicion and skepticism where every reading becomes itself the letter of a further reading.

It is just this problem of second-guessing that underlies the curious reemergence of Portia's mesh–and its opposition to the veil of Pauline allegory–in a scene that we might consider a Shakespearean analogue to Augustine's moment under the fig tree. I refer here to the scene of Portia's "conversion": act 3.2, the scene during which Portia's "curb'd will" is in a manner unbound, thanks to Bassanio's not inconsiderable hermeneutic skills. "My selfe, and what is mine," she tells Bassanio once he has correctly passed the casket test, "to you and yours / Is now conuerted" (3.2.173–74). In marriage Portia experiences a conversion exactly analogous to a religious conversion, her purse and her person becoming subject to a higher power just as the religious convert overcomes his own recalcitrant flesh in the name of the spirit.[25]

Significantly, like Augustine's *tolle, lege*, the moment of Portia's conversion of the will is also marked by a song that prompts interpretation–although it is a song that she herself bids play. The stage direction in the Folio reads:

Here Musicke.
A Song the whilst Bassanio *comments on the*
Caskets to himselfe.

(3.2.66–68)

Interestingly, the song takes the place of Bassanio's actual reading of the inscriptions on the caskets. Unlike Arragon and Morocco before him, Bassanio does not read aloud, and indeed it is unclear whether he reads the inscriptions at all–a crucial point, to which we will return in a moment. As we shall see, the question of how, or even *whether*, Bassanio reads has typically been elided by modern critics, who all too quickly adopt the perspective of the scroll Bassanio finds when he unlocks the leaden casket: "*You that choose not by the view / Chance as faire, and choose as true*" (3.2.138–39). Bassanio, it appears, is not swayed by appearances. But what then to make of Portia's song? It plays while he reviews the caskets; in what ways might the song sway his choice?

> *Tell me where is fancie bred,*
> *Or in the heart, or in the head:*
> *How begot, how nourished.*   *Replie, replie.*
> *It is engendred in the eyes,*
> *With gazing fed, and Fancie dies,*
> *In the cradle where it lies:*
> *Let vs all ring Fancies knell.*
> Ile begin it.
> *Ding, dong, bell.*
>   All. *Ding, dong, bell.*
>   (3.2.69–78)

Thematically the song attests to the same problem of appearances decried in the scrolls of all three caskets: all that glisters is not gold, and to choose by view is to fall prey to a short-lived and superficial "fancy"–to a passion engendered merely in the eyes. But there are perhaps even more superficial ways to choose than through the eyes; is it possible, for instance, that Bassanio is swayed by *sound*? Could a silly quibble, a shallow trick be responsible for Bassanio's success? In his 1978 *Harmonies of "The Merchant of Venice,"* Lawrence Danson notes with marked distaste the view that the song serves as "a trick to bring Bassanio, by way of the rhymes 'bred ... head ... nourished,' to the inevitable 'lead'" (117). As Danson tells us, the play's entire thematic harmony–or at least Danson's own argument about that harmony–hinges upon the legitimacy of Bassanio's trial. The song *cannot* be a trick. The scroll *must* be right: Bassanio does not choose by view; he alone of all the suitors is not swayed by mere appearances.

As we shall see, at stake with the question of Bassanio's choice is the status of allegory, and its relation to anti-Semitism, in the play.

If Portia's father's will is to retain its aura of the numinous, and *if* Bassanio's fitness as Portia's lover is to be affirmed; *if* the casket-trial is to be one in a series of trials that includes also the trial in Venice and the trial of the rings,

> and *if* those trials are to function as dramatic metaphors
> for love's harmony–for which the music of the song is
> itself a figure: *if* the play is to remain a romantic comedy
> rather than a farce or a neatly disguised satire, *then* the
> idea that Portia tips off Bassanio has got to be dismissed.
>
> (Danson, 117–18, emphasis added)

The passage, which stacks the entire edifice of Danson's argument
upon the shaky fulcrum of the "if," neatly exemplifies the problem
of post-Holocaust *Merchant* criticism. Like Coghill, Danson seems
driven to rehabilitate the play through allegory; like Coghill, Danson argues that the play's tensions are all resolved harmoniously
when viewed through the lens of Christian parable. Nonetheless,
the more Danson articulates the stakes of his argument, the less
persuasive it becomes: far from preempting a critical reading of the
play, Danson's *if*'s reinforce its validity. Danson, indeed, establishes an absolute symmetry between irony and allegory: if the
play is to be read as allegory, it cannot also be interpreted as social
satire; if it is read ironically, it cannot also portray love's harmonies. Each reading comes at the expense of the other, which
means that neither reading can ever be final since each invokes its
opposite, if only by negation.

As Richard Halpern points out in a brilliant reading of "The
Jewish Question" in Shakespeare, the recursive either/or we see
here in Danson's argument–a "logic of mutual exclusion," as
Halpern calls it (225)–is symptomatic of the modernist response
to the play. Halpern discusses the tendency of modern critics "to
divide themselves between those who . . . react primarily to the
hypocrisies and contradictions of Venetian society and those
who . . . respond instead to the play's harmonies" (211). Insofar
as *Merchant* examines Christian ideals, it also potentially exposes
Christian hypocrisy as the failure of real men and women to live
up to those ideals. In this way, allegory capacitates irony: the
allegorical reading of the play also makes available a critical,
ironic reading. Thus from Coghill's suggestion that an allegorical
reading of *Merchant* drives a wedge between social labels and
actual practice, we pass easily into an ironic reading like René
Girard's or Harold Goddard's, where Shylock becomes the
Christians' scapegoat "because he reminds them of their own
unconfessed evil qualities."[26]

Halpern's essay presents an incisive analysis of the either/or dilemma facing modern criticism of the play: in Coghill's disturbingly blunt terms, is Shakespeare pro-Jew or anti-Jew? Halpern's essay in many ways resolves the dilemma by demonstrating that the entire debate is founded upon the logic of anti-Semitism. I am indebted to Halpern's approach and conclusions, and my own reading of *Merchant* also examines the connection between the play's ambivalences and the structure of anti-Semitism. Yet the difference between our two accounts is crucial, and will need to be clarified upon more careful examination of Halpern's argument.

In a discussion that positions Shakespeare in relation to figures as diverse as Marx, Werner Sombart, and James Joyce, Halpern surveys the structural link between anti-Semitism and a modernist aesthetic. As the inversion of Danson or Coghill's harmonious allegories, ironic readings of the play serve to negate a presumed anti-Semitic content. Yet, as Halpern shows, such "anti-anti-Semitism" converges on its inverse, preserving the functional identity of the Jew. "Even if one accepts the view that the play's Christians are as bad as Shylock, and hypocritical to boot, one is still left with the fact that the Jew mirrors only society's vices and becomes thereby a standard of degeneration. 'See, they're even worse than the Jews!'" (Halpern, 161–62). Both irony and allegory alike position the Jew as *mirror*, and thus neither manages to challenge the logic of racism: both leave intact the Jew's structural position.

Allegory and irony reach the same conclusion in Halpern's account because, as critical modes, they operate according to the same hermeneutic principle of "disjunctive reading" (see Halpern, 180, 220): both deny the allure of surface, severing the symbolic ties between inner and outer, form and content, in order to cut through to truth. Furthermore, just as irony and allegory, anti-Semitism and anti-anti-Semitism, converge through a logic of mutual exclusion, so too, Halpern argues, does the modernist discourse of the Jew itself articulate two mutually exclusive poles: the Jew is at once criticized as supreme allegorist—overly abstract, excessively theoretical—*and* criticized as a practical-minded ironist unable to appreciate an aesthetic, spiritual realm (see Halpern, 224–25).

By analyzing the stakes and legacies of modernism, Halpern's argument provides a powerful context for interpreting post-Holocaust readings of the play. At the same time, however, because his discussion of the play's anti-Semitism is squarely situated in the modern, it implicitly confirms (if despite itself) the conclusions of historians like Goldhagen and Oberman and critics like Coghill, Hunter, and Danson that there simply is *no* Jewish question for Shakespeare–that anti-Semitism is itself a modern phenomenon. Most problematic, perhaps, is Halpern's discussion (and deconstruction) of the logic of mutual exclusion: *either* irony *or* allegory, *either* anti-anti-Semitism *or* anti-Semitism. The logic Halpern here describes is a specifically post-Romantic one; his discussion of allegory and irony begins with German Idealism and German Romanticism, and is explicitly attuned to the uses of Romanticism in contemporary criticism: "The bond between allegory and Judaism in post-Hegelian thought is suggestive for the development of literary theory in general and rich in ironic implications for the critical career of Paul de Man in particular" (219). If, however, our goal is to fill in the blanks in the history of anti-Semitism by understanding the *history* of allegory, then we will need to consider the possible logic of *non*-exclusion that allows hypocrisy and harmony to cohabit in this play.[27]

We will, in particular, need to question Halpern's association of allegory–and its inverted twin, irony–with what he calls *disjunctive reading*: a reading that rejects surfaces, treating them as deceptive veils. The casket game, Halpern argues, "teaches the necessity of disjunctive reading. The golden surface of the first casket acts not as symbolic embodiment but as allegorical negation of its hidden content" (220).[28] Here Halpern echoes the conclusions of the modern allegorists and ironists he examines. Thus, for instance, Danson characterizes the play's touches of sweet harmony as a lesson about the "limits of sensory experience and the folly of trusting to even the most reasonable shows of the world" (170). At the other end of the critical spectrum, Girard points to the very same disjunction when he describes "Shakespeare's ironic distance" (251): "Shakespeare is writing . . . that appearances, especially the appearances of beautiful language, are 'The Seeming truth which cunning times put on / To entrap the wisest'" (251). For Danson, Bassanio's success with the caskets reveals a Pauline faith in things unseen, and distinguishes Bassanio from the "worldly choosers" who rely on glistering appearances.[29] In contrast, for Girard, Bassanio's success exemplifies the irony that Shakespeare's message about appearances can only be grasped by the hypocritical. Less "naive" (Girard, 245) than the

foreigners in this play (e.g., Morocco, Arragon, Shylock), the Venetians know enough *not* to take appearances at face value.

Halpern is right: the principle of disjunctive reading supports
both a Girard and a Danson, both a critical and an allegorical reading of the play. Furthermore, *nothing changes* when we adopt one
reading over the other. The same lesson is taught—*all that glisters is
not gold*, the lesson contained in the golden casket—and that lesson
remains a "Christian" one. The problem, however, is that it is not
Bassanio who best exemplifies this lesson; rather it is Portia's *other*
suitors, Morocco and Arragon, who do so. It is they who read "disjunctively" in this play—not Bassanio. It is they who read allegorically, seeking to unveil the truth that lurks beneath the play of
mere appearances. Morocco and Arragon, and not Bassanio, read
for depth, passing quickly over the surface as such.

As is often noticed, Morocco, for instance, seems well aware of
the misleading nature of appearances before he ever reaches the
caskets. "Mislike me not for my complexion" (2.1.5), he bids Portia—a line that most readers, quick to cite his hermeneutical naivety,
appreciate as dramatic irony. Given the personal experience of the
"tawnie Moore"with superficial judgments, he of all people should
not be fooled by mere appearance! Yet, precisely, although he does
choose the golden casket, Morocco at no point relies "naively" on
outward show. Far from presuming the "organic unity of form and
content, image and spirit" (Halpern, 218), Morocco carefully questions the connection between outer form and inner content when
making his decision. He recognizes, in other words, that the casket
test amounts to a test in interpretation, and that the relationship
between the sign and what it signifies is neither immediate nor
obvious. In short, he recognizes that he might get it *wrong*:

> What saies the Siluer with her virgin hue?
> Who chooseth me, shall get as much as he deserues.
> As much as he deserues; pause there *Morocho*,
> And weigh thy value with an euen hand,
> If thou beest rated by thy estimation
> Thou doost deserue enough, and yet enough
> May not extend so farre as to the Ladie:
> And yet to be afeared of my deseruing,
> Were but a weake disabling of my selfe.
>
> (2.7.23–31)

To appreciate the ambiguity of the inscription is exactly to distrust the face value of appearances; far from naive or provincial, Morocco recognizes the limits of his own perspective, realizing that his personal "estimation" provides no sure or universal standard for judgment. Moreover, no sooner has he offered this first interpretation than he recognizes its limits as well. "And yet . . ." Ever mistrustful of first impressions, Morocco thus demonstrates nothing less than a capacity to read disjunctively—just as Arragon does, when he suspiciously confronts the gold casket: "Who chooseth me, shall gaine what many men desire: / What many men desire, that many may be meant / By the foole multitude that choose by show, / Not learning more than the fond eye doth teach" (2.9.26–29). Both Arragon and Morocco know enough to question what the fond eye teaches. The lesson of the golden casket is a lesson they have already learned.

Morocco, moreover, goes one step further than Arragon. He is the first suitor to attempt the test, and the suitor whom Portia perhaps favors the least.[30] Yet, of all Portia's suitors, Morocco alone seems cognizant of the full complexity of the casket test. He realizes that, in order to choose correctly, not only must he interpret the relationship between inner content and outer sign; he must also interpret the relationship between two different signifying codes: he must reconcile what the caskets "say" with the material out of which they are made. He is the only suitor who systematically interprets *both* codes, both the inscriptions and the metals, and who recognizes that both codes must point to Portia.[31]

And yet Morocco chooses incorrectly. Danson speaks for most modern interpreters of the play when he tells us that "Morocco, like Arragon later, confuses the outside with the inside . . . the literal with the spiritual" (99). For critics like Danson Morocco reads like a Jew, observing no disjunction between sign and thing. Such is indeed the sentence that the casket passes, with its death's head memento mori and enscrolled reminder: "*Guilded timber doe wormes infold*" (2.7.71). All that lives must die, passing from nature to eternity—and from the standpoint of eternity, all gold is fool's gold, all splendor is mere deceptive show, since every fair from fair sometime declines. The judgment of the casket is death in every sense: death as the unveiled content of golden beauty and death as the sentence for Morocco himself who, having sworn to forgo marriage if he chooses incorrectly, will now be assured of dying heirless, and hence dying absolutely. But is the judgment just? According to the casket's scroll, Morocco errs in mistaking transient value for enduring spiritual worth. His is the error of idolatry; a fair enough charge, perhaps, given his description of Portia as a "mortall breathing Saint," a "shrine" that draws pilgrims from every corner of the earth (2.7.41). Idolatrously worshiping the flesh instead of the spirit, his error is to confuse appearance with reality.

To accept the casket's judgment, however, is to presume that Morocco chooses the gold for what he takes to be its intrinsic value—that he chooses it for its face value. Yet indeed, in choosing the golden casket Morocco is, once again, self-conscious in his role as reader. He chooses not gold as such but gold as the signifier of Portia. Indeed, he reaches his decision only after he reminds himself of that distinction crucial to a disjunctive reading: the distinction between visible form and invisible content. "One of these three containes her heauenly picture," he muses, as he struggles to infer hidden contents by discerning the game's signifying logic.

> Is't like that Lead containes her? 'twere damnation
> To think so base a thought, it were too grose
> To rib her searecloath in the obscure graue:
> Or shall I thinke in Siluer she's immur'd
> Being ten times vndervalued to tride gold;
> O sinfull thought, neuer so rich a Iem
> Was set in worse than gold!
>
> (2.7.49–56)

Readers prepared to concede the justice of the scroll's sentence point out that Morocco here wrongly equates appearance with reality, shadow with substance. First, he confuses the representation of Portia with the woman herself. "One of these three containes her . . . *picture*," he begins, and in the next breath literalizes the image: "Is't like that Lead containes *her?*" The casket is a burial casket, with Portia immured within. He seems to recognize no difference between image and reality: the counterfeit Portia *is* Portia. His next mistake—as such readers would have it—is a related one, but even more deadly: "neuer so rich a Iem / Was set in worse than gold!" Morocco wrongly thinks to infer spiritual value from physical value, equating this gem among women with literal, material riches. "A golden minde stoopes not to showes of drosse," he has already argued in response to the leaden casket (2.7.21)– further evidence for readers like Danson that the prince confuses "'*shows* of dross' with real dross" (Danson, 99). If initially he does make a clear distinction between inner content and outer form, struggling to discern the logic of the casket signifying game, it would seem that the distinction immediately collapses.

But let us, like Morocco, pause here and likewise read more closely. "A golden minde stoopes not to showes of drosse." This is a play where mythological references are almost as prominent as biblical ones, providing an epic register for the "ideology of adventure" that the play associates with its merchants as well as its wooers.[32] Portia calls Bassanio her Hercules in the "conversion" scene and Morocco himself identifies with Hercules–and of course, at the heart of this adventure mythos is the epic metaphor that decisively links marriage with trade: the image of Portia as the golden *fleece* who later salvages Anthonio's *fleets*.[33] Given the mythological subtext, it seems at least conceivable that the shows of dross to which Morocco here refers are counterparts to Hippomenes' golden apples. Like Morocco, Hippomenes is a suitor who risks death to win the prize–in this case, the swift-footed Atalanta, whom he must outrun. He triumphs through a kind of trickery or feint: as they race, he drops three golden apples given to him by Venus in Atalanta's path; she stoops to pick them up, and thus he distracts her just enough to win. In 1596/7 when *Merchant* was likely composed, Shakespeare might still have been thinking about Hippomenes' story, having written *Venus and Adonis* only a few years earlier.[34]

In terms that Shakespeare would also certainly have known, Barnabe Barnes elaborated the Petrarchan dimensions of the golden apple story in his 1593 elegy:

> Swift Atalanta (when she lost the prise
> By gathering golden apples in her race)
> Shewes how by th'apples of thine heauenly eyes,
> (Which fortune did before my passage place
> When for mine hartes contentement I did runne)
> How I was hindred, and my wager lost.
>
> (Elegy 13, 1–6)[35]

Barnes's elegy reveals the link between Hippomenes' golden apples and a Petrarchan visual erotics. Just as Atalanta defeats her purpose when she stoops for shows of gold, so does Barnes's lover lose his wager and his heart's contentment because he is solely led, as Portia might put it, by nice direction of the eyes.[36] Atalanta is beguiled from her course by the allurements of her suitor; Barnes's lover is blinded by his lady's beauty, mortified by the shame of a fancy fed–and yet not sated–by gazing. To choose by view is indeed to lose one's way.

"Men that hazard all / Doe it in hope of faire aduantages: / A golden minde stoopes not to showes of drosse" (2.7.19–21). The golden mind that Morocco would presume he has–to presume less would be "but a weake disabling" (2.7.31) of himself–is a mind ready to risk all, but to do so with good cause. It is a mind-set "bold and hardye" that Ovid's Hippomenes also shares; before he sees Atalanta run, he asks in amazement of the other suitors: "Is any man so mad to seeke a wyfe / With such apparant perill and the hazard of his lyfe?" Yet once having seen her naked, "her golden locks" tossing upon her "whyght as snowe" back, he apologizes for his error: "In fayth / I did not know the wager that yee ran for." A golden mind will wager all for a golden fleece. Yet, as the Ovidian intertext demonstrates, the gold we stoop for may well be our undoing; even if it comes from a goddess, it may turn out to be dross after all. Such, indeed, is the nature of risk.

Morocco doesn't allude directly to the Ovidian story, but he doesn't have to. The complex thematics of beguilement and risk, of alluring surfaces and superficial lures addressed by the story is a thematics already structured into the casket game. On the one hand, the objective of the game is to find a hidden content: this is a game that, in asking its players to read for depth, presumes a disjunctive awareness. All that glisters is not gold–our relationship to content is mediated by superficial form. At the same time, like Atalanta's footrace, this is a game defined both by its tremendous prize and by its tremendous risk: to lose is to forgo heirs, which is to forgo life–"thou single wilt proue none" (sonnet 8.14)–and to win is to gain a gem of great price. All that glisters is not gold; men that hazard all do it in hope of fair advantages. Morocco knows exactly what the game knows. The values he espouses are the very ones that structure the game's objective and define the game as such: there can be only one winner, and Morocco knows this too.

"*Portia* adew, I haue too grieu'd a heart / To take a tedious leaue: thus loosers part" (2.7.78–79).

And yet it is precisely because he knows *only* what the game knows that Morocco cannot win. The game presumes an allegorical perspective–an ability to read disjunctively, to read for depth. But to win the game one needs to be able also to reflect upon that perspective: one needs to read the game's objective itself. One needs, in short, to recognize that this is a game *about* allegory. One needs, then, not to recognize *what* this allegory occludes but instead to take stock of the sheer fact *that* it occludes. In short, the winner of this game needs not to lift veils, seeking absent presences, but instead to see the veil itself–in all its formal reality–in the crisscross, absent-present surface of its mesh.

Morocco, in other words, knows how to play, but not how to win. In this way, he reads less "like a Jew" than like a "papist": he is the quintessential Christian allegorist.[37] The problem is that Shakespeare's Belmont seems to operate according to Lutheran rules. And thus we return to Bassanio in 3.2. Where the other suitors read for depth, Bassanio attends to the surface as such. The other suitors read by unveiling; for them, meaning is uncovered once appearances have been *lifted*: that is, both negated and sublated. For Bassanio, however, to uncover meaning is not to unveil hidden depth–discarding form for content–but rather to study that superficial form itself, interpreting its veil-like function *as such*. What distinguishes Bassanio from the others is thus not the recognition that things are signs–and sometimes misleading signs at that (i.e., "all that glisters is not gold")–but rather his recognition of the signifying nature of the sign per se. Bassanio, in other words, recognizes the casket not so much as sign but as *signifier*. What he thereby comprehends is the duplicity or doubleness inherent in signification: signs don't just direct our attention to signifieds, they also direct us to themselves as signifiers; in pointing to something else, they point to their own pointing. And, finally, in doing so they raise our suspicions, pointing not so much to hidden meanings as to hidden *intentions*: what, we find ourselves asking, is the point of this pointing?

In recognizing the function of the signifier, Bassanio knows more than the game knows–he knows the intention *behind* the game. Unlike Morocco and Arragon–who both view the trial more or less as a gamble, a game of chance with Portia as some

kind of Renaissance Carol Merrill revealing what lies behind cur-
tain number three—Bassanio recognizes that the "game" is in truth
a *test*. He strives not so much to determine the allegorical link
between insides and outsides as he works to infer the very *office* of
the game. In this way, Bassanio's relation to the caskets *as veils* is
exactly analogous to Luther's relationship to the Law *as letter*: the
Law as it is (as Luther tells us) *for others* whose ignorance and sin
it reveals. Like Luther vis-à-vis the Law, Bassanio realizes that the
casket's true purpose lies in what it unveils about those who read
it, and not what it veils beneath its surface. "Those who see Moses
clearly, without a veil . . . understand the intention of the law and
how it demands impossible things" (LW 35, 245): it is precisely
such an ability to recognize *intention* that distinguishes Bassanio
from the other suitors. But it is also this ability that leaves the
impression that the game was *rigged*—whether by Portia's song or
by some other means.[38] Bassanio has figured out the trick of the
game, and hence the game figures out nothing about him. Indeed,
it is Bassanio's ability to read the caskets suspiciously that makes
him victorious; he second-guesses the game, asking not what the
caskets hide but what their hiding *means*. Yet it is also this suspi-
cious, performative reading that awakens *our* suspicions, leaving a
lingering sense of bad faith.

It is thus significant that Bassanio's remarks about the caskets
begin mid-thought, without any indication of precisely what he is
interpreting: "So may the outward showes be least themselues /
The world is still deceiu'd with ornament" (3.2.79–80). Does his
"so" refer, as John Weiss first suggested in 1876, to conclusions
drawn from the hints in Portia's song? A fancy engendered in the
eyes dies quickly—so too is the world deceived by ornament. But
even if Bassanio does not refer to the song, the "so" with which he
begins indicates a conclusion sufficiently vague, sufficiently broad
to open out from the game itself into the world in which the game
is played. *So may the outward shows be least themselves; the world is
still deceived with ornament.* Morocco sought an analogy between
the caskets' outward shows and their precious inner contents. Bassanio's broad, all-encompassing "so" suggests a different starting
point. Bassanio begins with the analogy between the game itself—
a game that asks us to relate outward shows with inner truths—and
the world at large. He begins, that is, by considering how the game
fits into the world; or rather, he begins by asking what sort of

world it is that would make such a game—such a *test*—necessary. In short, he hits upon the only way to win the game: one must sec-ond-guess Portia's father's will, for, "who chooses his meaning," as Nerissa tells us, "chooses [Portia]" (1.2.30–31). To win, Bassanio will need to second-guess the purpose of the game; he will need, in other words, to reconstruct its *Morall.*

> In Law, what Plea so tanted and corrupt,
> But being season'd with a gracious voice,
> Obscures the show of euill? In Religion,
> What damned error, but some sober brow
> Will blesse it, and approue it with a text,
> Hiding the grosenesse with faire ornament :
> There is no voice [i.e., *vice*] so simple, but assumes
> Some marke of vertue on his outward parts;
> How manie cowards, whose hearts are all as false
> As stayers of sand, weare yet vpon their chins
> The beards of *Hercules* and frowning *Mars,*
> Who inward searcht, haue lyuers white as milke,
> And these assume but valors excrement,
> To render them redoubted. Looke on beautie,
> And you shall see 'tis purchast by the weight,
> Which therein workes a miracle in nature,
> Making them lightest that weare most of it:
> So are those crisped snakie golden locks
> Which makes such wanton gambols with the winde
> Vpon supposed fairenesse, often knowne
> To be the dowrie of a second head,
> The scull that bred them in the Sepulcher.
> Thus ornament is but the guiled shore
> To a most dangerous sea: the beautious scarfe
> Vailing an Indian beautie; In a word,
> The seeming truth which cunning times put on
> To intrap the wisest. Therefore then thou gaudie gold,
> Hard food for *Midas,* I will none of thee.
>
> (3.2.81–108)

Moralizing from the casket game to the "cunning times," Bassanio becomes a veritable fount of exempla, generating a flow of golden words with the ease of Midas himself. From law, to religion, to vice, to lily-livered cowards who frown like Mars, to beauty with its borrowed locks, to the guiling, gilded shore, to an actual veil itself: the whole world remains deceived with ornament. All that glisters is not gold. Yet, in keeping with his hermeneutic of suspicion and his attention to performative surfaces, Bassanio's moralizing differs significantly from those allegorical insights offered by Morocco and Arragon. Arragon and Morocco warn against the dangers of the "fond eye"–the very eye of fancy that "pries not to th'interior, but like the Martlet / Builds in the weather on the outward wall" (2.9.29–31). Bassanio's concern with ornament, however, goes beyond the problems of the foolish desiring eye; for Bassanio, what plagues the cunning times is not folly but a rather more direct *deception.* Arragon's martlet, after all, is not so different from the carnally minded Jew: both bird and Jew fail to look beyond appearance, and hence both build on insecure foundations. But Bassanio's ornaments are not simply signs taken as things; they are lures set to entrap the wisest. (These are, indeed, the sort of indestructible and irresistible ornaments a seducer might use to enmesh even the wariest and wisest of maids.) In short, if for Morocco and Arragon the problem is solved by reading disjunctively, *figurally,* for Bassanio, the problem is solved only by a hermeneutics of suspicion: who set this trap and why?

Hence Bassanio's examples are all examples of dissembling, where ornament serves not simply to obscure the truth, but to disguise the false *as* true. To put the issue yet another way: where the other suitors seek truth by distinguishing between seeming and being, Bassanio describes a world of *seeming truths.* His is a catachrestic world where the truth itself has been falsified, slandered with a false esteem: sweet beauty no longer hath a name. Thus, although all of Bassanio's examples hold forth the promise of possible revelation–the promise that a deceptive outer appearance might be stripped away–it is a promise necessarily foreclosed. "In Law, what Plea so tanted and corrupt / But being season'd with a gracious voice, / Obscures the show of euill?" The image, as many readers have noted, is a crucial one, given the various traps laid by the law in this play. Like a tainted bit of meat, a false plea is readily swallowed once it is seasoned well enough. The toothsome ornament masks a corrupt interior; strip away the spices and the rotten flesh will be revealed. But the metaphor is imprecise, for it is precisely such "seasoning"–the false pleas that confound good

and evil—that corrupts the Law from the start. The taint masked
by the seasoning of a gracious voice is, ultimately, the taint *caused*
by that seasoning, for what corrupts the Law, as Bassanio sees it,
can only be the very mingling of good and bad that poisons justice. Ornament here is both the cause and the effect of a corruption intrinsic to that substance which it amends.

Bassanio's further examples all appear similarly to establish a
simple opposition between false exterior and true interior. Yet, in
each example, it is the exterior show of truth that decisively compromises our faith in truth, confounding the opposition between
fair and foul that would allow us to strip away all ornament and
purge the world's corruption.[39] In his final examples, he invokes
the dilemma of ornament in the perhaps privileged terms of
Shakespeare's Petrarchism: in the context, that is, of the very discourse of ornament itself. The moment marks a subtle, but
definite, shift in his monologue. Where his terms have built slowly
until now, cadenced through repetition and rhetorical question
("In Law, what Plea . . . ?" "In Religion, what damned error . . . ?"
"How manie cowards . . . ?")—here for the first time Bassanio
invokes a second person, and adopts a hortatory stance.

> Looke on beautie,
> And you shall see 'tis purchast by the weight,
> Which therein workes a miracle in nature,
> Making them lightest that weare most of it:
> So are those crisped snakie golden locks
> Which makes such wanton gambols with the winde
> Vpon supposed fairenesse, often knowne
> To be the dowrie of a second head,
> The scull that bred them in the Sepulcher.

Bassanio's first declaration is paradoxical. *Look* on beauty and you
shall *see* 'tis purchased by the weight. . . . The phrasing conflates
two profoundly incompatible acts of seeing. To look on beauty is
precisely *not to see* the deception that renders it false. Once we recognize that beauty can be bought and sold, it is for us no longer
beauty. To look on beauty, then, is precisely *not* to see that cos-
metic commodification that fairs the foul and bewhores the hon-
est. The eye that beholds, that looks *on* surfaces, gazes *upon* beauty,
is not the eye that sees *through* that appearance; it is not the grave-

yard eye that views the skull beneath the painting and decries a
"beauty" that lies between quotation marks. A "beauty" that *lies*.
Within a traditional figural universe, however, those two eyes/I's
are joined within a narrative that yokes ends to beginnings, parts
to whole, all under the form of eternity and the eye of God. It is
the eye or I of allegory that speaks from within the golden casket:
"O hell! what haue we here, a carrion death / Within whose emp-
tie eye there is a written scroule" (2.7.64–65). This allegorical eye
is the eye of the *memento mori*; the I that overcomes the pull of
appearances, the dead weight of the flesh, by lifting the golden veil
of beauty and reading through, behind, or beneath it. This eye
reads for depth–*under* the eye of God, **sub specie aeternitatis**.

But Bassanio does not read under anything; his two eyes/I's
remain instead unreconciled and trained on seeming truths, just as
he remains ambivalently enmeshed by those "crisped snakie
golden locks"–the locks of a supposed fairness that also designate,
as we shall see in a moment, Portia's golden fleece. *Looke on beautie, / And you shall see 'tis purchast by the weight*. Bassanio's divided
vision of beauty reinvokes the critique of allegory we found in
Shakespeare's Sonnets, where no reconciliation was possible
between flesh and spirit, canker and rose, foul and fair. Beauty itself
was a thing of time, ripening on the path to rotting and ever different from itself. In such a world, the fair head of beauty is simultaneously "the dowric of a second head"–of, that is, the sepul-
cher's skull. It is, finally, in terms of such a critique of allegory that
we must read the last two examples of Bassanio's speech: "Thus
ornament is but the guiled shore / To a most dangerous sea: the
beautious scarfe / Vailing an Indian beautie."

The passage contains two notorious textual cruxes. In the first
place, readers dating back as far as 1632–the publication date of
the Second Folio–have wanted to construe "guiled" as *guilded* [i.e.,
gilded]. Furness cites several early editors who argue for *guilded* in
favor of the continued metaphor of falsely glittering surfaces. One
editor even notes the potential allusion to the golden locks of the
previous line.[40] We might here recall the flattering eye of the
"Sunne" in sonnet 33; an eye that ultimately reflects the work of
the poet's own flattering, alchemical praise: "Fvll many a glorious
morning haue I seene, / . . . / Guilding pale streames with
heauenly alcumy" (33.1, 4). The idea of a language that merely
flatters, whose figures corrupt what they ornament, links the world

of the *Sonnets* to the exegetical world of Bassanio's ornament where a sweet voice both taints and seasons the Law and where the devil can cite scripture for his purpose (cf. 1.3.102). Like the flattering voice that turns foulness into supposed fairness, the gilded shore would be that alchemical lure that turns mortal hazard into noble quest. For one nineteenth-century critic, the gilded shore even offered a direct reference to Raleigh's *Discovery of Guiana* and the tempting sands of the New World.[41] We might argue more simply that both Shakespeare and Raleigh draw their imagery from the same mythological source, for what else could this gilded shore be but the beach of Colchis, the home of the golden fleece, that tempts a new generation of argonauts into most dangerous waters? Bassanio himself makes the allusion explicit in the very first scene of the play:

> For the foure windes blow in from euery coast
> Renowned sutors, and her sunny locks,
> Hang on her temples like a golden fleece,
> Which makes her seat of *Belmont Cholchos* strond,
> And many *Iasons* come in quest of her.
>
> (1.1.178–82)

Just like Raleigh's 1596 *Discovery*, written to attract investors with the promise of New World gold, Bassanio's discourse of gold also gilds the risk of his venture. Raleigh's *Discovery* was unsuccessful; he found no financial backers to support further voyages to Eldorado. Bassanio's flattering, gilded words, however, are a success, convincing Anthonio to risk both purse and person (cf. 1.1.148) in order to furnish his Jason.

As *guiled* shore–the reading of both the 1600 Quarto and the First Folio–the strand that Bassanio describes in 3.2 poses a slightly different threat. A gilded shore deceives by obscuring hidden and dangerous depths with its glittering surface; but how are we to understand the quarto/folio reading? A *guiled* shore is presumably a shore that beguiles us; the passive participle denotes that which is full of guile, deceptive or treacherous. The formulation verges on tautology: a guiled shore beguiles. But how, exactly, does it do so? What is deceptive about this deceptive shore? The answer is offered only obliquely, in the apposite image–the passage's second textual crux–of "the beautious scarfe / Vailing an

Indian beautie." Like a beautiful scarf veiling an Indian beauty, the shore "veils" a dangerous sea. This shift to a figural register (the shore is *like* a veil) is significant, and even more complex than it first appears: both scarf and shore are offered not simply as examples of ornament's deception—not merely in the interest of enumerating the faults of a "world . . . still deceiu'd with ornament"—but as rhetorical ornaments themselves. Scarf and shore are ornament's ornament, ornament's metaphor: "Thus ornament is but the guiled shore / To a most dangerous sea: the beautious scarfe / Vailing an Indian beautie." Indeed, both scarf and shore offer versions of that most orthodox figure of figure itself: the veil. Yet it is a troubling version of this figure, eliciting two full pages of gloss in Furness's Variorum.[42] As Lisa Renée Lampert has recently pointed out, Bassanio's veil dramatically reinvents the gender politics of the traditional metaphor. Traditionally, either the veil or that which it covers is marked as feminine: either the ornamental surface of the text is a suspect, feminine veil that must be removed to reach the truth—or truth itself is a woman, her beauty chastely hidden. "In Bassanio's formulation, however," Lampert writes, "neither layer, the veil nor the woman shrouded beneath, represents any kind of idealized or sought-after beauty or truth. Instead both exterior and interior are beguiling and potentially dangerous."[43]

Lampert's analysis points to a crucial indeterminacy in the passage. The relationship between guiling shore and dangerous sea, or between beautious scarf and Indian beauty, is the vehicle meant to reveal the relationship beween vehicle and tenor in general: between ornament and that which it embellishes/hides/reveals. Yet an ambiguity unsettles these figures of figure; an ambiguity signaled, for instance, in the very oddity of the term *guiled* when we expect to read *gilded*. Presumably, as we have said, the guiled shore is the shore that beguiles us; presumably, as centuries of readers have also argued, the passive participle denotes an active force. But when we take the image at its passive letter, the guil*ed* shore becomes the shore that is itself deceived: the patient, and not the agent of deception; the secondary effect or target of beguilement and not its initial cause or source.[44]

Similarly, if, as Lampert argues, both the veil and the Indian beauty it shrouds are alike "beguiling and potentially dangerous," it is because an analogous indeterminacy between source and target, tenor and vehicle, agent and patient, unsettles this second figure of figure as well. For Furness, writing his 1888 commentary in a colonial spirit, the contours of the image are clear enough, even if the details are fuzzy: the beautious scarf ornaments "something repulsive; what that something is each student will have to decide for himself; for me the original suffices. An Indian beauty is assuredly not an English beauty." Furness cites a nineteenth-century estimation of Indian aesthetics: "'An Indian requires that his wife's face should be the color of good marketable sea-coal'" (Furness, 147 n). But if Indian beauty is indeed *black* beauty not only for Furness but also for Shakespeare–and a synonym for expressions Shakespeare uses unambiguously elsewhere (like "Ethiope" or "brow of Egypt")–then, as we know from sonnet 127, there is, strictly speaking, nothing deceptive or dishonest about it.[45] Black "beauty," Indian "beauty," does not beguile us, strictly speaking; indeed, if it is as ill-favored as marketable sea-coal then such "beauty" is the only truth in a marketplace world of *seeming* truths. It gives the lie to what we formerly called beauty; in other words, despite its scare quotes, Indian or black "beauty" is more true, more fair than that sweet beauty that no longer hath a name.

In its blackness, Indian "beauty" refuses to dupe us: it refuses to pose *as* beauty, and in the process it reveals beauty itself as mere pose, as "*supposed* fairnesse." The virtue of this foulness lies precisely in the way it lays no claim to virtue; black "beauty" is not beauty's dissembler but its belier. And because it refuses to dupe us, we'll forgo the scare quotes: Indian beauty is no pretender to that which the old age counted fair; instead, it is precisely the legitimacy of what passed for fair that is now in question–it is sweet "beauty" that has been slandered with a bastard shame. If scare quotes are needed (and the concept would have been foreign to Shakespeare, of course), they should serve to distance sweet "beauty" from her title.

Indian beauty–black beauty–is not true beauty, but neither is "beauty" true. Indeed, the blackness of Indian beauty, its foulness, manages to unsettle the very relationship between concealing veil and revealed truth, between inside and outside; in this way the image echoes the ambiguity of the "guiled shore"–the shore both affected by and effecting deception. Indian beauty is what the beauteous scarf masks; but in fact, it is such concealed foulness that unmasks the beauteous itself, exposing beauty as *mere* mask,

mere *veil*. In this way, Bassanio's figure of figure disrupts the allegorical logic of the golden casket. All that glisters is not gold: as
we have seen, the moral of the golden casket is that we must read
disjunctively; such a principle recognizes the sheerly conventional
status of the sign. But if Bassanio's beauteous scarf is false, it is so
not because it misleads us, pointing to a fair signified (i.e., fairness
itself), yet delivering only foulness; rather, this fair signifier is false
because there is no *true* signified to which it points. Fairness is only
sham, in the world of seeming truths common to *Shakespeare's Sonnets* and to Bassanio's Venice; all the lovely exteriors that Bassanio
enumerates—the beauteous scarf, the crisped snaky locks, the cos-
metic loveliness "purchast by the weight," and all the rest of his
dangerous ornaments—are "bastard signes of faire" (sonnet 68.3).
Unauthorized, unparented, these signifiers not only belie the genitive that links them to beauty (bastard signs *of* fair); more devastatingly, they reduce fairness itself to a mere bastard sign—to a
signifier without a signified. Such bastard signs make us look for
origin and lineage in a world where succession is, as it were, broken. They make us read for depth in a world that is all shallow.

We are now in a better position to understand Bassanio's first
figure of figure: the guiled shore to a dangerous sea. From the start
of the play we have known that seas are dangerous, but it is the
shore—or at least the shallows—that ultimately proves disastrous:
"*Anthonio* hath a ship of rich lading wrackt on the narrow Seas; the
Goodwins I thinke they call the place, a very dangerous flat, and
fatall" (3.1.3–6). If the shore is that margin where the sea yields to
the land, the dangerous, misnamed Goodwins are indeed a "guiled
shore": a margin of land in the midst of the ocean; a shore that we
fail to recognize as such. The danger of shallows is not what they
hide, but our false assumption *that* they hide; no matter how still
they run, these waters do not run deep: no ocean, no safe depth
underlies this flat surface. Indeed, the "very dangerous flat" to
which Anthonio's wealth succumbs is a shore mistaken for sea—a
surface that conceals only the fact that there is no depth to con-
ceal. Like the beauteous scarf that points to a false "beauty,"
Anthonio's dangerous flat—Bassanio's guiled shore—deceives us
when instead of taking it at face value, we instead construe it as
veil-like metonym: as, in other words, the figure of that which
remains hidden and unsounded.

Like the canker-rose in *Shakespeare's Sonnets*, Bassanio's figures of figure, the scarf and the shore, catachrestically undermine the difference between outside and inside, between vehicle and tenor, image and truth. Indeed, the "truth" "behind" these ornaments is that the search for inner truth, hidden meaning, sweet beauty is a *trick*: a trick to reveal our blind presumptions and our weakness. The caskets are not veils; they are instead *meshes*, seeming truths meant to entrap the wisest; meshes that are revealing not because they hide something but because, as our eyes take in the difference between knot and not—between the strings of the net and the holes those strings define—the mesh in its encompassing of both presence and absence, in its insistence on the profundity of surfaces, makes us look twice at what's right in front of us. And thus it should come as little surprise that once Bassanio does find his way into the casket's interior, what he finds is yet another mesh-like surface:

> What finde I here?
> Faire *Portias* counterfeit. What demie God
> Hath come so neere creation? moue these eies?
> Or whether riding on the bals of mine
> Seeme they in motion? Here are seuer'd lips
> Parted with suger breath, so sweet a barre
> Should sunder such sweet friends: here in her haires
> The Painter plaies the Spider, and hath wouen
> A golden mesh t'intrap the hearts of men
> Faster then gnats in cobwebs: but her eies,
> How could he see to doe them? hauing made one,
> Me thinkes it should haue power to steale both his
> And leaue it selfe vnfurnisht: Yet looke how farre
> The substance of my praise doth wrong this shadow
> In vnderprising it, so farre this shadow
> Doth limpe behinde the substance. Here's the scroule,
> The continent, and summarie of my fortune.
>
> (3.2.121–37)

"Here in her haires / The Painter plaies the Spider, and hath wouen / A golden mesh t' intrap the hearts of men." Under the ornamental mesh of the leaden casket is another mesh; the hidden "depth" Bassanio discovers—none other than the golden fleece—is itself another surface: Portia's counterfeit. The same readers who fault (or exonerate) Morocco for his presumed inability to distinguish between reality and counterfeit will tend to read this odd little speech as further evidence that Bassanio is the lifter of veils. For Danson the moment represents a brief lapse in Bassanio's "sense of proportion," as he momentarily "harks back to the mode of those who 'choose by show'" before decisively rejecting the lure of appearance (172). For Richard Halpern, who rejects readings like Danson's by way of Marx and Lacan, Bassanio's discovery of "faire *Portias* counterfeit" reveals the problem of fetishism: "At the very moment when Bassanio thinks to have discovered the hidden truth, he is confronted with another representation, another mediation" (Halpern, 199). Willingly or not, Bassanio has demystified the very idea of a "hidden essence or reality lying beneath the play of differential surfaces" (199) by revealing the empty sham that underlies the glitter. For Halpern no less than for Danson, Bassanio's "reaction to the image verges on idolatry or fetishism" (Halpern, 200); yet again, for Halpern no less than for Danson, Bassanio's speech ultimately reinforces the fundamental iconoclastic lesson of the play: *all that glisters is not gold.*

If Danson and other allegorizing readers of the play celebrate Bassanio's ability to distinguish between show and truth ("this shadow / Doth limpe behinde the substance"), Halpern's critical perspective cuts through the same distinction, revealing that *all* is show. Yet, thanks to their shared emphasis on a disjunctive reading that negates surface, Danson and Halpern alike presume the same distrust of image, the same fundamental iconoclasm, at the heart of the play.[46] The difference between their two readings of the play is, ultimately, analogous to the "difference" between an Erasmian Platonism and the asceticism of radical reformers like Zwingli and Karlstadt. Where Erasmus, following in the footsteps of Augustine, seeks to transcend the flesh "as on the steps of Jacob's ladder from the body to the spirit," Zwingli and the other "fanatics" strive to renounce the flesh outright.[47] Similarly, the "harmonies" that Danson discerns in *The Merchant of Venice* entail the transcendence of, as Lorenzo would put it in act 5, "this muddy vesture of decay," while the critical vision that Halpern both examines and deploys amounts to a distrust of such harmonies and the seductions they allow: "incisiveness is purchased at the cost of beauty" (225). Yet if Halpern and Danson replicate the dichotomy of puritan and papist, in Luther's eyes, as we've already seen, both extremes end up "drowning in the flesh"–fetishizing it in the name of avoiding idolatry. In their efforts to negate the flesh, both extremes elevate it to supreme importance. Paradoxically both views fetishize the flesh in the name of avoiding idolatry.

There can be no idols, however, without veils; what transforms the image into a fetish is the very act of un-veiling that invests it with an absent and esoteric mystical depth.[48] In the process of stripping away the outer image, the iconoclast fills the heart with "goetzen"–with idols–transforming, as Luther tells us, "das gering eusserlich ding," the least outwardly thing, into a god.[49] Bassanio, however, is no stripper of veils. Instead, as he gazes upon Portia's image he once again foreshortens that distance between surface and depth, between imitation and truth. In a scene that has strategically denied us evidence of Bassanio as reader, his lengthy ekphrasis of Portia's counterfeit–evidence that he is, indeed, a good looker–demands a second glance. We do not hear Bassanio read the caskets' inscriptions–but we do hear him *see*.

> What finde I here?
> Faire *Portias* counterfeit. What demie God
> Hath come so neere creation? moue these eies?
> Or whether riding on the bals of mine
> Seeme they in motion? Here are seuer'd lips
> Parted with suger breath, so sweet a barre
> Should sunder such sweet friends: here in her haires
> The Painter plaies the Spider, and hath wouen
> A golden mesh t'intrap the hearts of men
> Faster then gnats in cobwebs: but her eies,
> How could he see to doe them? hauing made one,
> Me thinkes it should haue power to steale both his
> And leaue it selfe vnfurnisht: Yet looke how farre
> The substance of my praise doth wrong this shadow
> In vnderprising it, so farre this shadow
> Doth limpe behinde the substance.

The careful distinction between shadow and substance, between the artist as demiurge and as Creator, frames Bassanio's verbal portrait of Portia's portrait, seeming to establish a descending order of imitation. Yet the portrait overwhelms its frame, leveling such distinctions to the single plane of sight where the eyes of the painter and the eyes that behold his painting cannot be distinguished. Both sets of eyes play the viewer, beholding surfaces, transfixed by the beautiful face; both are entrapped by beauty's mesh. And both sets of eyes play the painter, gilding and flattering their object—a fact borne out here in Bassanio's ekphrastic recourse to the gilt images of Petrarchan poetry: *sugar breath, golden mesh*. In this way, both painter and viewer are subject to the same confusion of agency and passivity we found in the figure of the "*guiled* shore"—the shore that is at once the alluring cause and the beguiled victim of appearance. To what extent does the eye effect what it sees; to what extent is it affected by it? Ultimately what collapses the distinction between shadow and substance, counterfeit and original, is the ambiguity of the eye/I as both painter and canvas of the image. It is an ambiguity that corresponds exactly to Shakespeare's catachrestic revision of Petrarchism: "Mine eye hath play'd the painter and hath steeld, / Thy beauties forme in table of my heart" (Sonnet 24:1–2).

Finally, it is this ambiguity of vision that seems to unsettle Bassanio in his long-deferred moment of reading. "*You that choose not by the view / Chance as faire, and choose as true*" (3.2.138–39). The scroll bids that he claim his lady with a kiss; instead Bassanio pauses, "doubtfull whether what [he] *see* be true" (3.2.154, emphasis added)—doubtful, perhaps, because the scroll has gotten it all wrong: it is indeed precisely "by view" that Bassanio chose; moreover, he did so by giving the lie both to fairness and to truth. *You that choose not by the view chance as faire, and choose as true*. In Bassanio's world—Shakespeare's world—there is only "supposed" fairness and "seeming" truth. The view is everything.

A last word about veils. When I characterized Luther's interpretation of the Pauline figure, I indulged in a bit of fanciful anachronism, imagining the reformer, as it were, at a microscope, revealing the veil as mesh and offering us a mosquito's-eye view. In truth, no anachronism was necessary. Half a century before Luther's ninety-five theses, Leon Battista Alberti had already offered his own extreme close-up of the veil in his famous treatise on perspectival painting:

> Nothing can be found, so I think, which is more useful than that veil [*velo*] which among my friends I call an intersection. It is a thin veil, finely woven [*un velo sottilissimo, tessuto*

raro] dyed whatever colour pleases you and with larger threads [marking out] as many parallels as you prefer. This veil I place between the eye and the thing seen, so the visual pyramid penetrates through the thinness [*rarità*] of the veil. This veil can be of great use to you. Firstly, it always presents to you the same unchanged plane [*superficie*]. Where you have placed certain limits, you quickly find the true cuspid of the pyramid. This would certainly be difficult without the intersection. . . . Secondly, you will easily be able to constitute the limits of the outline and of the planes. . . . On panels or on walls, divided into similar parallels, you will be able to put everything in its place.[50]

In its thinness, its *rarità*, the veil is simultaneously diaphanous and opaque; it allows the painter to represent depth, although he sees nothing but surface. Indeed, Alberti's veil works by transforming depth into surface, flattening–projecting–the visual "pyramid" unto a single unchanged *superficie*. In this way, the veil functions as a screen–a mesh–that strains the three-dimensional world, reticulating and organizing it as plane. As flat, perspectival space.

> Mine eye hath play'd the painter and hath steeld,
> Thy beauties forme in table of my heart,
> My body is the frame wherein ti's held,
> And perspectiue it is best Painters art.

> (24.1–4)

THE MELANCHOLY OF THE FLESH

Shylock, as many readers have argued, seems unable to tolerate what his son-in-law calls "tutches of sweet harmonie" (5.1.66). For him, as we shall see in a moment, the sweet melancholy of the bagpipe is a mere "whine" with unfortunate diuretic properties, just as he bids Jessica shut out the music of Christian masquers: "the vile squealing of the wry-neckt Fife" (2.5.32). Where others hear harmony he seems to hear only dissonant screeches; where others feel their spirits lifted, he imagines only a body sinking, deformed and offending, like the twisted neck of the fife player or the self-wetting humiliation of the bagpipe's auditor. For

Lawrence Danson and other readers, Shylock bears out Lorenzo's dictum at the end of the play: "The man that hath no musicke in himselfe, / Nor is not moued with concord of sweet sounds, / Is fit for treasons, stratagems, and spoyles" (5.1.93–95; see Danson, 181 ff.). But Lorenzo's discussion of harmony is exceptionally complex and deserves a closer look. The discussion, as we shall see, leads back to the melancholy that begins the play, leading us back to the problem of the flesh.

> Looke how the floore of heauen
> Is thicke inlayed with pattens of bright gold,
> There's not the smallest orbe which thou beholdst
> But in his motion like an Angell sings,
> Still quiring to the young eyed Cherubins;
> Such harmonie is in immortall soules,
> But whilst this muddy vesture of decay
> Doth grosly close in it, we cannot heare it.
>
> (5.1.67–74)

From the very start with Israel Gollancz's 1916 "The 'Shylock' of Shakespeare," modern interpreters of the play as Christian allegory have taken Lorenzo's lines to Jessica as a kind of gloss for the play as a whole, reinforcing the importance of transcending the flesh—that "muddy vesture of decay" that must be stripped away in the name of the spiritual harmony of "immortal souls."[51] Lorenzo's speech seems to summarize neatly the assumptions of a traditional allegorical perspective. Yet few have lingered on Lorenzo's odd metaphor for the starry heaven: "*pattens* of bright gold."[52] A paten is the plate on which the bread is laid at the celebration of the Eucharist; to imagine the stars as such gold dishes is to imagine them as fleshly containers for things spiritual. Both extrinsic ornament and enabling fundament, the stars support the heavens on a floor thick inlaid with gold, just as the golden communion plate supports the Host. Once again, Lorenzo's speech bespeaks the allegorical relationship between flesh and spirit. And yet, by alluding to the Eucharist, Lorenzo's image immediately complicates itself. If the ontology of the paten is clear-cut, the nature of the bread that it bears is not. Indeed, within a discussion that has seemingly decided the question of the flesh—it is nothing but a "muddy vesture"—Lorenzo manages to invoke the doctrinal controversy that, more than any other perhaps, becomes a flash-point for the sixteenth-century reconsideration of (the) matter. Ultimately, Lorenzo's image of a celestial harmony that reconciles body to soul like the bread on the paten plate is untenable, its tenor compromised by its much-debated vehicle—its spirit by its flesh, if you will. Perhaps it is small wonder, then, that Lorenzo's harmony brings only sadness to Jessica, his convert wife. "I am neuer merry when I heare sweet musique," the gentle Jewess tells him (5.1.78).

Jessica's melancholy, I want to suggest, reflects the play's concern with the unresolved problem of the flesh. From its consideration of usury and the mercantile venture to its examination of another kind of market—the business of marriage—to that most obvious emblem of the flesh-bond, *The Merchant of Venice* calls into question the relation between the material and spiritual worlds, showing us that any effort to try to peel away the veil of matter only ends up drowning us. At stake in the play is thus a sense of the flesh as fetish: as absolute and impossible to delimit. Indeed, it may well be that this problem underlies not only Jessica's melancholic response to her husband's harmonies but the melancholy that runs through the play as a whole—Portia's melancholy, to be sure ("By my troth *Nerissa*, my little body is a wearie of this great world"), but even more important, the sadness around which, ultimately, the worlds of both Venice and Belmont revolve: the sadness of Anthonio.

Certainly it is Anthonio's own contested flesh that positions him as "th' vnhappy subiect" around whom circulates the "quarrels" of the play's two main plots (cf. 5.1), but even the "Want-wit sadnesse" (1.1.9) with which he opens the play seems relevant to the problem of defining the flesh:

> *Sola.* Not in loue neither: then let vs say you are sad
> Because you are not merry: and 'twere as easie
> For you to laugh and leape, and say you are merry
> Because you are not sad. Now by two-headed *Ianus*,
> Nature hath fram'd strange fellowes in her time:
> Some that will euermore peepe through their eyes,
> And laugh like Parrats at a bag-piper.
> And other of such vineger aspect,
> That they'll not shew their teeth in way of smile,
> Though Nestor sweare the iest be laughable.
>
> (1.1.53–62)

As melancholy often works in Shakespeare, Anthonio's causeless sadness seems to evacuate meaning, leaving behind the world as an empty shell–think here of Jaques, sucking melancholy out of a song "as a Weazel suckes egges" (*As You Like It*, 2.5.13–14).[53] Solanio's figure for that shell is the two-headed Janus: the face that is always facing us, merry because it is not sad, sad because it is not merry. Structurally, Solanio's Janus presents something like the undecidable rabbit/duck ambivalence of Luther's critique of allegory, where presumption is just the other side of despair and the world must be a lie before it can be the truth. This face that is always facing us resists depth: behind one face is only another; for all its seeming three-dimensionality, the Janus head is nothing but masks.[54]

Despite its apparent flippancy, Solanio's mock raises a question about the nature of human nature that ultimately the play will have a hard time answering. Evacuated of their depth and meaning, what Shylock later refers to as human "affections" or "passions" (cf. 4.1.54, 55)–the inclinations or aversions that shape our conduct–reduce to mere physical idiosyncracies: the quirky, uncontrollable tics that meaninglessly distinguish one man from another. There is little to differentiate affections such as these from the mechanical repetitions of a parrot's voice. Solanio's merrymakers who can't help but laugh like parrots at a bagpiper, find their Janus-like inversion in the trial scene, in the men Shylock cites who "when the bag-pipe sings i'th nose, / Cannot containe their Vrine" (4.1.53–54). For Shylock the example of the bagpipe serves as recalcitrant response to the Duke's plea that the Jew drop his suit: "We all expect a gentle answer Iew" (38). The pun on gentle/Gentile, as many have noted, like related quibbling throughout the play on the meaning of "kind" ("This Hebrew will turne / Christian, he growes kinde" [1.3.183–84]), reveals the ways in which Shylock stands for a resistant particularity–for the principle of difference itself.[55] The Duke insists upon this difference at the same time that he appeals to the universal quality of "humane gentlenesse and loue" (4.1.29). Shylock's response is to push still further in the direction of meaningless particularity–a particularity that he identifies with the unruly flesh itself, "sway[ed] . . . to the moode / Of what it [i.e., 'affection'] likes or loaths" (55–56). Where the Duke hopes for depth and reason, Shylock insists instead on mask-like superficiality, confirming the Christians' sense that he is an obdurate shell of a man, "voyd, and empty / From any dram of mercie" (4.1.7–8).[56]

And ultimately, as figure for the cruel superficiality of the flesh, Shylock does contrast with a gentle Gentile depth—but as we shall see, in the process he also reveals the Janus mask that constructs such depth. In the conversion to which his flesh finally submits, a flesh that resists gentility at every turn, what Shylock reveals is the superficiality of Christian depth itself. He reveals, as we'll see, the necessarily *two-faced* nature of Christian mercy.[57]

"It will, of course, be argued," Coghill writes in 1949,

> that it is painful for Shylock to swallow his pride, abjure his *racial faith*, and receive baptism. But then Christianity is painful. Its centre is crucifixion, nor has it ever been held to be equally easy for all natures to embrace. . . . But from Anthonio's point of view, Shylock has at least been given his chance of eternal joy, and it is he, Anthonio, that has given it to him. Mercy has triumphed over justice, even if the way of mercy is a hard way.
>
> (23, emphasis added)

We should not be surprised that Coghill's strict separation of "race feeling" and theological doctrine collapses when he discusses the play's climax and refers to Shylock's "racial faith"—nor should we be surprised that Coghill's notion of a "hard mercy" seems to echo the *scharffe barmhertzigkeit*, the sharp or harsh mercy that Luther recommends against the Jews in his late writings (a "mercy" that includes forced labor; burning synagogues, homes, and schools; forbidding rabbis to teach; stealing Jews' cash and precious metals, and prohibiting usury).[58] After all, for Coghill it is the possibility of conversion that should mark the dividing line between a theological and a racial definition of the Jew—and yet there is something about Shylock's forced conversion, coming as it does in the wake of a scene that has sought to "out-Jew the Jew," that seems to trouble this dichotomy, calling into the question the firm boundary Coghill envisions between the Elizabethans and we moderns, just as Luther's sharp mercy confuses any sharp distinction between a modern eliminationist perspective and a pre-modern conversionist one.

Significantly, the conversion is one of the few plot elements of the trial scene that is entirely Shakespeare's own; while, for instance, Portia's distinction between flesh and blood is a regular feature of the flesh-bond plot, none of the known versions of the story involve the usurer's conversion. Why does Shylock's conversion become important for Shakespeare? And why is it that, as Coghill claims at least, of the various conditions Shylock must meet in order for his life to be spared, it is the forced conversion "that seems to modern ears so harshly vindictive" (Coghill, 22)? Why is it there, at the very moment that the play effaces the distinction between Jew and Christian in the name of the triumph of faith over flesh, that modern readers have most suspected the play's Christians of *bad* faith?

The problem begins, I think, with an often overlooked or misread moment of dialogue.

> POR.   Of a strange nature is the sute you follow,
>   Yet in such rule, that the Venetian Law
>   Cannot impugne you as you do proceed.
>   ....
>   Do you confesse the bond?
> ANT.   I do.
> POR.   Then must the Iew be mercifull.
> IEW.   On what compulsion must I ? Tell me that.
> POR.   The quality of mercy is not strain'd. . . .
>
> (4.1.185–94)[59]

Even admirers of the play as Christian allegory tend to view Portia throughout this scene, and especially at moments like this one, as a master tactician, skillfully maneuvering Shylock into an ever more rigid statement of the literalism and legalism for which he stands. Portia is "totally in control" of a situation "she has engineered" writes Lawrence Danson (62); her "final tactic" is to demonstrate to Shylock the untenability of a legalistic viewpoint (Lewalski, 341). The image of Portia as consummate strategist–as *lawyer* even– working in the name of mercy, offers an emblem of the bad faith so many modern readers have discerned in the play. Allegorical readers like Coghill, however, have argued that these "tricks" are not part of Portia's character but rather "devices" that serve to forward the symbolic movement of the plot (cf. Coghill, 21–22). Both views are inadequate, however, failing to take into account the seriousness of Portia's commitment to the Law as such. The law of Venice cannot impugn Shylock since his suit is completely in order.

Nor does Anthonio contest the bond; there, too, all is "in rule" with
Shylock's suit. "Then must the Iew be mercifull." The line is often
read as a casual remark (revealed later on as canny strategy): since
there is no legal remedy that can save Anthonio's life, the only
recourse is an appeal to mercy. But Shylock's response reveals, I
think, the genuine dilemma that Portia has no choice but to confront: "On what compulsion must I? Tell me that."

Mercy presents a problem—indeed, the central problem—
within a doctrine of justification by faith alone. Mercy is the grace
that imputes righteousness where none has been deserved; it is
that love, that faith that gives itself for nothing in return. As such,
as Portia tells us, mercy is by definition unconstrained and free. It
cannot be compelled and retain its character as mercy; it is, as Shylock recognizes, the very antithesis of "must"—the very opposite of
the Law, bearing out the truth of Luther's formulation: "No work
of law is done gladly and willingly; it is all forced and compelled."
While the work of Law is strained and grudging, revealing our disobedience as much as it reveals our compliance, mercy is liberal
and free. "It droppeth as the gentle raine from heauen / Vpon the
place beneath." We cannot earn God's mercy any more than we
can grant mercy to others on command. As the Law's antithesis,
mercy is also antithetical to good works; mercy, like faith, cannot
consist in an action that we perform, but rather is the result of
God's action within us. But if mercy gives itself for nothing, how
can we ensure its presence in our lives? We cannot earn it, we cannot perform it. How then can we be sure that our own deeds are
selfless and forgiving—and (it amounts to the same question), how
can we be sure that we are ourselves freely forgiven? How can we
ensure, in other words, that we are saved?

Portia encapsulates the logic of the problem, as well as the
dramatic structure of the trial scene, in the famous climax of her
speech:

> Therefore Iew,
> Though Iustice be thy plea, consider this,
> That in the course of Iustice, none of vs
> Should see saluation: we do pray for mercie,
> And that same prayer, doth teach vs all to render
> The deeds of mercie.

> (207–12)

If mercy cannot be compelled, Portia suggests, it can somehow be taught. Or, to put it more precisely, the *necessity* of mercy can be taught. Or, to put it even more precisely, the consideration that our works will never save us yields the realization that we rely on God's good graces alone. And *that* humbling realization is itself, Portia seems to suggest, a kind of grace that teaches us mercy. A *kind* of grace, yet not the enabling thing itself: the distance from teaching to action is, as Portia herself has already noted, not so quickly traversed. "If to doe were as easie as to know what were good to doe," Portia tells Nerissa in their very first scene, "Chappels had beene Churches, and poore mens cottages Princes Pallaces" (1.2.13–14). There are no shortcuts here, no direct routes either to salvation or to that liberal spirit of grace Portia seeks to embody in Belmont: "I stand for sacrifice," she tells Bassanio (3.2.60). There are no shortcuts because there is no real response to Shylock's question: "On what compulsion must I?" To get to mercy, Portia, like the Venetians stymied by their own legal precedent, must stumble first over the course of justice.

In sum, Portia's office in the courtroom is to perform the very office of the Law, serving not only as a "Daniel" (as Shylock first calls her), but as the lawgiver Moses himself, who unveils the Law not by treating the flesh as a veil, or the letter as an allegory, but instead by focusing ever more intently upon the flesh and the letter *as such*, revealing their fetishistic and infinite scope. Like the laws of Moses, bewildering (as Luther tells us) in their number and complexity, the Law proliferates wildly in Portia's hands, branching out in every direction, its reach ever more extensive, its satisfaction ever more patently impossible—and it does so in order to compel that which cannot be compelled.[60] Thus, with each new, exfoliating reading of the "flesh" nominated in the bond, Portia uncovers a new law:

> Tarry a little, there is something else,
> This bond doth giue thee heere no iot of bloud,
>
> . . . .
> . . . take thou thy pound of flesh,
> But in the cutting it, if thou dost shed
> One drop of Christian bloud, thy lands and goods
> Are by the Lawes of Venice confiscate
> Vnto the state of Venice.
>
> (319–26)

Shed thou no bloud, nor cut thou lesse nor more
But iust a pound of flesh: if thou tak'st more
Or lesse then a iust pound. . .
. . . .
Thou diest, and all thy goods are confiscate.

(341–48)

Tarry Iew,
The Law hath yet another hold on you.
It is enacted in the Lawes of Venice,
If it be proued against an Alien,
That by direct, or indirect attempts
He seeke the life of any Citizen,
The party gainst the which he doth contriue,
Shall seaze one halfe his goods, the other halfe
Comes to the priuie coffer of the State,
And the offenders life lies in the mercy
Of the Duke onely, gainst all other voice.

(363–73)

As the definition of "flesh" becomes fractally more complex, the Law widens its net, tightens its hold, until there can be no escape from justice: "Thou shalt haue iustice more then thou desirest" (332). And, at the moment of the Law's tightest, broadest hold and the flesh's greatest complexity, when it has become entirely impossible to delimit the flesh, to cut it away like a veil, since now it denotes "life" (368) itself–at that very moment, mercy reappears. "Downe therefore, and beg mercy of the Duke" (378). The Law has performed its office, constraining Shylock to forgo justice in the name of Christian charity. "Such blindness," Luther writes, "must be . . . compelled and forced by the law to seek something beyond the law and its own ability, namely, the grace of God promised in the Christ who was to come" (LW 35, 244). So does Shylock receive the answer to his question about compulsion.

Yet, of course, Shylock never does beg mercy; he is pardoned before he asks for pardon, and offers scarcely any reaction to the hard mercy of his conversion. But it doesn't matter, since neither the conversion nor the Duke's or Anthonio's mercy seem, in the final analysis, to be designed for the benefit of Shylock. It is, after all, the Christians who have a stake in the problem of mercy, for both their personal and their political salvation. It is they who can benefit from the way Shylock's defeat serves at its point of highest intensity to elicit the "mercy of the Duke," thereby demonstrating the correlation Portia cites between "temporall power" and divine grace. And it is they who, for their own peace of mind, will want to reconcile the tensions between presumption and despair, Law and Gospel, flesh and spirit, and ultimately between Jews and Christians. But in the Janus-headed world that Luther helps create, instead of the allegorical resolution of opposites, we find a constantly flipping coin. The Christians in this play cannot resolve the question of their own faith without performing the office of the Law; they need Shylock in order to stage the possibility of mercy. And yet, it is precisely this sense of staginess that engenders the concern of bad faith. The more Portia tries to compel mercy through demonstrating the failure of justice, the more the whole setup risks seeming rigged—the "mercy" that finally appears bearing no more authority or credibility than the ever-expanding readings of Shylock's bond and Venetian law. At issue here is just another version of Luther's particular brand of spiritual distress: if the truth is only founded on the recognition of a lie, it is thus itself always vulnerable to a further unveiling.

In the end, such Janus-like ambivalences render the difference between Jew and Christian undecidable, much as the flesh itself becomes impossible to define in clearly delimited terms. But rather than enable a new era of religious tolerance, such ambivalence seems only to render the Jew infinitely more dangerous because infinitely more slippery. And it is ultimately as the figure for a Christian bad faith that this slippery Jew becomes the alibi for a Law that is ever-expanding and a mercy that is growing ever more sharp.

NOTES

PREFACE

1. G. W. F. Hegel, *The Phenomenology of Spirit*, tr. A. V. Miller (Oxford: Oxford UP, 1977), 1, 11. Translation slightly modified. German cited from the Suhrkamp-Taschenbuch-Wissenschaft series collection of Hegel's works, vol. 3 (Frankfurt am Main: Surkamp Verlag, 1986 [1970]).

2. Michel Foucault, "What Is an Author?," in *Language, Counter-Memory, Practice: Selected Essays and Interviews*, ed. Donald F. Bouchard, tr. Donald F. Bouchard and Sherry Simon (Ithaca: Cornell UP, 1977), 115.

3. As Patricia Parker and others have pointed out in reference to the Renaissance fascination with inversions, with costards and bottoms: *Preposterous* is the name that George Puttenham gives to the figure hysteron-proteron: "Ye haue another manner of disordered speach, when ye misplace your words or clauses and set that before which should be behind" (3.13.6) (George Puttenham, *The Arte of English Poesie* [London: Richard Field, 1589]). See Patricia Parker, "Preposterous Reversals: *Love's Labor's Lost*," *Modern Language Quarterly* 54, no. 4 (1993): 435–82, and "Preposterous Events," *Shakespeare Quarterly* 43, no. 2 (Summer 1992): 186–213.

4. Gayatri Spivak's "preface" to her translation of *Of Grammatology* offers a useful and self-problematizing introduction to the Derridean deconstruction of the *prae-fatio*, the before-saying of the preface. See "Translator's Preface"

in Jacques Derrida, *Of Grammatology*, tr. Gayatri Chakravorty Spivak (Baltimore: Johns Hopkins UP, 1976 [1974]), ix–lxxxvii.

5. Thanks to Hugh Grady for encouraging this connection.

6. Foucault, "Nietzsche, Genealogy, History," in *Language, Counter-Memory, Practice*, 144.

7. "An examination of descent . . . permits the discovery, under the unique aspect of a trait or a concept, of the myriad events through which—thanks to which, against which–they were formed" ("Nietzsche, Genealogy, History," 146).

8. Bouchard and Simon's translation includes Foucault's prefatory remarks to this famous essay, which situate it more clearly in its own historical context. Delivered as a 1969 lecture at the Collège de France, the essay bears clearly the marks of the author-function it describes: at stake is Foucault's attempt to vouchsafe and delimit the intentions behind his own writing.

9. In terms not unrelated to my own concerns, Slavoj Žižek offers an incisive critique of Searle's "descriptivism" in *The Sublime Object of Ideology* (London: Verso, 1989), 92–95.

10. Of course, Hegel would never deny the teleological nature of historical discourse itself; even the most unsophisticated "historical account" tells its story, perforce, in retrospect–historical causes can only, after all, be identified as such in view of their purported succeeding effects. Nonetheless, such retrospection will never account for the kind of wholeness Hegel identifies as *die Wahre*.

11. Marc Norman and Tom Stoppard, *Shakespeare in Love: A Screenplay* (New York: Miramax, 1998), 9.

12. I consider Shapiro's argument at greater length in chapter 5. While I disagree in important ways with his methods and conclusions, I am much indebted to his work.

13. Unless otherwise noted, all references to Shakespeare's plays are taken from the Routledge facsimile of the first folio: *Mr William Shakespeares Comedies, Histories, & Tragedies: A Facsimile of the First Folio, 1623*, ed. Doug Moston (New York: Routledge, 1998). Line numbering follows Doug Moston's practice in this volume. A further technical, and ultimately theoretical, point: because my reading of Shakespeare will argue that we can neither evade nor resolve the crisis of authorial intent that his work provokes, I have decided to retain early modern spelling and punctuation throughout. My aim here is not to recapture the "original" text, nor to suggest that we can recuperate either an original textual indeterminacy or an original textual clarity. In this way, by calling into question the possibility of returning to an original text, I differ from proponents of both old and new textual criticism. At the same time, if it is impossible to return to origins, a modernized, emended edition of Shakespeare implies an equally impossible transcendence of those ori-

gins in the name of enduring truth. Shakespeare's texts, I argue, precisely thematize both impossibilities. By citing the original orthography I preserve nothing of origins, yet undermine any hope to transcend them: this "original" text can only appear alien to a modern reader, foregrounding both our own historicity and our historical distance from the text.

14. See 3.2, where Orlando chides Ganymede-Rosalind: "there's no clocke in the Forrest" (3.2.296–97)–although, just a few scenes earlier, we learn from Jaques that Touchstone has a "diall" in his pocket (2.7).

15. I quote here Ian Wilson's engaging account of the discovery in *Shakespeare: The Evidence* (London: Headline Book Publishing, 1993), 44. The following history of the testament is based on Wilson's account, as well as James G. McManaway's, "John Shakespeare's 'Spiritual Testament,'" *Shakespeare Quarterly* 18 (1967): 197–205. I have also consulted S. Schoenbaum's *William Shakespeare: A Documentary Life* (New York: Oxford UP, 1975), which offers facsimiles of both Malone's transcription and the 1638 English publication of Borromeo's Testament.

16. The echo in *Hamlet* of this phrase–"cut off in the blossom of my sins"–is striking, although perhaps of little import. On the one hand, the phrase is proverbial; on the other hand, since the authenticity of the Spiritual Testament has never been verified, the phrase could very well reflect a forger's conscious decision to echo the play. Even so, to my knowledge no one has investigated this parallel in any detail, nor considered the potential significance of John Shakespeare's Will for a reading of *Hamlet*. Stephen Greenblatt's gorgeous meditation on mourning, Passover, the Eucharist, and Catholicism does not, for instance, mention the Spiritual Testament, although the document would strongly support his argument. See Stephen Greenblatt, "The Mousetrap," *Shakespeare Studies* 35 (1997): 1–32.

17. The first article of the Testament, as transcribed by Malone and reproduced in facsimile in Schoenbaum's *Documentary Life* (42).

1. AUGUSTINE UNDER THE FIG TREE

1. With occasional modification to reflect the Latin of the Vulgate, biblical quotes throughout this chapter refer to the King James Version. In my treatment of Pauline and Johannine theology, I am less interested in "Paul" or "John" than in these figures as understood by Augustine. Rather than trying to reconstruct the definitive Pauline or biblical text, I would prefer to consult the texts that Augustine himself actually read. Unfortunately, these are no longer extant per se (although the Vulgate, to which I will occasionally refer, comes close).

2. As I have suggested in my preface, this conception of a simultaneously fulfilled and annulled law answers to Hegel's conception of the *Aufhebung*, by

which one stage of consciousness is both destroyed and preserved in the next. More than mere similarity, this structural homology between Christian grace and Hegelian dialectic reminds us of the extent to which a Christian hermeneutics, at least in its most Hellenized, least Semitic form, underlies what Heidegger, and so many others following him, would call the West's logocentrism. In her suggestive treatment of anti-Jewish attitudes in the Western literature of self and other, Jill Robbins has followed such a lead, bringing a poststructuralist sensibility to the tropes and materials of Christian revelation. See Jill Robbins, *Prodigal Son/Elder Brother: Interpretation and Alterity in Augustine, Petrarch, Kafka, Levinas* (Chicago: U of Chicago P, 1991).

3. Paul, of course, writes his epistles before the compilation and codification of Christian scripture, yet even for a later patristic thinker like Augustine, the question of scripture remains an open one. It is too easy for us to hear the title of a book in Augustine's references to the *novum* or *vetus testamentum*. Instead we must hear the uncertain borders between reading a *text* titled the New Testament and participating in an event that is the new testament. That is to say, we must "hear" the peculiar inflections of a written speech-act; we must hear the indecision between what has taken place *in facto* and what *in verbo*. For a lucid history of the process of scriptural canonization, see J. N. D. Kelly, *Early Christian Doctrines*, 5th ed. (London: Adman and Charles Black, 1977), 52–60, and Jaroslav Pelikan's discussion of apostolic continuity in *The Emergence of the Catholic Tradition (100–600)*, vol. 1 of *The Christian Tradition: A History of the Development of Doctrine* (Chicago: U of Chicago P, 1971), esp. 112–16.

4. Erich Auerbach, "Figura," in *Scenes from the Drama of European Literature: Six Essays*, tr. Ralph Mannheim (New York: Meridian, 1959), 51.

5. Auerbach notes the Latin Church fathers' use of the word *figura* to translate the Greek word *typos*, meaning imprint, form, mold, or model, and conveying the sense of prefiguration. In this way, *figura* is the Latin name for *type* (cf. "Figura," 44–45). But as almost every modern writer on the subject admits, no systematic or stable terminology for figurality exists in the patristic sources. Even so, most modern critics go on to propose just such a fixed vocabulary—most often in terms of the distinction between type and antitype. One needs instead, I think, to recognize the wide play of thought that the early church's "lack of systemacity" indicates. In patristic writings on allegory we don't simply find incoherence; instead we find a series of overlapping metaphors that, in various ways and with varying success, elucidate the relationship between old and new testaments. Thus: the old testament is the *typos*, the promise or the shadow (*umbra*), the image (*imago*), imitation (*imitatio*), exemplum, likeness (*similitudo*), form (*species*) of the new, which is in turn the antitypos of the old, its fulfillment, its completion, its truth (*veritas*) or revelation. (Cf. "Figura," 48).

6. See, for instance, Jean Daniélou, S.J., *From Shadows to Reality: Studies in*

the Biblical Typology of the Fathers, tr. Dom Wulstan Hibberd (London: Burns and Oates, 1960); "La typologie d'Isaac dans la Christianisme Primitif," *Biblica* 28 (1947): 363–93; "Les divers sens de l'Ecriture dans la tradition primitive," *Ephemerides Theologicae Lovanienses* 24 (1948): 119–26. See also J. N. D. Kelly, *Early Christian Doctrines*, 69–75, under the heading "Typology and Allegory." For an important critique of such discussions, see Henri de Lubac's "'Typologie' et 'allegorisme,'" in *Recherches de Science Religieuse* 34 (1947): 180–226, where the author argues that the term "typology" misses the dynamism implicit in Christian exegesis. In contrast, de Lubac reminds us that *allegoria* fundamentally denotes a dynamic relationship: "It establishes the relation of figure to truth, of letter to spirit, of old to new" (185). *Allegoria* is not simply that which the Old Testament *is*, but that relation which links old to new.

7. Joseph A. Galdon, S.J., *Typology and Seventeenth-Century Literature* (The Hague: Mouton, 1975), 30–31.

8. G. W. H. Lampe, "The Reasonableness of Typology," in *Essays in Typology: Studies in Biblical Theology* (Naperville, Ill.: Alec R. Allenson, 1957), 21. Cited in Galdon, 28.

9. Thus while the Antiochene exegetes do object to an Origenist, Alexandrian school of moral allegory on the basis of its ahistoricity, they do not question its legitimacy in terms of a greater "subjectivism." On the communal basis of reading and the "plurisignificance" of Scripture for Augustine, see Ralph Flores, "Reading and Speech in St. Augustine's Confessions," *Augustinian Studies* 6 (1975): 1–13, and Geoffrey Galt Harpham, "The Fertile Word: Augustine's Ascetics of Interpretation," *Criticism* 28, no. 3 (Summer 1986): 237–54. For a discussion of the Antiochene/Alexandrian debate, see Thomas M. Davis, "The Traditions of Puritan Typology," in *Typology and Early American Literature*, ed. Sacvan Bercovitch (Amherst: U of Massachusetts P, 1972), 25–26, and de Lubac (who shares Daniélou's desire for a spiritual sense of Scripture, but disagrees with some of his conclusions), "'Typologie' et 'Allegorisme,'" 200 ff.

10. It isn't until the late Renaissance that anything approaching a stable terminology of type and figure emerges. (And it isn't until the mid-nineteenth century that the word "typology," denoting a distinct form of scriptural interpretation, is first coined.) I am thinking here of the way in which the Swiss reformers–unlike Luther–critique a figural tradition not by rejecting the notion of the flesh as figure of the spirit but instead by insisting upon the flesh's *mere* figurality. In this way, they try, iconoclastically, to reject as mere artifice or ornament that symbolic capacity of figure, and yet maintain a typological approach to the Book. (Whence the possibility for these reformers–a possibility already imaginable in the 1520s–to conceive of the reformed church as a church *militans*, existing in this world as the necessary fulfillment of scriptural types.) I consider Luther's differences from the Swiss reformers–

whose critique of *figura*, I argue, is ultimately less radical, less thoroughgoing than Luther's–in chapter 3. However, the full-length study that would examine the ways in which the Reformation fractures a figural tradition by means of competing critiques of that tradition has yet to be written. The topic is a complex one but would help explain the history behind the terminological confusion within the modern discourse of allegory and typology.

11. Jean Daniélou, "La typologie d'Isaac dans la Christianisme Primitif," 369. Cited in Galdon, 67 n.

12. Marcion's work is primarily known through the writings of his detractors. For a brief but splendid account of Marcionite beliefs and their role in both the formation of the Christian canon and the early apologist efforts of the Church, see Pelikan, The *Emergence of the Catholic Tradition*, 68–81. See also E. C. Blackman, *Marcion and His Influence* (London: SPCK, 1948). The classic treatment of Marcion remains Adolf Von Harnack's *Marcion: Das Evangelium vom fremden Gott*, 2 vols. (reprint, Berlin: Akademie-verlag, 1960).

13. References to *Adversus Marcionem* as in the two-volume bilingual Oxford edition, ed. and tr. Ernest Evans (Oxford: Clarendon, 1972). I have modified Evans's translation.

14. My discussion of a distinction between "genetic" and "promissory" relations has been influenced by Jill Robbins's suggestive treatment of primogeniture and the reversal thereof in the parable of the prodigal son. See *Prodigal Son/Elder Brother*, esp. the introduction and chapter 1.

15. See ibid., esp. pp. 12–20, for the difficulty, if not the structural impossibility, of figuring the Judaic "otherwise"–as something *other* than the eclipsed Other, the Elder Brother to Christianity's Prodigal Son.

16. Daniel Boyarin analyzes the apparent contrast between this passage, with its universalizing and potentially liberating overtones, and the gendered and status-conscious discussions of 1 Corinthians. See Daniel Boyarin, "Paul and the Genealogy of Gender," *Representations* 41 (Winter 1993): 1–33. See also Boyarin, *A Radical Jew: Paul and the Politics of Identity* (Berkeley: U of California P, 1994).

17. Indeed, if freedom and slavery were simply traits to be *inherited*, then freedom would never be free of its enslavement to a natural order of succession and blood lineage.

18. One should note, however, that this insistence upon non-distinction becomes the very rationalization for that distinction without which Christianity would be unthinkable: namely, the distinction between Christian and Jew. This dilemma becomes crucial, as we shall see, in the historiography of anti-Semitism. See my remarks in chapter 5.

19. "Oliva" and "oleaster" are the terms used in the Vulgate. When Augustine cites the passage from Romans he refers to the "olea" and the "oleaster."

20. The Latin term for grafting is "inserere": to insert. See the Vulgate, Romans 11.17: "tu autem . . . insertus es in illis [ramis fracti]": you however are inserted in place of those broken branches. Augustine repeats this usage in his treatise *Adversos Iudaeos* (*Patrologia Cursus Completus,* 1st ser. [hereafter cited as PL], 42:51–64).

21. Throughout this chapter I deliberately avoid the pair of terms often used to distinguish a theologically driven animosity toward the Jews from a modern racist hatred: "anti-Judaism" versus. "anti-Semitism." In chapter 5 I will consider the stakes of such terminology in depth, arguing for a revised understanding of the relation between theology and discourses of "race."

22. Latin references to the *Tractatus Adversos Iudaeos* as in PL, ed. J-P Migne (Turnhout: Brepols, 1977), 42:51–64. English translation is a modified version of The Fathers of the Church edition: Saint Augustine, *Treatises on Marriage and Other Subjects,* ed. Roy J. Deferrari (Washington, D.C.: Catholic U of America P, 1969), 391–414.

23. Latin references to *De Civitate Dei* as in the *Corpus Scriptorum Ecclesiasticorum Latinorum* (Vienna: F. Tempsky, 1866–), ed. Österreichische Akademie der Wissenschaften, 40:1–2. English translation is a modified version of Henry Bettenson's Penguin Classics edition. *Concerning the City of God against the Pagans* (Harmondsworth and New York: Penguin, 1986 [1972]).

24. All references to *De Doctrina Christiana* as in the bilingual (French and Latin) *Bibliothèque Augustinienne* edition: *Oeuvres de Saint Augustin,* 1st ser., vol. 11 (Paris: Desclée De Brouwer, 1949). My English translation, a modified version of D. W. Robertson's, also draws upon Combes and Farges's French translation. See D. W. Robertson Jr., *On Christian Doctrine* (New York: Macmillan, 1958).

25. Robbins's point is somewhat different from mine, however. She, eager to deconstruct the logic of *figura,* sees this "image of an image" as that which "cannot definitively be said to belong to one of the two poles of figural interpretation" (8). If I find this deconstruction somewhat hasty it is only because I find that Augustine has himself addressed this problematic. Indeed, this "seepage" is central to his decisive revision of Paul.

26. This usage of *vox* remained ubiquitous among Latin writers through the Middle Ages and is carried over into English and the Romance languages in the Renaissance. One of the earliest such usages of *vox* in Augustine can be found in his discussion of language in Sermon 288. There he distinguishes between *vox* and *verbum* in figural terms, arguing that John the Baptist, the "voice clamoring in the wilderness," was the *vox* or signifier for Christ–the *Verbum* or signified. For a splendid discussion of the *verbum/vox* distinction in particular and Augustine's notion of *verbum* in general, see D. W. Johnson, "Verbum in the Early Augustine (386–397)," in *Recherches Augustiniennes* 8 (Paris: Études Augustiniennes, 1972): 25–53. A. D. R. Polman also discusses the distinction, usefully summarizing and citing large portions of a variety of

Augustinian tracts. A. D. R. Polman, *The Word of God According to St. Augustine*, tr. A. J. Pomerans (Grand Rapids, Mich.: Eerdmans Publishing, 1961), esp. his treatment of Augustine's neoplatonism in chapter 1. The text of Sermon 288 can be found in PL, 38:1302–6.

27. Unlike Saussure, Augustine makes no distinction between the *signified* as a specific mental content and the *referent* as the "real" thing in the world whose existence and nature, as precisely extra- and potentially pre-linguistic, must be bracketed by the semiologist. It is, however, clear that his definition of *res*–as that which we either use or enjoy–is oriented toward human understanding and endeavor. *Res* is the empirical object captured by human language and practice.

28. Brian Stock points out the tendency in modern discussions of orality and literacy to elide the special status of the *oral reader* in ancient culture. He reminds us that the unpunctuated form of scrolls and codices required such "sounding out," and argues that the distinction between oral and silent reading relates for Augustine to a broader neoplatonic program of ascent. Reading as empirical activity is a prelude to spiritual contemplation. As I argue above: *legere* is transcended in favor of *intellegere* in exactly the same way that Jewish carnality is superseded by Christian spirituality. My account of Augustine's "ethics of interpretation" differs from Stock's, however, insofar as I focus upon the way that the narrative of any such ascent or supersession entails, for Augustine, a problematic effacement of origins. For his discussion of oral reading, silent meditation, and reading as ascent, see Brian Stock, *Augustine the Reader: Meditation, Self-Knowledge, and the Ethics of Interpretation* (Cambridge, Mass.: Belknap Press, 1996), 5–11, 61–65, 113–14, 250–51.

29. References to the *Confessions* as in the two-volume bilingual Loeb edition (Cambridge: Harvard UP, orig. pub. 1912). Translation modified.

30. See Geoffrey Galt Harpham's insightful reading of Augustinian polysemy: "For Augustine in Book 12 truth is a principle of excess in language, a measure of meaning exceeding any possible interpretation, any coherent authorial intention. . . . Truth is a property of every right interpretation, of which there can be no limit (which is *not* the same as saying that all interpretations are right)" ("The Fertile Word," 246).

31. Brian Stock characterizes this difference between Paul and Augustine as the difference between *eschatology* and *hermeneutics*, arguing that Paul distinguishes between history (what the Israelites experienced) and text-as-figure (those events written "for our sake on whom the ends of the ages are come"), while for Augustine both sides of the exchange are textual: Paul's *historia* is understood as the Scripture's literal meaning. See Stock, *Augustine the Reader*, 167–68.

32. *De Catechizandis Rudibus* 4.8, as cited in Robbins, *Prodigal Son/Elder Brother*, 1.

33. References to *Contra Faustum* as in the *Corpus Scriptorum Ecclesiastico-*

rum Latinorum (Vienna: F. Tempsky, 1866–), ed. Österreichische Akademie der Wissenschaften, 25:1–2.

34. Augustine does, however, distinguish between *praecepta agendae vitae*, precepts that tell us how to lead life, and *praecepta significandae vitae*, precepts that signify life (*Contra Faustum* 6.2 ff.). The distinction here is between actual and figural precepts. The former sort of precept–paradigmatically one of the Ten Commandments–can not be construed figurally but must be taken at face value. Augustine's example of an actual precept is "Thou shalt not covet"; his example of a figural precept is "Thou shalt circumcise every male on the eighth day." Of course, not unlike Augustine's distinction between the translated and the proper, this distinction is untenable. In the final analysis we could demonstrate that even *praecepta agendae vitae* involve a normativity based in *figura*.

35. Except of course the Eschaton. We must remember that while the structure of *figura* always appears binary, it is also ever on the verge of expanding, of becoming a ternary structure that looks ahead to the end of time.

36. Eugene Vance, "Augustine's *Confessions* and the Grammar of Selfhood," *Genre* 6, no. 1 (March 1973): 5.

37. See, for starters, Brian Stock's *Augustine the Reader* and John C. Cooper's "Why Did Augustine Write Books XI–XIII of *The Confessions?*" *Augustinian Studies* 2 (1971): 37–46. For Stock, the shift is one from narrative to analysis: the two discourses in *The Confessions* (and elsewhere in Augustine's work) are nonetheless unified in their investigation of reading. John C. Cooper, on the other hand, argues less ambitiously that Augustine shifts from a *confessio peccati* to a *confessio fidei*.

38. See 10.31 for Augustine's rather subtle development of classical treatments of pleasure and pain in the context of eating: "But while I am passing from the annoyance of need to the peace of satiety, in that transition itself the snare of concupiscence lies in wait for me. The transition itself is pleasant." Augustine's treatment of a differential component to pleasure anticipates Freud's work with homeostasis in *Beyond the Pleasure Principle* and Lacan's vision of the symbolic ordering of *jouissance* in terms of the cross-referential, diacritical structure of a signifying system (see, e.g., *L'Éthique de la psychanalyse*, Seminar 7 [Paris: Éditions du Seuil, 1986], 22 ff.).

39. Brian Stock offers one of the most complete discussions of Augustinian time, memory, and self-consciousness available; see *Augustine the Reader*, esp. chapter 8. For a careful account of *Confessions* 11 in the context of analytic philosophy, see James McEvoy, "St. Augustine's Account of Time and Wittgenstein's Criticisms," *Review of Metaphysics* 38 (March 1984): 547–77. A broader and in some ways more compelling account of time in Augustine's work is Robert Jordan's essay, "Time and Contingency in St. Augustine," in *Augustine: A Collection of Critical Essays*, ed. R. A. Markus (New

York: Doubleday, 1972), 255–79. See in addition Eugene Vance's incisive essay, "Language as Temporality," in *Mimesis: From Mirror to Method, Augustine to Descartes*, ed. John D. Lyons and Stephen G. Nichols Jr. (Hanover, N.H.: UP of New England, 1982), 20–35.

40. See, for instance, Derrida's seminal arguments in "La pharmacie de Platon," in *La dissémination* (Paris: Éditions du Seuil, 1972).

41. Text of the *De Magistro* as in the bilingual *Bibliothèque Augustinienne* edition: *Oeuvres de Saint Augustin*, 1st ser., vol. 6, ed. François Joseph Thonnard (Paris: Desclée De Brouwer et Cie, 1941).

42. Cf. Johnson, "Verbum in the Early Augustine," and Polman, *The Word of God According to St. Augustine*.

43. I discuss this important episode at length in chapter 3.

44. Augustine discusses biblical sortilege in his Epistles 37 and 55. Mary Carruthers examines these letters in *The Book of Memory: A Study of Memory in Medieval Culture* (Cambridge: Cambridge UP, 1990), 333 n. 90.

45. See *Enarratio in psalmum* 4.8. I discuss this *enarratio* in the next chapter.

2. PETRARCH IN THE SHADE OF THE LAUREL

1. References to Petrarch's vernacular lyrics as in *Petrarch's Lyric Poems: The Rime Sparse and Other Lyrics*, bilingual ed., tr. and ed. Robert M. Durling (Cambridge: Harvard UP, 1976). I have occasionally modified Durling's prose translations.

2. See, for starters, Durling's concise discussion of the *Rime sparse*'s Augustinian motifs of recollection and dispersion in his introduction to *Petrarch's Lyric Poems*.

3. See my discussion of Romans 11 in chapter 1.

4. I am thinking here both of Socrates' asceticism–that is, as Plato depicts it, Socrates' insistence on the value of frustrating the senses in the pursuit of a higher good (cf. for instance his descriptions of the lover in the *Phaedrus* and the *Symposium*)–and I'm recalling his faith that to know the good is at once to desire and to serve it, an argument that Plato eulogizes most poignantly, because most ironically, in the *Apology*. Augustine inherits the Platonic view of a virtuous *ascesis* from Cicero, Plotinus, and Porphyry.

5. References to the *Commedia* as in Charles S. Singleton's three-volume bilingual edition with text and commentary: Dante Alighieri, *The Divine Comedy*, tr. Charles S. Singleton (Princeton: Princeton UP, 1982 [1973]).

6. Unless otherwise noted, throughout this chapter I will be citing the Bible in the version Petrarch would have consulted, the Vulgate.

7. The question of Abraham's "here I am"–and my notion here of an ethics of voice–immediately evokes a Levinasian ethics of responsibility. For

Emmanuel Levinas the call of the other is what constitutes the self as sub-ject—a subject who is therefore primordially ethical, responsible a priori for the other insofar as the self is a subject at all. A fundamental anachronism thus lies at the heart of ethical responsibility for Levinas: the subject comes into being *already* responsible, already indebted to the other, already from the start responding to alterity. Thus, for Levinas, any ethical action or concrete response that we make to that other is inadequate because it comes *after the fact* of the call: instead of confronting the radical priority of the other's claim upon us, ethical action seeks to translate the self's constitutive responsibility into meaning, into a representation that the self, in its freedom, commands. It is only for Levinas in a radically anachronistic response—the kind of infinite willingness to be bound attested to in Abraham's "here I am"—that we find the true passivity of Levinas's ethical subject. See *Otherwise Than Being: Or, Beyond Essence*, tr. Alphonso Lingis (Pittsburgh: Duquesne UP, 1997 [1981]), esp. 145–46.

Jill Robbins addresses Levinasian alterity as a specifically Jewish answer to the figural tradition in *Prodigal Son/ Elder Brother*. Levinas plays less of a role in my story, however, because of the centrality for him of the other's *proximity*—the other's face—as the anarchic (i.e., radically prior) nature of responsibility. For my purposes, the kind of responsibility I wish to address is one that has already—and necessarily—failed to face the other. Indeed, the very notion that I am called, that the other faces *me*, essential to an ethics of read-ing, signals precisely the effacement of alterity. In other words, insofar as I am a subject constituted by my reading, I have *already missed* my encounter with the other.

8. It is no accident that one sign of God's covenant is Abram's new name, Abraham. Abram's willingness to be renamed marks an extreme instance of his openness to discourse and to interpellation. "And I will place my covenant between me and you and will multiply you exceedingly much . . . nor will your name any longer be called 'Abram' but you will be called 'Abraham' because I have made you the father of many nations" (Gen. 17:2–5).

9. The classic modern text to consider this interpellative moment in reli-gious life is Martin Buber's *I and Thou*, tr. Walter Kaufmann (New York: Scrib-ner, 1970). Unlike Levinas, Buber finds no aporias in his efforts to articulate the moment of interpellation.

10. In what follows we will also refer to shifters as "deictics," although Émile Benveniste warns that the concept of deixis is misleading in this con-text "unless one adds that the deixis is contemporary with the instance of dis-course" (*Problèmes de linguistique générale*, 2 vols. [Paris: Éditions Gallimard, 1966], 1:253). I have consulted throughout and occasionally modified the translation of Benveniste as it appears in *Problems in General Linguistics*, tr. Mary Elizabeth Meek (Coral Gables: U of Miami P, 1971).

11. Benveniste, *Problèmes de linguistique générale*, 1:252. The French word

instance (e.g., *l'instance de discours*), used frequently by Benveniste and translated by Meek as its English cognate, conveys a range of meaning not present in the English. While Benveniste seems primarily to be conveying the sense of present time and circumstance, the French word also connotes *insistence*—a sense of solicitation or pressure.

12. Benveniste, however, argues that the third person is not a person at all: "it is really the verbal form whose function it is to express the *non-person.*" Unlike the first two persons, which find their reference in the concrete instance of discourse, the third person "in itself does not specifically designate anything or anyone." Instead, the third person as a "non-person" signals precisely the absence of what specifically qualifies the "I" and the "you" (*Problèmes de linguistique générale*, 1:228, 230).

While this distinction seems correct as far as it goes, it does fail to take into account the importance of the proper name. My name designates me neither as an "I" nor as a "you," but as an extra-discursive entity to be apprehended from the "objective" perspective of the third person. And as we've seen with Abraham's response to God's call, in an important sense the third-person designation ("Abraham?") intervenes between the "I" and the "you." By imagining discourse as an essentially dyadic phenomenon, Benveniste thus neglects the way in which the third person is included in discourse as excluded. Accordingly, the dyad of personal engagement is asymmetrical, mediated by and potentially disrupted with the non-person itself. Lacan suggests the importance of this asymmetry in terms of the individual's entrance into language in his opening remarks to "L'instance de la lettre dans l'inconscient ou la raison depuis Freud," in *Écrits*, 493–528, esp. 495 (Paris: Éditions du Seuil, 1966). The rough equivalences between Benveniste's non-person and the Lacanian "big Other" (i.e., the symbolic order) warrant further analysis.

13. Thomas Greene discusses this point from Benveniste in an important context that we shall consider shortly: humanism's ability simultaneously to appreciate and to overcome historical difference and hermeneutic anachronism. See *The Light in Troy: Imitation and Discovery in Renaissance Poetry* (New Haven: Yale UP, 1982), 15.

14. The existence of the vocative case in Latin suggests that the appellative use of proper names might more appropriately be described as a use of the second person than as an instance of the impersonal. "Et tu, Brute?" However, I'd like to suggest that such vocative usage precisely figures the way in which Benveniste's "non-person" mediates between persons; I would see the vocative as a kind of intermediate locution that demonstrates the overlap and interplay between language—as a more or less stable system of designations and substitutions—and discourse as an ever-shifting system of internal references.

15. I allude here to Augustine's remarkable reading of Exodus 12:35–36

(the Israelites' theft of Egyptian gold) as a figure for the figural interpretation of pagan texts. "Those however who are called philosophers, if by chance they have said things which are true and accommodated to our faith . . . , what they have said should be reclaimed [*in usum nostrum vindicanda*] from them for our use as from unjust possessors. For thus the Egyptians had . . . vases and ornaments of gold and silver and clothing which that people, in fleeing Egypt, took with them rather as if they were secretly reclaiming [*vindicavit*] it for a better use" (*Doctrina* 2.40.60).

16. For the sake of argument this distinction between spoken and written discourses is useful, although it cannot be maintained rigorously—as critiques of phonologocentrism have long reminded us. In "Signature Event Context" (in *Margins of Philosophy*, tr. Alan Bass [Chicago: U of Chicago P, 1982], 307–30), to cite just one famous instance of this critique, Derrida counters the notions of singularity and context-boundedness that animate Austin's view of the speech-act. There Derrida argues that, structurally, every mark, even an oral one, is a grapheme. A certain self-identity of the mark is required to permit its recognition—but this unity of the signifying form constitutes itself only by virtue of its iterability: by virtue, that is, of the possibility of being repeated in the absence not only of its referent but of any determined signified or intention of signification. In this way, Derrida argues that all signifying marks are a species of writing—all potentially proffered in the absence of a determinate signifying context.

17. This is, at any rate, how Benveniste envisions discourse transpiring: namely, as an essentially dyadic exchange between perfectly invertible persons. But this vision of a perfectly symmetrical exchange of places misses the important sense in which asymmetry and alienation attend the individual's entry into discourse, whether that discourse be spoken or written. As I've already indicated, both Lacan and Derrida offer important theoretical insights into the nature of this discursive asymmetry. Also extremely relevant is Maurice Blanchot's discussion in *L'Espace littéraire* (Paris: Gallimard, 1955), and elsewhere, of the "impersonal" and its relation to literature.

18. Peter Brown, *Augustine of Hippo* (Berkeley: U of California P, 1969), 174–75; Suzanne Poque, "Les Psaumes dans les 'Confessions'" in *Saint Augustin et la Bible*, Bible de Tous les Temps, vol. 3, ed. Anne-Marie la Bonnardière (Paris: Éditions Beauchesne, 1986), 155–66; cf. esp. 157. In terms resonant for our discussion, Poque describes Augustine's style as one of dialogue, of "écoute spirituelle" and response (155–56). For a more general discussion of the role of prayer in the *Confessions*, see Jose Oroz Reta, "Prière et Recherche de Dieu dans les Confessions de Saint Augustin," *Augustinian Studies* 7 (1976): 99–118.

19. The approach is well trod. "As is well known," Joel Fineman tells us in *Shakespeare's Perjured Eye*, "the poetry of praise is regularly taken to be, from Plato and Aristotle through the Renaissance, the master model of poetry"–

and, at least within a Judeo-Christian context, the master model for all praise, for an ideal/idealizing poetics of vision, is itself the Davidic psalm (*Shakespeare's Perjured Eye: The Invention of Poetic Subjectivity in the Sonnets*, [Berkeley: U of California P, 1986], 1). For Fineman it is the psalmist whose ideal language–a language *of* vision–brings together word and referent, subject and object, praiser and praised. But, as Fineman argues in his gloss of an engraving by the seventeenth-century Christian cabalist Robert Fludd (*Perjured Eye*, 111, fig. 1), such all-seeing visionary poetics must necessarily contain, as its organizing principle, that which enables sight but which cannot in itself be seen. Thus in the Fludd engraving, a kneeling David is depicted in prayer below the eyeball/sun of God; here, as Fineman argues, Fludd allegorizes the ways in which a comprehensive visual totality can be constituted only by dint of linguistic difference. For instance, Fludd inscribes the words that David sings ("In alarum tuarum umbra canam," "in the shade of your wings I shall sing" [Psalm 63:7]) as a ray of light directed upward to the Tetragrammaton YHVH–the unspeakable name of God (*Jehova*)–inscribed on the sun/eye's iris: "In Fludd's picture, where the verse of psalm and *Jehova* lie at oblique angles to each other (just as the Latin stands in translational relation to the Hebrew), it is clearly the case that King David does not literally voice the name of God. It is possible, however, reading either up or down, to take inscribed *Jehova* as a syntactic part of David's speech, either as its apostrophized addressee or as the direct object of its *canam*. This syntactic, but still silent, link between the Latin and the Hebrew is significant, for unspeakable *Jehova* thus becomes the predicated precondition through which or across which what the psalmist says is translated into what the psalmist sees" (113). If God is here presented as an all-seeing eye, there is, nonetheless, one thing that He *cannot* see: His own name, inscribed upon the eyeball's iris. But Fineman's reading also discloses the "deaf and dumb-spot," as it were, of a poetry of praise: the unspeakable, excluded (but included *as* excluded) graphesis: the Tetragrammaton, the name of God that can be voiced only through periphrasis (e.g., *Ha Shem* or *Adonai*). Thus Fineman signals the paradoxical logic by which an excluded sight or sound ensures the comprehensive totality of a visual or vocal field; or, in grander terms, the logic by which the *whole*, in order to be figured or thought as such, must nonetheless include a *hole*. This is the same logic that necessitates that a principle of difference be included, in its very exclusion even, within any systematic expression of sameness. Fludd thus figures the anagogic coherence of the psalmist's vision as including/excluding a navel of incoherence: namely, God's difference from Himself; i.e., the non-self-coincidence implied by the eyeball's inability to see itself. And, Fineman will argue, it is precisely by traversing this navel of incoherence or difference that "what the psalmist says is translated into what the psalmist sees" (113). Sight and sound, word and vision, come together in an integrated and integrating apprehension of truth. (I explore this logic, and its role in Fineman's reading of *Shakespeare's Sonnets*, at length in chapter 4.)

Of course, ultimately Fineman's interpretation foregrounds the fragility of any such integration, demonstrating the risk of disruption evoked by the possibility of speaking the unspeakable Name: "the 'Word' that *speaks* of difference will then become the paradoxical likeness of its difference from itself" (119). Fineman suggests that it is precisely in order to avoid this paradox that the Tetragrammaton is unspeakable. Once spoken, the Signifier of signifiers can't help but speak against itself, unraveling the integrated, integrative cosmos it also, simultaneously, bespeaks. To carry this logic one step further, however, we would need to revise our understanding of how Fludd conjoins a verbal futurity–the promise of a *future* singing, *canam*, "I shall sing"–with a vision of *present* singing. For Fineman, this conjunction allegorizes the holistic pretenses of a visionary poetics: image here makes present a deferred verbality. But one really needs, I think, to take the engraving at its word: the image of David singing sets before us the psalmist's voice, but only as something set aside, set ahead; only as something projected into an eschatological future structurally akin to a mythic Edenic past. Indeed, what Fludd here allegorizes is not the successful present rendering of a future voice, but rather the displacement of that voice *by dint of* its rendering. Fludd, in other words, represents David's voice as a *written* utterance.

For Fineman, Fludd's engraving reveals the extent to which a visionary poetics is graphically compromised at its very origin. I would contend, however, that this "compromise" is entirely unproblematic within the very tradition that Fineman cites: the tradition that takes David's voice as the very model of praise. Indeed, within the Christian tradition that elevates David to the status of exemplum, the linguistic wrinkle in his field of vision simply marks his role as *figure*. Fineman has, in other words, misunderstood the very nature of the psalmist's vision. Far from presuming to present presence in all its holistic fullness, the psalmist stands for a vision that is necessarily defined by/as an absent-presence. David's vision, that is to say, is understood in figural and chiastic terms; like the prophetic legislation of the patriarchs, the prophetic nature of David's vision is "visible" only in hindsight. To see it, David must look through an other's eyes–eyes that will no longer see *him*. The "blindspot," then, at the center of David's visual field is well understood within the figural tradition that, indeed, defines David as *visionary*. The problem Fineman identifies, in other words, poses no problem for *figura* (although presumably it poses a problem for *David*).

20. According to Ellen St. Sure Lifshutz, this view can be traced back to the first-century Jewish commentaries of Josephus Flavius and Philo of Alexandria. Later commentators took the poems to be written according to Greco-Latin metrical principles–a notion that contributed to the Renaissance belief that the psalter was originally written in hexameters. Furthermore, it

was not until the seventeenth century that serious doubts about David's authorship arose. Even though in the very titles to certain psalms other authors are mentioned, the idea of David's sole or primary authorship persisted. Cf. Ellen St. Sure Lifschutz, "David's Lyre and the Renaissance Lyric: A Critical Consideration of the Psalms of Wyatt, Surrey and the Sidneys" (Ph.D. diss., University of California, Berkeley, 1980), 5–6, 36–39 ; and A. J. Minnis, *Medieval Theory of Authorship: Scholastic Literary Attitudes in the Later Middle Ages* (London: Scolar, 1984), 43.

21. See Minnis, *Medieval Theory of Authorship*, 45.

22. References to the *Enarrationes in psalmos* as in the *Corpus Christianorum Series Latina* 38–40, *Aurelii Augustini Opera*, 10 (Turnhout: Brepols, 1954–1984).

23. As Brian Stock notes, medieval readers credited Augustine with the invention of the fourfold hermeneutic schema; see *Augustine the Reader*, 165 and 373 n. 187 (where Stock cites Henri de Lubac's treatment of the subject in *Exégèse médiévale*). Beryl Smalley traces the fourfold schema back to John Cassian's (360–435) *Conlationes*, which supplements the *De Doctrina Christiana* as a monastic guide for Bible study. In addition to the literal or historical sense of Scripture, Cassian distinguished three figural senses, the allegorical, the tropological or moral (what Augustine called the "aetiological" sense), and the anagogical. His example of the fourfold exegesis of the holy city, Jerusalem, captivated medieval exegetes and was often repeated: according to *history* Jerusalem is a city of the Jews; according to *allegory* it is the Church of Christ; according to *anagoge* it is the heavenly city of God; according to *trope* it is the soul of man. Cf. Beryl Smalley, *The Study of the Bible in the Middle Ages* (Oxford: Blackwell, 1952), 27–28.

In his essay "'Typologie' et 'Allegorisme,'" de Lubac—one of the Jesuit theologians whose work, roughly contemporaneous with Auerbach's, is responsible for the resurgence of contemporary interest in figural interpretation—cites a medieval tag, originating with Nicholas of Lyra, which neatly distinguishes the four levels: *Littera gesta docet, quid credas allegoria / Moralis quid agas, quo tendas anagogia* [The literal teaches deeds; allegory teaches what you should believe; the moral level teaches what you should do, and the anagogical level teaches where you are heading]. The most comprehensive treatment of the subject remains his four-volume *Exégèse médiévale* (Paris: Aubier, 1959–1964).

24. For mention of David's singing and playing before the ark of God, see 1 Chronicles 13:8 and 1 Chronicles 16.

25. The text of Psalm 4, as Augustine cites it in his *Enarratio*: "In finem, psalmus canticum David. / Cum inuocarem, exaudiuit me Deus iustitiae meae. In tribulatione dilatasti mihi. Miserere mei, et exaudi orationem meam. / Filii hominum, usquequo graues corde. Vtquid diligitis uanitatem, et quaeritis mendacium? / Diapsalma / Et scitote quoniam admirabilem fecit Dominus sanc-

tum suum. Dominus exaudiet me, dum clameuero ad eum. / Irascimini, et nolite peccare. Quae dicitis in cordibus uestris. In cubilibus uestris compungimini. / Diapsalma / Sacrificate sacrificium iustitiae, et sperate in Domino. Multi dicunt: Quis ostendit nobis bona? / Signatum est inquit in nobis lumen uultus tui, Domine. Dedisti laetitiam in cor meum. / A tempore frumenti, uini et olei sui multiplicati sunt. / In pace, in idipsum obdormiam, et somnum capiam. Quoniam tu, Domine, singulariter in spe habitare fecisti me."

26. See *Confessions* 9.4: "I wished that they [the Manichees] might hear without my knowing whether they heard me, lest they [*illa*] should think I spoke it on their account [*propter se*]."

27. The period corresponds with his priesthood and the early days of his episcopate. *De Doctrina Christiana* (396, 426), *Contra Faustum* (397–398), and *De Trinitate* (begun 399) all address figural interpretation as a central issue.

28. The situation is even more complicated than I am suggesting here since, in addition to the split that we would expect with any written first-person discourse between "author" and "speaker," Augustine's text forces us also to consider the distinction between the narrated "I" and the "I" as narrator. The two distinctions overlap and certainly reinforce each other, but it would be a mistake to confuse them. For one thing, unlike the first-person narrator, by definition the author is not a person *of* discourse, since he stands *behind* discourse as its source.

29. Interestingly, when Augustine cites the psalm within the complex discursive context of the *Confessions*, he transforms its first verse, changing the problematic third person to "you."

30. Structurally, the scene in book 9 where Augustine wishes to read before the Manichees resembles nothing so much as the Cretan Liar's paradox (in its purest form: "I am lying").

31. Henri de Lubac, "'Typologie' et 'Allegorisme,'" 193–94.

32. Particularly in its Pauline context, *figura* is often translated as "example" (cf. 1 Cor. 10:6). Auerbach discusses the word's inclination "toward the universal, lawful, and exemplary" in "Figura," 15.

33. See my discussion of Augustine's exhortation for hermeneutic charity–"legitime lege utamur," let us use the law lawfully (*Conf.* 12.30)–in the previous chapter.

34. "A son livre," ll. 41–42, as in Pierre de Ronsard, *Les Amours (1552–1584)*, ed. Marc Bensimon and James L. Martin (Paris: Garnier-Flammarion, 1981). Ronsard, having abandoned his first lover (Cassandre) in favor of a succession of new ones, is justifying both his sensualism and his pluralism. Interestingly, he argues that Petrarchism is more strict than Petrarch himself: even Petrarch didn't follow his own law. He was too smart for that. "Luy mesme ne fut tel: car à voir son escrit / Il estoit esveillé d'un trop gentil esprit / Pour estre sot trente ans, abusant sa jeunesse, / Et sa Muse, au giron d'une seule maitresse" (ll. 45–48).

35. For a good discussion of ancient theories of *imitatio*, see Greene, *The Light in Troy,* chapter 4. Greene's discussion of the famous Senecan version (*Ep. Mor.* 84) of the Lucretian-Horatian metaphor of the assimilative honeybee is particularly useful (cf. 73–76). While Greene notes that Seneca's apian simile "arguably" defines "a theory of reading as much as of writing" (73), he does not discuss the medieval persistence of the image as a model for the *florilegia*–i.e., those compilations of authoritative texts culled and copied (rarely verbatim) in the process of one's reading. Furthermore, Greene does not cite the influence of such compilations on Petrarchan humanism.

36. Thomas Greene's *The Light in Troy* remains the most valuable recent discussion of the relation between Petrarch's recognition of historical difference and his conception of *imitatio.* Nonetheless, Petrarch has long been credited with the transition to a modern conception of history–a conception that imbues imitation with the nostalgic recognition of loss. In his classic article, "Petrarch's Conception of the 'Dark Ages,'" (*Speculum* 17, no. 2 [April 1942]: 226–42), Theodor M. Mommsen connects this conception of history with Petrarch's urgent appeals to men like Cola di Rienzo and the German emperor Charles IV to revive Rome's glory through imitation.

37. Judson Boyce Allen, "Grammar, Poetic Form, and the Lyric Ego: A Medieval a Priori," in *Lois Ebin, ed., Vernacular Poetics in the Middle Ages,* 199–226 (Kalamazoo, Mich.: Medieval Institute Publications, 1984), 208.

38. For Paul Zumthor, however, this performative aspect of the medieval lyric renders its first person not so much normative or universal as *anonymous.* Zumthor thus distinguishes the medieval lyric from autobiography. In the first place, autobiographical discourse presumes a link between an "énonciateur," i.e., a speaker, and "the 'theme' of which the successive actions generating the narrative are the predicate," i.e., the subject of the statement (Paul Zumthor, "Autobiographie au Moyen Age?" in *Langue, Texte, Enigme* [Paris: Éditions du Seuil, 1975], 165–80. In autobiography, then, the "I" simultaneously designates the individual insofar as she is now speaking and insofar as her statements bespeak her, predicating actions and attributes to the grammatical subject of her discourse. In contrast, with medieval poetry, since the *jongleur* who sings or recites the lyric can change with each new performance, there can be no such functional link between speaker and bespoken. Thus, Zumthor tells us, the medieval lyric cannot count as autobiography. As Zumthor reminds us, the opposition so central to a modern narrative tradition between "history" and "fiction" is more or less inoperative for the medieval storyteller ("Autobiographie," 165) and thus, with the medieval lyric's "potential" first person, with an "I" whose actualization varies with each new speaker, the question of the author's place within or behind the discourse doesn't even arise. Completely transparent, the troubador lyric is performative rather than normative; actualized in a specific vocalization, the poem seems primarily to indicate its own generic presence, rather than any absent authorial figure or

substantial fictional persona. In this way, expressing an "I" whose reality is supported solely by the present discursive instance, the troubador tradition articulates the mere shifter of Benveniste's linguistics. As Zumthor writes, echoing the linguist's definition of the shifter, the medieval lyric ego is "a pure empty sign referring to the bearer of voice" (Paul Zumthor, "Le 'je' de la chanson et le moi du poète," in *Langue, Texte, Enigme*, 187).

39. "What Is Poetry?" in John Stuart Mill, *Essays on Poetry by John Stuart Mill*, ed. F. Parvin Sharpless (Columbia: U. of South Carolina P, 1976), 12.

40. See Barbara Herrnstein Smith, *On the Margins of Discourse* (Chicago: U. of Chicago P, 1978). By "fictive utterance" Smith means an utterance that transpires, could only be spoken, in a fictional world. She means, that is to say, a theatrical kind of speech. It seems significant to me, however, that, properly speaking, there is no such thing as a fictional utterance. There are only fictional contexts. Thus if I utter the marriage vow while in character on stage I am not actually married—but it is the setting, and not the utterance, that is feigned. The utterance remains what it is: a marriage vow. See J. L. Austin, *How to Do Things with Words* (Cambridge: Harvard UP, 1975), esp. 9.

Herbert F. Tucker usefully discusses the new critical approach to lyric as monologue in "Dramatic Monologue and the Overhearing of Lyric," in *Lyric Poetry: Beyond New Criticism*, ed. Chaviva Hosek and Patricia Parker (Ithaca: Cornell UP, 1985), 226–43. See Jonathan Culler's essay from the same volume ("Changes in the Study of Lyric," 38–54) for a complementary viewpoint.

41. Lifschutz, *David's Lyre*, discusses the history of the penitential psalms, as well as Petrarch's imitation, 40–45, 133–34. Robert G. Twombly provides a good discussion of the psalms' history of paraphrase with special attention to Thomas Wyatt. See his "Thomas Wyatt's Paraphrase of the Penitential Psalms of David," *Texas Studies in Literature and Language* 12 (1970): 345–80.

42. Stephen Greenblatt, *Renaissance Self-Fashioning: From More to Shakespeare* (Chicago: U of Chicago P, 1980), 117–18. See also his discussion of the penitential psalms in general and Wyatt's psalms in particular, 115–28.

43. Jerome made three translations of the Psalms—the "Roman" psalter, a corrected version of the Old Latin edition with reference to the Septuagint; the "Gallican" psalter, a revision of the Roman with reference to other Greek texts and perhaps the Hebrew; and a new translation of the Hebrew. Petrarch would have been reading the Gallican, which became standard, at least in France, in the medieval Vulgate. In *Familiari* 10.4 Petrarch faults Jerome for being unable to translate the psalms while retaining their meter and meaning. With the exception of the "Ascent of Mont Ventoux" (*Fam.* 4.1), references to the *Rerum familiarium libri XXIV* as in *Le Familiari*, ed. Vittorio Rossi and Umberto Bosco, 4 vols. (Firenze: Sansoni, 1933). English translations (modified) from *Letters on Familiar Matters. Rerum familiarium libri XXIV*, tr. and ed. Aldo S. Bernardo, 3 vols. (Baltimore: Johns Hopkins UP, 1975–1985).

44. Giles Constable, "Petrarch and Monasticism," in *Francesco Petrarca Citizen of the World. Proceedings of the World Petrarch Congress, Washington, D.C., April 6–13, 1974*, 53–99 (Padova: Editrice Antenore; Albany: SUNY Press, 1980), 53. Constable is drawing on Pietro Paolo Gerosa's argument in his *Umanesimo cristiano del Petrarca. Influenza agostiniana attinenze medievali* (Torino: Bottega d'Erasmo, 1966).

45. In the edition of the *Psalms* that I will be using, Giovanni Ponte writes that "Petrarch's interest in Biblical poetry, principally David's (but also Job's, Ecclesiastes' and Solomon's) matures in the decade of his most intense spiritual crisis (1340–1350)." *Opere di Francesco Petrarca*, ed. Emilio Bigi, Giovanni Ponte, and Giuseppe Fracassetti (Milano: Mursia, 1963–1994), 1192. The *Psalms* appear in this collection in Latin with Italian translation, 494–509. Late in life, either as disclaimer or as boast, Petrarch maintains having written the *Psalms* all in one day (cf. *Sen.* 10.1).

46. *Fam.* 10.4.

47. The text of the entire psalm:

> Heu michi misero, quia iratum adversus me constitui Redemptorem meum, et legem suam contumaciter neglexi.
>
> Iter rectum sponte deserui; et per invia longe lateque circumactus sum.
>
> Aspera quelibet et inaccessa penetravi; et ubique labor et angustie.
>
> Unus aut alter ex gregibus brutorum; et inter lustra ferarum habitatio mea.
>
> In anxietatibus cum voluptate versatus sum; et in sentibus cubile meum stravi.
>
> Et obdormivi in iteritum; et speravi requiem in tormentis.
>
> Nunc igitur quid agam? Quo me in tantis periculis vertam? Spes adolescentie mee corruerunt omnes.
>
> Et factus sum naufrago simillimus, qui, mercibus amissis, nudus enatat, iactatus ventis et pelago.
>
> Elongatus ego sum a portu, et viam salutis non apprehendo, sed rapior sinistrorsum.
>
> Video tenuiter quidem; sed hinc michi gravius duellum, quia irascor michimet, et anime mee sum infestus.
>
> Irascor peccatis meis, sed ingenti miseriarum mole depressus sum; nec est respirandi locus.
>
> Sepe fugam retentavi, et vetustum iugum excutere meditatus sum; sed inheret ossibus.
>
> O si tandem excidat a collo meo! Excidet confestim, si tu iusseris, Altissime.

O si michi sic irascar ut te diligam, vel sero!

Sed multum timeo, quia libertas mea meis manibus
labefacta est.

Iuste crucior, consensi. Labore torqueor dignissimo.

Quid michi procuravi demens? Cathenam meam ipse
contexui, et incidi volens in insidias mortis.

Retia michi disposuit hostis, quacunque ibam; et ped-
ibus meis laqueos tetendit.

Ego autem despexi, et incessi securus inter lubrica, et
in peccatis michi blanditus sum.

Credidi iuventutis decus non aberrare, et secutus sum
qua me tulit impetus.

Et dixi mecum: "quid ante medium de extremis cog-
itas? Habet etas quelibet suos fines.

Videt ista Deus, sed irridet; facillimus erit ad veniam.
Converti poteris cum voles."

Nunc consuetudo pessima suum vindicat mancip-
ium, et vincit manus frustra reluctanti.

Quo fugiam non habeo, nam et ego vinctus sum, et
refugium meum longe est.

Moriar in peccatis meis, nisi auxilium michi veniat ex
alto.

Non merui, fateor; sed tu, Domine, miserere, et
extende manum tuam pereunti.

Et, memor, promissionum tuarum, eripe me de fau-
cibus inferni.

Gloria Patri et Filio et Spiritui Sancto. Sicut erat in
principio, et nunc, et semper, et in secula seculo-
rum. Amen.

48. If Maureen Quilligan is correct, such prominence of the letter *qua* letter might be a formal feature of narrative allegory itself. See *The Language of
Allegory: Defining the Genre* (Ithaca: Cornell UP, 1979).

49. Like *versatus sum, anfractus* here turns between abstract and concrete
meanings, foregrounding in the process the "languageness" of Petrarch's language. Literally denoting a "breaking around," and so a curving circuit or a
coiling (e.g., *solis anfractus,* the revolution of the sun), the word has a special-
ized rhetorical sense as well: *anfractus* signifies that roundabout circumlocu-
tion with which, like Petrarch, one beats around the (thorn) bush.

50. Famously, in the *Confessions* Augustine himself plays with words that
denote *turning.* But for Augustine such turns convey that directionality which
grants translation its redemptive force: we never get caught in the turns themselves. See, for instance, the way his quibbling at the end of book 4 charts a
narrative movement through its prefixes: "vivit apud te semper bonum nos-

trum, et quia inde *a*versi sumus, *per*versi sumus. *Re*vertamur iam, domine, ut non *e*vertamur" (*Conf.* 4.16). To turn against God is to be perverse, and ultimately overturned; the convert, however, always *returns.*

51. "Letter to Posterity" ("Posteritati"), *Seniles* [*Sen.*] 13.1, as in *Opere di Francesco Petrarca*, ed. Bigi, 972–87. English translation of the *Seniles* as found in *Letters of Old Age: Rerum senilium libri I–XVIII*, 2 vols. tr. and ed. Aldo S. Bernardo, Saul Levin, and Reta A. Bernardo (Baltimore: Johns Hopkins UP, 1992).

52. A notable exception is Charles Trinkaus, *In Our Image and Likeness: Humanity and Divinity in Italian Humanist Thought*, 2 vols. (London: Constable, 1970), esp. vol. 2, ch. 12 and 15: "Italian Humanism and the Scriptures" and "From *Theologia Poetica* to *Theologia Platonica.*"

Of course, many critics take note of Petrarch's Augustinianism—although typically they do so in order to stress his "thoroughgoing voluntarism" (Constable, "Petrarch and Monasticism," 83), i.e., his emphasis on the role of will in sin and salvation in contrast to a Thomistic stress on the intellect. Courcelle's study, "Pétrarque entre Saint Augustin et les Augustins du XIVe siecle," *Studi Petrarcheschi* 7 (1961): 51–71, remains a classic treatment, as does P. O. Kristeller's "Augustine and the Early Renaissance," in *Studies in Renaissance Thought and Letters* (Roma: Editiori di Storia e Letteratura, 1956).

53. See, for instance, Theodor M. Mommsen's argument in "Petrarch's Conception of the 'Dark Ages.'" In two quite different ways, both Marguerite Waller and Albert Ascoli suggest structural analogies and continuities between a Petrarchan conception of history and a medieval Christian conception. Cf. Albert Russell Ascoli, "Petrarch's Middle Age: Memory, Imagination, History, and the Ascent of Mount Ventoux," *Stanford Italian Review* 10, no. 1, *Perspectives on the Italian Renaissance*, ed. Marilyn Migiel, 5–43; Marguerite Waller, *Petrarch's Poetics and Literary History* (Amherst: U of Massachusetts P, 1980).

54. "Augustine filled his pockets and his lap with the gold and silver of the Egyptians when he was about to depart from Egypt. Destined to be the great fighter for the Church . . . he girded his loins with the weapons of the enemy," ("On His Own Ignorance," in *The Renaissance Philosophy of Man*, tr. Hans Nachod, ed. Ernst Cassirer, Paul Oskar Kristeller, and John Herman Randall Jr. [Chicago: U of Chicago P, 1948], 114–15). About Petrarch's use of the fathers to support the use of pagan texts, Francis X. Murphy writes: "In this he was a medieval man." Cf. Francis X. Murphy, C.SS.R., "Petrarch and the Christian Philosophy," *Francesco Petrarca, Citizen of the World*, 237.

55. See Carruthers, *The Book of Memory*, esp. 156–220.

56. Minnis's argument is compelling, but ultimately and intrinsically unsatisfying as a causal explanation of the shift in author-concept. At issue here is the chicken-egg problem that bedevils so much intellectual history: do

the prologues *cause* a shift in intellectual attitudes, or *reflect* that shift, or simultaneously cause *and* reflect? Without a theory of the historical relationship between ideas and material praxis/conditions, this question cannot be resolved–yet any such metahistorical theory will necessarily find its justification *elsewhere*, outside of the historical materials it examines. My response to this familiar dilemma: I define my own narrative as a "reading," rather than as a story about cause.

57. Ernest Hatch Wilkins, *Life of Petrarch* (Chicago: U of Chicago P, 1961), 51.

58. The critics whose arguments, for the sake of argument, I am somewhat caricaturing are, respectively, Thomas Greene, in *The Light in Troy,* 104 ff.; Michael O'Connell, "Authority and the Truth of Experience in Petrarch's 'Ascent of Mount Ventoux,'" *Philological Quarterly* 62, no. 4 (Fall 1983): 507–20; Robert M. Durling, "The Ascent of Mt. Ventoux and the Crisis of Allegory," *Italian Quarterly* 18, no. 69 (Summer 1974), 7–28; and Albert Russell Ascoli, "Petrarch's Middle Age: Memory, Imagination, History, and the 'Ascent of Mount Ventoux.'"

59. *Fam.* 4.1, Latin text as in *Opere di Francesco Petrarca*, ed. Bigi, Ponte, and Fraccassati, 730–42.

60. Since Pierre Courcelle's *Les Confessions de St. Augustin dans la tradition littéraire* (Paris: Études Augustiniennes, 1963), 329–52, and Guiseppe Billanovich's "Petrarca e il Ventoso," *Italia Medioevale e Umanistica* 9 (1966): 389–401, scholarly consensus has taken the "Ascent" as an artful and fictive document, written as much as fifteen years after its purported date, April 26, 1336, and perhaps a decade after the death of its purported addressee, Dionigi da Borgo San Sepolcro.

61. Teodolinda Barolini, "The Making of a Lyric Sequence: Time and Narrative in Petrarch's *Rerum vulgarium fragmenta,*" *MLN* 104, no. 1 (January 1989), 5.

62. C .S. Lewis's observation that Petrarch takes up Dante's example, but loses the prose, has proved irresistible to more than one generation of critic. See his *English Literature in the Sixteenth Century, Excluding Drama* (Oxford: Clarendon, 1954), 327. Roland Greene discusses Petrarchan narrativity and the impact of Dante in particular and Menippean satire in general on Petrarch in *Post-Petrarchism: Origins and Innovations of the Western Lyric Sequence* (Princeton: Princeton UP, 1991).

63. Paul Zumthor discusses the *Vita nuova* as the culmination of the *vida/razo* tradition in his "Autobiographie au moyen age?" in *Langue, texte, enigme* (Paris: Editions du Seuil, 1975), 173–78. For an interesting general account of the tradition, see Elizabeth Wilson Poe, *From Poetry to Prose in Old Provençal: The Emergence of the Vidas, the Razos, and the Razos de trobar* (Birmingham, Ala.: Summa, 1984).

64. The term is Gianfranco Contini's, proposed in his "Preliminari sulla

lingua del Petrarca," which serves as introduction to his edition of the *Canzoniere* (Torino: Einaudi, 1964). Barolini also cites Contini, 5 n. 10.

65. For Roland Greene, Petrarch's retrospective deixis recalls the elegiac mode of Augustan Rome's lyric poets. For us, such retrospectivity is not only inevitably and essentially figural, but, more specifically, it is tied to Augustine's understanding of a lyric scriptural discourse: i.e., the Davidic psalm. To Greene, however, who sees the lyric as essentially non-figural, moored in a here-and-now temporality, such use of deixis cuts against the genre, rendering it narrativistic; he thus compares Petrarch's use of deixis to a novel's ability to construct a narrative fiction.

66. This paradox of requiring a first-person utterance to close down the third-person totality of past sighs is simply another version of Russell's paradox. The *suono/sono* of *Rime* 1 is analogous to that "class of all classes that does not classify itself" with which Joel Fineman associates Shakespeare's *Will*. The kind of deconstructive subjectivity Fineman ascribes to Shakespeare is, I would maintain, more properly descriptive of the Petrarchan subject. (I elaborate this point further in chapter 4.)

67. See Robert Durling, "Petrarch's 'Giovene donna sotto un verde lauro,'" *MLN* 86, no. 1 (January 1971): 1–20. Durling points out that "Padre del ciel" is the first anniversary poem to follow "Giovene donna."

68. 1338 because "Padre del Ciel" commemorates the eleventh anniversary of the *innamoramento*, which, according to the note on Petrarch's flyleaf to Virgil and according to poem 211, occurred in 1327. Oddly enough, however, Petrarch seems to assume that April 6 is *always* Good Friday (see, for instance, poem 3); he fails to take into account that 7 is not an integral multiple of 365, or even of 366. The minimal effect of the passage of time, then, would be to disjoint the connection between the erotic year and the liturgical one. Each year the magical date, April 6, falls on the very next day of the week.

69. See John Freccero's famous remarks on this score in "The Fig Tree and the Laurel: Petrarch's Poetics," in *Literary Theory/Renaissance Texts*, ed. Patricia Parker and David Quint (Baltimore: Johns Hopkins UP, 1986), 32.

70. Surely the ambiguity of the word *allor* is not incidental here. At once "then" and "laurel," it is no accident that it marks the failure of retrospection by citing that name around which the poet's turns keep turning.

71. Durling includes and translates Dante's sestina "Al poco giorno" in his edition of the *Rime sparse*. See Durling, 617–18.

72. The claim is implicit in both Durling's and Freccero's accounts, but is most fully developed in Nancy Vicker's influential treatment "Diana Described: Scattered Woman and Scattered Rhyme," *Critical Inquiry* 8, no. 2 (Winter 1981): 265–79.

73. See his "Petrarch's 'Giovene donna,'" 12 ff.

3. LUTHER DISFIGURING THE WORD

1. *D. Martin Luthers Werke, Kritische Gesamtausgabe (Weimar, 1883–)*, 30[1], 133. All German and Latin references of Luther's work are from this edition (also known as the Weimar edition, or the "Weimar Ausgabe," WA). The Weimar edition of his table-talk will be designated in the text as WAT.

2. The language of Exodus itself is somewhat ambiguous, seeming to stress not so much God's absolute reality but his preeminence among all other deities. Luther's translation of the actual commandment in the opening of the *Grosse Katechismus* reflects such ambiguity: "Du solt kein andere Götter haben neben mir," You shall have no other gods beside me. The word *neben* carries the same instability as the English word "beside(s)": is the issue at hand spatial proximity or exclusivity? Characteristically, however, Luther glosses the commandment in terms of the latter issue; that is, in terms of an absolute dictate to love an absolute, and absolutely singular God.

3. Without viewing its articulation as deeply paradoxical or giving it the central position I do in Luther's work, Heinrich Bornkamm discusses Luther's reading of the First Commandment as a privileged moment in Luther's account of faith and the Law. Bornkamm thus describes the "unity of the First Commandment": "It requires me to believe God's affirmation and to recognize him alone as my God. Thus the promise is the reason for the commandment" (*Luther and the Old Testament*, tr. Eric W. and Ruth C. Gritsch [Philadelphia: Fortress Press, 1969], 166). Here, as elsewhere throughout this essay, I am deeply indebted to Bornkamm's classic, and still exceptional, analysis.

Jaroslav Pelikan—whose work is also influenced by Bornkamm—views the First Commandment as the best example of Luther's vision of the double-sided word of God: the same word can both console and damn. The First Commandment is the most threatening statement ever made because it denounces all idolatry but also enunciates the doctrine of justification by faith alone because it puts God uppermost. *Luther the Expositor: Introduction to the Reformer's Exegetical Writings. Luther's Works*, American ed. (hereafter cited as LW), companion volume (St. Louis: Concordia Publishing House, 1959), 65–66.

4. See Erik Erikson's classic discussion of Luther's ambivalence in *Young Man Luther: A Study in Psychoanalysis and History* (New York: Norton, 1962 [1958], esp. 163 ff. According to Erikson, such ambivalence is produced by the absolutist demand—as Luther understands it—to love wholeheartedly. However, because Erikson relegates the ambivalence to psychosocial forces, he underplays its theological coherence and importance.

5. 1535 Commentary on Galatians, *Luther's Works*, American ed. (Philadelphia and St. Louis, 1955–), 27:73, 75.

6. *Martin Luther on the Bondage of the Will*, tr. James I. Packer and O. R. Johnson (Grand Rapids, Mich.: James Clarke, 1957), 103.

7. The insight cuts both ways: God's grace is also, and by definition, a free gift that cannot be earned or compelled. Luther's doctrine of justification by faith alone entails the necessity of grace: we can no more fulfill the Law than we can earn our own salvation.

8. *De Baptismo* 5: "semper carnalia in figuram spiritalium antecedunt." Cited in Auerbach, "Figura," 33.

9. Nonetheless, an anti-figural stance is of course central to Protestantism in all its forms, from Tyndale's critique of the fourfold method of scriptural exegesis in his *Obedience of a Christian Man*, to a seventeenth-century Puritan typological millenarianism, which tries to salvage one strand of *figura*–its insistence on an imitative, prophetic reading–while nonetheless rejecting the tropological basis of such hermeneutics.

10. I refer here to Kant's famous dictum in the *Critique of Pure Reason* that thoughts without intuitions are empty and intuitions without thoughts are blind.

11. For a discussion of Luther's conception of conversion, as developed in the critical early years beginning with the *Dictata Super Psalterium* (1513–1515), see Marilyn J. Harran, *Luther on Conversion: The Early Years* (Ithaca, N.Y.: Cornell UP, 1983). Harran is most interested in the subject of man's role in his own conversion: to what extent, as Luther sees it, is conversion within our power, and to what extent are we reliant on God's grace? As she notes, Luther is equivocal on this point, at times even suggesting that conversion consists solely in the recognition that we are sinners before God and incapable of any good work (cf. 57–59).

12. I am indebted to Richard Strier, who first helped me recognize the importance of Luther's redefinition of the flesh.

13. Our constitutive inadequacy to respond to God's word–to fulfill even the least of His commandments–underlies, I take it, the formulation that "whatever does not proceed from faith is sin." Luther will not rule out the possibility of *das gute Werk*, of a deed that is sinless insofar as it proceeds directly from God's grace acting within us. Indeed, faith is itself the greatest and most difficult of such good works, Luther will tell us, because it is the work of God alone acting in us, while all other works He effects through us and by us. Nonetheless, as the conception of *faith as work* itself suggests, our works are "good" only insofar as they serve as responses to God's call–to His infinite demand in the First Commandment that we obey Him; that we fulfill His Law with our love. Thus, when Luther argues in the 1520 sermon "Von den guten Werken" that good works are whatever God has commanded, while sin is whatever He has forbidden–we must remember that every attempt on our part to fulfill God's commandment will also amount to rebellion: failing to obey Him completely, *von hertzen*, our obedience is itself witness to disobedience.

14. Allen and Greenough usefully explain this "unstable" (their term) objective usage of the genitive: "This usage is an extension of the idea of

belonging to (Possessive Genitive). Thus in the phrase **odium Caesaris,** *hate of Caesar,* the hate in a passive sense *belongs* to Caesar, as *odium,* though in its active sense he is the *object* of it, as *hate*" (*Allen and Greenough's New Latin Grammar,* ed. J. B. Greenough et al. [reprint, New Rochelle, N.Y.: Aristide D. Caratzas, 1983], 348). Analogously, the *reliquae* do not *belong* passively to sin, but rather, in an active sense, these remnants are directed toward and definitive of sin itself. Instead of being the *subject* that possesses fragments, sin is itself the *object* of fragmentation.

15. Here Luther cites Augustine, who has also discussed the tame olive's failure to produce, of its own nature, other tame olives. See Augustine, *Ad Valerium de nuptiis et concupiscentis* 1.19 (Patrologia Cursus Completus [hereafter cited as PL 44, 426]). But where Luther foregrounds the *olea*'s unnatural sterility—its inability "of nature" to reproduce itself—Augustine highlights the organic link between roots and branches. For Augustine, the cultivated olive is indeed fertile, "fruitful in its root of the holy patriarchs" (*Adversos Iudaeos* 1.1). It is this natural fertility that the ingrafted Gentile branches disrupt. Thus Augustine's olive tree, unlike Luther's but like Paul's, still signifies the essential difference between fleshly (*secundum carnem*) and spiritual (*per repromissionem*) succession.

16. Luther discusses his breakthrough discovery—often referred to as the *Turm Erlebniss* (the Tower experience)—in the autobiography that appeared as the preface to the first edition of his Latin works (cf. WA 54). Many critics still accept Erich Vogelsang's argument that this breakthrough can be tracked as far back as Luther's 1513–1515 lectures on the Psalms. See Erich Vogelsang, *Die Anfänge von Luthers Christologie, Arbeiten zur Kirschengeschichte,* vol. 15 (1929). Roland Bainton's account of Luther's Reformation discovery is still valuable, but cannot compare to Heiko Oberman's superbly sensitive and lucid reading. See Heiko A. Oberman, *Luther: Man Between God and the Devil,* tr. Eilenn Walliser-Scwarzbart (New York: Doubleday, 1982), 151–74; and Roland H. Bainton, *Here I Stand: A Life of Martin Luther* (New York: New American Library, 1950), 48–50.

17. Luther's rejection of an essential difference between Old Testament Judaism and New Testament Christianity is, for him, not inconsistent with the pogroms he proposes in a late treatise like the 1543 "Of the Jews and their Lies" or the 1545 "Admonition Against the Jews." (I will discuss this point at much greater length in my reading of *The Merchant of Venice* in chapter 5.) In the opening pages of *Luther and the Old Testament,* Heinrich Bornkamm notes that "Luther refused to let his judgment of the Jews in his day confuse him in his conviction of the incomparable particularity of the history of the Old Testament people of God" (6). In other words, Luther's contempt for contemporary Jews—the cursed enemies of God—did not blind him to the workings of Christ in the sacred history of the sons of Abraham. The subject is not an incidental one for Bornkamm, even if his tone in this characteristically

oblique reference to anti-Semitism is mild to the point of indecipherability. As Bornkamm notes in his preface, the monograph's appearance was delayed until 1948 because the Nazi office of censorship, the Reichsschriftumskammer, refused its publication.

18. Luther's views on the question of the visible church are unique among those of the major reformers. As Heiko Oberman points out, Luther rejects the notion shared by the reform movements in Switzerland, in southern Germany, and with Calvin, that a militant church can become triumphant in this world. For Luther, the history of the Church is a history of the devil's persecution; against the devil's attacks, his Church is not triumphant but defenseless, eking out its survival only thanks to state protection. At the same time, however, in his 1530 *Grosser Katechismus* and elsewhere, Luther defines the Church as the communion of saints. His Church is a visible one—albeit one constantly threatened with corruption and dissolution, unable ever simply to embody God's kingdom on earth. See Oberman, *Luther*, 246–50, 270, 301–2. For a slightly different point of view, one that emphasizes Luther's attack not on the notion of militancy but rather on the equally problematic belief in an entirely personal revelation, see Jaroslav Pelikan's account in *Luther the Expositor*, 106–8. Pelikan cites Luther on the importance of ministry and ceremonies in the long history of faith: "God always establishes some outward and visible sign of His grace alongside the Word. . . . an outward sign and work or sacrament. . . . Thus the church has never been without outward signs" (WA 42, 184; quoted in Pelikan, 106). Ultimately, Luther's Church is an ambivalent union of visibility and disembodiment. Coextensive with its earthly institution, the Church nonetheless fails to embody God's Word. As a communion of saints, it is also a communion of sinners who daily fight the battle to live in the Spirit—a battle that is not ours to win in this life but that nonetheless is always ours to lose.

19. "That These Words of Christ, 'This Is My Body,' etc., Still Stand Firm Against the Fanatics," tr. Robert H. Fischer, LW 37, 147.

20. In the 1536 Wittenberg Concord, a settlement was reached between the Lutheran estates and Southern Germany (including Bucer's Strassburg) on the subject of the Eucharist, but it has taken until our day for Bucer's dreams of a larger union of reformed churches to be fulfilled. On August 18, 1997, an overwhelming majority of the Churchwide Assembly of the Evangelical Lutheran Church in America voted in favor of a unity plan with the U.S. Reformed Churches, including the Presbyterian Church, the United Church of Christ, and the Reformed Church in America.

Of Martin Bucer's unrealistic hopes for union between Lutheran and Reformed churches in his own time, Herman Sasse writes, "There was and there is no middle road between the 'est' and the 'significat' [i.e., between literal and figurative readings of the words of institution: "Hoc *est* corpus meum" (Luke 22:19)]. Not to have seen this in time and to have overestimated his ability to reconcile views which are irreconcilable–this was the tragedy of Bucer." See Herman Sasse, *This Is My Body: Luther's Contention for the Real Presence in the Sacrament of the Altar* (Minneapolis: Augsburg, 1959), 310–11.

21. See Fischer's discussion of Bucer's Eucharist views and translation of the *Postil*, LW 37, 147–48 nn. 256–59.

22. Suffering from physical constipation throughout his life and criticized, from his own day to the present, for the frequent scatological outbursts in his writing, Luther oscillated between anal retentiveness and an equally compulsive anal explosivity, a characteristic that has especially fascinated post-Freudian readers. Erik Erikson (*Young Man Luther*) and Norman O. Brown (*Life Against Death* [New York: Vintage Books, 1959]) have most famously focused on the psychohistorical dimensions of Luther's scatology. Erikson, in particular, reminds us that scholars have not adequately accounted for the 1532 fragment of Luther's table-talk in which the theologian asserts that his pivotal "Tower Experience" took place in the privy: "Diese Kunst hatt mir der Spiritus Sanctus auff diss Cl. [i.e., Cloaca] eingeben" (Erikson, 204–5).

Heiko Oberman and Stephen Greenblatt offer alternative views of Luther's scatology. Oberman points out the precise rhetorical function of Luther's scatology as a means to combat the devil, in this manner arguing against readers who either would condemn Luther for his "coarseness" or pyschoanalyze him for his pathology. See Oberman, "Teufelsdreck: Eschatology and Scatology in the 'Old' Luther," *Sixteenth Century Journal* 19, no. 3 (Fall 1988): 435–50. Greenblatt links Luther's scatology to the early-modern civilizing process detailed by Norbert Elias, as well as to the development of a uniquely Protestant notion of the individual. "The festive excess, the mingled degradation and exuberance" (11) of an earlier carnivalesque has been transformed into a doctrine of supreme self-hatred and paradoxical self-importance. See Greenblatt, "Filthy Rites," *Daedalus* 111 (Summer 1982): 1–16.

23. See Kevin Dunn's discussion of this point in a different context: *Pretexts of Authority: The Rhetoric of Authorship in the Renaissance Preface* (Stanford, Calif.: Stanford UP, 1994), 30.

24. *De Libero Arbitrio* 2.16.43, as translated by Dom Mark Pontifex, in *The Problem of Free Choice* (New York: Newman Press, 1955).

25. The influence of humanism on the Protestant Reformation–and particularly on the philologically minded reformist doctrine of *sola scriptura*–has been too broadly studied to offer a complete bibliography here; many of the more salient points have been usefully summarized by Alister McGrath in *The Intellectual Origins of the European Reformation* (Oxford: Basil Blackwell, 1987). H. Junghans discusses in particular the impact of humanism on Luther's early thought in "Der Einfluss des Humanismus auf Luthers Entwicklung bis 1518," *Luther-Jahrbuch* 37 (1970): 37–101. On the subject of nominalism and human-

ism at Erfurt, see Oberman, *Luther*, 116 ff., and W. Urban, "Die 'via moderna' an der Universität Erfurt am Vorabend der Reformation," *in Gregor von Rimini: Werk und Wirkung bis zur Reformation*, ed. H. A. Oberman (Berlin: De Gruyter, 1981), 311–30. Luther himself was wont to characterize his treatment of texts as "terminist" or nominalist, considering himself a follower of William of Ockham. In a frequently cited fragment from his table-talk, he declares the necessity of interpreting an author *in suis terminis*–according to the usage appropriate to that author's station and context. Otherwise, he declares, one "tortures" [*martert*] the text. See his *Tischrede*, *WAT* 5, no. 6419.

26. Note that the idea of following an example without setting one serves, for Kevin Dunn, to characterize not Petrarch but Luther, whose "posthumanist" model of authorship invokes the "flipside of *imitatio* theory": the effort to create a discursive space and seal it off from potential imitators (33). As Dunn puts it: "Luther wants to roll up the road to Damascus behind him" (50). Dunn's account of Lutheran authorship is compelling, but misleading. As I've tried to suggest, this flipside of *imitatio* is intrinsic to the humanist view of authorship from the start, bespeaking the pathos that Petrarch uncovers in a traditional Augustinian model of imitation. If Luther also seems to cast his life as inimitable example, we must recall that his doctrine of justification by faith alone constitutes a radical rejection of the very idea of imitation. Luther, as Paul's imitative successor, "rolls up the road to Damascus" by shattering the notion of succession itself. (For a discussion of Paul's own efforts to create an "inimitable authority" in 2 Corinthians, see Dunn, 38–40. Ultimately for Dunn, Luther's posthumanist model of authority is simply a further, unproblematic delineation of the Pauline model.)

27. My terms here recall Derrida's critique of Hegel through Bataille, where a "restricted economy" that redeems loss in the dialectical movement of *aufheben* finds its undoing in the "general economy" that posits absolute expenditure. See "From Restricted to General Economy: A Hegelianism Without Reserve," in *Writing and Difference*, tr. Alan Bass (London: Routledge and Kegan Paul, 1978), 251–77. I am also indebted to private conversation with Brian Manning Delaney, whose reading of Nietzsche's "eternal return" as a "circular dialectic"–a dialectic that disrupts the tropes of *aufheben*–might similarly characterize the negations at play in Luther's anti-figuralism.

28. See Bornkamm's discussion of this fragment (149), and his treatment of Luther's twofold understanding of Moses and the Mosaic Law. Bornkamm's account is deeply persuasive; however, it tends to domesticate Luther, reconciling his views to a stable figural narrative, where I would emphasize radical elements of ambivalence and incommensurability and connect Luther's opposition of Law and Gospel to the antagonism of flesh and spirit.

29. For Luther's account of his appearance at Worms, see WA 7 and LW 32. Kevin Dunn offers a compelling reading of the inconsistencies in this published account argument in *Pretexts of Authority*, 27–30.

30. Arthur J. Dewey offers an intelligent discussion of the theology of letter/spirit in *Spirit and Letter in Paul,* Studies in the Bible and Early Christianity, vol. 33 (Lewiston/Queenstown/Lampeter: Edwin Mellen Press, 1996). For the most part, Dewey seeks to illuminate the eschatological and social dimensions of Paul's opposition, and to entirely debunk an Origenist, spiritualizing view. For his brief historical overview of Origen and later theologians, see xii–xiii.

31. Heinrich Bornkamm, however, suggests that "Luther killed the four senses of Scripture at the moment he applied them" because he understood the "literal" sense in prophetic, christocentric terms, rather than in the historical-factual terms familiar since the early Church fathers (88). Yet, on the other hand, Wolfgang Schwab points out that Luther follows the precedent of late scholastic hermeneutics in this respect. See Schwab, *Entwicklung und Gestalt der Sakramentheologie bei Martin Luther* (Frankfurt: Verlag Peter Lang, 1977), 15–16.

32. Karl Holl also discusses this point, arguing that Luther's work corrects centuries of error by rejecting the connection between spiritual understanding and allegoresis. See Bornkamm's discussion of Holl's reading in *Luther and the Old Testament,* 89.

33. Luther consistently—both in the 1519 commentary on Galatians and elsewhere—singles Origen and Jerome out as the key proponents of a spiritualist interpretation of the Bible. Luther almost always considers Augustine as free from such reproach. However, as I have tried to suggest in chapter 1, Augustine's actual views on the subject of allegory were not at odds with an Origenist allegory but only systematized that exegesis into a coherent worldview—a view with far-reaching implications for and assumptions about not only texts but the nature of the human soul and human history.

34. Luther's concerns here echo, in certain ways, Augustine's (or Tertullian's) response to those like Faustus (or Marcion) who deny the Christian relevance of Jewish scripture. For Augustine and Tertullian, however, the crucial issue is the unity of the Bible and the way such unity endows Christianity with scriptural authority. For Luther, on the other hand, the Word of God is decisively *not* unified, but instead riven in two. Nonetheless, the ongoing persistence of faith in the face of this rift is an important message of consolation that is easily lost unless we hold on to the history recounted within the Old Testament.

35. A concern with such contingency is precisely what Paul is after when he formulates the notion that the Law is spiritual in Romans 7. There he considers the plight of fallen man, who is now unable to follow the commandments of God because his flesh contends with his spiritual self. Augustine follows Paul almost verbatim in *De Spiritu et Littera* when he writes that "we know that the law is spiritual; but I am carnal, sold under sin. For that which I work, I know not; for what I would, that do I not, but what I hate, that I do"

(25). See *The Spirit and the Letter*, in *Augustine: Later Works*, ed. John Burnaby (Philadelphia: Westminister Press, 1950), 215. Both Augustine and Paul imagine a straightforward or "clean" dualism between flesh and spirit, where the sinner is unable, despite himself, to follow the dictates of conscience. Such a sinner sins, as it were, against his will: the spirit is willing, but the flesh is weak. However, for Luther, once again, the dualism between flesh and spirit is no longer straightforward: we do not sin despite ourselves, but rather as fully willing, complicitous agents. (I discuss these topics at greater length in chapter 4 and especially chapter 5.)

36. Hence Luther glosses the Galatians 4 distinction between the progeny of Hagar—an enslaved people—and the legacy of the free wife, Sarah: to be bound by the Law is to receive it without grace, "for then we keep it either out of fear of threatened evil or out of hope of gain, that is, hypocritically" (LW 27, 314). To receive the Law without grace is to receive it without that spiritual understanding of its office. In itself, the spiritual Law serves precisely to liberate us by revealing the insufficiency of our works. Interestingly, Luther cites Augustine as his authority for the notion of the letter as the Law in the absence of grace (see LW 27, 312).

37. Although scholasticism, with its complex theology of merit, had considered the problem of a good work lacking in love long before Luther, nonetheless Luther's insistence on the utter worthlessness of such "good" works marks his radical departure from tradition. Indeed, it could be argued that Luther's insight into the nature of the Law was too novel to be thoroughly and rigorously assimilated in his own time. One does not find as probing an analysis of law until the Enlightenment and the rise of liberalism. I'm thinking here particularly of Kant, for whom the problem of the Law—of the possibility of freedom under constraint—serves as the starting point in the task to ground human knowledge transcendentally (that is, by recourse not to empirical contingency but rather to man's "free conformity" to the self-willed norms of thought). In *The Critique of Practical Reason*, Kant turns specifically to the problem of the moral law, and argues that the heteronomous conformity to an external rule cannot constitute a moral stance. Instead, Kant famously proposes the Categorical Imperative: at its base, the imperative that we act as if our actions were the product of a self-willed legislation, and thus were capable of universal application. In general, it could be argued that Kant's "transcendental idealism" replaces a Lutheran notion of grace with the self-reflecting work of philosophical critique.

38. Here Luther marks his distance from scholasticism in two distinct ways. In the first and most obvious sense he is rejecting a principle of merit—in particular the idea of *meritum de congruo*. According to this principle of congruent merit, we can render ourselves fit through the exercise of our free will for the gift of grace, which will save us. In this small measure, then, we can through our actions help affect our salvation. But Luther goes further by

rejecting the late scholastic notion of the efficacy of doing *quod in se est*–of doing one's very best. Luther's treatment of the Law would suggest that, rather than render us more fit for God's grace, the effort to earn salvation by doing all that we can, all that is in us, can only render us *less* fit: the more we strive for holiness, the more hate we engender against God's Word.

39. In his early writings Luther sounds a more optimistic note about regenerate man's ability to fulfill the Law. In editions of the Pentateuch before 1534, Luther claims that "through the grace of Christ the heart has now become good, loving the law and satisfying it." In the 1534 complete Bible edition and in later editions, however, he replaces this line with the more measured claim that "through Christ sin is forgiven, God is reconciled, and man's heart has begun to feel kindly toward the law." See LW 35, 244, n. 17.

40. As cited in Bainton, 228. Bainton sums up Luther's sentiment here neatly: "The very recognition that we are sinners is an act of faith."

41. In his 1530 *Grosser Katechismus*, Luther even renders this teaching catechetical doctrine. See Oberman's discussion of this point in *Luther: Man Between God and the Devil*, 176.

42. Cited in Bainton, 218. For Bainton, Luther's focus upon a God who works by contraries, damning where He means to save, reveals the "medieval" cast of the reformer's thought. What Bainton seems to miss, however, is how Luther's sense of a necessary ambivalence at the heart of Christian life utterly transforms a medieval understanding of the relationship between flesh and spirit.

43. Richard Strier helpfully discusses Luther's rejection of a Platonist "shell/kernel" thinking in his essay "Martin Luther and the Real Presence in Nature," *Graven Images* 1 (1994): 64.

44. Karl Holl (1866–1926) is the modern theologian most responsible for this interest in Luther's "totus homo"; see the first volume of his *Gesammelte Aufsätze zur Kirchengeschichte*, which has been recently translated: *What Did Luther Understand by Religion?*, ed. James Luther Adams and Walter F. Bense, tr. Fred W. Meuser and Walter R. Wietzke (Philadelphia: Fortress Press, 1977). Richard Strier's essay "Martin Luther and the Real Presence in Nature" alerted me to Holl's importance. See Strier's discussion of both Holl and the "whole man," 55.

45. Carl C. Christensen, *Art and the Reformation in Germany* (Athens: Ohio UP, 1979), 61–62.

46. Richard Strier has very lucidly described a humanist "*Phaedo*" tradition of transcending the flesh, which he tracks to Karlstadt and the Swiss reformers through Augustine and, especially, Erasmus ("Martin Luther and the Real Presence" 56 ff.). Strier's reading builds on Herman Sasse's classic account of Zwingli in *This Is My Body*, esp. 116–30. E. J. Devereux usefully documents the impact of Erasmus on, especially, the Henrician Reformation

in "Tudor Uses of Erasmus on the Eucharist," *Archiv für Reformationsgeschichte* 62 (1971): 38–52.

47. Christensen follows Ronald Sider in asserting Karlstadt's constant reference to John 6:63 (*Art and the Reformation*, 26–27). See also Sider, *Andreas Bodenstein von Karlstadt: The Development of His Thought, 1517–1525* (Leiden: Brill, 1974). See also Pelikan's characteristically intelligent discussion of the biblical verse, of its centrality in the sacramentarian controversies of the 1520s, and of Luther's reaction to it in the treatise "That these words" in *Luther the Expositor.*

48. Christensen uses this phrase in his discussion of Karlstadt, who, he argues, began polemicizing under the influence of Erasmian humanism as early as 1518 (*Art and the Reformation*, 26).

49. Strier, "Martin Luther and the Real Presence," 55. Strier is borrowing C. S. Lewis's phrase (in *Literature of the Sixteenth Century Excluding Shakespeare*) for William Tyndale's worldview.

50. Recall Augustine's words, cited earlier in this chapter: "These things [of the world] give way so that other things may take their places and the whole be preserved in all its parts" (*Conf.* 4.11).

51. Cited in John Phillips, *The Reformation of Images: Destruction of Art in England, 1535–1660* (Berkeley: U of California P, 1973), 39.

52. "Handbook of the Christian Soldier," as in Erika Rummel, ed., *The Erasmus Reader* (Toronto: U of Toronto P, 1990), 154.

53. Augustine evokes this Platonic dialectic of distraction and ascesis in characteristically sensuous terms, in his gloss of Wisdom 6:17: "Wherever you turn she [God's Wisdom] speaks to you by means of the traces she has left on her works, and calls you back within, when you are slipping away into outward things, through the very forms of these outward things" (*De Libero Arbtrio* 2.16.41).

54. See Christensen, *Art and the Reformation*, 23 ff., for a discussion of the charged events of 1522. Luther's initial response came in the form of sermons; his written treatise against Karlstadt ("Against the Heavenly Prophets")–emerged some two years later, 1524–1525, at the start of the Eucharistic controversy.

55. I am indebted here to Phillips's astute reading of this controversy and his discussion of the Thomastic epistemology it informs: "It is natural to man to reach the intelligibilia through the sensibilia because all our knowledge has its beginning in sense" (*Summa Theologica* I.Iq.1,a.9). See *Reformation of Images*, 11–15.

56. Heiko Oberman offers the best reading of Luther's reactionary politics I've seen to date. In *Luther: Man Between God and the Devil*, Oberman considers Luther's support of secular authority, intolerance toward other religions and sectarians, violent objections to Münzer and the Peasant Revolt, et cetera, as symptoms of a man believing himself on the brink of the Second

Coming. In these Last Days, the world was bound to be a chaotic place, given over to Satan. Amid such disarray, every Christian would need to fight to preserve order—if only to preserve God's Word and His Church until the very end (see esp. 289–93).

57. See Christensen, *Art and the Reformation*, 53–54. According to him, Calvin's later practice takes the injunction as the Second Commandment and thus strengthens the case for iconoclasm vis-à-vis all representations.

58. Of course, it is just such "vertrawen" that marks both Gott and Abgott, God and idol. To return to the *Grosse Katechismus* and its gloss of the First Commandment: "alleine das trawen und gleuben des hertzens machet beide Gott und abeGott. Ist der glaube und vertrawen recht, so ist auch dein Gott recht, und wideruemb wo das vertrawen falsch und unrecht ist, da ist auch der rechte Gott nicht. . . . Worauff du nu (sage ich) dein hertz hengest und verlessest, das ist eygentlich dein Gott" (WA 30^I, 133)

59. Quoted in Herman Sasse's excellent overview of Luther's role in the Eucharist controversies, *This Is My Body*, 146.

60. Karlstadt, Oecolampadius, and Zwingli were all alike influenced by the 1521 treatise of Dutch humanist Cornelis Hoen—a treatise that followed in the tradition of earlier critiques of the Eucharist (e.g., Wyclif's), but was first to introduce the sixteenth century to a purely figurative understanding of the words of institution. Nonetheless, each theologian interpreted Hoen's thesis in a slightly different way. Oecolampadius, for instance, pointed out that in the Aramaic that Jesus would have spoken, there is no copula. The trope would have rested upon the meaning of "corpus" and not on the interpretation of "est."

For Luther's own account of the differences among Karlstadt's, Oecolampadius's, and Zwingli's readings of "Hoc est," see LW 37, 41. See also Sasse's discussion of the Hoen letter (*This Is My Body*, 122–25); the medieval background of such figurative readings (13–77); and Zwingli's and Oecolampadius's accounts (116–33, 140–41).

61. Christ's discourse in John 6 took place at the synagogue at Capernaum (see John 6:24). "He that eateth my flesh, and drinketh my blood, dwelleth in me, and I in him" (John 6:56, KJV). In the sixteenth century, the reformers use the term "Capernaite" as a term of abuse for believers in transubstantiation.

62. One of Luther's most persuasive points in his attack on the Reformed Eucharistic doctrine is his assertion that, far from expressing celestial piety, the spiritualism of the Swiss derives ultimately from an excessively *carnal* vision. The motor driving their rejection of the Real Presence, Luther argues, is not their spirituality but instead their childlike literalism and inability to grasp spiritual truths: "I suppose they will dream up for us, as one does for the children, an imaginary heaven in which a golden throne stands, and Christ sits beside the Father in a cowl and golden crown, the way artists paint it. For

if they did not have such childish, fleshly ideas. . . . they surely would not allow the idea of Christ's bodily presence in the Supper to vex them so" (LW 37, 55). In this way, their spiritualism doesn't merely culminate in a fleshly-mindedness: it *emerges* from it.

63. Ultimately banished from Saxony because of his Eucharistic views, Karlstadt nonetheless found a safe haven in Switzerland, becoming a professor of theology in Basel. But Thomas Münzer "drowned in the flesh" in more ways than one. A radical in both his religious views and his politics, Münzer participated briefly in the Peasants' War (1524–1526) and was executed in 1525, after the collapse of the movement in Germany.

64. English translation from "The Pagan Servitude of the Church" [more commonly translated as "The Babylonian Captivity"], tr. Bertram Lee, in *Martin Luther: Selections from His Writings*, ed. John Dillenberger (New York: Doubleday, 1962), 274.

65. For the language of Christ's body and blood as "Sigill und Pfandt" see WA 8, 516. Robert C. Croken, S.J., discusses this seal and pledge in the context of Luther's theology of testament, and his rejection of the Mass as sacrifice. See Croken, *Luther's First Front: The Eucharist as Sacrifice* (Ottawa: U of Ottawa P, 1990), 33–34.

66. The "Babylonian Captivity" is often regarded as the irrevocable turning point in Luther's opposition to Rome. Written in Latin, it had an audience that was primarily clerical. Its figural title equated the papacy to Babylon, and the Jews' captivity in a foreign land to the Christians' removal from Scripture. In a letter discussing the treatise, Erasmus wrote that Luther's breach with Rome was now irreparable. See Bainton's discussion, *Here I Stand*, 137–40. For a fuller account not only of "The Babylonian Captivity" but also of Luther's attack on traditional sacramental theology in general, particularly with regard to the Lord's Supper, see Croken, *Luther's First Front*.

67. Ralph W. Quere, "Changes and Constants: Structure in Luther's Understanding of the Real Presence in the 1520's," *Sixteenth Century Journal* 16, no. 1 (1985): 45–78. Quere distinguishes "significationist" approaches–which he traces back to the neoplatonic formulations of Saint Augustine–from "transformationist" accounts like Ambrose of Milan's and the Fourth Lateran Council's doctrine of transubstantiation. Where significationists present the bread and wine, for instance, as signs signifying the crucified body of the risen Lord, transformationists see the bread and wine as having actually become that body (46). For Quere, Luther's own developing theology of sacrament begins with the significationist language of *signum* and *res*, but ultimately dismantles it via the insistence on the sacramental presence of Christ.

68. Aquinas's view of the Mass as sacrifice was a doctrine reaffirmed at the Council of Trent. Aquinas: "This sacrament is both a sacrifice and a sacrament; it has the nature of a sacrifice inasmuch as it is offered up; and it has

the nature of a sacrament inasmuch as it is received. And therefore it has the effect of a sacrament in the recipient, and the effect of a sacrifice in the offerer, or in them for whom it is offered." (Summa III. q.79, a.5; quoted in Croken, 91). For two excellent contemporary discussions of this doctrine, see Croken, *Luther's First Front*, and Ferdinand Pratzner, *Messe und Kreuzesopfer: Die Krise der sakramentalen Idee bei Luther und in der mittelalterlichen Scholastik* (Vienna: Verlag Herder, 1970). Both Croken (a Jesuit) and Pratzner adopt an apologist note, arguing that Luther radically misreads the traditional doctrine of sacrifice when he rejects that doctrine in the 1520s.

69. See Quere's cogent discussion of Zwingli's significationism, 57–64.

70. For a discussion of the evolution of Luther's concept of faith as hearing the word, see Kenneth Hagen, *A Theology of Testament in the Young Luther: The Lectures on Hebrews* (Leiden: Brill, 1974). Hagen follows Adolf Hammel's thesis that Luther first adopts the notion of a clinging to the Word of God–an *adhaesio verbo dei* (Ps. 73:28)–in his 1517–1518 Lectures on Hebrews. See Hagen, 11.

71. Compare this formulation to the one that Zwingli adopts from Cornelis Hoen's treatise on the Lord's Supper: the Eucharist is in essence a visible reminder to trust Christ's promise, just as a ring is a pledge from bridegroom to bride (cf. LW 37, xii). Where Luther would see the acceptance, and offering, of the pledge as itself constitutive of faith, for Hoen and Zwingli these material acts–like the ring itself–are merely prompts to a faith that is *elsewhere*. In itself, for Hoen and Zwingli, the giving and getting of the ring means nothing–a formulation with grave consequences for marital fidelity, as both J. L. Austin and Shakespeare's Portia would suggest.

72. Given the one experience of faith, common to patriarchs and Christians alike, it would seem that Luther makes no sharp distinction between the Old and the New Testaments–whether by these terms we mean two separate covenants or two separate books. "There is only one God who does not permit himself to be divided, praised at one place and chided at another, glorified in one word and scorned in another" (LW 37, 26). But as Heinrich Bornkamm points out, as often as Luther asserts the continuity or unity of the Old and New Testaments, he also insists on the difference between the two (cf. 86). In his "Preface to the Old Testament" he distinguishes between the two covenants, arguing that the Old Testament "did not stand upon God's grace, but upon men's works, [and thus] it had to become obsolete and cease" (LW 35, 246). Based in Law, the old covenant was annulled by the new covenant based in the promise of Gospel. And yet, every book of the Bible, whether a part of the Old or the New Testament, contains both law and promise: "There is no book in the Bible that does not contain both. God has placed them side by side in every way–law and promise" (*Postil*, WA 10$^{1.2}$, 159; quoted in Bornkamm, 83). God's Word is irrevocably double-sided, simultaneously damning and con-

soling. Any ability to differentiate between two historical covenants or epochs, any ability to recount a narrative of the Old succeeded by the New, is immediately undercut by the office of the Law according to which judgment reveals salvation, Law reveals Gospel.

73. Again, it is my contention—as I've argued in chapter 1—that a clear, sharp distinction between a so-called typological mode of reading and Origenist allegory was simply not available either for the Church fathers or for the sixteenth century. Luther's insistence upon the text's *historical* dimension does not line up neatly with a distinction between "literal" meaning and "figurative" meaning as we would today understand those terms. Instead, Luther is concerned to avoid rationalizing readings of any sort that would seek to render God's Word human-sized and thereby annihilate history *as* the history of that Word.

Thus, Luther relied on allegory—both a typological christology and a looser spiritualist allegoresis—in his own biblical interpretations throughout his life. He did, however, become more cautious after 1525. Bornkamm follows Gerhard Ebeling in arguing that the turning point for Luther vis-à-vis allegory was his struggle over biblical interpretations with the *Schwärmer* (Bornkamm, 94).

74. Here I follow Heiko Oberman's account of an "alien" faith or word in Luther. As Oberman points out, for Luther, the devil is "that master of subjectivity," exploiting our sense of self-reliance and sapping our confidence by leading us to self-doubt. In our fight against the devil, it is important that God is present—that the sacraments are external, "alien," not merely symbols (*Luther: Man Between God and the Devil*, 227). Oberman cites Luther: "'The Prince of Demons himself has taken up combat against me; so powerfully and adeptly does he handle the Scriptures that my scriptural knowledge does not suffice if I do not rely on the *alien Word*'" (226, emphasis mine).

75. In a sense the Eucharist, as Luther sees it, is the sacrament of sacrament. The Real Presence is a paradigm instance of sacramental unity itself. In other words, in the Eucharist God's Word becomes flesh in two ways: on the one hand, the physical eating and drinking of the sacrament allows us to cling to Christ's covenant with us. Thanks to the sacramental sign, we lay hold of the *verbum* of God. At the same time, what is physically consumed is itself the Word Made Flesh: Christ's presence in the bread and wine is another more fundamental instance of the unity of *verbum* and *signum*.

76. Catachresis, or *abusio*, as the Latin rhetors called it, is often defined by modern readers as implied or mixed metaphor. Such definitions, however, miss the structural necessity of this "abuse"; for Quintilian catachresis is *necessaria* as a way of generating neologisms within an all too impoverished Latin. Quintilian defines the figure as crucial when "non habentibus nomen suum accommodat quod in proximo est": lacking a proper name, we adapt

the nearest possible term. It is just this sort of *necessary* transfer of signification that informs Shakespeare's poetics, as we shall see at greater length in the next chapter. (See Quintilian, *Institutio Oratoria* 8.6.34, tr. H. E. Butler [Cambridge: Harvard UP, 1946], 3:320–21.)

4. WILLFUL ABUSE: THE CANKER AND THE ROSE

1. References to *A Lover's Complaint* are from the facsimile (Wright imprint) reproduced in Robert Giroux's commentary on the Sonnets. See Robert Giroux, *The Book Known as Q: A Consideration of Shakespeare's Sonnets* (New York: Random House, 1983), 296–306. The best two modernized editions of the poem are to be found in John Kerrigan's 1986 New Penguin *The Sonnets and A Lover's Complaint* and Katherine Duncan-Jones's 1997 Arden edition, *Shakespeare's Sonnets.* Hyder Rollins's notes in *A New Variorum Edition of Shakespeare: The Poems* (Philadelphia: Lippincott, 1938) are also invaluable (hereafter cited as *Variorum Poems,* followed by page number). Kerrigan's edition is widely credited with reigniting interest in the poem and with encouraging scholars to treat it as an integral component of Q.

2. George Puttenham, *The Arte of English Poesie* (London: Richard Field, 1589), 3.7.1 [128]. References to Puttenham taken from the electronic version of the short-catalogue title (STC 20519) available at *http://prod.library.utoronto.ca/utel/rp/criticism/artofp_all.html.* Quotes hereafter cited in text by book, chapter, and paragraph number–followed by page number in square brackets. Both here and in references to Shakespeare's poems, I have retained original spelling and punctuation, with a very few exceptions. E.g., I have modernized the long "s" throughout and eliminated doubled incipit capitals (e.g., "FRom fairest creatures we desire increase") and irregular spacing to avoid typographical confusion.

3. As I argued in the previous chapter, it is important here to remember that Luther's definition of "flesh" differs from that of his fellow reformers. For Luther the flesh is not merely the material world, but all of creation (including intangibles like mentation and desire) in distinction from the Creator.

4. A word here about italics and capitalization. By convention critics most often refer to the "Sonnets" when referring to Shakespeare's 154 lyrics (not all of which, by the way, are sonnets in the strict sense; famously 126 offers six rhymed couplets and 99 has fifteen lines): the capitalized word ("Sonnets") denotes a kind of overarching textual unity; the failure to italicize the word reflects the absence of an authorial title. Thanks to this convention, critics have sidestepped the question of authorization: we don't know that Shakespeare intended these poems to be read as a collection, and yet, suspending disbelief, we will read them *as if* he did. I will be arguing, however, that we cannot sidestep the authorization debate (thorny and tedious as it

certainly has become); indeed, I maintain that the poems' overarching unity emerges only in the process of reading, and only as supported by the existence of, a specific book: the 1609 quarto (Q) entitled *Shakespeare's Sonnets*. As I make my claim, I will follow convention when referring to the poems, in order to avoid confusion: i.e., "the Sonnets"–capital S but no italics. Once having developed the terms of my argument, however, I will refer to the work by its actual title: *Shakespeare's Sonnets* (or, abbreviated: the *Sonnets*) in order to stress the singular importance of the *book*.

5. Interestingly, Puttenham's term here–"abuse"–follows Latin usage (*abusio*) in providing a neutral and entirely direct translation of the Greek nomenclature (*kata* + *chresis*). For once Puttenham avoids his usual whimsy and "nouelties," eschewing the figurative language he uses elsewhere to personify the classical tropes and schemes. It's as if the danger that catachresis describes–the danger of misappropriating names and thus abusing figure–momentarily governs Puttenham's own nominating discourse.

6. Such readers have followed the author of the *Ad Herennium* more readily than Quintilian or those Renaissance writers like Puttenham whose definition reflects Quintilian's usage. Gideon Burton's online rhetoric handbook–in many ways a wonderful document and research tool–is typical in this respect. Catachresis, he writes, is the "use of a word in a context that differs from its proper application. Generally considered a vice; however, Quintilian defends its use as a way by which one adapts existing terms to applications where a proper term does not exist" (*Silva Rhetoricae*, "catachresis," *http://humanities.byu.edu/rhetoric/catachre.htm*). Quintilian is the defensive exception, not the rule.

7. See Richard A. Lanham, *A Handlist of Rhetorical Terms*, 2d ed. (Berkeley: U of California P, 1991), 31.

8. See Sister Miriam Joseph, *Shakespeare's Use of the Arts of Language* (New York: Columbia UP, 1947), 146.

9. Although this breach may well be, as Sr. Miriam Joseph suggests, a thrillingly masterful–masculine–moment in the hands of the right poet. See also Helen Vendler's similar treatment of catachresis as "mixed metaphor" in her commentary to sonnet 1 in *The Art of Shakespeare's Sonnets* (Cambridge: Harvard UP, 1997), 48.

10. References to the *Rhetorica ad Herennium* as in the Loeb edition: *Ad c. Herennium De Ratione Dicendi Libri IV*, tr. Harry Caplan (Cambridge: Harvard UP, 1954). Thomas Wilson echoes this definition, along with Donatus's definition of the trope, in the 1560 *Arte of Rhetorick*.

11. References to the *Institutio Oratoria* as in the Loeb edition, tr. H. E. Butler (Cambridge: Harvard UP, 1959). I have modified Butler's translation somewhat.

12. Compare, e.g., 8.2.6, 8.6.4–6, and 8.6.35–36.

13. For the charge that Quintilian is "inconsistent," see Eva Feder Kittay,

Metaphor: Its Cognitive Force and Linguistic Structure (Oxford: Clarendon, 1987), 296. To push my response to Kittay even further, I might argue that Quintilian's terminological inconsistency—his description of catachresis as both a version of metaphor and a necessary abuse that must be distinguished from metaphor—is a symptom of the way the trope glosses, and attempts to gloss over, the lack/rupture at the center of signification itself: the rupture that signals the "differance" within sameness. In his essay "White Mythology: Metaphor in the Text of Philosophy" (*Margins of Philosophy*, 207–71), Derrida describes the ultimately catachrestic structure of all metaphor, revealing the problematic rupture at the center of the Western metaphysics of identity and presence.

14. As I argued in chapter 1, this "linearity" is the paradoxical result of a circular structure: that is, the retrospective and revisionary framework provided by figural interpretation. The flesh is succeeded by spirit, the old by the new, the sign by the figure, only *after the fact.* The first comes "first" only insofar as it is understood to be *last.*

15. By subverting an economy of use, catachresis seems structurally analogous to usury—a topic that plays a central role in shaping Shakespeare's poetic imagination. Usury keeps surfacing in my account of figure, catachresis, and the relationship of Jew to Christian, but the complexity of the topic warrants a careful, book-length study of its own. Richard Halpern offers a brilliant account of usury in *The Merchant of Venice* that suggestively relates Marx's notion of use-value, problems of signification, and the circularity of capitalist exchange. (See chapter 5 for a detailed discussion of Halpern's argument.) Halpern never mentions Augustine's *uti/frui* distinction in his discussion of use/Iewes/ewes in *Merchant*, but the link between a labor theory of value and a Pauline theology of the Word is implicit in a number of recent discussions of early-modern literature. John Freccero's essay on Petrarchan poetics, "The Fig Tree and the Laurel," is perhaps the most famous and influential of these; R. A. Shoaf and Marc Shell have also written incisively on the topic. See Marc Shell, "The Wether and the Ewe: Verbal Usury in *The Merchant of Venice*," in Shell, *Money, Language, and Thought: Literary and Philosophical Economies from the Medieval to the Modern Era* (Berkeley: U of California P, 1982), and R. A. Shoaf, *Dante, Chaucer, and the Currency of the Word: Money, Images, and Reference in Late Medieval Poetry* (Norman, Okla.: Pilgrim Books, 1983). I address questions of labor and language from a Derridean perspective in "*Inferno* and the Poetics of *Usura*," *MLN* 107 (1992): 1–17. Finally, Peter C. Herman has usefully surveyed the question of usury in the procreation sonnets in "What's the Use? Or, the Problematic of Economy in Shakespeare's Procreation Sonnets," in *Shakespeare's Sonnets: Critical Essays*, ed. James Schiffer (New York: Garland Publishing, 1999), 263–83.

16. I discuss Augustine's distinction between use and enjoyment, and the ethics of desire it informs, in chapter 2. The distinction is essential for John

Freccero's celebrated discussion ("The Fig Tree and the Laurel") of an idolatrous Petrarchan poetics as well.

17. Puttenham's own example here is telling: *I lent my loue to losse, and gaged my life in vaine.* With its economic tenor, the example foregrounds the homology between catachresis and usury. The "loan" of meaning marked by catachresis is somehow excessive, unbalanced. There seems to be no possible return on meaning's investment; like the speaker's "loue," with catachresis meaning is lent quite literally "to loss": the proper name (whatever we would "properly" call a love that is "spent" in vain) is borrowed to compensate the very lack of name. Interestingly, Puttenham's text, which poses the question of catachresis in terms of a failure of *love*, echoes the constant refrain of his contemporaries' invectives against usury, as that financial practice which destroys charity. (The echo is all the more instructive since Puttenham's catachrestic loan apparently inverts the logic of usurious interest: if catachresis "gages" in vain, the problem with the usurer is that he *never* does so, staking his investment only in view of certain profit.) Ultimately at stake with both catachresis and usury is the *legitimacy of exchange.* If catachresis entails a misappropriation of language, it is because it constitutes a "borrowing" that structurally can never be repaid. By disrupting notions of origin and property/propriety at once, catachresis utterly disrupts the logic of redemption that aligns the quid-pro-quo world of love (think here of *charitas*'s Golden Rule: "do unto others . . .") with the equities of economic exchange. If charity begins at home, catachresis and usury both render us homeless. I examine Puttenham at length in my current research project ("The Use of Shakespeare"). (See also n. 14 above.)

18. As I explain in my preface, my methodological starting point is the notion of an unresolvable gap between the empirical and the transcendental: a breach that is essential to the way we create textual meaning and yet that such meaning routinely strives to disavow. If Luther is crucial to the story I want to tell, it is because his writings present historically the first influential effort to theorize this breach–in all of its constitutive unresolvability–per se.

19. With the exception of "A Lover's Complaint," all references to *Shakespeare's Sonnets* are from the facsimile (Aspley imprint) reproduced in *Shakespeare's Sonnets*, ed. with an analytic commentary by Stephen Booth (New Haven: Yale UP, 1977).

20. The division of the sequence into "young man" and "dark lady" sonnets has been the conventional view since the Malone and Steevens 1780 edition of the poems. Peter Stallybrass ("Editing as Cultural Formation: The Sexing of Shakespeare's Sonnets," *Modern Language Quarterly* 54, no. 1 [March 1993]: 91–103); Margreta de Grazia ("The Scandal of Shakespeare's Sonnets," *Shakespeare Survey* 46 [1994]: 35–49); and Heather Dubrow ("'Incertainties Now Crown Themselves Assur'd': The Politics of Plotting Shakespeare's Sonnets," *Shakespeare Quarterly* 47, no. 3 [Fall 1996]: 291–305) offer important recent critiques of this editoral history.

21. Following Booth, it is common to cite six uses of the word within the three so-called *Will* sonnets (135, 136, 143): (a) that which one wishes to do; (b) the auxiliary verb; (c) lust; (d) penis; (e) vagina; (f) William. Hyder Rollins summarizes the debate concerning other Williams in the poem (e.g., the young man or the cuckolded husband). See *A New Variorum Edition of Shakespeare: The Sonnets*, ed. Hyder Edward Rollins (Philadelphia: Lippincott, 1944), 1:345 (hereafter cited as *Variorum Sonnets*, followed by volume and page number).

22. Booth, 543.

23. See the influential recent discussions of copyright by Martha Woodmansee, "The Genius and the Copyright: Economic and Legal Conditions of the Emergence of the 'Author,'" *Eighteenth-Century Studies* 17 (1984): 425–48; Mark Rose, "The Author as Proprietor: *Donaldson v. Becket* and the Genealogy of Modern Authorship," *Representations* 23 (Summer 1988): 51–85; and Arthur F. Marotti, "Shakespeare's Sonnets as Literary Property," in *Soliciting Interpretation: Literary Theory and Seventeenth-Century English Poetry*, ed. Elizabeth D. Harvey and Katharine Eisaman Maus (Chicago: U of Chicago P, 1990): 143–73. Most recently, Max W. Thomas has offered an interesting challenge to the prevailing interpretation of copyright law and its impact on notions of authorship. See "Eschewing Credit: Heywood, Shakespeare, and Plagiarism Before Copyright," *New Literary History* 31, no. 2 (Spring 2000): 277–93.

24. Like every question concerning the book called *Shakespeare's Sonnets*, the significance of these thirteen extant copies remains unclear. A minority of critics maintain that the number is small, indicating that the edition was not only unauthorized but also quickly suppressed by Shakespeare and his friends. The case for suppression is made stronger by those–like Hyder Edward Rollins in the 1944 Variorum–who cite the "total silence" with which the publication of the volume was met. Robert Giroux cites Rollins in this matter of the Sonnets' neglect, following a line of reasoning to be traced back to Frank Mathew's 1922 study, *An Image of Shakespeare*: the quarto (Q) must have been suppressed because there is no direct reference to it in contemporary literature, no further editions of it, no copies of the text in the libraries of contemporary bibliophiles like Robert Burton. (See Robert Giroux, *The Book Known as Q*, 4–8). Giroux's text is a well-argued version of the kind of detective criticism I go on to discuss below. His work is *almost* taken seriously by the academic mainstream; Helen Vendler, for instance, cites him in the bibliography to her massive commentary on the sonnets, *The Art of Shakespeare's Sonnets*.) Increasingly, however, critics have argued that thirteen extant copies is quite a large number when we consider the delicate medium of the quarto. (For instance, in contrast to the thirteen copies of Q, Rollins cites only three surviving copies of the 1599 *Passionate Pilgrim*, one of which is imperfect. See *Variorum Poems*, 526.)

25. Five of the poems have been, since Edmund Malone's 1780 *Supplement to the Edition of Shakespeare's Plays Published in 1778 by Samuel Johnson and George Steevens* (London: Bathurst, 1780), definitively ascribed to Shakespeare. Five of the remaining twenty in the 1599 edition have been ascribed to other authors; most modern editors consider it highly unlikely that the remaining five poems belong to Shakespeare. See E. T. Price's discussion of the collection's publishing history in *The Poems*, ed. E. T. Price (London and New York: Routledge, 1996 [Methuen, 1961]), xxi–xxiii. See also Maurice Evans's analysis in the 1989 New Penguin edition of *The Narrative Poems*, 59–61, 244–52, and Rollins, *Variorum Poems*, 524–58.

26. In his *Palladis Tamia*, cited by Rollins in *Variorum Sonnets*, 2:53.

27. A striking fact, given the multiple editions that Shakespeare's two narrative poems, *Venus and Adonis* and *The Rape of Lucrece*, saw in the first decades of the seventeenth century.

28. Although Shakespeare's terms are ambiguous here–not least because of the "almost" that qualifies his statement. Is it paternity–or *maternity*–which is at issue? To show their birth could equally mean to show the pedigree that, like their "name," proceeds from the father–and also to show the site of a more literal birth, from the fertile conceit of the poet as mother.

29. As will hopefully become clear, I mean my remarks here to apply to methodologies as diverse as a poststructuralist focus on *écriture* (see Roland Barthes's classic essay "The Death of the Author") and a new textual critic's analysis of the material conditions of publication. Foucault's critique (in, e.g., "What Is an Author?") of Barthes applies equally well to the new textual criticism: to insist on textual indeterminacy in the place of a classical notion of authorial intention only renders the author-function more diffuse than ever, thereby inventing a new notion of authorial transcendence. A final note, in light of the Oedipal dimensions of this issue, the death of the Author: is it an accident of no significance that the exemplary instance of catachresis is, for Quintilian, the term *parricide*? In its proper usage the word means the murder of a father, and yet by abuse we apply it to murder in general. (See *Institutio Oratoria* 8.6.35). But can there ever be a proper name for the murder of a father? Isn't patricide/parricide *always* catachrestic, since to pronounce the death of God/Father/Author is ultimately to simultaneously acknowledge and deny our relation to our origins? Catachresis in this sense unmasks *figura*, naming the ambivalent relationship to origins–to the Jewish Patriarch–that defines the Christian figural tradition. At this point, we are only a step away from Freud's *Moses and Monotheism*.

30. Marotti discusses memorial transcription as the source for the versions of sonnets 138 and 144 that appear in *The Passionate Pilgrim*. See "Shakespeare's Sonnets," 51.

31. At the end of his 1612 *An Apologie for Actors*, Heywood appended a note to his current printer, attacking Jaggard for pirating his previous

work. "I must necessarily insert a manifest iniury done me in that worke [the 1609 *Troia Britanica*] by taking the two Epistles of *Paris* to *Helen*, and *Helen* to *Paris*, and printing them in a lesse volume [the 1612 *Passionate Pilgrim*] vnder the name of another [i.e., Shakespeare] which may put the world in opinion I might steal them from him" (quoted in Rollins, *Variorum Poems*, 535). See Max Thomas's interesting reading of Heywood's note in "Eschewing Credit."

32. See my discussion of the speaker/author distinction in Davidic psalm in chapter 2.

33. In W. K. Wimsatt and Monroe C. Beardsley, "The Intentional Fallacy," in *The Verbal Icon: Studies in the Meaning of Poetry* (Lexington: U of Kentucky P, 1982 [1954]), 4.

34. Indeed, almost *exactly* like that; as I have been trying to suggest throughout this study, our most mundane reading experiences are heirs to Augustine's moment under the tree. For Renaissance Petrarchism, however–and especially for William Shakespeare–the potential dissonance between little *a* and big *A* proves, in the end, more interesting than the promise of clarity and coherence that such reading proffers.

35. See *Variorum Sonnets*, 2:42–52, for a discussion of readers who have questioned the canonicity of Q.

36. Leona Rostenberg is the critic, cited in Katherine Duncan-Jones, "Was the 1609 Shake-speares Sonnets Really Unauthorized?" *Review of English Studies* 34:134 (May 1983): 152.

37. Duncan-Jones cites Sidney Lee's biography of Thorpe in the DNB (152).

38. See Heather Dubrow, "'Incertainties Now Crown Themselves Assur'd,'" 297–98.

39. Heather Dubrow analyzes the problems of a related form of "circular reading" in her discussion of the arguments supporting claims for the bipartite division of the sequence: "We assume that a given poem evokes one or the other of those personages [e.g., dark lady or young man], deduce certain traits from the text, and then assign lyrics concerned with the same traits or issues to the same character" ("Politics of Plotting," 297). Once again the presumption of coherence supports readings meant to provide the evidence for presuming coherence. Dubrow's essay marks an admirable effort in sustained skepticism: she refuses to read a narrative in the sequence.

40. Joseph Pequigney, *Such Is My Love: A Study of Shakespeare's Sonnets* (Chicago: U of Chicago P, 1985), 220.

41. Antedating Joel Fineman's book on the Sonnets by a year, Pequigney's case for the structural integration of the sequence depends in part on a reading of the unified psychoanalytic narrative contained within the poems. Where Fineman, albeit in a very different register and with quite dif-

ferent conclusions, argues that Shakespeare anticipates a Lacanian analysis of subjectivity, Pequigney argues that Shakespeare anticipates a Freudian analysis of the bisexual soul. See Pequigney, 81–101. Fineman's remarks on the relationship between Shakespeare and Lacan are made most explicit in his essays "The Turn of the Shrew" and "The Sound of O in *Othello*."

42. *Sonnets of Shakespeare*, ed. Sidney Lee (1905), 11. Cited in Duncan-Jones, 153.

43. On the question of homophobia in the editorial history of the Sonnets, see Margareta de Grazia, "The Scandal of Shakespeare's Sonnets" and Peter Stallybrass, "Editing as Cultural Formation."

44. Although it is difficult not to notice certain turns of phrase: "Readers with *normal* sexual tastes, with no knowledge of the poem's context, inevitably read sonnet 18 as a lover's poem to his lady." See Robert Giroux, *The Book Known as Q: A Consideration of Shakespeare's Sonnets* (New York: Random House, 1983), 18, emphasis added.

45. Of course, Giroux misconstrues the nature of the very fallacy he critiques. The problem for people like Wimsatt and Beardsley with biography is not whether poems have a connection to biography but whether we can ever know that connection from the text and, furthermore, whether meaning can ever be understood as a function of authorial intention.

46. Indeed, she cites Keats in this essay, comparing the seducer of *A Lover's Complaint* to the poet's mistress in Keats's *Ode to Melancholy* (170).

47. See Kerrigan's introduction to his New Penguin edition of the poems: *The Sonnets and A Lover's Complaint* (New York: Viking Penguin, 1986), 10.

48. Donald Foster points out that the address "TO.THE.ONLIE.BEGET-TER.OF.THESE.INSVING.SONNETS" is an *epigraph* and "not, however, as it is usually called, a 'dedication'" (42). Foster's point here reinforces his own reading of this prefatory language: if the preface is a dedication, and if Mr. W.H. is in truth Master William [S]Hakespeare, then the volume of poems would be, oddly, dedicated to its own author. See Donald W. Foster, "Master W.H., R.I.P.," *PMLA* 102 (1987): 42–54, and my discussion of Foster's arguments above.

49. Editions based on Benson's 1640 version of the text followed him in omitting the epigraph; indeed, it wasn't until after Malone annotated Q in 1780 that attention was drawn back to the inscription. See *Variorum Sonnets*, 2:166. Rollins also notes that neither George Steevens in 1766 nor Edward Malone in 1780 seems much impressed by the preface; both pass over it in silence. Foster–who fails to note that editions based on Benson's volume omit the preface–misleadingly broadens Rollins's claim, implying that no early reader (and, significantly, Foster fails to specify "early" in this context) would have found Thorpe's epigraph striking. "The earliest editors of the Quarto found nothing remarkable about Thorpe's epigraph–or, if so, gave no hint that they did" (Foster, 43). Thus Foster implies that our problems with the epigraph are artifacts of an anachronistic misreading of its language. How-

ever, if by the "earliest editors" of Q Foster means Benson and those following his lead, an equally likely assumption would be that the epigraph was
"remarkable" enough to suppress it: if Benson—as has often been charged—
sought to suppress the homoeroticism of Q, wouldn't he have been likely as
well to suppress a potentially homoerotic tribute to Mr. W.H.? Ultimately,
however, my point is simply that one cannot argue incontrovertibly either
way from the available evidence. Rollins discusses the history of readings of
the epigraph in appendix 7, 2:166–76. My discussion above recapitulates
many of the most influential readings he cites.

50. I allude here to the song with which Portia famously helps Bassanio
make his choice among competing inscriptions in *Merchant of Venice* 3.2. I discuss this scene at length in the following chapter.

51. The "adventurer" who "sets forth" alludes straightforwardly enough
to publishing as a risky, but potentially rewarding, venture: one *sets* a page in
type just as one *sets forth* on a merchant vessel, eager to turn a profit (i.e.,
"wishing [to do] well"). Nonetheless, there have been readers who have questioned both this apposition ("WELL-WISHING.ADVENTVRER" and
"T.T.") and the reference of T.T. to Thomas Thorpe. For alternative readings
of "T.T.," see *Variorum Sonnets*, 2:174–75.

52. The most industrious readers have managed to fold the syntax of the
entire inscription back upon itself, making Mr. W.H. the subject, and not the
object, of "wisheth": e.g., Mr. W.H. wisheth all happiness, and that eternity
promised by our ever-living poet, to the only begetter of the ensuing sonnets.
According to this reading, Mr. W.H. becomes the dedicator of *Shakespeare's
Sonnets*—perhaps, again, the person who procured the manuscript—but he is
not the sequence's dedicatee, who remains the poet's friend and inspiration.

53. G. Blakemore Evans offers the most cogent critique of Foster's arguments to date. See his remarks in *The Sonnets*, ed. G. Blakemore Evans (Cambridge: Cambridge UP, 1996), 115.

54. Foster cites Martin Spevack's count, *A Complete Concordance to the
Works of Shakespeare*, 9 vols. (Hidlesheim: Olms, 1968), 2:1255.

55. Park Honan, *Shakespeare: A Life* (Oxford and New York: Oxford UP,
1998), ix–x.

56. We should perhaps hear here the Shakespearean pun on *no-thing* as
vagina: literally it is the will of woman, the no-thing of woman, that authorizes his actions.

57. Ultimately—or perhaps preeminently—it is the distinction of gender
that gives way in the play's construction of authority. To cite but one central
instance of such ambiguity: as has often been noted, the witches are of indeterminate gender: as Banquo tells us, they *should* be women, but their beards
prevent one from saying so with certainty.

58. Thanks to Karen Jackson Ford for pointing out the strangeness of this
phrase's diction. According to the OED, the usage is indeed rare. A quick, and

by no means conclusive, survey of the Chadwyck-Healey English poetry database confirms this point. Out of 857 occurrences of the word "fault" in the 498 texts searched for the years 1590–1625, the phrase to "make fault" occurs only three times, including Shakespeare's usage in sonnet 35.

59. Rollins notes (*Variorum Poems*, 584–85) that the first edition to give the sonnets separately from the poems in *The Passionate Pilgrim* and various songs from the plays–Moxon's 1830 edition of the Sonnets–omits *A Lover's Complaint*, and Moxon's example is followed by future editors of Q. Even John Kerrigan, the first major editor who includes *A Lover's Complaint* within an edition of the Sonnets in order to make a case for the formal integrity of Q, entitles his volume *The Sonnets and a Lover's Complaint.* It is only with Katherine Duncan-Jones's 1997 edition for Arden that the book called *Shakespeare's Sonnets* is presented both with its original title and in its entirety.

60. Here, at last, we have the author's name cited in full–unlike the incomplete reference with which Q begins: *Shake-speares Sonnets*–and yet, this second title, not insignificantly, has only managed for most readers to further weaken the case for Shakespeare's authorization of Q.

61. Of course, as Giroux's facsimile immediately makes clear, the catch-word "A" at signature K also cues the reader: given the catchword, "finis" marks no end of the text but instead waves us on to the beginning of the next poem: "*A* Lovers complaint."

62. I am alluding here to the deliberate puns on a doubled, re-cited voice at the start of the *Complaint.* Like the superfluous bounty of the monarch who can only give absolutely ("where excesse begs *all*") and thus does not give where there is determinate need ("where want cries *some*"), the voice that fills this poem inflates itself on the reiterated experience of loss, overflowingly full insofar as it is eternally self-emptying. This is a voice that resonates only so far as it negates its surroundings. With the usual precision of his poetic imagination Shakespeare enfigures the self-perpetuating hollow-fullness of this voice in terms of the concavity that allows an echo. "From off a hill whose concaue wombe reworded / A plaintfull story from a sistring vale / My spirrits t'attend this doble voyce accorded." It would not be difficult, but would take us too far afield to do so now, to relate this double voice to the sound of O as Joel Fineman reads it in *Othello*, or to align the overflowing margents of the *Complaint* to the "superfluous moiety" Fineman discusses–the "phenomenology of the spurt," as he facetiously calls it–in his reading of poetic will ("The Temporality of Rape") in *The Rape of Lucrece.*

63. Interestingly, given the link I've been suggesting between authorization, poetry, and trespass, hypallage is usually understood as a species of the figure hyperbaton, a figure that Puttenham calls "the trespasser" (see 3.13.1).

64. In addition, Marotti notes, royal patents were sometimes granted to a specific printer, bestowing upon him the privilege of producing specific kinds of books (e.g., Common-Law texts). See Marotti, 143.

65. See Marotti, "Shakespeare's Sonnets as Literary Property," 65, as well as Max Thomas's recent critique of such a view in "Eschewing Credit."

66. See Freinkel, "Shakespeare and the Theology of Will," *Graven Images* 2 (1995): 31–47.

67. From my remarks here, it has perhaps become apparent that I disagree sharply with the "descriptivist" account of the proper name discussed, vis-à-vis Foucault and Searle, in my preface. Indeed, I follow Žižek in presuming, contra Searle, "the radical contingency of naming." See *The Sublime Object of Ideology*, 95.

68. In the face of such linguistic emptiness, however, some critics have tried to resuscitate the dead letter in various ways, insisting upon (for instance) a reference to the Rose Theater; an allusion to Master W.H.; and, defying typography altogether, a play on Wriothesley as "Rose-ly." See *Variorum Sonnets*, 1.7–8. In response both to New Critical and new historical readings, it has become easy to dismiss this sort of critical speculation as comically fussy, overly ingenious. I would argue, however, that we need to take this old-fashioned speculative criticism more seriously. Such speculation precisely reveals the ways in which Shakespeare's poetry mobilizes, as well as frustrates, our own desire for genealogy: for plumping out language with authoritative, figural coherence. Similarly, I have insisted upon reading *"Rose"* as a proper name, although many critics have plausibly argued that–with the possible exception of the plays on *Will* (although see my discussion of this point below)–Q's frequent use of italics cannot be understood as indications of proper nouns. As early as 1904, H. C. Beeching observed that all the italicized words in Q have capital letters, and other critics have pointed out that the list of italicized words includes words as various as *Audit* (4), *Statutes* (55), *Intrim* (56), *Alien* (78), *Satire* (100), *Hereticke* (124), and *Quietus* (126). (Cf. Rollins's discussion of William Hughes (Hewes), *Variorum Sonnets*, 2:180 ff.) To my mind, it is unclear how we can acknowledge the significance of Q's typography in one instance–e.g., the italicized *"Will"* of sonnets 135 and 136–and justifiably deny its significance elsewhere. Doesn't our reading presume a certain regularity? *Rose*, like *Audit*, might be a common noun after all–but the italics tempt us to consider otherwise, and *that* temptation–along with the desire for *figura* that it evinces–is, to my mind, the crucial issue.

69. See Viola-Cesario's version of these procreation arguments for Olivia in *Twelfth Night*: "Lady, you are the cruell'st shee aliue, / If you will leade these graces to the graue, / And leaue the world no copie" (1.5.237–39). With her teasing reply, Olivia points out the absurdity of a procreation understood in terms of mechanical reproduction: "O sir, I will not be so hard-hearted: I will giue out diuers scedules of my beautie. It shalbe Inuentoried and euery particle and vtensile labell'd to my will. As, Item two lippes indifferent redde, Item two grey eys, with lids to them: Item, one necke, one chin, & so forth" (1.5.240–45).

70. No wonder Helen Vendler begins her reading of the Sonnets with the reading of a catachresis (see n. 9 above): from the very start of this book a procreative *figura* has given way to an onanistic *abuse.*

71. Matthew 25:18, Geneva Bible. The annotation to this parable reads: "Christ witnesseth that there shall be a long time, betweene his departure to his Father, and his comming againe to vs, but yet not withstanding that, he will at that day take an account not onely of the rebellious & obstinate, how they haue bestowed that which they receiued of him, but also of his houshold seruants, what haue not through slouthfulnesse employed those gifts which he bestowed vpon them." See *The Geneva Bible (The Annotated New Testament, 1602 Edition)*, ed. Gerald T. Sheppard (New York: Pilgrim Press, 1989).

72. But compare 129 where "th'expence of Spirit in a waste of shame" enfigures the outpouring of "spirit" with a quite different valence.

73. It has long been noted that many of Shakespeare's arguments in the procreation sonnets derive from the version of Erasmus' "Epistle to persuade a young gentleman to marriage," that appeared as a rhetorical set piece in Thomas Wilson's *Arte of Rhetorique* (1553). Katharine M. Wilson discusses the conventionality of these arguments in *Shakespeare's Sugared Sonnets* (London: George Allen and Unwin, 1974), 146 ff.

74. The pun on "increase" is Joel Fineman's discovery. In *Shakespeare's Perjured Eye*, Fineman explores the in-creasing logic of increasing as a function of that differentiating fold in/through which sameness as such is reproduced. For Fineman, the increase we desire is that crease *of* desire–the crease that splits the Lacanian subject as he accedes to language, moving from a finite order of demand to the infinite register of desire.

75. For a brilliant reading of humanistic notions of *copia* in terms of linguistic proliferation and intertextuality, see Terence Cave, *The Cornucopian Text: Problems of Writing in the French Renaissance* (Oxford: Oxford UP, 1979), esp. 3–34.

76. See John Kerrigan's reading of the sonnet in his edition of *The Sonnets and A Lover's Complaint* (New York: Viking Penguin, 1986), 30–31.

77. On the somewhat scanty basis of a few recent lexical studies, the past ten or so years have seen a shift in consensus regarding the dating of the Sonnets. The trend has moved toward a later dating of the Sonnets' composition, or at least their revision, but the evidence remains circumstantial and inconclusive. More important, like all empirical arguments about Q, shifting interpretations of the available evidence do not fundamentally affect my thesis. Temporality, succession, belatedness are themes that Q problematizes so deeply, that questions of dating are ultimately built into our interpretation of the sequence as such. See Donald W. Foster, "Reconstructing Shakespeare Part 2: The Sonnets," *Shakespeare Newsletter* (Fall 1991): 26–27, and A. Kent Hiett, Charles W. Hieatt, and Anne Lake Prescott, "When Did Shakespeare Write *Sonnets 1609?*" *Studies in Philology* 88 (1991): 69–109.

78. E. M. W. Tillyard, *Shakespeare's History Plays* (reprint, New York: Barnes and Noble, 1964). Tillyard originally published the work in 1944.

79. The catachrestic idea of beauty's veil directly glosses that crucial topos of Christian allegory: the letter of Mosaic Law as veil, as we shall see in the next chapter.

80. The only real exception is sonnet 99, where the poet accuses flowers of having stolen the "purple pride" of the young man's cheeks and "marierom [marjoram]" of his hair. But even in this poem the floral catalogue of the young man's beauties seems to serve as mere prelude to the canker in line 13 that consumes flowers, beauty and all.

81. E.g., the kind of catalogue Olivia jokingly gives in response to Cesario's procreation arguments in note 69 above.

82. See Fineman's brilliant discussion of sonnet 105 in *Shakespeare's Perjured Eye*, 254–55.

83. See sonnet 121.9–"Noe, I am that I am, and they that leuell / At my abuses, reckon vp their owne"–for the famous allusion to God's self-predicating tautology in Exodus 3:14.

84. Without recognizing its evocation of a post-Reformation universe, critics usually emend the line in terms of an avoidable conflict between nature and morality–"All men make faults and even I in this, / Excusing *thy* sins more than *thy* sins are": i.e., the poet corrupts himself by exculpating the young man's moral failing as if it were more intrinsic to the young man's identity than it is.

85. Fineman is not the first reader to note that the sonnets are filled with puns on the difference between the unitary phallus–that *one thing* the poet expresses so proudly in a sonnet like 105–and the vaginal *no-thing* of the dark lady, a black hole capable of encompassing and negating countless wills, even that *some-thing/nothing* of the poet in sonnet 136.

86. "The Structure of Allegorical Desire," in *Allegory and Representation*, ed. Stephen J. Greenblatt (Baltimore: Johns Hopkins UP, 1981), 26–60.

87. Marshall Grossman's remarkable treatment of narrative poetry in the English Renaissance came to my attention as this study was already in press, unfortunately precluding any substantial engagement with his argument here. Like my reading of Shakespeare's will, Grossman's treatments of Spenser, Donne, Marvell, and Milton are explicitly indebted to *Shakespeare's Perjured Eye*–and Grossman, also like me, seeks to historicize and contextualize Fineman's insights through, among other things, extended readings of Petrarch and, especially, Augustine. Yet, where my reading of Luther leads me to examine a poetics that constitutively undermines the presentation of narrative–or of a self sustained by narrative's chiastic turns–Grossman's locates the Renaissance's poet's continuing commitment to narrative, now sustained by the folds of a Protestant typology. On the basis of Grossman's study (and my remarks here are, perforce, still provisional) one might then confirm my asser-

tion in chapter 3 that Luther's critique of *figura* is unique in its radical challenge to narrative; other Protestant versions of the critique enable a differentiation between suspect allegory and acceptable typology (the basis, for Grossman, of historical narrative itself) that allows (in my view) the essentially unbroken transmission of a figural legacy. See *The Story of All Things: Writing the Self in English Renaissance Narrative Poetry* (Durham: Duke UP, 1998).

88. In chapter 1 I examine the ways in which a grammatical present tense literally drops out of the scriptural tag Augustine employs in his *Contra Faustum*: "nisi credideritis, non intellegetis": unless you *have believed* you *will* not *understand.* The tag is not itself a true chiasmus, but it captures precisely the troping structure I describe above.

89. We have a new just-so story in sonnet 127–a new myth of origins– but it is important to recognize that at stake here is not a new origin itself but simply a new way of talking about the "old" origin that was itself a symptom and not an origin. And even this "new" way of talking about the "old" origin is not new: the terms of sonnet 127 have already been spoken in poems like 35, where the poet's comparisons are what authorize trespass to begin with. Hence, once again, I disagree with Fineman in characterizing the shift from young-man to dark-lady sonnets as an allegorical unfolding (e.g., *implicare* to *explicare*). Indeed, we haven't gotten anywhere by changing our stories; nothing has unfold*ed*, since the discourse of beauty is inseparable from, and defined from the start by, the unfoldable folds within it: i.e., the cankerous creases in the budding rose. Ultimately the problem that these poems recount is indeed that we cannot ascribe priority of blame; we cannot tell a consistent story. Who's at fault? the authorizing poet, the young man for not procreating, the foul people for pretending to be fair? At stake in all of these ascriptions of fault is, once again, the catachrestic breakdown of a difference between the ornament and what it ornaments: between beauty as painted and painted beauty. And, again, it is precisely this breakdown that signals the impossibility of assigning a temporal cause/origin for the breakdown itself.

90. This formulation approaches a description of the problem of usury as Shakespeare construes it, both in the sonnets and in *The Merchant of Venice*. Again, it would take another book to explore adequately the link between the economy of use and the question of figure, but for now we might say that usury entails just that strangely productive wastefulness that characterizes the poet's lack of "quicke change" in his sonnets.

91. Fineman's discussion of the "heliocentrism" of visionary poetry offers a careful summary of this familiar logic (*Perjured Eye*, 68–70). See Derrida, "White Mythology," for an extended discussion of "heliotropism" and the sun as metaphor's metaphor.

92. By my count, *will* in some form–including *wil, willing(ly), wilt, wilful(ly)* and *wild* [willed]) appears nearly one hundred times in Q–a frequency

of about one *will* every twenty-five lines of verse, or every two hundred words. Twenty-two of those *will*'s occur in the three so-called *Will* sonnets: 135, 136, 143. Like all the terms that Q italicizes, the italicized form of *will* is also capitalized. This form appears—eleven times in total—only in the *Will* sonnets. A non-italicized but capitalized *will* appears as well in sonnet 57.

93. "Frankly bawdy," says G. Blakemore Evans (253), whose explication of the puns in his 1996 edition of the sonnets (Cambridge UP) offers nonetheless, despite the supposed "frankness" of the wordplay, one of the only comprehensive paraphrases of the poems that I've found.

94. What's in a name? Crucial to Fineman's discussion of *will* is his contention that, in speaking out his name the poet identifies himself with the split subject of his language, recognizing himself as both a first-person and a third-person subject, as both (to return to Benveniste's terms) the subject of his utterance and of his statement. Moreover, because the name *Will* also designates that sexual desire that puts one will—or sex organ—inside another, the name also identifies the poet's subjectivity with the "missing copular connection," the third person of desire, which mediates, as well as disrupts, the purely imaginary unity of "I" and "you" (see 292 ff.). I invoke these more subtle details of Fineman's argument in order to point out the structural similarities between this description of *Will* as a third-person split in subjectivity and my own description of the impact of the third person on the translated "I" of *figura* in Petrarch. Ultimately the subjectivity that Fineman defines can be ascribed to Petrarchan lyric—as a *written utterance*—per se. My point is not that Petrarch "got there first" but that Fineman's discussion misses the ways in which Shakespeare gets *somewhere else*.

95. Booth's 1978 commentary on this point remains the most thoughtful I've come across: "I have not followed [Q's] suit because a modern reader's susceptibility to orthographical signals is so acute that Q's capitals and italics can make the poems sound even more archly precious than they were for Shakespeare's reader; a modern reader may also incline toward the folly of trying to dredge meaning from Q's selectivity in singling out some *will*'s typographically and printing other in ordinary roman" (466). Yet even Booth, the most typographically "democratizing" of recent editors, decides to capitalize the final *Will* of sonnet 136: "And then thou louest me for my name is Will."

96. As cited in Albert Feuillerat's facsimile edition of *Astrophil and Stella* in volume 2 of *The Complete Works of Sir Philip Sidney*, 4 vols. (Cambridge, Eng.: University P, 1922–1926).

97. See my discussion in chapter 1 of the syntactical linearity of reading (*legere*, as Augustine calls it) in contrast with a figural and revisionist exegesis (what Augustine calls "understanding" or *intellegere*, punning on the seeming etymological relation to *legere*). Sidney's affirmation by negation reminds me of equally chiastic moments in *Twelfth Night* (Feste's "if your foure negatiues make your two affirmatiues" in 5.1) and, more strikingly, in *Richard II*.

Richard's "I, no; no, I" at the center of the deposition scene (4.1), with its puns on aye/I, negation and affirmation, offers in miniature the problematic relationship that Richard bears to language. In a reading I have pursued elsewhere, Richard's abuse of language in his insistence upon a metaphoricity that would be sheerly performative, marks–or perhaps allegorizes–the political consequences of *figura*'s collapse.

98. Critics have adopted an array of readings for this line without, of course, decisively resolving its ambiguities. "Let 'no' unkind, no fair beseechers kill": thus read Booth, Kerrigan, and Evans, following T. G. Tucker's 1924 and Ingram and Redpath's 1964 editions of the Sonnets: the mistress's unkind denial must not kill any beseechers who are fair (the unfair beseechers, one imagines, are another matter). Another reading, dating back at least as far as Edward Dowden's 1881 edition, construes the line somewhat differently: "Let no unkind 'no' fair beseechers kill": by implication, all beseechers are fair, and it is the unkind "no" that is negated. Still other readers–including, most recently, Walter Cohen in his annotations for the 1997 *Norton Shakespeare*–have chosen to avoid the question of citation and have interpreted "vnkind" as a substantitve: e.g., let not unkindness of yours kill fair beseechers (see also *Variorum Sonnets*, 1:135).

99. The legendary ribald exchange between Johnny Carson and Zsa Zsa Gabor is an obscene case in point, aptly demonstrating the double take, from propriety to impropriety, of the double entendre. With feline companion in her lap, Zsa Zsa is reported to have purred to Johnny, "Would you like to pet my pussy?" Johnny's reply: "Sure, but move the cat first." Consider this a twentieth-century "lite" version of Hamlet and Ophelia in act 3.2, where the "groaning" of pun (e.g., "Doe you thinke I meant Country matters?") wields its most misogynistically sexual force: "You are keene my Lord, you are keene . . ." "It would cost you a groaning, to take off my edge" (3.2.124, 250–51).

100. Editors commonly cite the early-modern proverb that a woman is wedded to her will, as a gloss of line 1.

101. Margareta de Grazia's 1980 essay "Babbling Will in *Shake-speares Sonnets* 127–154" offers an interesting reading of the theology behind Shakespeare's "babbling will" (*Spenser Studies* 1 (1980): 121–34).

102. As we've already seen with sonnet 135's double negatives, the poet reinforces this problematic in other ambiguities within the poem. Thus, for instance, the undecidability of "sute" and "sweet" in line 4: not only do the words, almost certainly homophonic for Shakespeare, conflate beginning with end–wishful desire (the lover's suit) with desire's fulfillment (the sweetness of consummation)–but the word also ambiguously serves as both name (e.g., the sobriquet *sweetie*), adverb and adjective. *Love* is similarly undecidable both in the *Will* sonnets and throughout the sequence.

103. The fantasy of such "combined summes" articulated here repeats the economic terms of that more famous articulation of the same fantasy:

"When to the Sessions of sweet silent thought, / I sommon vp remembrance of things past, / I sigh the lacke of many a thing I sought, / And with old woes new waile my deare times waste:/ . . . / But if the while I thinke on thee (deare friend) / All losses are restord, and sorrowes end" (30.1–4, 13–14). The treasury of the beloved's love–the precious "chest" that is his/her heart–is conceived in blatantly economic terms as that plenitude, that *summum bonum* (another "sum" word, like Shakespeare's sum, summer, and summons) that completes everything. See also sonnet 31.

5. WILL'S BONDAGE: ANTI-SEMITISM AND *The Merchant of Venice*

1. All references to the play as in *New Variorum Edition of Shakespeare: The Merchant of Venice*, ed. Horace Howard Furness (New York: Dover, 1964 [1888]). Spacing has been regularized and the long "s" has been modernized throughout, but otherwise orthography has been retained. For the most part, character names also follow the Folio spelling. Furness's edition is based on the Folio version of the play and where the 1600 Quarto (Q1) reading seems more intelligible, I have substituted it in square brackets. Both the folio version and Q1 are available online at *http://web.uvic.ca/shakespeare/index.html.*

2. I quote here from the published version of Coghill's 1949 lecture "The Basis of Shakespearian Comedy," in *Essays and Studies 1950* (London: John Murray, 1950): 1–28. Coghill's argument proved enormously popular, especially with the following generation of *Merchant* critics. Barbara K. Lewalski cites the essay as the inspiration behind her own allegorical interpretation of the play in her influential study "Biblical Allusion and Allegory in *The Merchant of Venice*," *Shakespeare Quarterly* 13 (1962): 327–43. Similarly, Lawrence Danson mentions a special indebtedness to Coghill–citing, indeed, the very passage I've quoted above–in his book-length study: *The Harmonies of The Merchant of Venice* (New Haven: Yale UP, 1978), 17.

As Danson himself notes, the Anglo-Jewish critic Israel Gollancz was apparently the first modern critic to offer a Christian allegorical reading of the play. Danson, whose study opposes ironizing readings of the play, finds it ironic that Gollancz first presented this Christian reading in a 1916 lecture to the Jewish Historical Society (14). James Shapiro, however, reads the fact as symptomatic not only of Gollancz's double bind as the first Jewish professor of English literature in England but also of the modern effort to repress the role of Jews and of anti-Semitism in England's national self-definition. See his important study *Shakespeare and the Jews* (New York: Columbia UP, 1996), 78–80. Gollancz's lecture "The 'Shylock' of Shakespeare" was reprinted posthumously in a volume titled *Allegory and Mysticism in Shakespeare. A Medievalist on "The Merchant of Venice." Reports of Three Lectures by Sir Israel Gollancz* (London: Geo. W. Jones, 1931).

Richard Halpern also cites Gollancz in the context of modern/modernist readings of the play in his provocative essay "The Jewish Question: Shakespeare and Anti-Semitism," in *Shakespeare Among the Moderns* (Ithaca: Cornell UP, 1997), 219. My own reading of *Merchant* differs from Halpern's in certain ways—most centrally, I think, in terms of the question of allegory—nonetheless, I am deeply indebted to it, both for its formulation of the "Jewish Question" and for its reading of Shylock in relation to Marx's money-form.

3. G. K. Hunter, "The Theology of Marlowe's *The Jew of Malta*," *Journal of the Warburg and Courtauld Institutes* 27 (1964): 215. James Shapiro discusses Hunter's work at length. See *Shakespeare and the Jews*, 83–85.

4. Shapiro, *Shakespeare and the Jews*, 85–86.

5. I'm alluding here to Goldhagen's chapter title, "The Evolution of Eliminationist Antisemitism in Modern Germany," in *Hitler's Willing Executioners: Ordinary Germans and the Holocaust* (New York: Vintage, 1997), 49–79.

6. Heiko A. Oberman, *The Roots of Anti-Semitism In the Age of Renaissance and Reformation*, tr. James I. Porter (Philadelphia: Fortress Press, 1984), xi.

7. Here, Elizabethan orthography will already suggest to us something of the instability for Shakespeare of this figure: *Iew* recalls not only the *use* of usury (or of Jacob's breeding *ewes* in Genesis 30: 32–42, to which Shylock compares his own usufruct [1.3.74–86) but also the celebrated *hew* [hue] (color, appearance, beauty, desirability) of, e.g., the young man in sonnet 20 ("A man in hew all *Hews* in his controwling"), as well as the incisive mark—the *hew*—with which such monumental alabaster is inscribed, compromised, and exposed (cf. for instance, the insistent quibbling on *hew* as "hue" and as "hew" in Shakespeare's most violent play: *Titus Andronicus*). In my current project, I explore just such a homonymic nexus, examining the question of economies linguistic, sexual, and financial in Shakespeare's work. Marc Shell offers an important lead in this effort with his essay "The Wether and the Ewe: Verbal Usury in *The Merchant of Venice*," in *Money, Language, and Thought* (Berkeley: University of California P, 1982): 47–83.

8. Many writers indeed distinguish between anti-Judaism and anti-Semitism, in order to stress the absolute nature of this religion/race dichotomy; before the nineteenth century, such formulations imply, there is literally no such thing as anti-Semitism. Indeed, as many writers are quick to point out, the word *Antisemitismus* itself wasn't coined until the latter part of that century. Wilhelm Marr, author of a number of anti-Semitism treatises, including the 1879 *Der Sieg des Judenthums über das Germanenthum* ("Jewry's Victory Over the Teutonic World"), is generally credited with coining the term. The OED cites an 1881 essay in the *Athenæum* as the earliest English usage of the word.

9. The context of the quote is indeed one of Žižek's frequent references to anti-Semitism. In general, I am greatly indebted to Žižek's work, which

played an early, formative role in my thinking about both anti-Semitism and ideology.

10. Indeed, one could argue that the prevailing understanding of anti-Semitism and its history needs to be turned, precisely, on its head. It is not a modern theory of racial identity that allows for the objective definition of the Jew, but rather a patristic and medieval theological conception that defines Jewish identity in the concrete, observable terms of practice and belief. It is the theological view that fixes the essence of Jewishness–albeit in the mutable terms of religious affiliation. It is the objectivity of this *theological* view that shifts in the sixteenth century, with Martin Luther's critique of a traditional allegorical framework.

11. Even James Shapiro, who rigorously questions the dichotomy of religion/race when applied to Elizabethan texts, seems to accept the dichotomy when it comes to characterizing a modern anti-Semitism: "those expecting a definitive answer to the question of whether Shakespeare was anti–or philosemitic will not find that answer here. I try to show instead that these anachronistic terms, inventions of nineteenth-century racial theory (and, since they are premised upon an imaginary racial category, uncapitalized here) are fundamentally ill-suited for gauging what transpired three hundred years earlier" (*Shakespeare and the Jews*, 11).

A word is in order here about the relationship between Shapiro's arguments and my own. In critiquing the formulations of G. K. Hunter and other modern critics, Shapiro suggests that "in late sixteenth-century England theology is not juxtaposed with racial thinking; in fact, it helps produce and define it" (84). For Shapiro, there are no clear boundaries between the categories of religion, race, and nation in early-modern England–indeed, Shapiro suggests that the early-modern Jewish question precisely consists in this categorical fluidity: just what *is* the Jew? I agree with Shapiro in many ways, and am indebted to his formulations in many respects–not least for his splendid reading of G. K. Hunter and other critics like him (83–88). I, too, maintain that the confusion of categories (especially insofar as that confusion frustrates the search for essences) is central to the Jewish question, but it is a confusion that I would argue extends into the modern period despite the emergence of race theory. Moreover, in my account I argue not that the religion/race dichotomy is anachronistic, exactly, but rather I draw attention to the ways in which the dichotomy is built into the Christian *theology* of Jewry from the start. It is, in fact, owing to the paradigm shift that theology undergoes in the wake of Martin Luther that the dichotomy becomes suddenly problematic for the early modern period.

One last point: I use the term "anti-Semitism" throughout this essay for two reasons. In the first place, because I see race theory as a response to an earlier shift in the theological understanding of Jews, and not as marking an absolute break with that view, I do not find the use of the term unduly anachronistic when applied to the early modern period. Nineteenth-century race theory attempts to *fix* an uncertainty in the relation between Jew and Christian that dates back, I argue, to the Reformation; my use of the nineteenth-century terminology for early modern texts is not meant to suggest that similar racial theories were available as such to those authors, but only to stress the continuity between early-modern and modern formulations of the problem. In the second place, unlike Shapiro (and other recent writers) I *do* capitalize "anti-*S*emitism." The category of race is certainly imaginary, but (as I argue above) one has misunderstood the structure of racism if one believes that it can be defeated by pointing out its lack of substantiating evidence. Such misunderstandings can afford a dangerous sense of complacency.

12. I touch briefly on this debate in chapter 4 as well, in the context of sonnet 35 ("No more bee greeu'd").

13. *On Free Will* serves as a response to the Manichean theory of evil, with its dualistic vision of the world. The burden of the treatise is to demonstrate how evil can exist if God is all good and omnipotent. The basic premise of the text is that "Evil is a turning of the will away from the unchangeable good, and toward changeable good" (2.18.53). Similar arguments pervade the *Confessions*, of course, and are particularly notable in book 8's discussion of the will (see especially 8.10). Notably, however, at the end of his life, in the 427 *Retractions* and in the face of the Pelagian heresy, Augustine saw fit to qualify his discussion of free will in order to emphasize the role of grace. Erasmus in many ways replicates this qualifying position when he argues that the proper approach to the subject of the *liberum arbitrium* is one that steers a path between presumption and despair, human ability and divine grace.

14. E. Gordon Rupp, P. Watson, tr., *Luther and Erasmus: Free Will and Salvation* (Philadelphia: Westminster Press, 1969), 86–87; 78. (All references to Erasmus' diatribe as in this edition.)

15. Martin Luther, *On the Bondage of the Will* [i.e., *De servo arbitrio*], tr. James I. Packer and O. R. Johnson (Grand Rapids, Mich.: James Clarke and Company, 1957), 102.

16. Cited in Rupp, *Luther And Erasmus*, 191.

17. "Preface to the Old Testament," LW 35, 242. The passage refers not specifically to Deuteronomy 30 but instead to the "office of the Law" more generally. See chapter 3 for an extended discussion of this passage and of the Law's office.

18. John Russell Brown reprints both the Moral and an excerpt from the tale as found in Richard Robinson's 1595 translation. Cf. *The Merchant of Venice*, ed. John Russell Brown (London: Routledge, 1991 [Methuen, 1955]), 174.

19. Barbara K. Lewalski, "Biblical Allusion and Allegory in *The Merchant of Venice*," *Shakespeare Quarterly* 13 (1962): 336. Lewalski (and later critics who

build on her observation) seem unaware that the *Gesta* moral offers a conflation of Deuteronomy 30 with a passage from the apocrypha–Sirach (also
known as "Ecclesiasticus"): "Before man is life and death; and whether him
liketh shall be given him" (KJV, see 15:14–17). The Sirach passage also plays
a central role in Erasmus' discussion. It is the text with which he begins his
scriptural argument and the text from which he draws his definition of free
will.

20. See Douglas Anderson, "The Old Testament Presence in *The Merchant of Venice*," *ELH* 52, no. 1 (Spring 1985): 119–32.

21. Furness follows Folio reading–"it is no *smal* happinesse"–but notes
the preferability of the Q1's play on *mean*.

22. Its "fullness," in other words, fails to count as plenitude; to be "full" of
holes is to be decisively (wholly, shall we say?) lacking in depth, interiority: to
be decisively *not* a container.

23. Portia's plural usage–*meshes*–is significantly ambiguous as well. She
could be denoting a multiplicity of holes, or a collective singularity (i.e., a netting comprising the knotted threads). She could also be describing more than
one netting: despite continual failure, the brain keeps devising mesh*es*, keeps
devising *decrees*, to ensnare the hot blood.

24. To follow through my metaphor of Luther's Law as mesh: these
"holes" are nothing other than the gap that separates infinite demand from
finite performance. As the history of the Talmud would suggest, there are
always ways to get around the Law, because there is no exhaustive way to
specify–much less to perform–the immeasurable obedience it commands.
Even our most diligent efforts only reveal the Law's loopholes; even our most
righteous deeds "get around the Law," falling short of absolute compliance.

25. Mary Janell Metzger discusses the homology between marriage and
religious conversion in a recent essay that focuses on Jessica's assimilation.
See Metzger's "'Now by My Hood, a Gentle and No Jew': Jessica, *The Merchant of Venice*, and the Discourse of Early Modern English Identity," *PMLA*
113, no. 1 (January 1998): 52–63. Metzger's basic argument is that Jessica
mediates the oppositions within the play by differing from both her father and
the Christians. She is the fair Jewess–an oxymoronic identity (like the "Indian
beautie" Bassanio invokes as he faces the casket trial–see below). As a living
oxymoron, Jessica is able to negotiate the difference between race and faith.

26. Harold Goddard, "The Three Caskets," reprinted in *Shakespeare: The
Merchant of Venice. A Casebook*, ed. John Wilders (London: Macmillan, 1969),
144. See also René Girard, "To Entrap the Wisest: Sacrificial Ambivalence in
The Merchant of Venice and *Richard III*," reprinted in *A Theater of Envy: William
Shakespeare* (New York and Oxford: Oxford UP, 1991): 243–55. Halpern discusses Girard's ironic reading of the play in *Shakespeare Among the Moderns*,
176–84.

27. Indeed, even among modern readers of the play, a harmonizing, alle-

gorizing reading has appeared to be compatible with an ironic view. An important case in point: John Weiss, the nineteenth-century critic that Danson credits with originating the ironic reading of Portia's song, is himself aware of no ironies. Even while conceding that Portia has (albeit "unconsciously") broken her oath, Weiss nonetheless insists as strenuously as Danson on the harmonious power of love: "A hint indeed! It is the very breadth of broadness, and a lover is not dull. . . . The strain reminds Bassanio of notices in his experience. . . . The melody woven out of air glides into his hand, and becomes a clew to bliss" (John Weiss, *Wit, Humor, and Shakespeare* [Boston: Roberts Brothers, 1876], 312, quoted in Furness, 141–42).

28. Note here Halpern's deployment of that famous Romantic antithesis: allegory and symbol. The two would certainly have been at odds for a Coleridge (or for a de Man, for that matter), but not for an Augustine.

29. See Danson, 170. The phrase "worldly chooser," a favorite with readers like Danson, is taken from Stephen Gosson's 1579 anti-theatrical treatise *School of Abuse*. Gosson refers to a non-extant play–*The Jew*–that has long been cited as the precursor to *Merchant.* See Geoffrey Bullough, *Narrative and Dramatic Sources of Shakespeare,* 8 vols. (London: Routledge, and New York: Columbia UP, 1957–1975), 1:445–46.

30. See, for example, her two notorious comments about his skin color. Indeed, Portia's rejection of Morocco amounts precisely to an explicit, knowing rejection of disjunctive reading: "If he haue the condition of a Saint, and the complexion of a diuell, I had rather hee should shriue me than wiue me" (1.2.126–27). (Portia's other, often remarked comment closes 2.7: "Let all of his complexion choose me so" [81]). The sharpest disjunction imaginable between inside and outside–black versus white, devil versus saint–only serves to *confirm* the rule of appearances by radically curtailing the influence of internal virtues. Inner saintliness may have its uses in the inner, private space of confession–but the mere complexion of the devil is enough to damn Morocco out in the open.

31. Arragon alludes to the baseness of lead and the preciousness of silver, but in effect he bases his decision on a reading of the inscriptions only. Bassanio, as we've already noted, explicitly comments on only the metals themselves, ignoring the inscriptions. Certainly dramatic expediency plays a role here; to have three different characters rehearse exactly the same clues with the same level of deliberative detail would have been tedious theater, and so a good playwright must vary the formula somewhat, attenuating the deliberations in order to keep the interest of an audience that, no doubt, already has figured out the right answer. Yet the *manner* in which Shakespeare varies and attenuates the scene is crucial, and requires interpretation.

32. See Michael Nerlich's important Marxist reading of the play, "The Merchant Adventurer Leaves the Ship," in *The Ideology of Adventure* (Minneapolis: U of Minnesota P, 1987): 108–82. Nerlich reads the play as drama-

tizing the triumph of capitalism–associated with a bourgeois celebration of economic risk and venture–over a feudalism that offers no chance for individual freedom.

33. Portia calls Bassanio both *Alcides* and *Hercules* as he faces the casket test, alluding to the Ovidian story of the virgin-tribute Hesione's rescue from the sea monster (see *Metamorphoses* 11.199 ff.): "I stand for sacrifice / The rest aloofe are the Dardanian wiues" (see 3.2.60–61). Morocco also compares himself to Hercules when he complains about the casket trial as a game of chance: "If *Hercules* and *Lychas* plaie at dice / Which is the better man, the greater throw / May turne by fortune from the weaker hand" (2.1.37–39). Lychas was the servant who was thrown by Hercules into the sea after he unwittingly brought Hercules a shirt dipped in venom (see *Metamorphoses* xi.155). Bassanio likens Portia's "sunny locks" to the golden fleece in (1.1.179–82). The pun on *fleece/fleets* occurs in 3.2.254–56: "*Gra.* We are *Iasons*, we haue won the fleece. / *Sal.* I would you had won the fleece [fleets] that hee [Anthonio] hath lost."

34. In Ovid's version, Venus tells Adonis the story of Atalanta and Hippomenes in order to dissuade Adonis from the hunt. Stirred to acts of "Uenerie" by Venus herself, Atalanta and Hippomenes profane a temple consecrated to Cybele. For punishment they are turned to lions. Venus tells Adonis to shun such fierce and wild creatures–but the story itself sounds more of a cautionary note about the very acts of venery that the love goddess now prompts Adonis to commit. Small wonder that Adonis does not heed her advice; the choice he has been offered is to hunt lions or be transformed into one. (All references to the *Metamorphoses* as in Arthur Golding's 1567 translation.)

35. Barnabe Barnes, *Parthenophil and Parthenophe. Sonnettes, Madrigals, Elegies, and Odes* (London: J. Wolf, 1593).

36. See Portia's equivocating response to Morocco's suit, earlier in the play: "In tearmes of choise I am not solie led / By nice direction of a maidens eies: /. . . / But if my Father had not scanted me, /. . . / Your self (renowned Prince) than stood as faire / As any commer I haue look'd on yet" (2.1.17–25).

37. Indeed, far from naive or un-Christian in their hermeneutic methods, readers like Morocco (and the presumably Catholic Arragon) follow the same rhetorical principles outlined by the Church fathers, exploring the conventions that align literal and figural meanings. "Is't *like* that Lead contains her?" Morocco asks. He seeks the hidden content by analyzing probabilities and similitudes; the single principle of *likeness* governs his reading. In this way, rather than presume the immediate givenness of meaning, Morocco defines and tests a rule to guide his allegorizing. Indeed, the rule he identifies is the very same rule Augustine articulates in *On Christian Doctrine*: "And when [an expression] is shown to be figurative, the words in which it is expressed will

be found to be drawn either from *like* objects or from objects having some *affinity*" (3.25.34, emphasis added). What ensures the disjunctive nature of allegory is, in fact, this principle of likeness, for it is precisely insofar as the external sign is a mere reflection—an *imago* or *speculum*—that it is ultimately to be discarded as veil. When our hearts turn to God, "the vaile shal be taken away": "For now we see through a glasse darkly: but then *shall we see* face to face. Now I know in part: but then shall I know euen as I am knowen" (2 Cor. 3:16, 1 Cor. 13:12, Geneva Bible).

Finally, the analogy with which Morocco concludes his reflections reveals the sophistication of his hermeneutic approach. "They haue in England / A coyne that beares the figure of an Angell / Stampt in gold, but that's insculpt vpon: / But here an Angell in a golden bed / Lies all within" (2.7.56–60). In effect, Morocco has already treated the caskets as coins by considering their value in terms of not only their metal substance but also their inscriptions. Here, however, the analogy between a coin and its engraved exergue becomes explicit. Portia's hidden image is envisioned here as something like the limit case of engraving. Where the coin's angel is only superficially insculpted, Portia's image is inscribed *so* deeply that it "lies all within": it is an engraving that doesn't just mark a surface; it defines interiority itself. And thus it is an image that can never be abraded in the usurious course of exchange. In this way, the golden casket becomes something like a super-coin: a token of enduring worth and value. Portia's portrait is thus put to good use. Echoing centuries of Western sign theory—and anticipating a modern semiotics—Morocco "solves" the riddle of the caskets by noting the analogy between signs and money.

For Richard Halpern, who reads the casket subplot in terms of Marx's analysis of economic value, Morocco's lines here indicate his reluctance to accept the tautologous nature of exchange value by positing a hidden essence—Portia herself—"lying imperturbably beneath the ephemeral and differential play" of surfaces. Morocco's mystification, Halpern argues, reproduces the logic of commodity fetishism where the "interiorized reflection" of the play of difference yields a mystical notion of depth (Halpern, 193). But if Morocco's analogy replicates the sort of commodity fetishism that transforms qualities into quantities, use values into exchange values, it does so not as a rejection of disjunctive reading—as Halpern maintains—but rather as its culmination. Indeed, what Morocco's exegesis reveals is the lesson taught by Luther's critique of *figura*: the effort to strip away the flesh in the name of spiritual content only transforms the flesh into fetish, making us drown in it all the more. It is indeed to combat this sort of fetishism that Luther critiques the traditional reading of the flesh as figural veil.

38. In her introduction to the *Norton Shakespeare* edition of the play, Katharine Eisaman Maus offers a canny example of such "other means" to rig the game: "Because every suitor gets the same chance, the casket test seems

to be fair; in fact, it is rather like those 'objective' intelligence tests that, in subtler or not-so-subtle ways, reward the belief systems of dominant groups while stigmatizing outsiders" (1086).

39. Thus in lines 83–94, Bassanio runs through examples of biblical exegesis, general virtue, and epic valor in consistently catachrestic terms. The biblical exegesis that blesses "damned error" is qualitatively no different from those interpretations grounding true faith; instead, it is the very confusion and proliferation of "seeming truths" that makes all exegetical "ornaments" suspect. Likewise, if vice is not "simple," neither can it be simply distinguished from that virtue whose mark it carries. And again, since so many can play the part of Hercules or Mars and assume "valors excrement," how can we distinguish the lily-livered cowards from men like Bassanio himself who also take the part of "yong *Alcides*" (3.2.58)? In these examples, what damns and taints the interior is not a *false* exterior but rather an exterior show of *truth*. Such "seeming truths" call into question the very opposition between inside and outside, true and false.

40. See Furness, 145 n. 103.

41. In his treatment of the line, Furnesss cites William Nanson Lettsom's note to W. S. Walker's *Critical Examination of the Text of Shakespeare*, 3 vols. (London: J. R. Smith, 1860), 1:291.

42. The two centuries of critics cited in Furness's gloss are most often troubled by the jingling repetition of *beautious* and *beauty*, and by the apparent oxymoron of an Indian beauty (cf. 146–47).

43. Lisa Renée Lampert, "After Eden, Out of Zion: Defining the Christian in Early English Literature" (Ph.D. diss., University of California, Berkeley, 1996), 235. Ultimately Lampert interprets Bassanio's veiled Indian in terms of the play's consideration of race and religion, exposing the implicit threat of miscegenation that troubles the play's construction of normative (i.e., white, male) Christian identity. "Bassanio's speech," writes Lampert, "shows how the discourse of exploration seems to eat like an acid at the discourse of exegesis in *The Merchant of Venice*" (237). Lampert's work builds on Carolyn Dinshaw's reading of the veil in *Chaucer's Sexual Poetics* (Madison: U of Wisconsin P, 1989). I am indebted to Lampert, who shared her work with me at a crucial moment in my research, reminding me of the significance of Bassanio's veil.

44. A related ambiguity attends the relationship between shore and sea in the image. Which comes first? Is the shore what leads us out into the sea, or is it the harbor that welcomes us from it? Are we deceived when we head out into dangerous waters, or in our homecoming–or in neither, or in both?

45. While, as Furness notes, Montaigne cites the "blackness" of Indians in the *Apology for Raymond Sebond*, and while modern editors without exception follow Furness's reading of "Indian" as denoting swarthy, the intriguing possibility of an alternate reading is raised when one considers associations

dating back to the middle ages of India with gold and saffron. Saffron was used in the middle ages not only to tint the vellum of manuscripts but also as a blond hair dye. (Thanks to Elizabeth Szalnic for this point.) Although allusions to "Indian gold" were also common in Shakespeare's time, I've been unable to locate any contemporary references to saffron used as hair coloring or to Indian beauty as a falsified fairness. For Montaigne's reference to Indian beauty, see *Essais* 2.12, cited from the 1595 edition: "Les Indes la [i.e., la beauté du corps] peignent noire et basannée, aux levres grosses et enflées, au nez plat et large." Significantly, Montaigne is here discussing the relativism of standards of beauty, precisely rejecting the language of idealism that Shakespeare both sustains and problematizes.

46. Following Jean-Joseph Goux's analysis of Jewish culture, the proscription against images and the birth of theory in Marx and Freud, Halpern discusses iconoclasm in *Merchant* at great length, and situates the play's ambivalence toward such demystification ultimately, embodied and chastened, in the figure of the Jew. See Halpern, 216.

47. See my discussion of this point in chapter 3.

48. Furness cites one nineteenth-century reader who interestingly bears this point out in his emendation of 3.2.105: "Let me attempt to restore the antithesis of the passage: 'Veiling an Indian *Deity*,' the Oriental idols being, as travellers tell us, gaudily attired and awfully ugly" (147 n).

49. See my discussion of Luther's response to Karlstadt in chapter 3.

50. Leon Battista Alberti, *Della pittura*, ed. Luigi Malle (Firenze: Sansoni, 1950), 83–84. English translation taken from *On Painting*, tr. John R. Spencer (New Haven: Yale UP, 1966), 68–69. Spencer's translation collates the Latin and Italian versions of Alberti's text.

51. Shapiro discusses the way Gollancz uses these lines to insulate himself from the play's potential anti-Semitism. *Shakespeare and the Jews*, 79.

52. Where they don't seek to emend the term (as, e.g., "pattern"), editors often, but not always, gloss *paten* as sacramental plate. (W. Moelwyn Merchant and John Russell Brown both, for instance, gloss the term in this way, but Katherine Eisaman Maus, editor of the 1997 *Norton Shakespeare* edition, glosses it as "disk.") Danson mentions the sacramentalist connotation of the *paten* but does not elaborate on it (*Harmonies*, 186–87).

53. But compare John Russell Brown's argument in the 1955 Arden edition of *Merchant* that it was entirely conventional for melancholics to be ignorant of (or at least tight-lipped about) the cause of their sadness.

54. As W. Moelwyn Merchant notes in his gloss of these lines for the New Penguin edition, there is nothing in the surviving effigies of Janus to suggest that the Romans saw his two faces as alternating between happy and sad. (See *The Merchant of Venice*, ed. W. Moelwyn Merchant (Harmondsworth: 1995 [1967]). Shakespeare seems, Merchant argues, to be conflating Janus with the two masks of comedy and tragedy. I would argue that the connec-

tion to theater is perhaps an intentional elaboration of Janus's function as the god of entrances and exits. To return to melancholy Jaques: in a world of theatrical masks, all the men and women "have their entrances and their exits." Like Jaques and Hamlet, Anthonio's melancholy is immediately conjoined with a recognition that the world's a stage: "I hold the world but as the world Gratiano, / A stage, where euery man must play a part, / And mine a sad one" (1.1.86–88).

One last note about the Janus head. For Lawrence Danson, the two-headed Janus offers an emblem for the allegorical "harmonies" of *Merchant*; like the two-faced god, the play embodies a balance of opposites, reconciling the competing principles it sets forth in a single figure (cf. *Harmonies*, 1–18). Given my own rabbit/duck reading of Janus, it should be clear that I differ with Danson here.

55. See, e.g., Stephen Greenblatt's discussion of the bagpipe speech as exemplifying the ways in which Shylock "seems to embody the abstract principle of *difference* itself" ("Marlowe, Marx, and Anti-Semitism," *Critical Inquiry* (Winter 1978): 295). To a certain extent, Greenblatt qualifies his earlier discussion of Jews in Shakespeare's England, in his review of Shapiro's *Shakespeare and the Jews*. See Stephen Greenblatt, "An English Obsession," *New York Times Book Review*, August 11, 1996, 12–13.

56. Shylock will give no reason for his obstinacy, except to cite the same obstinate particularity with which he, as Jew, is identified. Yet of course, for Shylock it is this particularity of the flesh that Jews and Christians most share in common; his "Hath not a Jew eyes?" speech suggests that the universality to which the Duke appeals may only, in the final analysis, be conceivable through the flesh. If Shylock speaks for the Jews' particular, fleshly resistance to a language of Christian "kindness" or universalism, he does so only by transforming the predicament of the flesh into a new universal.

57. Halpern discusses such superficiality, and its relation to depth, in terms of Marx's critique of the special fetishism of the money-form, 193 ff. My only quibble with this reading would be to point out that if the money-form only gives the illusion of depth, the "veils of mystification" (Halpern, 195) that Marx strips away in order to reveal that illusion are veils in the terms that Luther decries. In this way, the revelatory critique manages to strip away illusion only by creating its own sense of a depth that goes beyond surface. Whence the ease with which the critical gesture becomes fetishized in its own right (and whence too, perhaps, both the appeal of and the resistance to Theory that Halpern describes in the final section of his essay, 210–26).

58. Luther discusses harsh mercy in the most widely-quoted passage from his longest and most virulent treatise against the Jews: the 1543 "On the Jews and their Lies" (written just two years before his death). See LW 47, 268 ff. As Shapiro points out, this 1971 edition of *Luther's Works* is the first complete English translation of the polemic–although there is evidence that the Eliza-

bethans had indirect knowledge of Luther's anti-Semitic writings (Shapiro, 233 n. 27). The German text, "Von den Juden und ihren Lügen," and in particular the passage on harsh mercy, can be found in the Weimar Ausgabe of Luther's works: *Werke: Kritische Gesamtausgabe* 53 (Weimar, 1968 [1920]), 522.

59. Louise M. Bishop has suggested to me a possible pun between a "strained" mercy and the mesh that entraps the wisest, arguing for a connection between the reticulated structure of a strainer and the crisscross netting of the mesh.

60. Both Barbara Lewalski and Lawrence Danson have noted the office of the Law in 4.1. But neither critic recognizes the ways in which that office becomes indispensable and at the same time thoroughly problematic for the Protestant believer. For Lewalski the notion of the Law as our "schoolmaster" in Christ (Galatians 3:24) is merely a "tactic" that Portia uses to defeat the Jew (341–42). Danson, for his part, recognizes the "apparently irreconcilable tendencies toward grace or toward law" (80) for Shakespeare's contemporaries, yet still wants to imagine Portia and the play's other Christians as standing at a didactic remove from the lesson they teach Shylock. "In making sin appear *as* sin, God's law performs the crucial didactic function that Portia will make Venice's law perform, making man aware of his inevitably sinful nature (since no man can perform all the works of the law), and hence of his dependence upon God for salvation" (77). Neither Lewalski nor Danson see the treatment of the Law in 4.1 as jeopardizing the play's profoundly allegorical nature. Interestingly, Lewalski questions the idea that Shylock's conversion is even forced (she places quotation marks around the phrase *forced conversion*): "his brief 'I am content' suggests, I believe, not mean-spiritedness but weary acknowledgement of the fact that he can no longer make his stand upon the discredited law" (341).

SELECTED BIBLIOGRAPHY

PRIMARY TEXTS

Ad C. Herennium. De Ratione Dicendi (Rhetorica ad Herennium). Book 4. Latin and English. Tr. Harry Caplan. Cambridge: Harvard University Press, 1954.

Alberti, Leon Battista. *Della Pittura*. Ed. Luigi Malle. Firenze: Sansoni, 1950.

——. *On Painting*. Tr. John R. Spencer. New Haven: Yale University Press, 1966.

Alighieri, Dante. *The Divine Comedy*. Tr. Charles S. Singleton. 1973. Reprint, Princeton: Princeton University Press, 1982.

Augustine. *De Civitate Dei*. In Österreichische Akademie der Wissenschaften, edited by *Corpus Scriptorum Ecclesiasticorum Latinorum*. Vol. 40. Vienna: F. Tempsky, 1866–.

——. *Confessions*. 2 vols. English and Latin. Tr. William Watts. Cambridge: Harvard University Press, 1912.

——. Contra Faustum Manicheum. In Österreichische Akademie der Wissenschaften, ed. *Corpus Scriptorum Ecclesiasticorum Latinorum*. Vol. 25, pts. 1–2. Vienna: F. Tempsky, 1866–.

——. *De Doctrina Christiana (Le Magistère Chrétien)*. Latin and French. In *Bibliothèque Augustinienne: Oeuvres de Saint Augustin*. 1st ser., vol. 11. Tr. and ed. Gustave Combes and Jacques Farges. Paris: Desclée de Brouwer, 1949.

——. *De Magistro(Dialogues Philosophiques: De L'âme à Dieu)*. Latin and French. In *Bibliothèque Augustinienne. Oeuvres de Saint Augustin*. 1st ser., vol. 6. Ed. François Joseph Thonnard. Paris: Desclée de Brouwer, 1941.

——. *The Problem of Free Choice*. Tr. Dom Mark Pontifex. New York: Newman Press, 1955.

——. *The Spirit and the Letter*. In *Augustine: Later Works*, edited by John Burnaby, 193–250. Philadelphia: Westminster, 1980.

——. *Tractatus Adversos Iudaeos*. In *Patrologia Cursus Completus* [PL], edited by J-P Migne. 1st ser., 42:51–64. Turnhout: Brepols, 1977.

——. *Treatises on Marriage and Other Subjects*. Ed. Roy J. Deferrari. Washington, D.C.: Catholic University of American Press, 1969.

Barnes, Barnabe. *Parthenophil and Parthenophe: Sonnettes, Madrigals, Elegies, and Odes*. London: J. Wolf, 1593.

Erasmus, Desiderius. "Handbook of the Christian Soldier." In *The Erasmus Reader*, edited by Erika Rummel, 138–54. Toronto: University of Toronto Press, 1990.

Heywood, Thomas. *An Apology for Actors*. London: Nicholas Okes, 1612.

Luther, Martin. *D. Martin Luthers Werke: Kritische Gesamtausgabe* [WA]. Weimar: H. Böhlau, 1883–.

——. *D. Martin Luthers Werke: Kritische Gesamtausgabe*. Tischreden [WAT]. Weimar: H. Böhlau, 1912–1921.

——. *Luther's Works*. American ed. [LW]. Vols. 1–30, ed. Jaroslav Pelikan. Vols. 31–54, ed. Helmut T. Lehman. Philadelphia: Fortress Press, 1955–1976.

——. *Martin Luther on the Bondage of the Will*. Tr. James I. Packer and O. R. Johnson. Grand Rapids, Mich.: James Clarke, 1957.

——. "The Pagan Servitude of the Church." In *Martin Luther: Selections from His Writings*, edited by John Dillenberger and translated by Bertram Lee Woolf, 249–59. New York: Doubleday, 1961.

Luther, Martin, and Desiderius Erasmus. *Luther and Erasmus: Free Will and Salvation*. Tr. E. Gordon Rupp and P. Watson. Philadelphia: Westminster Press, 1969.

Petrarca, Francesco. *Le Familiari*. 4 vols. Ed. Vittorio Rossi and Umberto Bosco. Firenzi: Sansoni, 1933–1942.

——. *Letters of Old Age: Rerum senilium libri I–XVIII, [Sen.]* 2 vols. Tr. and ed. Aldo S. Bernardo, Saul Levin, and Reta A. Bernardo. Baltimore: Johns Hopkins University Press, 1992.

——. *Letters on Familiar Matters. Rerum familiarium libri XXIV*. 3 vols. Tr. and ed. Aldo S. Bernardo. Baltimore: Johns Hopkins University Press, 1975–1985.

——. "On His Own Ignorance." In *The Renaissance Philosophy of Man*, translated by Hans Nachod and edited by Ernst Cassirer, Paul Oskar Kristeller, and John Herman Randall Jr., 114–15. Chicago: University of Chicago Press, 1948.

——. *Opere di Francesco Petrarca*. Ed. Emilio Bigi, Giovanni Ponte, and Giuseppe Fracassetti. Milano: Mursia, 1963–1994.

——. *Petrarch's Lyric Poems: The Rime Sparse and Other Lyrics*. Italian and English. Tr. Robert M. Durling. Cambridge: Harvard University Press, 1976.

Puttenham, George. *The Arte of English Poesie*. London: Richard Field, 1589.

Quintilian. *Institutio Oratoria*. Latin and English. 3 vols. Tr. H. E. Butler. Reprint, Cambridge: Harvard University Press, 1976.

Ronsard, Pierre de. *Les Amours (1552–1584)*. Ed. Marc Bensimon and James L. Martin. Paris: Garnier-Flammarion, 1981.

Shakespeare, William. *The Narrative Poems*. Ed. Maurice Evans. Harmondsworth, Middlesex, Eng.: Penguin, 1989.

——. *A New Variorum Edition of Shakespeare: The Poems*. Ed. Hyder Edward Rollins. Philadelphia: Lippincott, 1938.

——. *A New Variorum Edition of Shakespeare: The Sonnets*. Ed. Hyder Edward Rollins. Philadelphia: Lippincott, 1944.

——. *A New Variorum Edition of Shakespeare: The Merchant of Venice*. Ed. Horace Howard Furness. Reprint, New York: Dover, 1964.

——. *The Norton Shakespeare*. Ed. Stephen Greenblatt, Walter Cohen, Jean E. Howard, Katharine Eisaman Maus, and Andrew Gurr. New York: Norton, 1997.

——. *The Merchant of Venice*. Ed. John Russell Brown. London: Routledge, 1994.

——. *The Merchant of Venice*. Ed. W. Moelwyn Merchant. Reprint, Harmondsworth, Middlesex, Eng.: Penguin, 1995.

——. *The Poems*. Ed. E. T. Price. Methuen, 1961. Reprint, London: Routledge, 1996.

——. *Shakespeare's Sonnets*. Ed. with analytic commentary by Stephen Booth. New Haven: Yale University Press, 1977.

——. *Shakespeare's Sonnets*. Ed. Katherine Duncan-Jones. Nashville: Thomas Nelson, 1997.

——. *Sonnets*. Ed. W. G. Ingram and Theodore Redpath. London: University of London Press, 1964.

——. *The Sonnets*. Ed. G. Blakemore Evans. Cambridge, Eng.: Cambridge University Press, 1996.

——. *The Sonnets and A Lover's Complaint*. Ed. John Kerrigan. New York: Viking Penguin, 1986.

——. *Sonnets of Shakespeare*. Ed. Sidney Lee. Oxford: Clarendon Press, 1905.

——. *The Sonnets of Shakespeare*. Ed. T. G. Tucker. Cambridge, Eng.: University Press, 1924.

——. *The Sonnets of William Shakespeare*. Ed. Edward Dowden. London: K. Paul, Trench, 1881.

Sheppard, Gerald T., ed. *Geneva Bible (The Annotated New Testament, 1602 Edition)*. New York: Pilgrim Press, 1989.

Sidney, Sir Philip. *Astrophil and Stella*. In *The Complete Works of Sir Philip Sidney*, edited by Albert Feuillerat, 2:241–301. 4 vols. Cambridge, Eng.: University Press, 1922–1926.

Tertullian. *Adversus Marcionem*. 2 vols. Latin and English. Ed. and tr. Ernest Evans. Oxford: Clarendon Press, 1972.

Wilson, Thomas. *The Arte of Rhetorique for the Use of All Suche as are Studious of Eloquence*. London: Richardus Graftonus, 1553.

SECONDARY TEXTS

Allen, Judson Boyce. "Grammar, Poetic Form, and the Lyric Ego: A Medieval A Priori." In *Vernacular Poetics in the Middle Ages*, edited by Lois Ebin, 199–226. Kalamazoo, Mich.: Medieval Institute Publications, 1984.

Anderson, Douglas. "The Old Testament Presence in *The Merchant of Venice*." *English Literary History* 52, no. 1 (Spring 1985): 119–32.

Ascoli, Albert Russell. "Petrarch's Middle Age: Memory, Imagination, History, and the 'Ascent of Mount Ventoux.'" *Stanford Italian Review* 10, no. 1 (1991): 5–43.

Auerbach, Erich. "Figura." In *Scenes from the Drama of European Literature: Six Essays*, translated by Ralph Mannheim, 11–76. New York: Meridian, 1959.

Austin, J. L. *How to Do Things with Words*. 2d ed. Cambridge: Harvard University Press, 1975.

Avni, Ora. *The Resistance of Reference: Linguistics, Philosophy, and the Literary Text*. Baltimore: Johns Hopkins University Press, 1990.

Bainton, Roland H. *Here I Stand: A Life of Martin Luther*. New York: New American Library, 1950.

Barolini, Teodolinda. "The Making of a Lyric Sequence: Time and Narrative in Petrarch's *Rerum vulgarium fragmenta*." *Modern Language Notes* 104, no. 1 (January 1989): 1–38.

Benveniste, Émile. *Problèmes de linguistique générale*. 2 vols. Paris: Éditions Gallimard, 1966.

——. *Problems in General Linguistics*. Tr. Mary Elizabeth Meek. Coral Gables: University of Miami Press, 1971.

Billanovich, Guiseppe. "Petrarca e il Ventoso." *Italia Medioevale e Umanistica* 9 (1966): 389–401.

Blackman, E. C. *Marcion and His Influence*. London: SPCK, 1948.

Blanchot, Maurice. *L'Espace littéraire*. Paris: Gallimard, 1955.

Bornkamm, Heinrich. *Luther and the Old Testament*. Tr. Eric W. and Ruth C. Gritsch. Philadelphia: Fortress, 1969.

Boyarin, Daniel. "Paul and the Genealogy of Gender." *Representations* 41 (Winter 1993): 1–33.

——. *A Radical Jew: Paul and the Politics of Identity.* Berkeley: University of California Press, 1994.

Brown, Norman O. *Life Against Death: The Psychoanalytic Meaning of History.* New York: Vintage Books, 1959.

Brown, Peter. *Augustine of Hippo.* Berkeley: University of California Press, 1969.

Bullough, Geoffrey. *Narrative and Dramatic Sources of Shakespeare.* 8 vols. London: Routledge; New York: Columbia University Press, 1957.

Carruthers Mary. *The Book of Memory: A Study of Memory in Medieval Culture.* Cambridge: Cambridge University Press, 1990.

Cave, Terence. *The Cornucopian Text: Problems of Writing in the French Renaissance.* Oxford: Oxford University Press, 1979.

Christensen, Carl C. *Art and the Reformation in Germany.* Athens: Ohio University Press, 1979.

Coghill, Nevill. "The Basis of Shakespearian Comedy." In *Essays and Studies,* edited by G. Rostrevor Hamilton, 1–28. London: John Murray, 1950.

Constable, Giles. "Petrarch and Monasticism." In Aldo S. Bernardo, ed., *Francesco Petrarca Citizen of the World. Proceedings of the World Petrarch Congress, Washington, D.C., April 6–13, 1974,* 53–99. Padova: Editrice Antenore; Albany: SUNY Press, 1980.

Contini, Gianfranco. "Preliminari sulla lingua del Petrarca." Introduction to *Canzoniere.* Torino: G. Einaudi, 1964.

Cooper, John C. "Why Did Augustine Write Books XI–XIII of *The Confessions?*" *Augustinian Studies* 2 (1971): 37–46.

Courcelle, Pierre. *Les Confessions de St. Augustin dans la tradition littéraire.* Paris: Etudes Augustiniennes, 1963.

——. "Pétrarque entre Saint Augustin et les Augustins du XIVe siecle." *Studi Petrarcheschi* 7 (1961): 51–71.

Croken, Robert C., S.J. *Luther's First Front: The Eucharist as Sacrifice.* Ottawa: University of Ottawa Press, 1990.

Culler, Jonathan. "Changes in the Study of Lyric." In *Lyric Poetry: Beyond New Criticism,* edited by Chaviva Hosek and Patricia Parker, 38–54. Ithaca: Cornell University Press, 1985.

Daniélou, Jean, S.J. "La typologie d'Isaac dans la Christianisme Primitif." *Biblica* 28 (1947): 363–93.

——. "Les divers sens de l'Ecriture dans la tradition primitive." *Ephemerides Theologicae Lovanienses* 24 (1948): 119–26.

——. *From Shadows to Reality: Studies in the Biblical Typology of the Fathers.* Tr. Dom Wulstan Hibberd. London: Burns and Oates, 1960.

Danson, Lawrence. *The Harmonies of "The Merchant of Venice."* New Haven: Yale University Press, 1978.

Davis, Thomas M. "The Traditions of Puritan Typology." In *Typology and Early American Literature,* edited by Sacvan Bercovitch, 11–45. Amherst: University of Massachusetts Press, 1972.

De Grazia, Margareta. "Babbling Will in *Shake-speares Sonnets* 127–154." *Spenser Studies* 1 (1980): 121–34.

——. "The Scandal of Shakespeare's Sonnets." *Shakespeare Survey* 46 (1994): 35–49.

De Lubac, Henri. *Exégèse médiévale: Les quatre sens de l'écriture.* 4 vols. Paris: Aubier, 1959–64.

——. "'Typologie' et 'Allegorisme.'" *Recherches de Science Religieuse* 34 (1947): 180–226.

Derrida, Jacques. "From Restricted to General Economy: A Hegelianism Without Reserve," In *Writing and Difference,* 251–77. Tr. Alan Bass. London: Routledge and Kegan Paul, 1978.

——. "Signature Event Context." In *Margins of Philosophy,* 307–30. Tr. Alan Bass. Chicago: University of Chicago Press, 1982.

——. "White Mythology: Metaphor in the Text of Philosophy." In *Margins of Philosophy,* 207–71. Tr. Alan Bass. Chicago: University of Chicago Press, 1982.

Devereux, E. J. "Tudor Uses of Erasmus on the Eucharist." *Archiv für Reformationsgeschichte* 62 (1971): 38–52.

Dewey, Arthur J. *Spirit and Letter in Paul.* Studies in the Bible and Early Christianity, vol. 33. Lewiston, N.Y.: Edwin Mellen Press, 1996.

Dubrow, Heather. *Captive Victors: Shakespeare's Narrative Poems and Sonnets.* Ithaca: Cornell University Press, 1987.

——."'Incertainties Now Crown Themselves Assur'd': The Politics of Plotting Shakespeare's Sonnets." *Shakespeare Quarterly* 47, no. 3 (Fall 1996): 291–305.

Duncan-Jones, Katherine. "Was the 1609 Shake-speares Sonnets Really Unauthorized?" *Review of English Studies* 34, no. 134 (May 1983): 151–71.

Dunn, Kevin. *Pretexts of Authority: The Rhetoric of Authorship in the Renaissance Preface.* Stanford, Calif.: Stanford University Press, 1994.

Durling, Robert M. "Petrarch's 'Giovene donna sotto un verde lauro.'" *Modern Language Notes* 86, no. 1 (January 1971): 1–20.

——. "The Ascent of Mt. Ventoux and the Crisis of Allegory." *Italian Quarterly* 18, no. 69 (Summer 1974): 7–28.

Erikson, Erik. *Young Man Luther: A Study in Psychoanalysis and History.* 1958. Reprint, New York: Norton, 1962.

Fineman, Joel. "The Structure of Allegorical Desire." In *Allegory and Representation,* edited by Stephen J. Greenblatt, 26–60. Baltimore: Johns Hopkins University Press, 1981.

——. "Shakespeare's Will: The Temporality of Rape." *Representations* 20 (Fall 1987): 25–76.

——. "The Turn of the Shrew." In Shakespeare and The Question of Theory, edited by Patricia Parker and Geoffrey Hartman, 138–59. New York: Methuen, 1985.

——. *Shakespeare's Perjured Eye: The Invention of Poetic Subjectivity in the Sonnets.* Berkeley: University of California Press, 1986.

——. "The Sound of O in *Othello*: The Real Tragedy of Desire." In *Critical Essays on Shakespeare's Othello*, edited by Anthony Gerard, 104–23. New York: G. K. Hall, 1994.

Flores, Ralph. "Reading and Speech in St. Augustine's Confessions." *Augustinian Studies* 6 (1975): 1–13.

Foster, Donald W. "Master W.H., R.I.P." *PMLA* 102 (1987): 42–54.

——. "Reconstructing Shakespeare Part 2: The Sonnets." *Shakespeare Newsletter* (Fall 1991): 26–27.

Foucault, Michel. *Language, Counter-Memory, Practice: Selected Essays and Interviews.* Ed. Donald F. Bouchard. Tr. Donald F. Bouchard and Sherry Simon. Ithaca: Cornell University Press, 1977.

Freccero, John. "The Fig Tree and the Laurel: Petrarch's Poetics." In *Literary Theory/Renaissance Texts*, edited by Patricia Parker and David Quint, 20–32. Baltimore: Johns Hopkins University Press, 1986.

Freinkel, Lisa. "*Inferno* and the Poetics of *Usura.*" *Modern Language Notes* 107 (1992): 1–17.

——. "Shakespeare and the Theology of Will." *Graven Images* 2 (1995): 31–47.

Galdon, Joseph A., S.J. *Typology and Seventeenth-Century Literature.* The Hague: Mouton, 1975.

Gerosa, Pietro Paolo. *Umanesimo cristiano del Petrarca; Influenza agostiniana attinenze medievali.* Torino: Bottega d'Erasmo, 1966.

Gilbert, Allan H. *Literary Criticism: Plato to Dryden.* Detroit: Wayne State University Press, 1967.

Girard, René. "To Entrap the Wisest: Sacrificial Ambivalence in *The Merchant of Venice* and *Richard III.*" Reprinted in *A Theater of Envy. William Shakespeare*, 243–55. New York and Oxford: Oxford University Press, 1991.

Giroux, Robert. *The Book Known as Q: A Consideration of Shakespeare's Sonnets.* New York: Random House, 1983.

Goddard, Harold. "The Three Caskets." Reprinted in John Wilders, ed., *Shakespeare: "The Merchant of Venice." A Casebook.* London: Macmillan, 1969.

Goldhagen, Daniel. *Hitler's Willing Executioners: Ordinary Germans and the Holocaust.* New York: Vintage, 1997.

Gollancz, Israel. "The 'Shylock' of Shakespeare." Reprinted in *Allegory and Mysticism in Shakespeare. A Medievalist on "The Merchant of Venice." Reports of Three Lectures by Sir Israel Gollancz*, 13–34. London: Geo. W. Jones, 1931.

Greenblatt, Stephen. "Marlowe, Marx, and Anti-Semitism." *Critical Inquiry* 5 (Winter 1978): 295–96.

——. *Renaissance Self-Fashioning: From More to Shakespeare.* Chicago: University of Chicago Press, 1980.

——. "Filthy Rites." *Daedalus* 111 (Summer 1982): 1–16.

——. "An English Obsession." *New York Times Book Review*, August 11, 1996, 12–13.

——. "The Mousetrap." *Shakespeare Studies* 35 (1997): 1–32.

Greene, Roland. *Post-Petrarchism: Origins and Innovations of the Western Lyric Sequence*. Princeton: Princeton University Press, 1991.

Greene, Thomas. *The Light in Troy: Imitation and Discovery in Renaissance Poetry*. New Haven: Yale University Press, 1982.

Grossman, Marshall. *The Story of All Things: Writing the Self in English Renaissance Narrative Poetry*. Durham: Duke University Press, 1998.

Hagen, Kenneth. *A Theology of Testament in the Young Luther: The Lectures on Hebrews*. Leiden: Brill, 1974.

Halpern, Richard. "The Jewish Question: Shakespeare and Anti-Semitism." In *Shakespeare Among the Moderns*, 159–226. Ithaca: Cornell University Press, 1997.

Harpham, Geoffrey Galt. "The Fertile Word: Augustine's Ascetics of Interpretation," *Criticism* 28, no. 3 (Summer 1986): 237–54.

Harran, Marilyn J. *Luther on Conversion: The Early Years*. Ithaca: Cornell University Press, 1983.

Herman, Peter C. "What's the Use? Or, the Problematic of Economy in Shakespeare's Procreation Sonnets." In *Shakespeare's Sonnets: Critical Essays*, edited by James Schiffer, 263–83. New York: Garland Publishing, 1999.

Hieatt, A. Kent, Charles W. Hieatt, and Anne Lake Prescott. "When Did Shakespeare Write *Sonnets 1609*?" *Studies in Philology* 88, no. 1 (1991): 69–109.

Holl, Karl. *What Did Luther Understand by Religion?* Ed. James Luther Adams and Walter F. Bense. Tr. Fred W. Meuser and Walter R. Wietzke. Philadelphia: Fortress Press, 1977.

Honan, Park. *Shakespeare: A Life*. Oxford and New York: Oxford University Press, 1998.

Hunter, G. K. "The Theology of Marlowe's *The Jew of Malta*." *Journal of the Warburg and Courtauld Institutes* 27 (1964): 211–40.

Iliescu, Nicolae. *Il Canzoniere petrarchesco e sant'agostino*. Roma: Società Accademica Romena, 1962.

Johnson, D. W. "Verbum in the Early Augustine (386–97)." *Recherches Augustiniennes* 8 (Paris: Études Augustiniennes, 1972): 25–53.

Jordan, Robert. "Time and Contingency in St. Augustine." In *Augustine: A Collection of Critical Essays*, edited by R. A. Markus, 225–79. New York: Doubleday, 1972.

Joseph, Sister Miriam. *Shakespeare's Use of the Arts of Language*. New York: Columbia University Press, 1947.

Junghans, H. "Der Einfluss des Humanismus auf Luthers Entwicklung bis 1518." *Luther-Jahrbuch* 37 (1970): 37–101.

Kelly, J. N. D. *Early Christian Doctrines.* 5th ed. London: Adman and Charles Black, 1977.

Kittay, Eva Feder. *Metaphor: Its Cognitive Force and Linguistic Structure.* Oxford: Clarendon, 1987.

Kripke, Saul. *Naming and Necessity.* Cambridge: Harvard University Press, 1982.

Kristeller, P. O. "Augustine and the Early Renaissance." In *Studies in Renaissance Thought and Letters.* Roma: Edizioni di Storia e Letteratura, 1956.

Lacan, Jacques. "L'instance de la lettre dans l'inconscient ou la raison depuis Freud." In *Écrits,* 493–528. Paris: Éditions du Seuil, 1966.

——. *L'Éthique de la psychanalyse.* Paris: Éditions du Seuil, 1986.

Lampe, G. W. H. "The Reasonableness of Typology." In *Essays on Typology: Studies in Biblical Theology,* edited by G. W. H. Lampe and K. J. Woolcombe, 9–38. Naperville, Ill.: Alec R. Allenson, 1957.

Lampert, Lisa Renée. "After Eden, Out of Zion: Defining the Christian in Early English Literature." Ph.D. diss., University of California, Berkeley, 1996.

Levinas, Emmanuel. *Otherwise Than Being: Or, Beyond Essence.* Tr. Alphonso Lingis. 1981. Reprint, Pittsburgh: Duquesne University Press, 1997.

Lewalski, Barbara K. "Biblical Allusion and Allegory in *The Merchant of Venice.*" *Shakespeare Quarterly* 13 (1962): 327–433.

Lifschutz, Ellen St. Sure. "David's Lyre and the Renaissance Lyric: A Critical Consideration of the Psalms of Wyatt, Surrey and the Sidneys." Ph.D. diss., University of California, Berkeley, 1980.

Marotti, Arthur F. "Shakespeare's Sonnets as Literary Property." In *Soliciting Interpretation: Literary Theory and Seventeenth-Century English Poetry,* edited by Elizabeth D. Harvey and Katharine Eisaman Maus, 143–73. Chicago: University of Chicago Press, 1990.

McEvoy, James. "St. Augustine's Account of Time and Wittgenstein's Criticisms." *Review of Metaphysics* 38 (March 1984): 547–77.

McGrath, Alister. *The Intellectual Origins of the European Reformation.* Oxford: Basil Blackwell, 1987.

McManaway, James G. "John Shakespeare's 'Spiritual Testament.'" *Shakespeare Quarterly* 18 (1967): 197–205.

Metzger, Mary Janell. "'Now by My Hood, a Gentle and No Jew': Jessica, *The Merchant of Venice,* and the Discourse of Early Modern English Identity." *PMLA* 113, no. 1 (January 1998): 52–63.

Mill, John Stuart. "What Is Poetry?" In *Essays on Poetry by John Stuart Mill,* 3–22. Ed. F. Parvin Sharpless. Columbia: University of South Carolina Press, 1976.

Minnis, A. J. *Medieval Theory of Authorship: Scholastic Literary Attitudes in the Later Middle Ages.* London: Scolar, 1984.

Miriam Joseph, Sister. *Shakespeare's Use of the Arts of Language.* New York: Columbia University Press, 1947.

Mommsen, Theodor M. "Petrarch's Conception of the 'Dark Ages.'" *Speculum* 17, no. 2 (April 1942): 226–42.

Nerlich, Michael. "The Merchant Adventurer Leaves the Ship." In *The Ideology of Adventure*, 108–82. Tr. Ruth Crowley. Minneapolis: University of Minnesota Press, 1987.

O'Connell, Michael. "Authority and the Truth of Experience in Petrarch's 'Ascent of Mount Ventoux.'" *Philological Quarterly* 62, no. 4 (Fall 1983): 507–20.

Oberman, Heiko A. *Luther: Man Between God and the Devil.* Tr. Eilenn Walliser-Scwarzbart. New York: Doubleday, 1982.

——. *The Roots of Anti-Semitism In the Age of Renaissance and Reformation.* Tr. James I. Porter. Philadelphia: Fortress Press, 1984.

——. "Teufelsdreck: Eschatology and Scatology in the 'Old' Luther." *Sixteenth Century Journal* 19, no. 3 (Fall 1988): 435–50.

Oroz Reta, Jose. "Prière et Recherche de Dieu dans les Confessions de Saint Augustin." *Augustinian Studies* 7 (1976): 99–118.

Parker, Patricia. "Preposterous Events." *Shakespeare Quarterly* 43, no. 2 (Summer 1992): 186–213.

——. "Preposterous Reversals: *Love's Labor's Lost." Modern Language Quarterly* 54, no. 4 (1993): 435–82.

Pelikan, Jaroslav. *The Emergence of the Catholic Tradition (100–600).* Vol. 1 of *The Christian Tradition: A History of the Development of Doctrine.* Chicago: University of Chicago Press, 1971.

——. *Luther the Expositor: Introduction to the Reformer's Exegetical Writings.* LW Companion Volume. St. Louis: Concordia Publishing House, 1959.

Pequigney, Joseph. *Such Is My Love: A Study of Shakespeare's Sonnets.* Chicago: University of Chicago Press, 1985.

Phillips, John. *The Reformation of Images: Destruction of Art in England, 1535–1660.* Berkeley: University of California Press, 1973.

Poe, Elizabeth Wilson. *From Poetry to Prose in Old Provençal: The Emergence of the Vidas, the Razos, and the Razos de trobar.* Birmingham, Ala.: Summa, 1984.

Polman, A. D. R. *The Word of God According to St. Augustine.* Tr. A. J. Pomerans. Grand Rapids, Mich.: Eerdmans, 1961.

Poque, Suzanne. "Les Psaumes dans les 'Confessions.'" In *Saint Augustin et la Bible,* 155–66. edited by Anne-Marie la Bonnardière. Vol. 3 of Bible de Tous les Temps. Paris: Éditions Beauchesne, 1986.

Pratzner, Ferdinand. *Messe und Kreuzesopfer: Die Krise der sakramentalen Idee bei Luther und in der mittelalterlichen Scholastik.* Vienna: Verlag Herder, 1970.

Quere, Ralph W. "Changes and Constants: Structure in Luther's Understanding of the Real Presence in the 1520's." *Sixteenth Century Journal* 16, no. 1 (1985): 45–78.

Quilligan, Maureen. *The Language of Allegory: Defining the Genre*. Ithaca: Cornell University Press, 1979.

Robbins, Jill. *Prodigal Son/Elder Brother: Interpretation and Alterity in Augustine, Petrarch, Kafka, Levinas*. Chicago: University of Chicago Press, 1991.

Rose, Mark. "The Author as Proprietor: *Donaldson v. Becket* and the Genealogy of Modern Authorship." *Representations* 23 (Summer 1988): 51–85.

Sasse, Herman. *This Is My Body: Luther's Contention for the Real Presence in the Sacrament of the Altar*. Minneapolis: Augsburg, 1959.

Schoenbaum, S. *William Shakespeare: A Documentary Life*. New York: Oxford University Press, 1975.

Schwab, Wolfgang. *Entwicklung und Gestalt der Sakramentheologie bei Martin Luther*. Frankfurt: Verlag Peter Lang, 1977.

Shapiro, James. *Shakespeare and the Jews*. New York: Columbia University Press, 1996.

Shell, Marc. "The Wether and the Ewe: Verbal Usury in *The Merchant of Venice*" In *Money, Language, and Thought: Literary and Philosophical Economies from the Medieval to the Modern Era*, 47–83. Berkeley: University of California Press, 1982.

Shoaf, R. A. *Dante, Chaucer, and the Currency of the Word: Money, Images, and Reference in Late Medieval Poetry*. Norman, Okla.: Pilgrim Books, 1983.

Sider, Ronald. *Andreas Bodenstein von Karlstadt: The Development of His Thought, 1517–1525*. Leiden: Brill, 1974.

Smalley, Beryl. *The Study of the Bible in the Middle Ages*. Oxford: Basil Blackwell, 1952.

Smith, Barbara Herrnstein. *On the Margins of Discourse*. Chicago: University of Chicago Press, 1978.

Spevack, Martin. *A Complete Concordance to the Works of Shakespeare*. 9 vols. Hidlesheim: Olms, 1968.

Stallybrass, Peter. "Editing as Cultural Formation: The Sexing of Shakespeare's Sonnets." *Modern Language Quarterly* 54, no. 1 (March 1993): 91–103.

Stock, Brian. *Augustine the Reader: Meditation, Self-Knowledge, and the Ethics of Interpretation*. Cambridge, Mass. and London: Belknap Press, 1996.

Strier, Richard. "Martin Luther and the Real Presence in Nature." *Graven Images* 1 (1994): 52–72.

Thomas, Max W. "Eschewing Credit: Heywood, Shakespeare, and Plagiarism Before Copyright." *New Literary History* 31, no. 2 (Spring 2000): 277–93.

Tillyard, E. M. W. *Shakespeare's History Plays*. Reprint, New York: Barnes and Noble, 1964.

Trinkaus, Charles. *In Our Image and Likeness: Humanity and Divinity in Italian Humanist Thought*. 2 vols. London: Constable, 1970.

Tucker, Herbert F. "Dramatic Monologue and the Overhearing of Lyric." In *Lyric Poetry: Beyond New Criticism*, edited by Chaviva Hosek and Patricia Parker, 226–43. Ithaca: Cornell University Press, 1985.

Twombly, Robert G. "Thomas Wyatt's Paraphrase of the Penitential Psalms of David." *Texas Studies in Literature and Language* 12 (1970): 345–80.

Urban, Wolfgang. "Die 'via moderna' an der Universität Erfurt am Vorabend der Reformation." In *Gregor von Rimini: Werk und Wirkung bis zur Reformation*, edited by Heiko A. Oberman, 311–30. Berlin: De Gruyter, 1981.

Vance, Eugene. "Augustine's *Confessions* and the Grammar of Selfhood." *Genre* 6, no. 1 (March 1973): 1–28.

——. "Language as Temporality." In *Mimesis: From Mirror to Method, Augustine to Descartes*, edited by John D. Lyons and Stephen G. Nichols Jr., 20–35. Hanover, N.H.: University Press of New England, 1982.

Vendler, Helen. *The Art of Shakespeare's Sonnets*. Cambridge: Harvard University Press, 1997.

Vickers, Nancy J. "Diana Described: Scattered Woman and Scattered Rhyme." *Critical Inquiry* 8, no. 2 (Winter 1981): 265–79.

Vogelsang, Erich. *Die Anfänge von Luthers Christologie*. Vol. 15 of *Arbeiten zur Kirschengeschichte*. Berlin: W. de Gruyter, 1929.

Von Harnack, Adolf. *Marcion: Das Evangelium vom fremden Gott.* 2 vols. Reprint, Berlin: Akademie-verlag, 1960.

Waller, Marguerite. *Petrarch's Poetics and Literary History*. Amherst: University of Massachusetts Press, 1980.

Wilkins, Ernest Hatch. *Life of Petrarch*. Chicago: University of Chicago Press, 1961.

Wilson, Ian. *Shakespeare: The Evidence*. London: Headline Book Publishing, 1993.

Wilson, Katharine M. *Shakespeare's Sugared Sonnets*. London: George Allen and Unwin, 1974.

Wimsatt W. K., and Monroe C. Beardsley. "The Intentional Fallacy." In *The Verbal Icon: Studies in the Meaning of Poetry*, 3–18. Reprint, Lexington: University of Kentucky Press, 1982.

Woodmansee, Martha. "The Genius and the Copyright: Economic and Legal Conditions of the Emergence of the 'Author.'" *Eighteenth-Century Studies* 17 (1984): 425–48.

Žižek, Slavoj, *The Sublime Object of Ideology*. London and New York: Verso, 1989.

Zumthor, Paul. *Langue, texte, enigme*. Paris: Éditions du Seuil, 1975.

INDEX